for Jane and Nick

Dreams and dreaming

A list of acknowledgments is given on
page 349 but the author wishes to
express special appreciation to Dr. R. A.
Sandison of Knowle Hospital, Fareham,
Hampshire, England, the Medical
Superintendent and staff of Powick
Hospital, Worcester, for the opportunity
of studying the clinical use of LSD-25;
Dr. William Dement of the Department
of Psychiatry, Stanford University, U.S.A.,
Dr. Charles Fisher of Mount Sinai
Hospital, New York, and the Art Therapist
at Netherne and Fairdene Hospital,
Coulsdon, Surrey; Nicolas Bentley for
editorial advice, Valerie Leach, who
designed the book; and Morwenna Arthy,
who has provided invaluable research help.
Norman MacKenzie

Aldus Books · London

Dreams and dreaming

Norman MacKenzie

"Of all the hard facts of science, I know
of none more solid and fundamental than
the fact that if you inhibit thought (and
persevere) you come at length to a region
of consciousness below or behind
thought, and different from ordinary
thought in its nature and character—a
consciousness of a quasi-universal quality,
and a realization of an altogether vaster
self than that to which we are accustomed.
And since the ordinary consciousness,
with which we are concerned in ordinary
life, is before all things founded on the
little local self, and is in fact self-
consciousness in the little local sense,
it follows that to pass out of that is to die
to the ordinary self and the ordinary
world."

Edward Carpenter

My days and dreams (1916)

©1965 Aldus Books Limited, London
First published in 1965 by Aldus Books Limited
Aldus House, Conway Street,
Fitzroy Square, London W1
Distributed in the United Kingdom
and the Commonwealth by
W. H. Allen & Company,
43 Essex Street, London WC2
Printed in Holland by
N. V. Drukkerij Senefelder, Amsterdam.

contents

1 The world of fantasy

What are dreams? There is no simple answer to this simple question. It has been asked in all ages by all peoples, from the ancient Assyrians to the contemporary aborigines of Australia, because the dream is a universal human experience. All men sleep, and all men dream. About a third of a normal lifetime is spent in sleeping, and much of that time is devoted to the process we call dreaming. Yet, although sleep and dreams are commonplace facts of life, they remain mysteries, and in each generation men have tried to puzzle out their cause and meaning.

This is true of our own time. Since 1899, when Sigmund Freud published *The Interpretation of Dreams*, the analysis and therapeutic use of dreams has been significant in the treatment of mental disorders. Many of Freud's theories about dreaming have profoundly influenced our thinking about art, literature, politics, and other matters far removed from clinical psychiatry. Since 1953 the scientific, and in particular the physiological, study of sleep and dreams has produced some astonishing results. But this development has scarcely had time to make any impact on public opinion, though in the course of time it may prove to be as revolutionary as Freud's psychological theory of the dream. In little more than 10 years, scientific research has begun to provide answers to certain questions that have been regarded as riddles since the dawn of history. Before long, it could well transform our views about dreaming, for

The Dream, a painting by Marc Chagall. From earliest times artists, writers, and philosophers have been fascinated by their dreams, often using them as material for their work. Recent scientific research into dreams and the dreaming process has already produced such promising results that physiologists and other medical specialists have turned their attention to dreams.

even in its early stages it clearly has implications that go far beyond the specific problem of dreams. For dreams are not an isolated phenomenon in man. They are products of the human brain, and the more we discover about them, the more we shall understand about the way that the brain works, about the relation between physical and mental states, about the physiology of sleeping and waking, about the psychology of mental illness, and about rational thought processes—as well as the imaginative faculty we call fantasy.

This book describes how these discoveries have come about and discusses some of their results. But it often happens that a superstition continues to survive long after science has made it obsolete, and superstitions about dreams are no exception.

In ancient and primitive societies, dreams were usually thought to be the work of gods or demons, appearing to mortals with messages of hope or despair. Some peoples, especially those of the Orient, believed that the soul left the body in sleep and wandered in a spirit world. It was generally accepted that in some occult fashion dreams could provide a glimpse of the future, reveal events happening at a distance, or indicate a necessary course of action. There were magic spells for inducing dreams, or for averting their evil consequences. Dreams were used as curses and cures, as the source of religious ideas, poems, and works of art, and as a basis for military and political decisions.

Such beliefs are not merely antique oddities. Just as many Englishmen feel a little uneasy if they walk under a ladder or spill some salt, so they may well respect the old adage that "Friday's dream on a Saturday told, will always come true, be it never so old." A Frenchman says that to speak of a dream before breakfast brings bad luck—saying it with a smile, but taking care not to tell you his dreams before he has eaten. A Greek girl, on St Catherine's Eve, bakes a cake with salt and wine, explaining that it is no more than an old custom, but secretly hoping it may help her to dream of her future husband. Traditional beliefs and practices of this kind have their counterpart in every country and in every age, as is shown by historical records that date back as far as Rome, Greece, and the Egypt of the pharaohs. It is said in one of the books dealing with the assassination of President Kennedy that, on the previous night, a woman telephoned the secret service duty officer at the White House, saying she had dreamed that the president would be killed in Dallas. The story reminds us that Abraham Lincoln dreamed of his own imminent death.

The public interest in dream oddities never flags. Only a few years ago, an English newspaper regularly published the dreams of a man who forecast the results of horse races, and there are frequent press reports of cases in which it is claimed that a lost person or a stolen object has been recovered by following the clues given in dreams. There was a famous example of this in 1932, when the small son of Colonel Lindberg, the famous American flyer, was kidnapped; newspaper readers were asked to submit any dreams that might help to find the baby. Hundreds were studied, but less than a dozen bore any resemblance at all to the facts. After Goya's portrait of the Duke of Wellington was stolen from the National Gallery in London in 1961, eager dreamers claimed to have "solved" the crime. In 1958, even the American Atomic Energy Commission considered a proposal that it should employ dream clairvoyants to predict where Soviet bombs might fall in the event of war!

As long as such superstitious ideas are still widely accepted, it is scarcely surprising that many people find it hard to distinguish between scientific facts and imaginative guesswork when they talk about dreams. They read in a newspaper that an Italian scientist thinks it may be possible to use infra-red rays to photograph dream images on the retina of the eye, or that American physiologists are measuring the duration of dreams in small children. But they have no means of telling whether such experiments are valid or merely nonsense. The English author J. B. Priestley appeared on a television program in 1962, asking any viewers who had had apparently prophetic or telepathic dreams to send them to him for use in a book he was writing about man's conceptions of time. Thousands of people, who took their dreams as seriously as did Mr. Priestley, responded to his request—although another B.B.C. program, the satirical *That Was The Week That Was*, had mocked the idea. In 1964, Arthur Koestler published a best-selling book called *The Act of Creation*, in which he spoke of dreaming as a "sliding back towards the pulsating darkness, of which we were part before our separate egos were formed." He was rebuked for this by the eminent zoologist and Nobel Prize winner J. P. Medawar, who scathingly put forward "the idea that the content of dreams may be totally devoid of 'meaning.' There should be no need to emphasize, in this century of radio sets and electronic devices, that many dreams may be assemblages of thought-elements that convey no information whatsoever."

What is the ordinary dreamer to make of such confusion? When eminent men are in such disagreement, how is he to decide whether his dreams are meaningful or meaningless, or what they mean if they are meaningful, or why they occur if they are meaningless? Even if he thinks his dreams are significant, how is he to tell the difference between one kind of dream interpretation and another? It is hard for the dreamer to answer, for he seldom understands what happens when he dreams. His dreams seem little more than passing fancies from some limbo between sleeping and waking, irrational, illogical, sometimes frightening, and almost always incomprehensible. Most people are not even sure whether they dream or not, or, if they do, how much they dream, or whether one kind of dream differs from another, because dreams are hard to remember and quickly vanish as one emerges from sleep.

Throughout most of man's history little has been discovered about the facts of dreaming, though the first chapters of this book will show the wide variety of guesses that were made. Aristotle and Plato really knew as much about dreams as Kant or Schopenhauer. But three great changes have shifted the dream debate away from speculation and toward science.

The first was the emergence of modern psychology toward the end of the 19th century, and the subsequent development of psychoanalytic theories about the hidden processes of the mind. Freud and his contemporaries enabled us to see the dream in a much wider context, as one of many apparently "abnormal" phenomena that range from quite common hallucinations through various states to the delusions of the mentally ill. It had long been suggested that some such relationship existed, but no one before Freud had offered an adequate theory of what that relationship might be. The psychoanalysts thus gave a new impetus to the interpretation of dreams, and to the collecting of them in large numbers. Their aim was to discover whether there were any common dream patterns or recurrent symbols that would help confirm the new techniques of interpretation.

The second change came little more than a decade ago, when scientific research into the nature of sleep unexpectedly threw up some dramatic new evidence about the physical process of dreaming, enabling experimenters to tell when a person was experiencing what we loosely call a dream—and this opened a completely new field for dream experiments.

The third and equally significant breakthrough has come with the recent discovery of drugs that have the capacity to induce mental states apparently very like those of dreaming, or of certain types of mental illness—the hallucinogens, or "mind-revealing" drugs such as mescalin, psilocybin, and LSD 25. Some of these drugs, or crude forms of them, have long been used by primitive societies as dissimilar and as widely separated as those in Central America and in Siberia, but it is only in the last few years that they have come into controlled experimental and clinical use. They provide another window on the dark antechambers of the mind, where one may encounter when awake many of the fantasies previously experienced only by the sleeper or the psychotic. At the same time, other new drugs have been found that seem able to damp down our fantasies—by restricting the amount we dream or the horrific possibilities of dreams, or by helping the mentally distressed to emerge from states of hallucination and establish closer touch with reality.

These three developments are discussed in the later chapters of this book, which deal with psychoanalytical, physiological, and chemical theories of dreaming. This division of the subject is merely a convenient device; it has no scientific significance and it should be borne in mind that the scientific objective in each case is to define and explain essentially the same phenomena. Whether the evidence comes from the analyst's consulting room, the sleep laboratories of scientists in New York, Chicago, and California, or the clinics in which the hallucinogenic drugs are being used for the treatment of mental illness, it is all part of a common and accumulating body of knowledge.

In 1953, Eugene Aserinsky, a postgraduate medical student in Chicago, made the decisive discovery upon which physiological research on sleep and dreams now rests. In that same year, Dr. Glenn V. Ramsey, of the University

Powerful hallucinogenic drugs are now used in psychotherapeutic treatment. Two paintings by a patient in a German clinic illustrate the drugs' effect. One picture (above) was painted before the drug psilocybin was administered, the second after. The action of the drug has produced changes in the structure of the picture.

of Texas, had summarized all the studies of dreaming then available. He lamented "the relatively small number of major research studies" on dreams. "The lack of scientific interest and data on the topic," said Dr. Ramsey, "has contributed to the myriads of speculations and the plethora of unscientific publications in the field. The topic of dreaming is largely shunned by current research workers and is given only the briefest of treatments or entirely omitted in most contemporary psychological textbooks."

Dr. Ramsey's strictures were a little severe at the time, and much has happened in the 10 years since he wrote them. But he was right in noting that even as recently as 1953, the ratio of fact to fancy in dream theory was extremely low. There was, he reported, "fairly consistent data regarding the nature of imagery appearing in dreams." Studies of dreaming in blind and deaf persons gave good grounds for believing that sensory deprivation had some influence on what one dreams—though the notable case of Helen Keller, blinded in infancy, showed that there were exceptions to the general rule that persons who go blind before the age of five seem not to "see" in their dreams. There were attempted estimates of the length and frequency of dreams; of the way dream patterns may change with the age or health of the dreamer; of the effect of such external stimuli as heat and cold, or such internal stimuli as certain kinds of food and drink; of the influence of high altitudes, fatigue, or wartime terrors on dream habits; and—in the Kinsey report—a link was shown between men's sexual dreams and nocturnal emissions.

The research was clearly scrappy; much of the work done by psychologists produced evidence that was difficult to compare—either with other psychological material or with the mass of highly subjective and largely unclassified dream reports published by psychoanalysts. Of the few studies that had then been published, the best known was that undertaken by Professor Calvin S. Hall, who now directs an Institute of Dream Research in Miami, Florida. Professor Hall's summary, based on an analysis of 10,000 dreams of present-day Americans, answers some of the common questions about what we dream. It may therefore be useful to glance at some of his conclusions.

First of all he investigated the setting of the dream. In five per cent of the dreams the dreamer had no sense of the locale. In 15 per cent, the setting was a conveyance of some kind, such as a car, aircraft, or boat; in 10 per cent, the dreamer was walking along a road; in another 10 per cent, the dream was set in a party, at a beach, a dance, or some other kind of entertainment; a further 10 per cent had some kind of rural location (rather more men than women dreamed of scenes out-of-doors). About a third of all the dreams took place inside a house, with the living room as the most popular setting, followed in descending order by the bedroom, kitchen, stairway, basement, bathroom, dining room, and hall. Though the rest of the dreams were scattered over

These drawings from an early edition of *The Interpretation of Dreams* illustrate Freud's belief that the dream is "the guardian of sleep." The drawings depict the dream of a nursemaid whose charge cries during the night because he wants to go to the lavatory. The dream tries to guard her sleep by showing him doing so. But the child continues to cry and she dreams that the pool of urine floods the town and becomes a sea, until finally the dream can no longer prevent her waking.

many locales, it was noted that comparatively few of them dealt with places of work—where people spend much time—and a surprisingly high proportion of them related to conveyances and places of entertainment, in which most people spend only a relatively small part of their time. Exotic or bizarre settings were very rare.

It will be noticed that the emphasis is on familiar scenes and objects, with a tendency to stress some of them more than might be expected from their relative importance in ordinary life. The dreams were also about familiar persons as well as familiar things. In 15 per cent of those studied by Professor Hall the dreamer was the sole character; in most of the other cases there were only two persons besides the dreamer and these were usually members of the family or close acquaintances; total strangers, or composite characters, accounted for only four out of 10 dream characters.

What do we do in our dreams? According to Professor Hall's study, there is a notable absence of situations related to work, to buying or selling, or to any kind of household chores. On the other hand, dreams involving sports, games, dancing, and so on are quite common. Professor Hall also reported that unpleasant dreams are more common than pleasant ones, fear more usual than anger, and sadness than happiness.

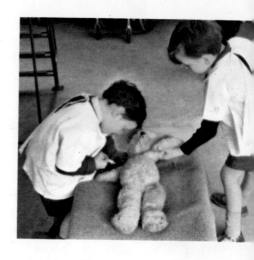

Children act out their fantasies openly in their play. Here, they are pretending to be doctors and operating on a toy.

Dream statistics of this kind do not in themselves help to explain why dreams are concerned with so many common elements, but they do indicate two important assumptions. The first is that dreams are not simply random collections of images; they seem to have very definite patterns, both in what they include and what they exclude. The second is that by examining these patterns and setting them in the context of the life and problems of the dreamers, we can see that certain symbols occur again and again in the dreams of different people and that they always seem to indicate much the same kind of feeling or problem.

Such assumptions, of course, are not accepted by those who deny that dreaming has any meaningful or discoverable pattern, or that symbolic significance may be attached to dream images. But they are the point of departure for anyone who believes that the imagery of dreams is open to interpretation. The language of dreams may be different from the language in which we express our conscious thoughts, but if it is decipherable it must have an inner structure and a definite vocabulary. What is true of even the most complicated code must equally be true of dreams—once we grant the assumption that somehow they make sense in terms of our total physical and mental processes.

This view underlies such research as that being conducted by Professor David Schneider, an anthropologist at the University of Chicago, who has collected over 2000 dreams from 70 societies, devised a means of coding them on cards which can be run through an electronic calculating machine, and then searched for patterns that may transcend the obvious differences of culture. He has been especially interested in discovering the frequency of sexual or aggressive dreams, or dreams with such themes as flying, falling, or the loss of teeth, and to estimate how far these vary from one society to another, or between men and women or the young and the old.

A similar project was undertaken in the United States by Dr. Richard Griffith, and also by two Japanese scientists. Dr. Griffith studied the dreams of 250 college students in Kentucky and the Japanese gave a similar questionnaire to 223 in Tokyo; over 7000 dreams were thus collected. It was found when the dreams were examined to see how often certain themes occurred that there was a remarkable similarity between the two groups. There were 34 such themes, ranging from sexual experience to being nude, from being buried alive to swimming, missing a train, falling, flying, or seeing strange animals. The differences, it seemed, were much less significant than the likenesses. About 80 per cent of both groups had dreams of falling; little more than half dreamed about the death of someone they loved. In almost every case, certain types of dream occurred with similar frequency. The differences in dream content were often more marked between American men and American women, or Japanese men and women, than between American and Japanese men. Variations in dream patterns, it appeared, might depend more on distinctions of sex than cultural factors, even when the societies were basically as different as those of America and Japan.

Studies of this kind have been strongly influenced both by the work of Freud and his successors and by the evidence that anthropologists have provided about the dreams of people in primitive societies. But all such studies, and indeed all forms of dream interpretation since antiquity, depend on the belief that dreams reveal much about the personality and life situation of the dreamer, and that their meaning is expressed in symbolic terms. To emphasize this point, which is crucial to the argument of this book as well as to the understanding of dreams, it will be useful to pause here and examine briefly what symbolism means.

Dream images are products of what we call fantasy—a mental process differing from that which governs our conscious thinking and behavior. The essence of fantasy is that it is not subject to the logical rules governing rational thought about real objects and real situations. It is a mental process whereby the mind escapes from reality and pictures the world as it might be, rather than as it is. We may say it is a child's picture of the world, or even a way of looking at life that is older and more primitive than the perceptions of what we call consciousness. By comparison with rational thought, it is immature, fanciful, and often fearful. It is a state into which the mind easily relapses when concentration is relaxed, or when concentration on what is real becomes unpleasant or painful. It is an intensely private experience, yet it can be as vivid as a real one. In his fantasies, the individual can play parts and obtain the vicarious satisfaction of feelings and desires that are denied to him in ordinary life, or that he may not even consciously admit. Fantasy allows him to praise or condemn others without fear of the consequences, to pretend that he is successful or destructive, even to commit crimes; in short, to compensate for feelings of inadequacy.

Each of us can recognize, if we are honest with ourselves, some such elements of fantasy in our own behavior. Most people who are emotionally stable and adjusted to their environment have fairly modest fantasies. But the more a person is exposed to external stress or is subject to mental disturbance, the more powerful and unlike everyday life the fantasies become. Some people are overwhelmed and as a result suffer from psychotic delusions, illusions, or hallucinations. But in all of us the private and differently ordered world of fantasy is the permanent and inescapable counterpart of the outer world with which we are so much more familiar. It is, indeed, an invaluable counterpart, for in healthy persons fantasy is a vital regulator of our lives.

We can see at once how it serves this function if we watch the ways in which a child uses it, partly as a means of learning, partly as a means of release from frustration, external pressure, or a situation that produces anxiety. The child has a stock of information and feelings. From these it selects known facts and emotions and in fantasy combines them in new ways, testing out a wide range of combinations or estimating the possibilities that lie ahead. In this fashion, what seems to be play is actually employed as an aid to growing up or to adjustment to the world. Play is enjoyed as an end in itself because fantasy is actually gratifying in itself; but it also serves a larger purpose. It cushions the child against situations it does not understand, or may find intolerable, and also offers a kind of dress rehearsal for life.

It is when the pressures become too strong, or when the substitute gratifications of fantasy are consistently preferred to the joys and sorrows of real

life, that fantasy takes on neurotic forms and leads to distortions of both body and social function—in other words, to psychosomatic illness and neurotic behavior. In extreme cases, a mentally disturbed person may be unable to distinguish between his fantasies and the reality of his life.

When this happens, fantasy becomes the stage on which he acts out his problems. The parts he plays will reflect aspects of his own character that he does not admit in normal life; the wishes he reveals will be those he usually hides; the rewards he seeks will be those denied to him in everyday life, and his fears will be of situations or persons that in the ordinary way seem too dangerous to be confronted. He will see himself as a conquering general, a great lover, a sadist, a gambler, an orator, or a wretch awaiting execution.

All the images employed in fantasy are symbolic. The man who toys with the image of himself as a general or a millionaire seldom wishes actually to be one; he wishes to be what that role represents—powerful, important, decisive, or rich. The woman who imagines herself as the victim of a torturer is feeling what that situation imples—that she is being victimized and ill-treated. In each case a conventional symbol has been appropriated from life because it expresses a wide spectrum of emotional associations. To say one wishes to be a general is to conjure up a much wider range of images than to say one wishes merely to be strong or successful or feared. Those characteristics, and many others—martial glory, blood, death, victory, the power to command, the satisfaction of wearing a uniform, regimental camaraderie—are all immediately evoked by the one symbolic word "general." This is clearly shown

The Balcony, a play by the modern French writer Jean Genet, is centered on a brothel—called "The House of Illusions" —in which the clients are able to act out their fantasies. These three scenes are from the 1963 American film of the play. Far left, a client impersonates a general. Left, a man and a prostitute enact a scene between a judge and a criminal. Right, a third client is enabled to act out his fantasy of being an archbishop.

It has been said that man is a "symbolizing animal"—a description that is as true of 20th-century man as of his forebears. For instance, the tiger is symbolic of power and speed, and it is used today by a flying club, above, and as a tattoo, right.

in Jean Genet's play, *The Balcony*, in which three ordinary men come to a brothel to act out their fantasies—one plays a general, one a judge, and one an archbishop. Genet has dramatized the kind of images that fantasy employs.

Every symbol expresses many ideas. It has certain common meanings—that is why we are able to communicate with each other—so that the word "general" conjures up for all of us the specific concept of a military commander. But it also has particular meanings for each individual. For a man who has spent years in the army the word obviously has a set of associations different from those it has for a pacifist. It is the wealth of secondary and emotionally potent meanings, many of which may be far removed from the immediate idea of a high-ranking soldier, that determine how each individual responds to the symbolic image.

This is a simple but psychologically crucial fact on which much depends. It is, for instance, the basis of a good deal of advertising. When an oil company uses the symbol of a tiger for one of its brands of gasoline, it is hoping to evoke in the motorist some of his unconscious associations with the idea of a tiger—its power and alacrity, its ability to spring forward suddenly. A tobacco company may employ symbols associated with masculinity—a tattoo on a hairy arm, the bearded face of a sailor, or a football player reaching for a cigarette package. In using symbols such as these the advertising agency is simply exploiting techniques that are used in every walk of life—in politics, religion, literature, and art.

Much of the symbolic ritual of the coronation ceremony is lost on the average Englishman, but the occasion may arouse deep feelings within him.

An American understands much more by the words "The White House" than "the official residence of the President of the United States"; the image summarizes a system of government and represents a focus of leadership. The devout Christian may well be unable to articulate fully all the emotions that he feels before the Cross. In each case, the individual is adding his emotions to the objective fact of the image. The same is true of a poem or a novel. It is not just the plain meaning of the words on the page that matters; those words are appealing or effective because of the associations they evoke in the reader, and the writer of genius is one whose mastery of symbolism enables him to engage the emotions of his public.

Symbolism is the subjective means whereby we organize our objective experience of life, fusing our inner emotional reactions with our perception of our environment. Without it, reality would be nothing more than a collection of inanimate objects and meaningless phenomena. Symbolic imagery thus appears to be one of the ways in which we store our memories, and the form in which they emerge in our dreams.

The most familiar form of imagery is the visual. Most dreamers "see" their dreams. At least, the eyes of the dreamer move as if he is watching something happen, and the whole optical system is stimulated. This fact has latterly provided one of the most important clues for scientists investigating dreaming. But the dream is something more than a succession of remembered visual images. Impressions of sound, taste, touch, and smell may occur, though apparently less often. And in dreams these sensory impressions appear to be accompanied by strong feelings; we are all aware of this when we wake sweating, trembling, or even weeping after a nightmare. But there is good reason for believing that every dream image is linked to a distinct feeling or group of feelings. The images and emotions that arise in sleep express deep psychological processes that affect us in both waking and sleeping. They seem to be the product of distinct physical functions within the human organism, much of which never "sleeps" and is regulated by vital and continuous rhythms of which we are consciously unaware.

The delicate relationship between the psychological and physiological processes can easily be disturbed. When we labor under strong feelings, our ability to notice what is happening around us is affected and often impaired. A grief-stricken person, for instance, may not respond to noises or sights that in normal circumstances would produce a marked reaction. Conversely, if anything cuts us off from the outside world, strange things happen to our feelings. A man imprisoned alone in a dark cell will experience hallucinations, seeing and hearing things that are not there. Such disturbances can be caused by physical or psychic stress, by drugs, by mental illness, or simply by the normal process of losing consciousness when we go to sleep. Whenever this happens we become aware of symbolic imagery that is very different from the thought processes of waking life.

A riderless horse often appears in myths, folk-tales, and dreams as a symbol of death. Above, the funeral of President John F. Kennedy, assassinated in November 1963. In this traditional ritual a riderless horse follows the coffin: empty boots reversed in the stirrups signify its master will not ride again. Left, a painting from a 16th-century French manuscript—*Death on a Black Horse.*

It was this view of symbolism that led Freud, Jung, and other pioneers of psychoanalysis to the study of man's symbol-making capacities in all their diverse expressions, from the dream to myths and primitive rituals, from the arts to the theory of numbers and the conceptions of nuclear physics. They believed that the only way to get at the meaning of a dream was to treat its imagery as something personally significant of the dreamer but at the same time, like all forms of fantasy, symbolic in character. It was not enough, however, simply to record the images of a dream; it was essential to discover what emotional charge was carried by each image, to ask what hidden feelings or memories lay behind the dream story.

We shall see later on how they set about this task. Meanwhile, the point can be simply illustrated by an example given by Robert Graves in his book *The Meaning of Dreams*. He cites the case of a woman who dreamed that she was having difficulty turning a large car in a narrow lane. Such a dream, Graves suggests, could symbolize the anxiety of the woman, who was not a good driver, about turning her car. It could also represent a problem in her life. She was living above her income (the large car), she felt constricted by this (the narrow lane), and felt she must change her style of life (to turn round), even though such a change would be difficult for her to make. Or the dream might well epitomize the problem of checking and redirecting any powerful emotional impulse where the road of habit is a narrow one.

Let us take a few more examples of dreams and see what psychologists have to say about the significance of their symbols:

"I dreamed that I was awakened by the sound of a horse's hooves in the street. I saw a white horse, with no rider, stopping at midnight in front of our house. I knew it came for my younger sister. I went to the door and opened it to call her, when suddenly I saw her coming down the stairs, all dressed in white. She did not say a word to me, but walked with stately steps down the stairs, through the hall, and out of the door. She mounted the horse and rode away. I woke up crying."

The woman who had this dream did not know that in many folk tales and myths a riderless horse is a symbol of death. True, it can also be taken to symbolize many other things, from powerful sexual feelings to a beast of burden, and the psychoanalyst's interpretation would depend upon the problems and passions of the dreamer. But in this case the woman who had the dream thought that it foretold the death of her sister (which in fact occurred a month later) whom she hated for marrying the man that she herself loved. The dream occurred just before the sister was due to have a child, and the dreamer made a point of telling her about the dream. If in fact it contained an element of prophecy, it was a prophecy that revealed her own secret wishes.

A different type of dream was reported by a man who had been making love to a girl and had found it difficult to stop short of sexual intercourse.

"I was in my car driving along and I wanted to stop the car immediately, but my brakes would not work. This went on and on until I wakened. I remember very vividly stepping on the brake, knowing I must stop the car to avoid some danger, but the car would not stop. Horror-stricken and afraid, I kept applying my foot to the brake, but nothing seemed to happen. There seemed to be a force or drive that made me keep moving in spite of the fact that I realized I must stop and that this could be accomplished only by application of the brake."

Symbols, however, cannot be divorced from either their cultural or their personal context, even if they appear to have a more general meaning. Fire, for instance, represents warmth in any society; but to someone living in a district menaced by forest fires, it means warmth of a dangerous kind, whereas to an Eskimo it means life-giving warmth. A dream of eating pork would clearly have different implications for a Jew and a Gentile, while the idea of a long journey would have one sort of association for a globe-trotting journalist and quite another for a peasant who has never left his village. Any study of symbols—whether they appear in dreams or in literature—has to take this fact into account. If fixed meanings are attached to symbols, they degenerate into mere signs with strictly limited connotations, conveying information but devoid of any power to evoke a response from our feelings. Their interpretation then degenerates also, becoming little more than a kind of parlor game.

Much dream interpretation, however, has depended in the past on the use of fixed symbols. Even today all popular dream books rely almost entirely on standardized interpretations.

Some people would say the same about crude popularizations of psychoanalytic dream theories. A man may have been told, for instance, that, to Freud, such objects as sticks, keys, and tools are all phallic symbols, and boxes, rooms, and pockets symbols of feminine sexuality. Why then, he might ask, should the male organ appear in one dream as a sword and in another as a fountain pen? One critic of Freud, when told that to dream of putting a key in a lock symbolized the sexual act, asked whether dreaming of sexual intercourse meant that he was actually dreaming of putting a key in a lock.

There are, of course, sensible answers to witticisms of this kind. But the fact that such jokes can be made underlines the difficulty of drawing a line between superstitious and serious attempts to understand dream symbolism. This difficulty led the noted American psychoanalyst Dr. Karl Menninger forcefully to assert his objection to popular dream interpretations.

"The telling and interpreting of dreams at teas, informal gatherings, and in drawing rooms, have exactly the same scientific status as horoscope reading, fortune-telling by cards, and ouija board predictions. Even a trained analyst cannot attempt with any certainty to interpret the dreams of a patient until he is thoroughly familiar with the case history."

Dr. Menninger was expressing understandable resentment. He and his professional colleagues are anxious to distinguish between their type of dream interpretation and the type that assumes that the meaning of dreams can be found simply by looking up the appropriate symbols in a reference book.

Yet, as critics of Freud have consistently pointed out, though psychoanalysis may now be a recognized form of therapy, it is by no means a science. It may be highly effective in dealing with people who are mentally ill, or even in providing plausible explanations of mental processes, but it is extremely difficult to test Freudian theories by any experimental method. Attempts have been made, it is true. And these experiments, almost all of them conducted by people who hoped to prove that Freud was right in his theories about symbolism, are claimed as confirmation of Freudian ideas. But they are no more convincing or less controversial than the reports of anthropologists that the dreams of distant tribal societies reveal universal symbolic patterns, or than Jung's attempt to show that comparable motifs can be found in the dreams of modern neurotics and of children, in the folk tales of peasant communities, and in the myths of antiquity. Any one of these theories may be right—or wrong. All the studies on which they are based are fascinating and suggestive; none, so far, is definitive.

This does not mean that they should be discarded, or that all dream interpretation is valueless because the interpreters disagree. On the contrary, despite the difficulties that the interpretation of dreams involves, and for all the passionate arguments it evokes, it is one of the ways in which man can continue the exploration of his inner nature. In years to come, now that the scientific investigation of dreaming has become possible, we should increasingly be able to distinguish fact from fancy, and either confirm or modify the theories of Freud and other psychologists. But in the meantime we must think skeptically rather than dogmatically about dreams.

Skepticism, however, does not impose a rule of silence upon us. It merely demands that as we examine the ways man has regarded his dreams throughout history, down to the latest discoveries made by American scientists, we must never lose sight of the real objective. This is not to prove one theory or disprove another. It is to use dreams, the manifestation of man's hidden mental processes, to achieve a greater understanding of the way he thinks, feels, and behaves, to seek out the sources of his hopes and fears, his loves and hates, so that he may live more richly and responsibly.

This is the century in which man has probed the riddle of matter by the techniques of nuclear physics, and reached out into space with radar and rockets. It is also the century in which men are beginning to explore the enigmas of human personality more rewardingly than ever before. In that search, the study of dreams has already played a vital part and it will continue to do so. For few routes lead us so directly to the fantasies of man's inner world as that which Freud called the "royal road" of dreams.

2   Gods and demons

As soon as human beings developed a written language, they began to set down their dreams and record ways in which they might be interpreted. Few early records survive, but even in the fragments that have been preserved from ancient Egypt—written in hieroglyphs that were themselves a series of picture symbols—we find evidence of the importance that the Egyptians attached to dreams and to oneirology, or dream interpretation. Almost 4000 years ago, Egypt had a flourishing and sophisticated civilization, an elaborate system of government, complex religious ideas, and a widespread belief in magic. In all these aspects of life dreams clearly played an important part. This is common knowledge to every reader of the Bible, in which the dreams of Joseph and Pharaoh are reported and interpreted in detail.

Archaeology has revealed even more about the Egyptian attitude to dreams. We now know, for instance, that the Egyptians believed that the gods revealed themselves in dreams; but, unlike other peoples in the Near East, and in the Orient, they do not seem to have thought that the soul could leave the body and travel abroad while a man was sleeping. To them, dreams were relatively straightforward. They were simply the perception of things that existed but could not be seen or heard in waking life. By various means, ranging from divine inspiration to ritual incantations, and even the use of potions and ointments to summon the "invisible spirits," Egyptians tried to make contact

A painting from the 12th-century Lambeth Bible shows Jacob's dream of a ladder linking earth and heaven with angels ascending and descending. God stood at the top of the ladder and promised that the land on which Jacob slept would be his, and that his seed would multiply and spread throughout the world. The Bible records many such "divine" dreams. In common with other peoples of the Near East the Hebrews believed that some dreams were divinely inspired messages whose guidance men should accept.

with this other world. They believed that from such contacts they derived warnings, advice, success in love or other ventures, recovery from illness, or merely pleasurable experiences.

Such beliefs go back deep into the history of Egypt. Dream interpretation was already an advanced technique by the time of the earliest extant record—the first, as far as we know, of the thousands of dream books to which men have turned to look for the meaning of their dreams. Now in the British Museum, it is usually called—after its donor—the Chester Beatty papyrus. It comes from Thebes in Upper Egypt and was written around 1350 B.C., although it incorporates material dating back probably to 2000 B.C. It makes the distinction between "good" and "bad" dreams that crops up again and again in all forms of dream interpretation up to modern times, and in two other ways also it anticipates later techniques.

It uses the idea of contraries—to dream of death, for example, is an omen of long life—which occurs in dream books from the very earliest to those of today, and which also appears in Freud's psychological interpretation of dreams. And it relies on verbal or visual puns or on hidden associations. The Egyptian word for buttocks resembles the word for orphan; and the papyrus dream book states that to dream of uncovering one's buttocks is an omen of one's parent's death. Probably, in more recent dream books, entries that seem peculiarly arbitrary in English had their origins in such verbal likenesses in languages long dead.

Some 200 *omina*, or dreams, are preserved in the Chester Beatty papyrus. It is good, we are told, to dream of copulating with one's mother; for this signifies that one's relatives will be loyal. It is good to dream of sawing wood, for this portends the death of enemies. But it is bad to dream of teeth falling out, which means death at the hands of one's dependents.

The papyrus includes several incantations for warding off the effects of unpleasant or threatening dreams. In one of these the dreamer recites a dialogue between the god Horus and his mother Isis:

"Come to me, come to me, my mother Isis. Behold, I am seeing what is far from me in my city."

"Here I am, my son Horus, come out with what thou hast seen, in order that thy afflictions through thy dreams may vanish, and fire go forth against him that frighteneth thee. Behold, I am come that I may see thee and drive forth thy ills and extirpate all that is filthy."

A papyrus from an Egyptian Book of the Dead (*c.* 1300 B.C.), showing a funeral procession with some of the rituals that ensured the safe arrival of the dead in the spirit world. From here they could still communicate with the living—principally through dreams.

Incantations seem to have played a substantial part in Egyptian ritual, though—like the practices that accompanied them, they often appear to have been closer to magic than to the religious spirit of the appeal to Horus and Isis. For example, the formula for ensuring that a friend (or an enemy) is sent a special dream will be more effective if it is stuffed into the mouth of a dead cat. In another case, which reminds us that the roots of what Europe called witchcraft lie far back in the past, an appeal to the "dark" god Seth could be made in these terms: "Take a clean linen bag and write upon it the names given. Fold it to make a lampwick and light it by pouring oil upon it. The words are Armuith, Lailamchonch, Arsenophrephren, Phtha, Archentechtha. Then, in the evening, going to bed without food, do thus: approach the lamp and repeat the formula seven times, put out the light and lie down to sleep. The formula is: Sachmu . . . eparma Ligotereench. The Aeon, the Thunderer, thou that hath swallowed the snake and dost exhaust the moon, and raiseth the sun in his season, Chtetho is thy name. I ask, O Lord of the gods, Seth, Chreps, give me the information I require."

Naturally, most of the dreams recorded are dreams of important persons, such as priests and kings. They fall into three main groups. The first are dreams in which the gods appear to demand some pious act. A large stone inscription placed before the giant sphinx at Giza tells of the dream of King Thutmose IV, who reigned about 1450 B.C., in which the god Hormakhu promised him the kingdom; in return, on becoming ruler, Thutmose cleared the sands away from the sphinx. The historian Plutarch notes a similar dream in which Ptolemy Soter saw a colossal statue, which ordered him to take it back to its original site in Alexandria. On waking, he ordered a search to be made for the statue, and when it was found, he had it returned.

In the second group of important dreams, the gods give unsolicited warnings or revelations. Some of these (as in the Books of the Dead and in the earliest medical papyri) reveal the hiding place of religious inscriptions used in funerary or medical magic. Others are predictive, like the dream of Tanutamon, the Ethiopian conqueror of Egypt, who saw a serpent to his left and another to his right. This was interpreted as an omen that he would rule the two Egypts, North and South.

Among these unsolicited dreams is one of the type that the Swiss psychologist C. G. Jung called "great" dreams, in which the dream content repeats a great mythological theme. The wife of Setme Khamuas, a great Egyptian magician, was barren. In a dream she was advised to go to her husband's privy and make a potion from the plant colocasia to give to her husband. The remedy apparently succeeded. Then, in a subsequent dream, the father was told how to name the child, who would become a great magician himself, leading and helping his people. This dream contains many of the elements of the "world-savior" myths —prophecying the coming of a miraculous leader —that were widespread in antiquity throughout the Near and Far East.

In contrast to such unexpected dreams, there was a third category: dreams invoked by elaborate rituals for specific purposes. A whole caste of priests, called "Masters of the Secret Things" or "Scribes of the Double House of Life," devoted themselves to such services, and practiced their mysteries in special temples. The most important was the temple at Memphis, dedicated to Imhotep, the god of healing. Imhotep, known to the Greeks as Imouthes, lived about 2980-50 B.C., was a noted architect (he built the Saqqara pyramid), an important medical man, and one of the astrologers of the priests of Ra. After his death he was gradually elevated to the status of a deity, and his temple became the center of a healing cult whose beliefs have persisted almost to modern times. For the priests at Memphis, like those in the sanctuary of Isis at Philae, and at the oracles of Khimunu and Thebes, practiced "incubation." This simply meant that sick persons were brought to sleep in the temple, where they fasted, or took potions, to induce beneficial dreams.

Like many of the Egyptian attitudes to dreams, the idea of incubation was passed on to later civilizations (the Greeks especially borrowed heavily, taking over gods, magic learning, and medicine from Egyptian traditions.)

But the Egyptians themselves had borrowed from earlier societies. In the millennia before the birth of Christ, men throughout the whole of the Near East were beginning to experiment with urban life and the creation of empires, with religious, philosophical, magical, and scientific ideas. One after another, in the crescent that stretched from the Mediterranean to India, civilizations rose and fell, cross-fertilizing each other with concepts and techniques that were carried by conquest and trade. The later Egyptian forms of dream interpretation, possibly even the cult of incubation, resemble earlier practices in Mesopotamia (and significantly differ from the main Egyptian tradition) closely enough to suggest that the Egyptians had grafted Assyrian ideas and methods on to their own concepts—as they certainly did with astrology.

Above, the stone inscription on the giant sphinx at Giza tells how Thutmose IV cleared the statue of sand in obedience to a dream sent by the god Hormakhu.

A wooden statue (*c.* 1250 B.C.), of the Egyptian god Bes, who was believed to protect sleepers against the demons of the night and send them pleasant and good dreams. Appeals to Bes took the form of rituals and magic spells involving strange ingredients. One papyrus declared that the ink for a petition must be made from the blood of a white dove, mulberry juice, cinnabar, rainwater, and myrrh.

One image that recurs in both the recorded dreams and art of the ancient Near East is that of giant creatures—half man, half beast—like the winged bull with a human head (left) from the palace of the Assyrian king Sargon II (eighth century B.C.).

Right, Gilgamesh, the most famous of all Assyro-Babylonian heroes—part-man, part-god—shown watering a bull (on a cylinder seal from the third century B.C.). The epic poem describing his exploits—composed before the Bible and probably dating back to 2000 B.C.—contains the earliest known series of dreams.

Yet there were important differences between the Sumerian-Babylonian view of the cosmos, and man's place in it, and that of the Egyptians. The peoples of Assyria and Mesopotamia were animists—that is, they saw themselves surrounded by natural forces that represented gods to be propitiated and devils to be feared. Anxious in the present, fearful for the future, feeling themselves the prey of powerful forces beyond their comprehension or control, they turned to a whole armory of devices for protection and reassurance—amulets and magic spells, prophecy, divination, and dream interpretation. The Babylonians, regarding the cosmos as a whole, concluded that events occurring in one part of it were reflected in another, and sought continually for causal connections between events. They believed that if one event (such as the birth of a freak, the appearance of a comet, or even a particular type of dream) was followed by another event (such as death, invasion, or conception by a barren woman), the repetition of the first event might be a signal that the second was about to recur. With this belief, every kind of omen became significant to them. They seem, however, to have divided omens into two main classes: those that concerned the ruler, the priests, and other high officials, which were the peculiar province of astrology; and those relating to private persons, for whom dreams were specially relevant.

The dreams of eminent men were treated seriously. As we find later in both Greece and Rome, a distinction was made between "divine" dreams, that had to be interpreted and obeyed, and "ordinary" dreams. The latter were often divided into "good" dreams sent by the gods and "bad" dreams sent by demons, which demanded some kind of cleansing or protective ritual. One of the functions of the priests or magicians was to enable the dreamer to tell whether a dream was "good" or "bad." This could well be difficult. Even in the Christian era, St. Augustine worried about how to tell pious dreams from mere delusions; and as late as the 13th century St. Thomas Aquinas drew a line between dreams of "divine revelations" and "unlawful and superstitious" divinations from the dreams inspired by demons.

Generally, in the pre-Christian Near East "divine" dreams were messages sent to a king or priests; many are recorded, but most are in a form so stereotyped that it is clear the dream has been edited to a conventional pattern. The irrational or symbolically complex contents customary in dreams rarely appear; when they do—the dreams of Nebuchadnezzar and Pharaoh in the Old Testament are typical examples—they are accompanied by rational or divinely confirmed interpretations.

Dreams from the whole of the Near East in this period contain frequent references to giants, or to gigantic hybrid creatures that seem to resemble the winged lions and other composite beasts found today among ruined palaces and temples. A Sumerian inscription, *The Dream of Gudea*, which dates back to the third millennium B.C., describes one of these figures:

"In the dream, the first man—like the heaven was his surpassing [size], like the earth was his surpassing [size], [according] to his wings he was Imduged [the bird of the weather-god], [according] to his lower parts [?] he was the storm-flood . . ."

Another example comes from a later religious poem: "In a dream as well as in a vision at dawn was shown a man surpassing in size, of glorious form, beautifully clad." And in the Gilgamesh epic, the oldest series of dreams known to us, the image of cosmic man again plays an important part. It is difficult to interpret these dreams, or to set them fully in their cultural context, because our knowledge of them and of the period is fragmentary. But the similarity of such dreams, especially the emphasis on these towering phantoms, suggests that they may all be incubation dreams, in which the dreamer has been sleeping at the foot of an enormous idol or within a sanctuary containing strange statues. If such dreams were assisted by hallucinatory drugs— and the only evidence at present is the resemblance between certain ancient visions and those seen by modern patients under the influence of hallucinogens—it is even more likely that the dreamer's fantasies would accommodate such emotionally affective elements as the idol of a god he was invoking.

There seems to be little doubt that in Assyria, as in Egypt, dreams were used in therapeutic processes. There are many rituals for dispelling the effect of evil dreams: about 1700 B.C., a poem from Babylon describes how a noble has been made ill by demons coming from the nether world, and how three dreams lead to his recovery. This is why the interpretation of bad dreams was more important than the deciphering of pleasant or obvious dreams—something had to be done about them. Anticipating contemporary psychoanalysis, the Assyrians believed that once the enigma presented by the dreams had been worked out the disturbing symptoms or the affliction would pass. But whereas modern psychoanalysis uses the dream to illuminate the hidden conflicts and repressed anxieties of the patient, the Assyrians believed either that a demon must be exorcized, or that the appropriate deity would reveal the means by which the sufferer could be treated.

The Assyrians certainly depended on dream books for help. This much we know from clay tablets found at Nineveh, in the library of the Assyrian king Ashurbanipal, who reigned between 669 and 626 B.C. This library, the oldest

Two Biblical dreams. Left, a medieval picture of the prophet Zechariah's vision of horses patrolling the world. The horses, according to a modern interpreter, represent different periods of ancient history. The vision was God's promise that, just as he had sent peace to other peoples in other times, so he would send peace to the Jews. Right, a representation from a 13th-century manuscript of Pharaoh's dream of seven fat and seven lean kine. When Egyptian wise men were unable to tell the meaning of this dream, Joseph the Jew was summoned. His interpretation was that seven years of plenty would be followed by seven years of famine.

directly known to us, was a repository of learning reaching back to the dawn of civilization—possibly to 5000 B.C. The Nineveh tablets, in fact, provide the link in a chain of dream theory that stretches from the most remote past to our own time. It is believed that Ashurbanipal's dream book was used by the Roman soothsayer Artemidorus (about A.D. 140), whose work has in turn inspired almost every subsequent compiler of dream books.

The Ashurbanipal tablets tell us, for example, that if a man flies repeatedly in his dreams, whatever he owns will be lost. In *Zolar's Encyclopedia and Dictionary of Dreams*, published in New York in 1963, we read: "Flying at a low altitude: ruin is ahead for you." Another idea that persisted is that dreams go by contraries. If an Assyrian dreamed that he was blessed by a god, he expected to experience that god's wrath; but "if the god utters a curse against the man, his prayer will be accepted." If you are cursed in a dream, Zolar tells us in 1963, "ambitions will be realized."

For most people, the dreams of antiquity are best known through the many examples in the Old Testament—the dreams of Joseph and Pharaoh, of

Daniel and Nebuchadnezzar, of Jacob and Solomon. But all these dreams, and the attitude of the Jews toward them, fit into the pattern of dream theory current throughout the Near East in the pre-Christian era. Nor is this surprising. The Jews, after all, had been in captivity in Babylon, where dream cults were widespread, and the largest collection of Jewish sacred writings—the Babylonian Talmud—was set down between the sixth and second centuries B.C. It is full of references to dreams, rules for interpreting dreams, and means of avoiding evil dreams. For, like other peoples in this region, the Jews distinguished between good dreams and those that were the work of malevolent spirits.

But there is one important difference between the Jewish view of dreams and that of the pre-Christian Near East. The Jews had become monotheistic, worshipers of one god rather than of many special gods. This difference, so vital in the development of religious ideas, was reflected in their view of dreams. For if there was only one god, he and he alone could be the source of the divine revelations that came in dreams. Since, moreover, he was the God of the Jews, he would usually—or at least on important occasions—speak clearly to them. His messages might seem garbled or enigmatic to non-Jews, such as Pharaoh or Nebuchadnezzar, and then Jews like Joseph or Daniel would be required to interpret them. Some such reasoning seems to lie behind the fact that almost all symbolic dreams in the Old Testament are dreamed by gentiles. It is true that the Talmud lays down principles of dream interpretation for ordinary people, and that there were many dream interpreters in old Jerusalem. But this popular interest in dreams may well have been a survival of Babylonian and Egyptian practices: the fact that several Jewish prophets gave warnings against false dreams and false interpreters suggests that there was a systematic effort to sharpen the distinction between divine and significant dreams and those that were either evil or without significance. Recognizing the traditional importance that was attached to dream interpretation, and the danger that religious heresy might arise from it, the orthodox prophets gave specific warnings against listening to such teaching. In Deuteronomy (XIII: 1-3) we read:

"If there arise among you a prophet, or a dreamer of dreams . . . saying, Let us go after other gods, which thou hast not known, and let us serve them, thou shalt not hearken unto the words of that prophet, or that dreamer of dreams; for the Lord your God proveth you, to know whether ye love the Lord your God with all your heart and with all your soul."

Despite the special emphasis which the Jews had begun to give to dream theory, they continued to classify dreams in much the same way as the peoples in neighboring territories. In some cases, when the wishes of Jehovah are made known through an angelic messenger, it is hard to distinguish between dreams and waking visions. In other cases, the dreamer hears the voice of God, or may even, like Solomon in Gideon, see the Lord himself. It seems clear that

A romanic sculpture depicting the dream of the Three Wise Men. In their dream God warned them not to return to tell Herod where to find the infant Christ.

Solomon's dream was in fact an incubation dream. He went to Gideon "to sacrifice there: for that was the great high place." So, too, was Samuel's dream when he slept in the temple of the Lord "where the ark of God was."

It is, of course, possible to read these biblical dreams in the light of modern conceptions. Psychological writers like Jung and Erich Fromm have analyzed ancient dreams to show how they may reveal much about dream patterns, and even the degree to which the ancients used their experience of dreams to reach certain insights into the dream process. Fromm has pointed out, for instance, that the Talmud says that three types of dream are fulfilled—dreams in the early morning, just before waking; a dream of a friend about oneself; and a dream that is interpreted by another dream. The modern psychoanalyst would concede that each of these three types of dream is significant. And if we assume that ideas and possibilities appear in our dreams of which, awake, we are unaware, it is possible to see the dreams of both Joseph and Pharaoh as examples of intuitive knowledge expressed in the symbolic language of the dream. Joseph's image of the sheaves bowing down may reveal his inner realization both of his talents and of the ambition that would carry him to great eminence. Pharaoh, too, could have been "unconsciously" aware of climatic factors that could lead to a seven-year period of rich harvests followed by seven years of famine, but the awareness broke through dramatically only in the form of the dream allegory of seven fat and seven thin kine.

Prophetic dreams are also found in the New Testament. Some of the most significant are found in St. Matthew's gospel (I: 20). "Behold, the angel of the Lord appeared unto him in a dream, saying, Joseph, thou son of David, fear not to take unto thee Mary thy wife; for that which is conceived in her is of the Holy Ghost." The flight into Egypt is linked to three dreams: in the first, the wise men are warned not to return to Herod; in the second, an angel appears in a dream, telling the Holy Family to go into Egypt to escape Herod; and, after Herod's death, an angel again appears in a dream to Joseph in Egypt, telling him to return to the land of Israel. Finally, we are told that the wife of Pontius Pilate urged her husband to release "that just man" Jesus, rather than Barabbas, "for I have suffered many things this day in a dream because of him."

The last of these dreams is curious. The dreams in the Bible are almost all fulfilled, for the dreamer answers the divine message; in this one, however, Pilate remains unmoved and Jesus is crucified. We are left wondering whether,

A Persian miniature painting of one of the many appearances of the Archangel Gabriel to the prophet Mohammed. The ancient world accepted such miraculous experiences as facts, but today many people would regard them as dreams.

behind this brief report, there lies a fragment of an older tradition such as we find in the early Coptic Church, in which both Moses and Jesus are seen as powerful magicians with the gift of miracles, visions, and even faith healing. There are good reasons why, in the account attributed to the apostle Matthew many years later, this aspect of the Christian story should have been played down, for the early Christians waged a long struggle against magic, divination, and other pagan practices.

More striking evidence of this is found in the apocryphal books of the Bible. Not only was the early Christian movement greatly taken up with the struggle between Moses, Aaron, and Pharaoh's magicians, and with the dreams of Daniel and Joseph; it was also concerned with the magical numbers of seven and twelve, the first of which is linked in astrology to the number of planets, and the second to the signs of the zodiac. Thus, in the Bible, we read of the seven-branched candlestick and the twelve cakes of shewbread. And to return to the dream of Pilate's wife, in the apocryphal Gospel of Nicodemus the Jews actually tell Pilate that Jesus is a conjurer. Pilate's wife then gives him the dream warning, but the chief priests reply: "Did we not say unto thee, he is a magician? Behold, he hath caused thy wife to dream."

If appears that throughout the ancient Near East there was a common tradition of oneiromancy strong enough to link the dream theories of peoples as different in other ways as the Assyrians, Egyptians, Jews, and, as we shall see, the Greeks of the classical period. There were local variations; there was undoubtedly borrowing and modification of ideas from one culture to another. There is not enough evidence to trace this process in detail, but all the surviving material points to the existence of this powerful, widespread, and historically continuous tradition of dream interpretation. Its persistence is further emphasized by an examination of the role dreams played in the Mohammedan religion, which sprang from the same area.

Drawing on and modifying Judaic concepts, using similar sources and some texts now lost to us, Mohammed's sacred book, the Koran, essentially embodies the same beliefs about dreams. There is the same effort to make a distinction between true, or divine, dreams, and false dreams; the same dependence on certain rituals to induce good dreams or to defend oneself against the dangers of bad ones; the same reliance upon holy interpreters and suspicions of false and misleading prophets; the same recourse to sanctioned dream books, usually the Koran, or texts based closely upon it. There was, too, the decline in the therapeutic use of dreams begun by the Jews (the healing aspects of oneiromancy survived more strongly among the Greeks and Romans). And there was the growing awareness, which we noted in Isaiah, that some dreams at least might have a physiological cause. Four types of dream, at least, were considered false, but not inspired by demons: those of persons of evil disposition; of wine drinkers; of eaters of depressing foods such as lentils and salt meat; and of children.

The prophet Mohammed himself attached great significance to dreams. Each morning he would ask his disciples what they had dreamed during the night, interpret the dreams he thought of value, and tell them his own dreams. And from the Koran and the numerous Mohammedan dream books it is plain that the principles of dream interpretation that the prophet used were those already familiar to us from other Near Eastern religions. His followers attached much importance both to truthful telling of the dream—and believed, incidentally, that it was best told immediately on waking—and to the quality of the interpreter. To aid his task, they thought he should take into account the name of the dreamer, his age and place of origin, and his occupation, religion, rank, and condition in life. This emphasis on the personal characteristics of the dreamer represents an advance over the mechanical interpretation of dreams, in which the dreamer or interpreter simply turns to the dream book to find the meaning of a symbol (a crude technique on which many modern dream books rely), and it is much closer to contemporary psychological practice, where the dream is examined for the insight its symbols give into the whole personality of the dreamer.

Certainly this stress on individual circumstances gave much greater sophistication to the process of interpretation. Not only did it permit the same symbol to mean different things to different dreamers; it also opened the way to a more elaborate symbolic system. The interpreter was no longer confined to the use of similarities or contraries; the distinction between good but self-evident dreams, and enigmatic but false dreams, became less significant; and more subtle interpretations were possible. Quite apart from a hierarchy of importance, which gave great prestige to the dreams of rulers and little authority to those of poor people ("they are constantly in grief and anxiety . . . and if they have good predicted, its fulfillment is distant"), Mohammedan dream codes gave priority to the dreams of men, and among women to the dreams of married women who were chaste and dignified. The matter was taken so seriously that interpreters were held in high favor and magnificently rewarded for beneficial interpretations. And where the interpreters differed, the consequences could be grave. A religion based on the Koran (the first part of which had been revealed to Mohammed in a dream), a movement whose possession of the holy city of Mecca had been promised in a dream, and a people to whom dream interpretation was an everyday affair, were likely to express any schism of faith in the same manner. The division of Islam into conflicting factions—a split that threatened the whole Mohammedan empire—was actually based on the dream of Mohammed, which the Sunnis used to justify the rights of his successors.

The ways in which Arabic dream theories worked are clearly seen in the writings of Gabdorrachaman, which became known in Europe through a French translation in 1664. If an egg appeared in a dream, it concerned women, for the Koran says: "Women are like an egg hidden in the nest."

Because Mohammed once called a shrew "a little adulteress," all dreams about shrews relate to faithless wives. If a word appears in a dream, it will be realized literally, or in precisely the contrary sense. If a man of probity dreams that his hands are tied, this merely indicates his aversion from evil, but in a wicked man such a dream prognosticates his final damnation. Later Mohammedan dream theory also introduced astrological ideas, relating dreams to the phases of the moon and planets, to the day of the week or the month. These concepts—as they spread eastward through Asia—fused with rather different oriental attitudes to dreams.

Classical Greece left an immense heritage to the modern world, in philosophy and politics, literature and architecture—a heritage in which the creative genius of the Greeks was enriched by the thinking of Egypt, and, through the Greek colonies in Asia Minor, with that of Babylon, Persia, and even beyond. The Greeks were original; but they were also brilliantly eclectic, adopting whatever seemed useful or interesting from the peoples with whom war or trade brought them into contact. The traces of this process are clearly shown in their attitude to dreams, which contains much that we can recognize as being of Egyptian or Babylonian origin, as well as much that was unusual, sophisticated, and peculiarly their own contribution.

The dream experience of the Greeks had themes similar to other Near East dream patterns. They, too, had dreams that they believed were divine, originating in Homeric times from Zeus, and, in later centuries, from others of their numerous gods. Sometimes the god himself appeared; more often a messenger was the emissary. Again, they made the customary distinction between "true" and "false" dreams, though they also faced the consequent problem of how to distinguish one from the other. Homer tells us that "true" dreams come through the gate of horn, and "false" dreams through the gate of ivory (a difference that was based upon a Greek pun), and later writers sustain this distinction. The Greek dreams contain famous prophecies, some of which are preserved for us by Herodotus. He tells, for instance, how Xerxes came to make his disastrous expedition into Greece. Two dreams convinced him that the planned attack was sensible.

There are many stories of important dreams in Greek legends, most of them taking a highly conventional form. The special interest in the Greek dream experience, however, lies less in the rich stores of dreams preserved in their literature and history than in two other aspects. The first is the widespread use of the cult of incubation—which was then passed on to the Romans and acquired from them by early Christians. The second is the emergence of a more rational and, indeed, inquiring attitude to dreams as natural phenomena: Plato, Aristotle, and some other philosophers seem to have approached more nearly to the modern conception of dreams than most writers in the intervening centuries. One might say, in fact, that the division between oneiromancy as a mystical or magic system and the serious treatment of

The early Greeks assumed the figures in
dreams to be people who lived near
the underworld. They entered the world,
Homer said, by the two Gates shown in
this 17th-century French engraving.
True dreams came through the Gate of
Horn, false through the Gate of Ivory.

dreams really begins in classical Greece, and that our own separation of dream attitudes into the popular and the scientific stems from this period.

The Greek cult of incubation, like the Egyptian, combined the search for divine or "true" dreams, relevant to many problems of everyday life, with a strong emphasis upon the therapeutic function of dreaming. In Greece, this cult may have superimposed practices taken from the Egyptians upon an older and more primitive fertility religion. The most famous oracles seem originally to have been earth oracles, related to the worship of underworld gods. And it is significant that the practice of incubation—which has been found in many cultures, from Central America to that of the Australian aborigines, from China to North Africa—has the cure of sterility as its central and original theme.

There is a great deal of evidence on this point, and it is underlined by the fact that many of these oracles assumed some sort of sexual union with a god or goddess during sleep in the temple—with Isis and Seraphis in Greece and Rome, with Diana in Ephesus, or Ino in Sparta—or through forms of sacred prostitution. Though the original theme may be sexual, it is understandable that a healing cult could extend from the treatment of sexual inadequacy to the cure of a variety of other ills. Incubation became such an element in everyday life that it was among the most popular and persistent of religious rites—the gods associated with it proving to have so strong an appeal to the public that the early Christians found them the most difficult to eliminate.

Many sacred places in Greece were used for incubation—remote hillsides, lonely caverns, gorges, streams, even ordinary temples in or near cities. They were dedicated to different gods, and the practices differed. The common elements were some form of anointment or purification and sleep induced by drugs, herbs, or other potions, or simply by the poor air in the place; and then either the interpretation of the dream by the priests of the oracle or, in medical cases, the administration of the cure indicated by the dream. The most famous of these oracles was that of Aesculapius of Epidaurus, whose cult spread rapidly until there were over 300 incubation centers devoted to Aesculapian therapy alone. Significantly, in view of the sexual theme associated with incubation, the symbol of Aesculapius was the serpent, one of the most potent religious symbols of the ancient world and one that modern psychoanalysis indentifies not only with the male sex organ but specifically with the sex organ of the father. Snake worship and ancestor worship are closely associated in many primitive societies, and the snake is seen as a token of strength, tradition, fertility, and health. Here again is evidence that Aesculapian concepts were built on much earlier foundations.

Aesculapius himself was a real person who had been deified (in the same way as the Egyptians had earlier elevated Imhotep into the god of healing). He lived about 1100 B.C., before the Trojan wars, and Homer calls him a hero who had been instructed in the art of healing by Cheiron. Worshiped originally as an earth spirit, with the serpent symbol, he was steadily elevated to the rank of son to Apollo, which entitled him to share in the sun symbol.

The incubation center at Epidaurus was in use for several centuries; the earliest inscriptions suggest that the worship of Aesculapius began there in the fifth century B.C. and continued for hundreds of years. Most of our knowledge of the practices employed there comes, in fact, from the end of the period, and especially from the *Sacred Orations* of Aristides, written about A.D. 150, in which the writer tells how Aesculapian therapy cured him of a long illness. The methods he describes may have changed during the centuries, as indeed they varied from place to place. Sometimes sacrifices were expected; in other places gifts of money or food, according to means; sometimes sleep was induced by ointments or potions; sometimes the patients were put into hypnotic trances, or at least, when they were in a receptive frame of mind, given suggestions by the priests or encouraged to develop forms of auto-suggestion.

What remains common to all such cults, however, is the central role assigned to the dream, in which the god appeared to indicate a remedy.

Those who slept in the Aesculapian temples to be cured of their illnesses first took part in various preparatory ceremonies. These ceremonies varied from temple to temple, but often the patient was shown the tablets put up by former patients recording their cures—like the relief (left), dating from the fourth century B.C., of Aesculapius and his family. Shortly before he slept the patient was taken to see a statue of the god so that it might inspire him with feelings of awe (below left, detail of statue of Aesculapius from the second century A.D.).

Then the patient prayed and sacrificed an animal, usually a ram, to the god. Above, a carving from an urn (early second century A.D.) shows a similar sacrifice.

Aristides tells us that he was given, in dreams, many odd commandments: to go barefoot in winter, to use emetics, and even to sacrifice one of his fingers. A modern writer, E. R. Dodds, has said that these dreams look like "the expression of a deep-seated desire for self-punishment," and that "obedience to such dreams may well have procured a temporary abatement of neurotic symptoms." The symptoms Aristides describes certainly sound like those of severe neurosis. He suffered from indigestion and insomnia, perpetual sweating, and choking in the throat. A modern doctor might diagnose a chronic anxiety state. Yet, at that time, the Aesculapian dream therapy was the only resort for such persons. And Aristides movingly describes the intensity of his emotional experiences while he was undergoing this primitive form of psychoanalysis:

"One listened and heard things, sometimes as in a dream, sometimes as in a waking life. One's hair stood on end; one cried and felt happy; one's heart swelled but not with vainglory. What human being could put this experience into words? But anyone who has been through it will share my knowledge and recognize the state of mind."

Finally, the patient lay down to sleep on the skin of the sacrificed animal beside the god's statue (left). Evidence suggests that often the priests returned later in the night, dressed as gods, to give medical treatment. Below, a relief (c. 400 B.C.) shows a patient being treated by Aesculapius. In the morning the priests interpreted his dreams and gave instructions for the future care of his health.

There was, no doubt, a great deal of charlatanism in such dream cults, especially when the priests took over the task of dreaming for the supplicants and mixed various forms of magic in their ceremonies to make them more obscure and therefore more impressive. And the cures—mostly, one suspects, of hysteria or other psychosomatic conditions—were almost certainly offset by the failures. If one puts many people at the mercy of their own unconscious, disguised as divine advice, there are bound to be tragedies.

Yet enough cures took place for the practice to survive; as in prediction, one success in faith healing outweighs a thousand failures. And it survived, through Rome, into Christianity. The new religion rejected much of the pagan world's customs and beliefs; yet it took over some part of them. Christian saints replaced pagan deities; Christian festivals were grafted on to pagan festivals; Christian miracles replaced the miraculous healing of Aesculapius. And the practice of incubation also remained, though in an attenuated form. Union with the god or goddess in sleep was replaced by prayers, often directed to the patron saint of a shrine noted for its healing powers, sometimes to the Archangel Michael, who took over some of the attributes of Apollo. The element of fertility ritual remained, but its form changed. The serpent, now identified with Satan and with sexuality, disappears back into the underworld, and the new holy places are not caves or sacred groves—long associated with fertility rites—but wells and springs; the unconscious association here seems to mark a shift of emphasis from the act of procreation to the act of

Today, pilgrims still sleep in the church at Tenos in Greece, where a picture supposedly by St. Luke—and discovered through a series of dreams—is believed to have healing powers.

Below, abandoned crutches testify to successful cures at the Grotto at Lourdes (France), famous for its healing waters since 1858, when the Virgin is said to have appeared to a peasant girl.

birth. But the search for dreams, later generalized into divine inspiration, continued: the practice of sleeping in a church, often after fasting, long survived. The belief that certain places are endowed with the power of miraculous healing is still with us, not only in such famous centers as the grotto at Lourdes, but in southern Italy, Greece, and Asia Minor.

While the Greeks were developing the cult of dreams into a popular therapeutic exercise, some Greek philosophers had begun to take a more speculative and less credulous view. Heraclitus, who lived from 540-475 B.C., was the first man known to have made the simple but vital statement that each man retreats in sleep into a world of his own. In one sentence, he thus detached the phenomenon of dreaming from the supernatural and made it a common human fact—but a fact, he seemed to think, that had no special meaning, for he advises us to follow in our conduct what we have in common, rather than subjective experiences. Another philosopher, Xenophanes, who lived shortly after Heraclitus, simply dismissed all forms of divination. But this was scarcely enough. Dreams plainly occurred, and had to be explained. They might be regarded simply as the carry-over into sleep of the cares and intentions of waking life, as Heraclitus suggests. Or, following the views of Democritus—the father of the atomistic view of the universe—dreams might be emanations from all persons and objects able, in a manner that seems to anticipate the idea of telepathy, to penetrate the dreamer's body and to enter his consciousness. Hippocrates, the founder of modern medicine, seems to have admitted a whole class of "divine" dreams, without caring much about them; what interested him—to judge from a Hippocratic treatise of about four centuries before Christ—were dreams whose symbolic form reveals what we now would call a morbid physiological condition. Such dreams, usually called "prodromic" (from the Greek word *prodromos*, "running before"), are in a distinct category. The appearance of symptoms of illness in dreams, long before they are evident in consciousness, is a phenomenon that has attracted much notice.

It is, however, in Plato and Aristotle, the greatest of the Greek philosophers, that a fundamentally new approach to dreams can be discerned. Plato, in *The Republic*, uses a phrase that strikingly anticipates Freud's theory of the relation between dreams and human instinct: "In all of us, even in good men, there is a lawless wild-beast nature, which peers out in sleep." And Aristotle, in his treatise *On Divination*, notes that physicians "tell us that one should pay diligent attention to dreams, and to hold this view is reasonable also for those who are not physicians but speculative philosophers."

Aristotle's most significant contribution, showing brilliant insight and a cool common-sense attitude, is found in three short essays: *On Sleep and Dreams, On Sleep,* and *On Divination Through Sleep.* Together they make up the earliest and one of the most interesting of all theories. Sleep, Aristotle suggests, reduces the activity of the senses; but residual sensory activity continues

The way specific dream symbols have been interpreted in four different cultures.

Greek

Different birds symbolize different types of people, thus eagles stand for people in power but wild pigeons for wicked women.

Pouring wine from vessels means peace of mind: draining a cup is a lucky token.

Trees from which ships are made are good omens for carpenters and mariners, but for other people they signify misfortune.

A snake signifies sickness and enmity: a powerful snake means a severe illness.

Bird on a fifth-century B.C. Greek coin.

Assyrian

To meet a bird in a dream shows that a lost belonging will be returned to the dreamer.

To be given an empty pot in a dream means the poor man will become poorer, but to be given a full goblet means the dreamer will be famous and have many children.

To be cutting down date palms signifies that the dreamer's problems will be solved.

To seize a snake means that the dreamer will receive protection from an angel.

Snake on a Sumerian vase (*c.* 3000 B.C.)

Jewish

It is unlucky to dream of an owl, but lucky to dream of any other kind of bird.

A dream of a cooking pot means peace (an interpretation based on a biblical text).

A dream of a palm tree means that the dreamer's sins will be punished.

To see a snake means the dreamer's livelihood is assured: if it bites him his livelihood will be doubled; if he kills it he will lose his livelihood.

Palm tree in a Jewish mosaic (*c.* 3000 A.D.)

Egyptian

A dream of catching birds signifies that some possessions will be lost.

To fill pots in a dream is a bad sign: it means the dreamer will experience great pain. Pouring beer from a vessel indicates that the dreamer will be robbed.
To be sitting on a tree shows that the dreamer's troubles will soon be overcome.

It is lucky to dream of a snake for it means that a dispute will be settled.

Egyptian vessel (*c.* 1000 B.C.).

even after the body has lapsed into torpor. Aristotle shows, by analyzing the nature of after-images, that the activity of sense organs such as the eye continues after the actual moment of perception. The senses, that is, can produce images that are not strictly dependent on external stimulation, and these images can be mistaken for real objects, especially under emotional stress. But why cannot a man appreciate this fact? Aristotle's answer is remarkable. He argues that our ability to judge perceptions and our capacity to have them—in the form of fantasies—are distinct functions. A man's mind may, therefore, be full of images in sleep, but be lacking in power to realize that these images are not reality. This process of absorbing sensations or impressions goes on all day, but passes without notice because the mind is subject to the much more obvious and powerful stimulus of waking experience. Finally, Aristotle understood that the effect of a dream on the dreamer after he wakes may be considerable, if only to set a mood which governs his behavior. "The movements set up first in sleep," he says, "should also prove to be starting points of actions to be performed in daytime, since the recurrence by day of the thought of these actions has also had the way prepared for it by the images which came before the mind at night."

Such rational considerations led Aristotle away from much of the superstitious muddle that surrounded dreams three centuries before the Christian era. Understandably, he thought little about divinely inspired prophetic dreams; if the gods wished to communicate with man, he suggested, they would do so in daylight and take more trouble in choosing the recipients. But he did see three ways in which dreams might be linked to the future. The first was the "prodromic" dream, in which small symptoms of an impending illness would be perceptible to the sleeper. The second, as we have noted, were cases in which the dream was the source of an idea or state of mind governing waking actions. Thirdly, in a point that recurs over and over again in later discussions of dream precognition, he observed that since there were so many dreams of such infinite variety, some of them were bound to resemble later events.

Aristotle has been one of the most influential figures in European thought, but his philosophy has fared better than his reflections on dreams. Relatively little attention was paid to them for 2000 years, until it was noticed how similar they were to modern theories—even his suggestion that the hallucinations of the insane, the illusions of the waking, and the fantasies of dreams are not merely similar, but may actually have a common origin. This is a more sophisticated theory than Plato's, but Plato's link between dreaming and hidden desires is not to be overlooked. When the rule of reason is suspended in sleep, Plato says, the two other elements of the soul—desire and anger—break through with all their unmitigated power, and the soul is prepared to accept incest, murder, and sacrilege. Here Plato approaches the idea of repressed aspects of personality that emerge only in dreams.

After such insight, his comments on morally superior dreams, and his apparent belief in demons as intermediaries between gods and men in sleep, both seem tamely conventional. Yet he did not pursue his insight further, or suggest how it might be applied to dream interpretation. The closest he came to that is in the *Timaeus*, in which he remarks: "It is sufficient proof that God coupled divination with human witlessness, that no one in his sober senses sets about divination of the really inspired sort unless he is asleep, when the intellectual faculties are tied up, or in an abnormal state through disease or some kind of enthusiasm." It was to be two millennia before the full force of that observation could be understood. Between the Greek philosophers and Freud stretched centuries in which men failed to come to grips with the essence of the dream process.

In those centuries the Greek states declined, and a new power rose to dominate the Mediterranean—Rome. But the Greek influence in the realm of ideas and art remained strong. The Romans were great soldiers and colonizers, carrying their standards to the ends of the known earth. But they borrowed religions and superstitions from others as easily as they imposed their political hegemony on them.

From Rome we have a mass of dreams, conflicting views of dreams, and contrasting forms of interpretation. For the Romans were addicted to divination of all kinds. The emperor Augustus who succeeded Julius Caesar took dreams so seriously that he made a law that anyone who dreamed about the commonwealth must proclaim it in the market place. The wife of Caesar himself, Calpurnia, was said by Plutarch to have dreamed of his assassination the night before he was stabbed to death. Tiberius, Caligula, and Domitian in turn had their deaths foretold in dreams. Many of these imperial dreams are reminiscent of the "official" dreams in other cultures; some sound as though they were invented by historians after the event, soothsaying being so widely accepted in Rome that its credit might seem undermined if an emperor's death or other important event had come and gone without such dream omens. Others may have been modified by the emperors or their advisers to fit a particular need of state: the emperor Constantine, trying to cope with the problems of the conversion of Rome to Christianity, certainly had some conveniently apposite dreams.

The dreams of Nero, however, sound more convincing. He dreamed of being covered by swarms of ants, of being dragged by his wife into a dark place, of being enclosed by the Roman national images and being unable to pass beyond them, and of various anatomical distortions. These dreams, though unpleasant, strike one as less official and more human than those recorded by other emperors: Nero clearly had psychological difficulties of some magnitude. This, indeed, may be one reason why his adviser Petronius was led to take such a common-sense attitude towards dreams: "It is neither the gods nor divine commandments that send the dreams down from the

Dream interpretation in Rome was mixed with forms of divination taken over from the Egyptians and the Greeks. Among these were astrology and palmistry. This magic hand of the third century A.D. is a typical occult device: carved with religious symbols it was supposed to avert the evil eye.

heavens", he said, "but each of us makes them for himself." Nero's was a case history from which Petronius could well have made this deduction.

Some Romans tried to liberate themselves from unthinking subservience to the occult. Titus Lucretius, living in the century before Christ, observed in terms that recall Aristotle's rationalism: " ... the mind is visited in sleep by the same images that it sees when awake, but we seem really to see, for instance, a dead man: this is because all the senses are at rest and cannot distinguish true from false. Moreover, memory is dormant and raises no objection. The figures seen in sleep seem to move and walk and gesticulate because one image succeeds another and so the former appears to change its position. Men dream about the activities and circumstances which occupy them in waking life ... repeat in their dreams the acts, emotions, and passions of life."

Yet, almost two hundred years later, the great classical physician Galen, who bitterly attacked many irrational methods of treatment, showed some lingering belief in the occult; he had, at the age of 17, turned from the study of philosophy to that of medicine specifically as a result of a dream. He appears to have been moving toward the idea of "prodromic" dreams, in which impending illness gives warning of its onset in the dream: the dream, that is, can be affected by daily life or physiological condition. Galen observes that dreams of fire are caused by yellow bile—what we might call a "liverish" state—while dreams of darkness indicate black bile. His attitude seems to have been very ambivalent. At times he attacks the idea of diagnosis through dreams, but he also mentions occasions when dreams guided him to cures. Nevertheless to do him justice, we should note that no modern psychoanalyst would wish to quarrel with his concluding statement: "It is necessary to observe dreams accurately both as to what is seen and what is done in sleep in order that you may prognosticate and heal satisfactorily."

Pliny, the historian who lived some 50 years earlier, was also taken with the idea that medical remedies might be disclosed in dreams. In his *Natural History* he tells of the discovery that the root of the wild rose is a cure for hydrophobia. The mother of one of the soldiers in the praetorian guard dreamed of it, and sent her son to find it. The cure is said to have worked. This sounds like a tale invented by Pliny or credulously accepted by him. Folk remedies of this kind were widely known, but associated with magic. To make them acceptable in Roman culture it was better that they should be introduced by means of a dream than by the less dramatic means of an old wives' tale.

None of these references, however, comes near in sophisticated reasoning to the analysis Cicero made in his essay *On Divination*—though even his rationalism had an unfortunate, even fatal, flaw. He was skeptical about dreams, but he took very seriously a dream in which he saw Octavius as a man who would rise to supreme power in Rome. He therefore cultivated him, and could well have expected reward when, from the struggle after the death of Julius Caesar, it was Octavius who emerged as the victor. But Cicero and his brother Quintus had provoked the enmity of Mark Antony, and when the purge lists were being drawn up Antony successfully demanded the killing of the brothers. This was an unhappy conclusion for a man who had challenged so forcefully the accepted dream theory of his time. Why, Cicero asked, if the gods can warn us of impending events, should they not do so clearly

Some dream interpretations by Artemidorus. Trees: a bay tree signifies a rich wife (top left: first-century A.D. terracotta lamp with tree). Birds: falcons stand for thieves (bottom left: Roman mosaic bird).

Snakes signify a long illness (top right: first-century A.D. bronze Roman snake). Cooking utensils: pots symbolize the dreamer's life—large pots, a long life (bottom right: silver saucepan A.D. 200).

when we are awake, rather than obscurely in sleep? How can one distinguish between true and false dreams? Either all come from nature, or none. "If, then, dreams do not come from God," he wrote, "and if there are no objects in nature with which they have a necessary sympathy and connection, and if it is impossible by experiments and observations to arrive at an interpretation of them, the consequence is that dreams are not entitled to any credit or respect whatever."

Much of what Cicero says clearly anticipates later criticism of all forms of dream interpretation and it is worth looking at some of his other points. He was dubious about prophecies. "From the visions of drunkards and madmen one might, doubtless, deduce innumerable consequences by conjecture, which might seem to presage future events. For what person who aims at a mark all day will not hit it? We sleep every night, and there are very few on which we do not dream; can we wonder then that what we dream sometimes comes to pass?" Cicero took little account of cures indicated in dreams: he thought the physician better for the sick than the dream interpreter. "The gods," he said, "have for our own sake given us intellect sufficient to provide for our own future welfare. How few people then attend to dreams, or remember them? How many, on the other hand, despise them and think any superstitious observation of them a sign of a weak, imbecile mind? Why should God take the trouble to consult the interest of this man, or to warn that one by dreams, when he knows that they do not only think it useless to attend to them but do not even condescend to recall them?"

Yet such skepticism was not the common view, then or later. In the middle of the second century A.D. there lived the man to whom almost all dream interpreters up to the time of Freud are indebted. This was Artemidorus, a Roman soothsayer whose *Oneirocritica* remains the essential source book. It is the most complete treatise on dream interpretation surviving from the ancient world, and just as it drew upon Greek, Assyrian, and Egyptian dream books, so it proved to be the foundation of many subsequent collections down to the present day. Editions were printed in Greek at Venice in 1518, in Latin at Basel in 1539, in French at Lyons in 1546. Its popularity is proved not merely by new translations and editions in most European languages, but by its continual re-publication. It was translated into English in 1644, and by 1740 it was already in its 24th English edition.

Artemidorus took dreams seriously. He gave full attention to the lessons of observation and experience in the art of dream interpretation; it was also important to know how skilled the interpreter might be. For the essential principle in Artemidorus is one common to many magical and occult practices, the principle of association—what the dream image evokes in the conscious mind. This, of course, was to be the vital principle in Freud's technique of dream interpretation, but with a difference he himself noted. Whereas in antiquity it is the association in the mind of the *interpreter* that is significant, in the psychoanalytical approach it is the association in the mind of the *dreamer*. Yet Freud, and later Jung, paid tribute to the work that has given Artemidorus such a key place in the history of oneiromancy. But for him, we should lack the crucial link between the dream interpretations of the ancient world and those of our own time. The interpretations given by Artemidorus in the second century A.D. provide us with a valuable basis of comparison when we examine the dreams reported by contemporary anthropologists from African, Asian, and Melanesian societies that are still pre-scientific.

When Artemidorus wrote that "dreams and visions are infused into men for their advantage and instruction," he was in fact recognizing that this symbolic language carried messages of importance—perhaps from the gods, but, whatever their origin, full of meaning. He also realized that arbitrary dream interpretation was misleading. Each man's dreams vary with his condition: "the rules of dreaming are not general, and therefore cannot satisfy all persons, but often, according to times and persons, they admit of varied interpretations." He goes on to warn of the dangers of over-simplification:

"A man may dream both good and bad dreams in one and the same night. Nay more, in the selfsame dream he may see both good and bad things, which the interpreter must separate in judgment. And this is no marvel, since the life and affairs of one particular man are such; that is, they ordinarily

The title page of the 1644 English edition of *The Interpretation of Dreams* by Artemidorus, a second century A.D. Roman soothsayer. Since its first printing—in Greek at Venice in 1518—the book has appeared in many languages and editions.

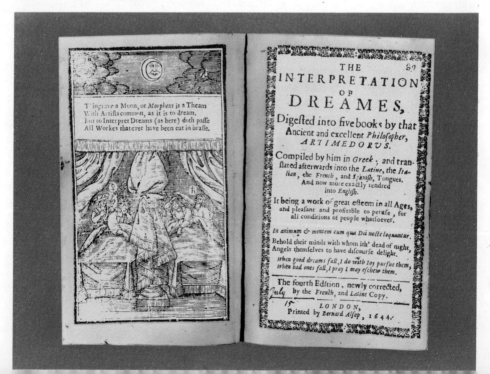

have evil mingled with good . . . Wherefore we must not always rest at one point or effect . . . but we must be ingenious to devise every day divers things . . . for our spirits and our nature are fertile, and recreate and sport themselves in variety."

The trouble taken by Artemidorus ("I have done no other by day and night but meditate and spend my spirit in the judgment and interpretation of dreams") made him a sophisticated commentator. He was interested in the question of recurrent dreams, in the intensity of emotion that different dreams evoked, in the manner in which prodromic dreams seemed to anticipate illness, and in the way in which dreams were related to such similar phenomena as visions, oracles, fantasies, and apparitions. But, above all, he was concerned with the distinction between two classes of dream: the *somnium*, which was a reference to the future; and the *insomnium*, the product of ordinary life, indeed of current states of mind or body. "The lover occupies himself with his sweetheart, the fearful man sees what he fears, the hungry man eats, the thirsty one drinks." The *somnium* is similar to what Jung was later to call the "great" dream, rich in symbolic material, loaded with powerful numinous effects, and normally beyond the comprehension of the dreamer.

In endeavoring to interpret such dreams, the interpreter must consider six critical points: *natura, lex, consuetudo, tempus, ars, nomen*. He must, that is to say, ask whether the events in the dream are natural, lawful, and customary for the dreamer, the conditions under which it was dreamed, and the occupation and name of the dreamer. These points analyzed, a variety of techniques must then be applied, from the lists given in the dream book, to the associations and, not least, the word plays or puns that can be discovered in the dream. We have already seen that puns provide the link between dream symbol and interpretation in many standard dream interpretations: the language in which one dreams is relevant. The psychologist Sandor Ferenczi, a colleague of Freud, remarked in 1910 that every tongue has its own dream language. And Artemidorus was well aware of the verbal and visual tricks the mind can play in dreams. To his son he said: "Do not be deceived into thinking that logical connections control the outcome. We believe that we discover fulfillment for past experience, but we build up reasons for ourselves alone, each according to his own ability."

How Artemidorus actually handled problems is seen in this extract from a chapter called "On Dreaming of Having One's Head Shaved" (in a modern translation by H. G. McCurdy):

"To dream of having one's whole head shaved, except in the case of priests of the Egyptian gods, and those who study how to raise a laugh, and those whose custom it is to shave, for whom it is good, is in general a bad dream, because it signifies the same thing that nudity does, and indeed foretells sudden and dire misfortune. To sailors it clearly portends shipwreck, and to the sick a most critical collapse, but not death. For the shipwrecked, and men preserved from a serious illness are shaved; the dead not at all. As to the former, it is a good dream because of their custom of shaving. To have one's hair cut by a barber, however, presages good to everyone equally."

At this point Artemidorus notes, characteristically, that the Greek word for being barbered differs only in one letter from the word meaning joy or welcome, and observes with a dash of irony that people overtaken by misfortune do not take the trouble to have their hair cut. But, all the same, the dream must show that a barber shaves the head; those who are preoccupied by evil or calamity have to see to their own shaving. Finally, in a passage that clearly shows how Artemidorus went about analyzing dreams, he adds:

"In addition, to have one's scalp scratched signifies a cancellation of interest in the case of a debtor, but for others it means a loss through those by whom they have been scratched, if indeed they have dreamed of having their scalp scratched by others. For we say that a man has been scalped if he has suffered a loss and been deceived by another person."

Almost two thousand years later we use the same phrase—and possibly the same image in our dreams.

Even at this distance in time we must feel a good deal of respect, not merely for the labors of Artemidorus, but also for the shrewd and far-from-mechanical interpretation he put on some dream symbols that still confront us today. The idea that the mouth may represent a house and the teeth the inhabitants of it can be found in the dream reports made in psychoanalysis today; the dream of losing a tooth thus logically becomes a symbol that a person in this household is dead, or that one wishes him dead. Almost all the main types of dream in modern psychoanalytical research have their parallels in the work of Artemidorus, though his interpretation was less profound and sophisticated. But it does provide us with a valuable check, over a long period of time, on the persistence of certain fundamental types of dream and of particular dream symbols. Artemidorus, in short, is the link between the ancient and modern schools of dream interpretation, and his work is not rivaled by anyone in Europe in the following centuries. Other writers put forward interesting ideas or wrestled with the theological and philosophical problems raised by dream phenomena, but none of them came close to him in importance.

Synesius of Cyrene, a Platonist of the fourth century A.D. who wrote a charming *Discourse on Dreams*, had some fascinating insights. He suggested, for instance, that "by images we conjecture the action of the future" because the dream images are the way in which the mind identifies a chain of events; he compared the dreamer to the sailor who suddenly sees a familiar headland and knows that beyond it lies a city full of men, or the soldier who knows that an army lies encamped out of sight when he stumbles upon its outposts. And he urged that we should write down "visions of sleep as well as day-dreams, together with chance events, so that we do not handle the unforeseen

The ritual of incubation is still practiced today in Asia as well as in Europe. Above, a Shinto temple at Itsuku-Shima in Japan where pilgrims come to spend the night.

as rustics do ... to record everything, not to overlook anything, even the slightest, but to relate it all, whether trivial or important." Yet such insights are no more than those of a sophisticated man who by experience had found his way to seeing some significance in what he dreamed. No one could match the classic Artemidorus; almost all borrowed heavily from him.

The dream theories we have so far examined all belong to a single major group—the tradition that stems from the Near East in the millennia before Christ. This tradition has links with the dream concepts of India, and in modern times ideas from Asian religion and philosophy have been assimilated into European thought. Yet the distant cultures of the Orient have a set of dream theories that are basically different from those we have traced back to Assyria and Egypt, and contain some fundamental similarities among themselves—whether we consider Hindu India, ancient China, or classical Japan.

Common to Hindu and Buddhist religions, and to other and less elaborate oriental faiths, is the idea that man has a soul which abandons the body in sleep and roams at will. It may wander among other men and in distant places—and the dream is the form in which this experience is registered. This idea, found among many simple societies in various parts of the world, explains why people are often reluctant to wake a sleeping man. His soul may not have found its way back into his body. The soul may wander in a nether world, or it may revert to a timeless unity with the cosmos.

The problem of reality, raised by such ideas, perplexed many oriental thinkers. How could a man tell what was a dream? The Chinese sage Chuang-tzu, an exponent of the doctrine of Lao-tzu, raised this point about 350 B.C.:

"While men are dreaming, they do not perceive that it is a dream. Some will even have a dream in a dream, and only when they awake they know it was all a dream. And so, when the Great Awakening comes upon us, shall we know this life to be a great dream. Fools believe themselves to be awake now.

"Once upon a time, I, Chuang-tzu, dreamed I was a butterfly, fluttering hither and thither, to all intents and purposes a butterfly. I was conscious only of following my fancies as a butterfly, and was unconscious of my individuality as a butterfly. Suddenly I was awakened, and there I lay myself again. Now I do not know whether I was a man dreaming I was a butterfly, or whether I am a butterfly now dreaming I am a man."

In these two short paragraphs, Chuang-tzu expressed an issue which still fascinates anyone concerned with the nature of dreams.

Chinese ideas of dreams are fascinating in the way they shift the focus of attention from magical and religious aspects toward ethical and philosophical problems of this kind. It is considered, for instance, that the "flowery" nature of the Chinese language is itself, as one writer puts it, "a kind of fossilized dream imagery," and almost all Chinese works on dream interpretation seem to combine practical observation with a distaste for the cruder forms of superstition in the Mediterranean and Near Eastern dream cults. Where later Chinese ideas show a concern with the supernatural, this usually is related to Buddhist teachings, which arrived in China from India. Buddhists, for example, believe that before his enlightenment the Buddha had five dreams, which warned him of this great event. In one of the dreams he saw four birds of different colors coming from the four quarters; they fell at his feet and became white. They were believed to represent the four laymen of four castes who would become his disciples. The symbolism of this dream is, as a matter of fact, rich and pregnant. Without noting the parallels that can be found in many myths, it is enough to note that C. G. Jung believed that such emphasis on the number four is almost always associated with a tendency toward integration, the discovery of wholeness in a personality, the emergence of a profound meaning in life.

Yet Chinese sources, for all their emphasis on the ethical and for all the changes that followed the spread of Buddhist concepts, tell of deep belief in the distinction between the material soul *(p'o)*, which regulates the functions of the body and dies with it, and the spiritual soul *(hun)* which leaves the body at death, carrying the appearance of the body with it. From this distinction, the Chinese developed their theory of dreams. They believed that the dream is caused by a temporary separation of the body and the *hun*—a separation which also accounted for trances, visions, and fits of various kinds. Once the soul is free, it can communicate with spirits, with the souls of the dead, or with gods, and return to the body bearing these impressions. Holding such a belief, the Chinese developed forms of dream interpretation not greatly different from those of the Near East. And, in addition, they practiced various kinds of incubation. This reached its peak under the first Ming emperor,

In a dream that predicted the Buddha's birth, Queen Maya, his mother, saw a child riding a sacred white elephant—shown in this 10th-century Chinese painting.

in the 14th century A.D. At that time any high official who visited a city had to spend the first night in the temple of the city god, so that he might receive his instructions in a dream. It was customary, too, for judges and other officials to go regularly to the temple for guidance—and again, as with the Mediterranean cultures, incubation was usually accompanied by fasting, bathing, and other rituals.

Perhaps because it is complex, mystical, and contemplative, Indian philosophy gave a significant place to the dream in its description of man's states of mind. In the *Brihadarmyaka-Upanishad*, (about 1000 B.C.,) we read:

"And there are two states for that person, the one here in this world, the other in the other world, and, as a third, an intermediate state, the state of sleep. When in that intermediate state, he sees both those states together, the one here in this world, and the other in the other world."

A carving from a Hindu temple in South India (*c.* A.D. 1900) built by an untrained villager in imitation of one seen in a vision. The vision—experienced while on a pilgrimage to the river Ganges—might explain the temple's original design.

But these three states are not regarded as equal. The waking state, "common to all men," is less real than the dream state, which is one in which a man's inner knowledge of himself is undisturbed by everyday sensations. The third stage is the highest. This is dreamless sleep. In this condition, the same *Upanishad* tells us, a man fully achieves the unity of his self with the infinities of time and space. It describes this condition in poetic imagery:

"A man in the embrace of a well-beloved woman knows nothing, neither inside nor outside, so does this man when in the embrace of the intelligent self know nothing within or without. That is the form in which his desire is fulfilled, in which the self is his desire, in which he has no desire and has passed beyond sorrow."

Indian practitioners of yoga, and of other trance-inducing techniques, aspire to achieve this blissful state and in their efforts to do so pass through various strange states of mind. We know of these from many descriptions in Indian mystic literature, but it is only in recent years that Europeans have come to realize that such passages describe mental states as accessible to them as to the yogi, and that far from being merely an esoteric cult, the Vedantic wisdom of India represents the most advanced thinking about the nature of the Self, and about man's whole inner but hidden life, that has been developed by an ancient civilization known to us. The three states of mind, for example, place the dream world (to use modern terms) midway between the conscious and unconscious parts of the mind and suggest that the dreamer is able to observe both simultaneously. To put it another way, the dream mediates between consciousness and the unconscious.

This is exactly the experience induced by the use of hallucinogenic drugs such as mescalin or LSD 25. The person who takes such drugs induces a dreamlike state without sleep, and is able to observe his conscious actions and deeper feelings from the vantage point between them. We shall see later what light these experiments in psychopharmacology shed on the dream process. It is important to note here, however, that the Indian dream theory comes closest to describing what seems to be a basic structural process in the human mind. What is more, the hallucinatory experiences reported by those who take these drugs often closely parallel the blissful visions recorded in Indian literature by those who passed beyond the gates of normal consciousness into the mysterious inner world.

It is this insight that accounts for the presence of two seemingly contradictory concepts of the dream in Indian literature. One—which seems to spring from an older common stock of ideas—is the belief that the soul leaves the body and goes in search of other experiences. But there is also the more sophisticated conception that the material of dreams comes from real life, even though it may be from aspects of real life of which, when he is awake, man is unaware, and that the dream weaves this material into new scenes, situations, and images. Early in the Christian era, King Milinda of northern India was asking what made a dream, what types of dream there were, and how they could be interpreted. A man's own mind, he observed, "does not itself seek the omen, neither does anyone else come to tell him of it. The prognostication comes of its own accord into his mind." The point is very similar to the Talmud precept: "The dream provides its own interpretation."

It is possible that the degree of contact between ancient societies was greater, over long periods of time, than it is easy for us to believe. So many cultural similarities are found between peoples inhabiting different parts of the globe that anthropologists developed the theory of cultural diffusion to account for the appearance of similar weapons, agricultural practices, art forms, and ideas. Yet there are many difficulties about this theory, and many ways in which some of these similarities could be explained by causes other than physical contact. In fact this is the basis of one of the main controversies in present-day anthropology. One could certainly find some evidence in dream theory to support either side of the argument. It is, nonetheless, an argument that is scarcely relevant here. The important fact for us in this book is not how various peoples in antiquity came to share certain beliefs, or even the significant differences between them. It is the emphasis of interest, respect, and mystery that they placed on dreams, which they saw as a vital part of man's inner, spiritual, or—as we should say—psychological experience.

3   The superstitious centuries

The coming of Christianity led to profound changes in European philosophy and morality. A new religion, drawing on the heritage of Judaea, Rome, and Greece and influenced by esoteric cults from the eastern Mediterranean, had arisen. How much of that heritage would be adopted, how much rejected, and how much of it modified to fit the new religion's needs? Many pagan ideas and customs were, in fact, taken over by the early Christians; and questions that had troubled pre-Christian thinkers—among them the nature of dreams and the extent to which they were of divine origin—began to exercise the founding fathers of the Church.

Early Christians had to accept the idea that at least some dreams had a divine inspiration. The Bible contained too many references to dreams to permit total skepticism, though some of the early Christian writers were bothered by what seemed to them superstitious and magical emphases on dream divination. The Platonist critic of Christianity, Celsus—who had denounced Jesus as a "wicked and God-hated sorcerer"—condemned the Jews as charlatans, "blinded by some crooked sorcery, or dreaming dreams through the influence of shadowy specters." Origen, one of the more important of the early Christian bishops, replying to Celsus two centuries later, denied that the Jews were obsessed with magical divination, and maintained that some dreams *were* divinely inspired prophecies. He quoted the dream that warned Joseph

Scholarly interest in the subject of dreams has varied from age to age, but a steady flow of dream books provides evidence of the ordinary man's continual occupation with them. Right, the frontispiece from a 19th-century dreambook, *The Dreamer's Oracle and Faithful Interpreter.* Despite the post-Renaissance reaction against the irrational, dream interpretation still retained its hold on popular opinion.

to flee into Egypt and observed that such a dream warning was not surprising: "in many other cases it has happened that a dream has shown persons the proper course of action."

Origen's difficulty was one that plagued many Christian writers at this period—how to separate dream prophecies from rational prediction, and also how to account for the fact that many dreams seemed silly or wicked. They could not attribute all dreams to heaven-sent inspiration.

The most sophisticated attempt to resolve this dilemma had been made long before Origen, by Tertullian, writing about A.D. 203. Sleep, he suggested, is a kind of temporary death, in which the soul is absent from the body, and dreaming is the form that the soul's activity takes when its physical instrument—the body—is at rest:

"This power we call ecstasy, in which the sensuous soul stands out of itself, in a way which even resembles madness. Thus in the very beginning sleep was inaugurated by ecstasy: 'And God sent an ecstasy upon Adam, and he slept' (Genesis II: 21). The sleep came upon his body to cause it to rest, but the ecstasy fell upon his soul to remove rest: from that very circumstance it still happens ordinarily that sleep is combined with ecstasy. In fact, with what real feeling, and anxiety, and suffering do we experience joy, and sorrow, and alarm in our dreams."

Almost two centuries later, Gregory of Nyssa, in his treatise *On the Making of Man*, revived the naturalistic approach to dreaming that we saw had characterized Plato and Aristotle: the faculties of nutrition, sensation, and reason could all play their part in the making of the dream. But, like all the early Christians, distinguishing between the independent soul and its corporal and temporary habitation, the body, he drew a line between dreams that were miraculous expressions of the will of the Deity (his comments on the dreams of Daniel and Joseph imply that, for him, these were not really dreams in the normal sense) and those directly related to the digestive process. Both sensation and intellect are at rest in sleep; the nutritive faculty of the soul thus dominates them, though the images it creates may well have been inspired by some experience while the sleeper was awake. Gregory believed not merely that dreams could be prodromic, but that they could also indicate the dreamer's personality—whether he was lustful or chaste, generous or greedy. In this he anticipated later psychologists, such as Jung and Alfred Adler, who sought to ascribe definite personalities to certain types, according to their dreams. In another sense, too, Gregory showed remarkable perception. He believed that man's passions expressed themselves in dreams; more, the source of the passions was the drive toward sexual reproduction. The passages in which he states this view are so similar to the essential view of Freud that

Left, *The Dream of the Falling Waters*, a painting by the German artist Albrecht Dürer (1471-1528) of one of his own dreams. Dürer interpreted the dream as representing a cosmic disaster; but it could also be seen as "prodromic," since Dürer suffered from a chronic ailment that three years later caused his death. The abstract quality of the picture contrasts strongly with the realism of Dürer's other work.

Right, a representation from a 15th-century manuscript of Nebuchadnezzar's dream. He saw a tree—so large that it provided food and shelter for all living things—cut down by God's command, and he heard God say: "let a beast's heart be given unto him; and let seven times pass over him" (Daniel IV: 16). The dream was interpreted by Daniel who saw that the tree symbolized Nebuchadnezzar, who would be driven from his kingdom to live like a wild animal for seven years. A modern psychologist has suggested that this dream indicated the approach of a mental illness.

The religious figures of medieval times
were often troubled by satanic visions.
Above, *The Temptation of St. Anthony* by the
16th-century artist Mathäus Grünewald.

it seems extraordinary that Freud made no reference to them in *The Interpretation of Dreams*. Consider these two extracts:

"For those qualities with which brute life was armed for self-preservation, when transferred to human life, become passions; for the carnivorous animals are preserved by their anger, and those which breed largely by their love of pleasure."

"Thus the rising of anger in us is indeed akin to the impulse of the brutes; but it grows by the alliance of thought: for thence come malignity, envy, deceit, conspiracy, hypocrisy."

Gregory was far closer to the modern view than St. Augustine, who lived from 354 to 430. In his *Confessions*, Augustine tells of a dream in which his mother foresaw that he would be converted from heresy. Yet, after his conversion, the problem of demons in dreams continued to harass him. He believed that they existed, that they could predict the future and accomplish marvels— though he doubted that they could transform men into animals, as Apuleius, in his book *The Golden Ass*, claimed to have happened to him. Augustine thought that such strange experiences, reported by persons he regarded as reliable, were the products of dreams and hallucinations. Therefore he tried to sort out the visions of "pious and holy men" from those "of men misguided by delusion, or, most commonly, by impiety." He was not notably successful in this and lamented in a letter: "I have not solved but complicated the question." He plainly did not wish to commit himself on a subject that troubled rather than illuminated his soul, for he concluded:

"Every day man wakes, and sleeps, and thinks; let any man, therefore, answer whence proceed these things which, while not material bodies, do nevertheless resemble the form, properties, and motions of material bodies; let him, I say, answer this if he can. But if he cannot do this, why is he in such haste to pronounce an opinion on things which occur very rarely, or are beyond the range of his experience, when he is unable to explain matters of daily and perpetual observations?"

The anxieties of theologians about the nature of dreams and the validity of divination seem to have been as acute in the mid 13th century as in the days of the early Christians. Pious men were afflicted with satanic hallucinations, hermits dreamed of seductive women, and the nightmarish gargoyles in many medieval cathedrals may illustrate the unpleasant visions that visited the devout. Modern psychologists have suggested that the frequency of such visions was due to an increase in sexual repression. The religious emphasis on chastity, they believed, led to the translation of sexual drives into other forms; the stress on humility led, equally, to the conversion of aggressive feelings into demonic shapes. The Devil, in these terms, was a symbol of the evils of the flesh; witches became an expression of sexual temptation and its dangers. Many medieval dreams, visions, and trance-like states seem to be of this kind. Pope Leo IX, when he was Bishop of Toul in the 11th century, dreamed of a hag who persecuted him with her attentions; the more he shrank from her, the closer she clung to him. But when he made the sign of the cross, she became transformed into an angel.

Other accounts tell of medieval nuns who felt they were married to the Church in a more than metaphorical sense, dreaming of themselves as literal brides of Christ. Pondering on such things, St. Thomas Aquinas reached this conclusion in his *Summa Theologica*:

"It seems that divination by dreams is not unlawful. To make use of divine instruction is not unlawful. God instructs men through dreams: for it is said in Job XXXIII : 5: 'Through a dream in a vision by night, when sleep comes over men and they slumber in bed, then He opens the ears of men, and teaching them imparts instruction'."

Aquinas also insisted that dreams have a prophetic character: "It is the experience of all men that a dream contains some indication of the future. Therefore it is vain to deny that dreams have efficacy in divination." This conclusion left Aquinas confronting the perennial difficulty: how to tell good dreams from bad, or true from false. He escaped the dilemma by asserting that nobody but the dreamer could tell one from the other. Moreover, dreams were not simply one or the other. The first category of dreams was those coming from within. They might be from the soul—"those things that have occupied a man's thoughts and affections while awake recur to his imagination while asleep." Or they might be from the body—"the inward disposition of the body leads to the formation of a movement in the imagination consistent with the disposition." The second category was dreams inspired from without, either from heavenly sources or from demons.

The interesting thing is that this analysis covered almost every explanation of dreams then conceivable. Very few writers on dreams in the following centuries did more than elaborate on one or more of these themes. But St. Thomas Aquinas actually gave little positive guidance. He reassured Christians that many dreams were purely a function of sleep, but stressed that others were more significant and their use in divination permissible, and he warned that people should be careful lest they were deluded by demons.

All through this period theologians had similar problems. Martin Luther feared that the Devil "may occasion many harms by evil dreams," and was so afraid of getting divine and demonic messages confused that he prayed to God not to speak to him in dreams. Calvin observed that "the usual plan of dreams is for God to speak by them allegorically and obscurely"—a proposition that made dreams very puzzling to the devout person.

Things were further complicated by the strange practices indulged in by the devout. Medieval records contain a good many references from which we may infer that the old habit of incubation had by this time assumed extreme forms. One such record concerns an Augustinian monastery in Donegal. This community was founded on the tradition that God had appeared to St. Patrick—the patron saint of Ireland, who died in the fifth century—and led him to the entrance of a cave, saying:

"Whoever confesses his past sins and will enter this place with good heart and firm faith will see here the punishments which are to be the lot of the wicked and the rewards which will be given to the righteous, and will come out having gained complete remission of his sins. But whoever enters merely to satisfy his curiosity will . . . remain until the Day of Judgment."

Five centuries later the monks had reduced this prophecy to organized practice. Before entering the cave, a postulant would fast for seven days; on the eighth day he entered a cell like a vertical coffin, in which he could not move. On the ninth day he received the last rites of the Church, and was led to the entrance of the cave. If, after a day spent in the cave, the pilgrim emerged, he was (understandably) on the point of insanity, but his visions were treated with reverence. Some never came out. One who did, an adventurer called Louis Ennius, left an account of his visions:

"Hardly had I taken up this position than frightful howls were heard, and from all sides terrible monsters rose up out of the earth. They seemed to be under the command of a black man whose head and feet were those of a goat,

Right, a 16th-century woodcut of the prior of the Lough Derg monastery in Ireland giving instructions to a knight about to enter a sacred cave (where legend says the devout may obtain forgiveness of their sins). Pilgrims still visit the cave; below, a group approaches by boat.

From antiquity to the present day the dream
has been a common literary device.
Above, a 15th-century painting of the
French allegorical poem, *The Romance of
the Rose*, in which the hero, the Lover,
dreams of his search for love—symbolized
by the Rose. The painting depicts the
Lover being admitted to a park where he
finds the Rose, but is driven away by
Danger, Scandal, and Shame. Right, a
woodcut from the romance *The Dream of
Poliphilus* (1499) by Francesco Colonna. It
shows Poliphilus fleeing from a dragon,
one of the many adventures that befell him
during a long dream journey.

beating his enormous bat's wings exactly as one sees Satan depicted by paint-
ers . . . Then I felt myself carried as if by a great wind across freezing clouds
of fog into an immense and gloomy plain, black as a burnt-out forest. It
seemed to me as if I were flying at some considerable height over this desolate
plain, and thus I was able to contemplate the most terrible of scenes. A host
of men and women of every condition peopled this plain. All these wretches
were being submitted to all kinds of torture, the forms varying according to
the crimes they had committed in their lifetime. Some were chained face-
downwards to the earth, their bodies studded with huge red-hot nails which
demons were driving in with hammers. Others were being eaten away by
lizards and serpents . . ."

Strictly speaking, such psychic experiences are not dreams, but for many
centuries men found it difficult to separate experiences of this kind from so-
called "normal" dreams. The late Middle Ages abound with stories of sor-
cerers, superstitions, and the significance of dreams. The magic spells of this
period often center around sleep and dreams. But one of the difficulties about
spells was the strange ingredients they needed. A French spell of this period,
for procuring "diabolical dreams," required the sleeper "to rub his eyelids
with bat's blood and place laurel leaves under his pillow." Another, to induce
a dream of loving someone unattainable in real life, prescribes the use of two
ounces of scammony (an oil made from the flowers of morning-glory or convolvulus, whose seeds are known to be hallucinogenic) and Roman camomile,
three ounces of cod-bone and tortoiseshell, and five ounces of beaver fat, all
to be boiled with opium. The resulting potion had to be sealed for 12 weeks,
buried through the winter in a cool cellar, and then rubbed on the navel
and nape of the neck before one went to sleep.

At the end of the 15th century, occultism was widespread. The alchemists,
the astrologers, the fortune tellers, the experts on magic numbers, were often
well-known. Sometimes they suffered imprisonment or death, but often they
were highly esteemed. Men such as the German Cornelius Heinrich Agrippa,
who was a writer, diplomat, physician, magician, and lawyer, or the Italian
Jerome Cardan, mathematician, astrologer, and doctor, are characteristic of
this period. Cardan (who died in 1576) not only wrote much about his own
dreams—and the near-miraculous elements in these must be discounted
because he was a notorious liar—but also gave recipes for various herbal potions
and ointments that would produce extravagant visions. There is little
doubt that a knowledge of primitive drugs that could induce trances or hallucinations was fairly widespread in Europe in the late medieval period.

But those who used or transmitted such knowledge had varying views about
the source and nature of the illusions thus created. Cardan, in the middle
of a long passage about the prophetic nature of dreams, suddenly breaks off
to observe: "I am convinced that it is very necessary to be careful of sleep,
for it is essential to the health of a man and occupies a third part of his life."

And, in an acutely perceptive phrase, he concludes: "For the meaning of the impression is the prime cause, and the meaning is in the man." Such a mixture of superstition, drugs, astrology, and insight was fairly typical of the time: European thinking had yet to be transformed by the rationalist revolution. Yet it was clearly beginning to react to the opening of communication with the Orient, either directly or through the revival of interest in the classical past. The ideas of Philippus Paracelsus (pseudonym of the Swiss alchemist and physician Theophrastus Bombastus of Hohenheim, who lived from 1493 to 1541) show a marked likeness to certain Vedic concepts from India—and in many ways seem like an anticipation of what, in the late 19th century, became known as Theosophy.

Paracelsus distinguished between the physical body of man and its ethereal counterpart, which wakes in sleep and in that condition can communicate with the spirits of other men or of the dead. This *evestrum*, as Paracelsus called it, could leave the sleeper's body, but if it lost contact altogether, the sleeper would die. During this astral life, which connects man to the Macrocosm, the experience of the evestrum is communicated to the sleeper in the form of dreams. Paracelsus elaborated this conception. He considered, first, that some dreams were "natural": it was unnecessary to say much about them "because they are known to all. They may be caused by joy or sadness, by impurities of the blood, by external or internal causes. A gambler may dream of cards, a soldier of battles, a drunkard of wines, a robber of theft. All such dreams are caused by the lower principles of such persons, which play with their imagination, heat their blood, and stimulate their fantasy."

Thus Paracelsus had come back to the age-old problem of true or false dreams, and, in essence, his views of "true" dreams were the same as those of the ancients. "There are supernatural dreams, and they are the messengers from God." Persons whose "nature is so spiritual, and their soul so exalted, that they can approach the highest spiritual sphere at a time when their bodies are asleep ... have seen the glory of God, the happiness of the redeemed, and the torture of the wicked."

Yet, even more than Cardan, Paracelsus reveals a substantial insight into the relation between the dream and the dreamer's psychological condition:

"That which the dream shows is the shadow of such wisdom as exists in the man, even if during his waking state he may know nothing about it; for we ought to know that God has given us our own wisdom and knowledge, reason, and the power to perceive the past and the future; but we do not know it, because we are fooling away our time with outward and perishing things, and are asleep in regard to that which is real within ourself."

This passage shows so clear an understanding of the way in which the hidden aspects of the personality are revealed in dreams that it is surprising to find no mention of Paracelsus in Freud's account of dream interpretation: it was C. G. Jung who rediscovered this revealing reference.

A good illustration of the vogue such concepts had is found in the long account by Rabelais of dream interpretation, from Plato to Artemidorus, that he puts in the mouth of Pantagruel. In contrast to such relatively serious attempts to grapple with the mystery of dreams, there was also a vogue for dream books and for various forms of numerology. The idea of lucky numbers, or magic squares, or mysterious ciphers, was an old one, and examples can be found far back in antiquity. A book published at Troyes, in France, in 1654, called *The Palace of the Curious*, explains how "algebra and the laws of chance give an interpretation of the most puzzling questions, in which dreams and nocturnal visions are explained according to the doctrines of antiquity."

How this was done may be seen from a later cipher book of 1830 published in England by the astrologer Raphael, who claimed that it was based on "an ancient and curious manuscript, which was buried in the earth for several centuries, containing one thousand and twenty-four oracles of answers to dreams." We may doubt whether its method of discovering "these secrets of fate, which the universal fiat of all nations in every age and clime, has acknowledged to be portended by dreams and nocturnal visions," was in fact lost to sight for centuries, only to be discovered by chance in a decaying courthouse in Somerset. The method was similar to that known in the 17th century in France; what is more, it has a curious resemblance to an ancient Chinese oracle book known as the *I Ching*, used for divination for many hundreds of years.

CARMEN Tho. Venatorij in laudem Cardani.

Ebibit hic Sophiæ fontes, & flumina Mufis,
  Et Phœbo, & doctis non inamœna uiris.
Hinc medicos mifcet fuccos, & corpora regum
  Illi creduntur, fummaʠ cura, Fides.
Deinde Syracufij funt nata Mathemata ciuis,
  Cætera funt terris cognita, & aucta polis.

A woodcut of Jerome Cardan—16th-century Italian philosopher, mathematician, astrologer, and man of letters—from his most famous work *De Subtilitate Rerum*, which was written because of a recurring dream. In the dream Cardan was shown in detail the plan and subject matter of a large book: the dream was so insistent that he decided it must be written. While he was doing so the dream continued to recur, being especially frequent when he was indolent, but entirely ceasing after publication of the first edition.

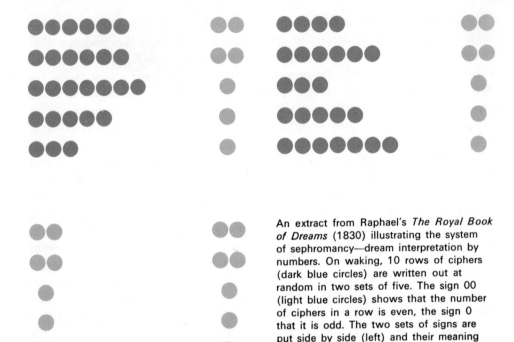

An extract from Raphael's *The Royal Book of Dreams* (1830) illustrating the system of sephromancy—dream interpretation by numbers. On waking, 10 rows of ciphers (dark blue circles) are written out at random in two sets of five. The sign 00 (light blue circles) shows that the number of ciphers in a row is even, the sign 0 that it is odd. The two sets of signs are put side by side (left) and their meaning found in the oracle book. The ciphers here mean the dreamer will gain new friends.

The alliance between dreams and divination is an ancient one; wherever magic, superstition, and the occult flourish, this link will be found. But in Europe during the last four centuries the occultist tradition has steadily diminished—one might say it has been driven underground. At the time of the Renaissance, superstitious ideas, dream divination, and magical practices were common in the highest social and intellectual circles, and a great deal of rubbish was mixed up with some sound intuition. Since then, however, astrology, numerology, dream books, and the like have become popular crazes. They endured—witness the fashion for astrological predictions in French or English newspapers—but they have survived, like all forms of magic, as something slightly disreputable or even fraudulent, lacking the appeal of the magical practices of the past, but retaining many of them in an emasculated and ritualized form.

Dream theory suffered from this same process; it also became a subject that most people with a claim to rational intellect regarded as something fit only for superstitious servant girls. Yet, though rationalists dismissed dreams as meaningless phenomena, the mass of the population continued to show faith in them. Nothing else can explain the continuing popularity of dream books, from the revival of Artemidorus in the 16th century down to the present day. This popular tradition, in all its essentials, has changed little from the time of Artemidorus.

While the work of Artemidorus was being published in Venice in the early 16th century, there appeared in the same city a Latin dream book called *The Dream Book of Daniel*, combined with the *Dreams of Solomon;* this book continued to appear in various editions—in English, for instance, in 1542. Like later 16th-century books published elsewhere, it made the familiar attempt to distinguish between divine, natural, and diabolical dreams.

Through succeeding centuries little was done to alter the basic interpretation derived from Artemidorus and other ancient sources, except to modify the idiom and a few of the symbols. The interpretation was fairly straightforward: to dream of swimming in tempestuous waters was a sign of impending trouble, to dream of gold denoted the prospect of riches. Cheaply printed pamphlets or chapbooks were widely circulated in London at this period; they had such florid titles as *The Old Egyptian Fortune-Teller's Last Legacy, The Royal Dream Book, The Golden Dreamer,* and *A Groatsworth of Wit for a Penny.* Most of these were 24-page books, a few having colored frontispieces. These are the kind of books that Frank Seafield, in the middle of the last century, was referring to when he complained that what was "once the revelation of the divine" had now become "an instrument by which a chapbook pedlar may best ascertain what is the smallest number of lies which Cinderella will insist on in return for her penny, without considering herself cheated."

The readers of such books were simple people, often living in the country and buying chapbooks from pedlars who went from village to village selling ribbons and fairings. For country people clung to old beliefs about the importance of dreams, especially of dreams on such special occasions as St. Agnes' Eve, Midsummer Eve, Halloween, or All Saints' Night. Certain rituals, such as sleeping with a sprig of mistletoe under the pillow or (in the Hebrides) eating a salted herring, were believed to procure dreams of the future, and particularly of future husbands or brides. It is to this custom that Keats refers in the lines:

> They told her how, upon St. Agnes' Eve,
> Young virgins might have visions of delight,
> And soft adorings from their loves receive,
> Upon the honey'd middle of the night,
> If ceremonies due they did aright;
> As, supperless to bed they must retire,
> And couch supine their beauties, lily white;
> Nor look behind, nor sideways, but require
> Of heaven with upward eyes for all that they desire.

The rituals varied from one district to another: those who had no local tradition to guide them could consult such sources as *Mother Bridget's Dream Book and Oracle of Fate*—which was printed in London, Manchester, Glasgow, Dublin, and other cities, and went on selling for decades. One can picture country girls faithfully carrying out the prescription for Candlemas Eve:

"On this night let three, five, seven, or nine young maidens assemble in a square chamber. Hang in each corner a bundle of sweet herbs, mixed with rue and rosemary. Then mix a cake of flour, olive-oil, and white sugar; every maiden having an equal share in the making and expense of it. Afterwards it must be cut into equal pieces, each one marking the piece as she cuts it with the initial of her name. It is then to be baked one hour before the fire, not a word being spoken the whole time, and the maidens sitting with the arms and knees crossed. Each piece of cake is then to be wrapped up in a sheet of paper, on which each maiden shall write the love part of Solomon's song. If she puts this under her pillow she will dream true. She will see her future husband and children, and will know besides whether her family will be poor or prosperous. . . ."

All kinds of different sources seem to have been drawn upon for such rituals—some from antiquity, some from medieval magic, some from local folklore, some plainly the invention of the author; they seem to contain both pagan and Christian elements, and even the pagan elements in Europe are a mixture of Roman, Greek, Egyptian, Teutonic, and Celtic traditions. Many

Two examples illustrating the popular interest in dreams. Left, an 18th-century engraving of a pedlar girl selling oracle and dream books. Right, the legend of St. Agnes depicted on the early medieval royal cup of the kings of England and France. St. Agnes (d. 304 A.D.) refused to marry the Prefect of Rome's son, declaring she was dedicated to a heavenly spouse. She was condemned to be raped and then burned, but was saved by divine intervention. A popular legend grew up that on St. Agnes' Eve (January 20-21) young girls could see their future husbands in their dreams. The British poet John Keats (1795-1821) based a poem on this superstition.

of these rituals and spells can be found in similar form in places as far apart as Hungary and Ireland, Spain and Norway.

As one traces these dream books over the years, it is evident that massive borrowing went on. The first American dream book, *The New Book of Knowledge*, published in Boston in 1767, contains astrological as well as dream information, and was probably pirated from an earlier copy brought from England. A *Book of Knowledge*, printed in 1795, gives seven pages of dream interpretations, many dealing with parts and conditions of the body. The first serious dream book to appear in America was *The Universal Interpreter of Dreams and Visions*, published in Baltimore in 1795. This book not only discusses the nature of sleep, somnambulism, divine dreams, and extraordinary dreams; it also includes a dream dictionary giving interpretations of various dreams by Artemidorus, Lord Bacon, and others. Later American dream books—and there were many in the next half century—drew heavily on this one, though the cheaper the publication, the cruder the interpretation.

In order to widen the appeal of such books, other themes were included— fortune telling by cards, palmistry, phrenology, moles, lucky numbers, etc.

Songer avoir une maladie de peau, comme la gale, des pustules, des poux.

Signifie : or, argent, richesses en proportion de la violence de la maladie.

The dream books on sale in countries throughout the world today have scarcely changed since those of antiquity—the earliest known dream book comes from the Egypt of the second millennium B.C. Above, 19th-century dream books from Scotland, Germany, France, and America. Right, a 20th-century collection of dream books.

The Golden Wheel Dream Book, published in New York in the middle of the 19th century, offered no interpretations, but simply gave a list of words accompanied by supposedly lucky numbers. The superstitious gambler, it seems, was presumed to be a buyer of such books. He would dream, say, of asparagus; according to whichever dream book he used he would then back the relevant number, or buy a lottery ticket bearing the same figures. The persistence of this habit is shown by the fact that a relatively modern book, *The Magical Spiritual Dream Book*, published in 1937 by Madame Fu Futtam—"a mysterious, scientific East Indian Yogi"—prints this incantation on its cover:

Now I lay me down to Slumber.
When I sleep and when I wake,
Pray God I hit the Number.

Harry B. Weiss, an American expert, found that most dream books on sale in the United States provided numbers rather than interpretations, and that some of their interpretations were remarkably similar, the various publishers simply reissuing slightly modified versions of books that had already sold in considerable numbers. For instance, in a book published in Cincinnati in 1835, it is stated that, "to dream of knives is unpropitious; it betokens lawsuits, poverty, disgrace ... shows your sweetheart to be of a bad temper, and unfaithful, and that if you marry, you will live in enmity and misery."

The same theme is repeated in the *Witch Doctor's Illustrated Dream-Book* of 1891, but with the significant difference that whereas in 1835 an unhappy marriage led to misery, in 1891 it could lead to divorce.

Mr. Weiss also found another significant change, reflecting an alteration in social customs. Between 1804 and 1909 there was little change in the interpretation of dreams about making pies. The makers of the later dream books, however, seemed to have realized that people no longer made their own pies, but bought them from bakers. References were changed accordingly—to dreams of *eating* pies. Not all publishers were as frankly opportunist as this. One remarkably honest dream book, published in Glasgow about 1850, ended by saying: "The foregoing pages are published principally to show the superstitions which engrossed the mind of the population of Scotland in a past age, and which are happily disappearing before the progress of an enlightened civilization. It is hoped, therefore, that the reader will not attach the slightest importance to the solutions of dreams rendered above, as dreams are usually the result of a disordered stomach, or excited imagination."

Contemporary dream books, of which large numbers are still published, do not normally contain such disclaimers. Their publishers are content to continue a well-tried and rewarding formula, with as few changes as possible. Older words, older concepts, drop out; there are no longer interpretations of dreams in which the dreamer is playing the spinet or the virginals. New ideas and new objects are given interpretations; telephones, subways, and stock certificates are now included. But, as Mr. Weiss points out, "over a period of a hundred and fifty years many interpretations have remained remarkably uniform."

The modern dream book represents the most degenerate form of what was once regarded as a divine art; it lacks any real religious or magical sanction, and is simply an expression of popular superstition, like the belief in lucky numbers, lucky colors, or birthstones. Whatever meaning may once have lain behind the symbols and the interpretation has long been lost.

Yet the reaction against purely superstitious attitudes to dreaming is nothing new. In England over 300 years ago the eloquent Jeremy Taylor—a cleric who picked the losing side in Cromwell's rebellion—argued in one of his sermons that "dreams follow the temper of the body and commonly proceed from trouble or disease, an active head and a restless mind, from fear or hope, from wine or passion, from fullness or emptiness, from fantastic remembrances or from some common demon, good or bad; they are without rule and without reason." Such a skeptical, though naturalistic, view was becoming more prevalent in this period. A century later John Wesley could state flatly that "we know the origins of dreams, and that with some degree of certainty," but his explanation did not go much beyond that suggested by St. Thomas Aquinas—some from the condition of the body, some from the passions of the mind, some by good angels, and "others undoubtedly are owing to the power and malice of evil angels." But Wesley had failed to keep up with advanced thinking. Robert Burton, author of the *Anatomy of Melancholy*, had said that "as a dog dreams of an hare, so do men on such subjects as they thought on last," and had added, "the gods send not our dreams, we make our own." And Thomas Hobbes, one of the greatest political philosophers of the 17th century, and the author of *Leviathan*, was also reacting against more flighty theories. "There is no doubt," he conceded, "but God can make unnatural apparitions. But that he does it so often, as men need to fear such things, more than they fear the stay, or change, of the course of nature, which He can also stay, and change, is no point of Christian faith."

Hobbes, like many after him, inclined to a somatic theory of dreams—the belief that physical factors can affect one's dreams, so that the man who sleeps in a draft may dream of being caught in a blizzard, and a mustard plaster on the chest may make him dream that he is consumed by fire. "Our dreams," Hobbes tartly observed, "are the reverse of our waking imagination." And he went on to consider the same question that had troubled Chuang-tzu, many centuries before. How does a man know that he dreams? Hobbes felt he knew, "because waking I often observed the absurdity of dreams, and never dream of the absurdity of waking thoughts; I am well satisfied that, being awake, I know I dream not; though when I dream, I think myself awake."

In France, the great rationalist philosopher René Descartes was finding this question more difficult to answer:

"I must . . . consider that I am a man, and that, consequently, I am in the habit of sleeping, and representing to myself in dreams those same things, or even sometimes others less probable, which the insane think are presented to them in their waking moments . . . I perceive so clearly that there exist no certain marks by which the state of waking can ever be distinguished from sleep, and that I feel greatly astonished; and in amazement I almost persuade myself that I am now dreaming . . ."

A similar thought had struck another French philosopher, Blaise Pascal, who lived at the same time as Descartes. In his *Pensées* he wrote:

". . . half our life being passed in sleep, we have, by our own avowal, no idea of truth, whatever we may suppose. Since, then, all our sentiments are illusions, who can tell but that the other half of life wherein we fancy ourselves awake be not another sleep somewhat different from the former, from which we awake when we fancy ourselves asleep? . . . In a word, as we often dream that we dream, and heap vision upon vision, it may well be that this life itself is but a dream . . . from which we wake at death . . . ."

The change of emphasis in these passages is significant. The inquiring mind no longer asks what a dream means: the inclination is to dismiss the interpretation of dreams as a superstitious pastime. But questions are now being asked about the dreaming process itself, about the nature of sleep and consciousness.

Another sharp-spoken contemporary, Sir Thomas Browne, in his essay "Of Dreams," makes no bones about his distrust of dream contents:

"Half our dayes we passe in the shadow of the earth, and the brother of death exacteth a third part of our lives. A good part of our sleepes is peeced out with visions, and phantastical objects wherein we are confessedly deceaved. The day supplyeth us with truths, the night with fictions and falsehoods...."

The tide of educated opinion was now setting against dream interpretation. "This art does not deserve the application of a wise man," said Pierre Bayle, author of the famous *Dictionary*. Every dream, he argued, was open to many interpretations, and dream diviners simply deceived themselves as well as others. The German philosopher Leibniz, in his *New Essays Concerning Human Understanding*, took the argument a stage further. The human personality, he suggested, contains the sum of all its past thoughts and experience— a view with which many modern psychologists would agree. "Many things can be forgotten," he therefore concludes in a striking hint to later pioneers in psychology, "but they could also be remembered long afterwards, if they were recalled as they should be."

Sterner rationalists, however, had no doubt that dreams were part of a superstitious frame of mind that the world could well do without. Thomas

The dream form was used by the English writer John Bunyan in the allegory *Pilgrim's Progress* (first published in 1678 and since translated into 108 different languages). An engraving shows the pilgrim Christian dreaming of his long and arduous journey through the Slough of Despond and the Valley of the Shadow of Death to the Celestial City.

Paine, in *The Age of Reason*, took a stern view of so-called miracles and visions, believing that a rational explanation could always be found for them. His analysis of the dreams and visions of Ezekiel and Daniel exemplified his approach. Such dreams, he argued, meant merely that the writers were prisoners-of-war in a foreign country. This fact "obliged them to convey even the most trifling information to each other, and all their political projects and opinions, in obscure and metaphorical terms. They pretended to have dreamed dreams and seen visions, because it was unsafe for them to speak facts or plain language."

Despite the rationalist reaction against any form of dream divination—a reaction that persists in the search for any explanation of dreams that will deprive them of hidden emotional significance—interest in dream interpretation, and in various forms of dreams, was not wholly discredited. There was, to begin with, a long and respectable literary interest in dreams, starting, in England, with *The Vision concerning Piers Plowman* (the first literary work of importance in anything that resembles the present English language), and continuing with Chaucer and then with Shakespeare. The dreams in *Julius Caesar* and the nightmare in *Richard III* are vital to the plots of these plays, and the most charming of all Shakespeare's fantasies, *A Midsummer Night's Dream*, is full of references to the love-dream rituals. One of the greatest of English prose works, John Bunyan's *Pilgrim's Progress*, is also cast in dream form. And it is obviously more than a literary device: Bunyan's allegory is so much a spiritual and psychological pilgrimage that the dream form must have been deliberately chosen to express the inner experiences by which Bunyan felt himself to have been changed.

Dreams that have played a vital part in the creative process were fairly well-known in the late 18th and early 19th centuries. The sense of beauty and terror, of mystery and illumination in dreams, was kept alive by poets, from Spenser to Tennyson in England, from Dante to Goethe in Europe. For Goethe, the dream had the magic of healing. "There have been times," he wrote, "when I have fallen asleep in tears; but in my dreams the most charming forms have come to cheer me, and I have risen fresh and joyful."

Almost 1500 years separate Goethe from St. Augustine—a millennium and a half in which no really important new ideas about the dream entered European thought; a period in which, according to experience, education, and religion, men largely repeated the insights or prejudices of much earlier writers; a period in which rationalism and intellectualism steadily triumphed over irrationalism, dogma, and superstition; in which science drove magic and superstition out of intellectual life and into the dark corners of the popular mind. The dream was treated increasingly as a bore, an illusion, a literary whimsy, at best the product of dyspepsia, and at worst a foolish superstition. Yet as the 19th century dawned, the ground was already prepared for the most striking developments in dream theory since the time of Aristotle.

4   Rationalists and romantics

In 1900, when Sigmund Freud published *The Interpretation of Dreams*, the book provoked much hostile criticism. The subject itself, let alone Freud's serious treatment of it, seemed a ludicrous one, not merely to other medical men but to many intellectuals trained in a rationalist tradition. Freud's book, however, began the last of the series of revolutions in thought which, in the course of the 19th century, transformed man's view of himself and of the world in which he lived.

The century began with a revolution in philosophy; it ended with the revolution in psychology; and in the intervening years there were equally important developments in physics, chemistry, biology, medicine, engineering, politics, and sociology. In 1800, Hegel was in his prime; by 1900, Darwin and Marx were dead; but Einstein and Freud were only on the threshold of their careers. Man had reached back through time to establish his own natural history and his relation to all living things; he had located himself in a vast expanding universe of space; he had begun to probe the mysteries of matter and energy; and he had turned inward to explore himself.

In the last of these explorations, dreams were to play a vital and controversial role. Yet the study of dreams was so out of keeping with the scientific temper of European thought in this century that, to many of the men who were expanding the frontiers of knowledge, it was intellectually disreputable

Dreams played an important role in the life and work of the 18th-century British artist and poet William Blake. Right, one of his paintings entitled *Queen Katherine's Dream*. His fascination by the symbols of fantasy was shared by other writers, philosophers, and artists of the period. Like Blake, they believed that dreams revealed the hidden creative and inspirational potential in human beings.

to talk seriously about dreams, and ridiculous to suggest that they could ever
be scientifically investigated. To rational, practical men, dreams were irrational and impractical, the stuff of which the poet's work was made rather
than the raw material from which to fashion a new theory of the human
mind. The scientist could measure, the surgeon dissect, and the naturalist
read the evidence of the fossil record. But what could the student of dreams
do? He had nothing solid with which to work, no scientific precedents to guide
him; and the reputation of his subject matter was clouded by its association
with superstition, astrology, clairvoyance, and numerology.

In the centuries after the Renaissance, the old traditions of oneirology
had become discredited among the educated classes. Dreams were usually
explained as the result of psychological disturbance, bad digestion, or external
stimuli such as heat, cold, and noise. They were certainly not regarded as
something integral and important to the human personality. Science was
interested in the conscious mind, and the physical organism it appeared to
control, not in the nebulous riddle of dreams.

It is against this background that one must set the attitude to dreams in
the 19th century. For it helps to explain why, when Freud came to summarize
previous work in this field, he felt that nothing very substantial had been
achieved. In the first chapter of *The Interpretation of Dreams* he remarked:

"It is difficult to write a history of the scientific study of the problem of
dreams because, however valuable that study may have been at a few points,
no line of advance in any particular direction can be traced. No foundation

has been laid of any secure findings upon which a later investigator might build; but each new writer examines the same problems and begins again, as it were, from the beginning."

In saying this, Freud did his predecessors rather less than justice. A few lines of advance can in fact be traced. They did not necessarily lead toward Freud's own work; some pointed toward modern findings in neurology, body chemistry, and the study of sleep. And it is true that, in the work of Freud's predecessors, speculation and introspection were often jumbled up; it was hard to tell where superstition ended and science began. But the science of dreams did not begin all at once, with the publication of Freud's book. The book itself drew heavily, though selectively, upon the reservoir of ideas about dreams that had been steadily accumulating throughout the previous century. While Freud's own contribution certainly contained revolutionary insights, it also had a significant intellectual ancestry.

Between the end of the 18th century and the beginning of the 20th there was a decisive change in the attitude toward dreams. The traditional view was that some, if not all of them, had divine or supernatural origins. Even when they were not simply regarded as the work of gods or demons, they were treated as manifestations of some external force. This traditional view was fast being replaced by another: increasingly the source of dreams was being attributed to man himself, not to external causes. Philosophers like Hobbes and Voltaire, as well as later medical and scientific researchers, argued that dreams were purely physiological in origin. But though they dismissed the

Oh! How I Dreamt of Things Impossible,
an engraving done by William Blake to
illustrate one of his poems. Blake appears
to have experienced many vivid dreams and
visions. On one occasion he saw God's face
looking at him through the window, on
another a tree full of angels.

Mad House, the last of a series of paintings
called *A Rake's Progress* by the 18th-
century artist William Hogarth, records
the cruel conditions of Bedlam—the first
English lunatic asylum. Society amused
itself by visiting the asylum—left,
two ladies watch the hero's death.

idea that dreams might offer significant clues to the dreamer's personality
or to the problems that confronted him in waking life, they recognized that
the dreamer made his own dreams.

This was a vital shift in emphasis, and one without which any scientific
attempt to understand the nature of dreams would have been impossible.
Once the source of dreams was located within, rather than outside, the dreamer,
the way had been opened for serious research. Dream theory was reflecting
the crucial changes that were going on in European thought at this period.
There was an increasing emphasis on the individual, a growing awareness
of man as a separate person, distinct from nature and society though he was
the child of both, a thinking animal responsible for his own fate. Modern
philosophy really began when Descartes said: "I think, therefore I am."
Modern psychology begins when Freud was able to say, in effect: "I am,
therefore I dream."

One reason why this idea took so long to germinate was the fact that the dominant theories of the mind took little account of irrational phenomena. An age which treated the mentally ill with little insight and human sympathy found it hard to take the ephemeral fantasies of sleep very seriously. The mystics, such as Emanuel Swedenborg, were dismissed as heretics or unbalanced people. Even the poets, such as Novalis, Wordsworth, Gérard de Nerval, William Blake, or Coleridge—men who could tolerate and reflect on experiences that did not fit neatly into contemporary scientific thought— were believed to have a streak of divine madness; while among writers, it was those who had a rich and troubled dream life, like William Hazlitt, Emerson, and Robert Louis Stevenson, who felt that dreams must signify something more than fleeting images of waking impressions. Much the same was true of the philosophers; it was those who were concerned with man's inner nature and spiritual aspirations who speculated about the nature of dreaming, rather than the positivists who sought to reduce all human experience to the logical and the measurable. But even those who were fascinated by dreams usually treated them as something subjectively important, or as no more than marginal evidence in some larger controversy about the nature of man and his mind. It is hard to see what else they could have done when they lacked, to an even greater degree than Freud, the systematic material on which to base their opinions. They had to rely heavily on introspection. The idea of an unconscious mental life for man, sleeping or waking, was only beginning to pass from the realms of poetry and philosophy into those of neurology and psychology.

For this reason it is hard to find typical or generally accepted views of dreams and dreaming in this period. We find, for instance, that the German philosopher, Arthur Schopenhauer, was asking the same profound but metaphysical question that Chuang-tzu had raised two thousand years before:

" . . . may not our whole life be a dream? . . . is there a sure criterion of the distinction between dreams and reality? Between phantasma and real objects? . . . The only sure criterion by which to distinguish them is in fact the entirely empirical one of awaking, through which, at any rate, the causal connection between dreamed events and those of waking life is distinctly and sensibly broken off."

For all this effort at a distinction, however, Schopenhauer was far from satisfied, concluding that "life and dreams are leaves of the same book" and that "we are forced to concede to the poets that life is one long dream."

Such an approach, however, was unlikely to commend itself to conventional or medical opinion. A physician, François Magendie, writing at about the same time as Schopenhauer—his book *Physiology* was published in 1844— stated flatly: "It may be doubted if dreaming ever occurs in a perfectly normal state. There are reasons for considering this phenomenon as always indicative of a morbid condition, though often slight and transient." To such a man, whose down-to-earth conception of the human mind seems trivial compared to the insight of Schopenhauer, all dreams, nightmares, visions, and hallucinations seemed abnormal. Magendie would have been incapable, with his emphasis on an apparently realistic but actually erroneous view of mental processes, of comprehending what Schopenhauer was talking about when he said that "the origin of madness . . . will become more comprehensible if it is remembered how unwillingly we think of things which powerfully injure our interest, wound our pride, or interfere with our wishes; how easily . . . we unconsciously break away or sneak off from them again . . . ." What Freud was to call a "resistance" was clearly identified by Schopenhauer, and in this recognition lay more than one clue to the nature of dreams as Freud was later to conceive it.

The same line of thought can be found in other German philosophers and writers in the early part of the 19th century, especially those influenced by the nature-philosophers like the physician and painter C. G. Carus. While Magendie and his medical contemporaries were regarding all that was not conscious as irrational, if not actually morbid, men such as J. G. Fichte, F. W. J. von Schelling, and the romantic novelist J. P. F. Richter, were already familiar with the concept of the unconscious. Richter, for instance, had asked a vital question:

"Why should everything come to consciousness that lies in the mind since, for example, that of which it is already aware, the whole great realm of memory, only appears to it illuminated in small areas, while the entire remaining world stays invisible in the shadow? And may there not be a second half-world of our mental moon which never turns toward consciousness?"

The idea of the unconscious—the dark side of our mental moon—was essentially the work of German philosophers. The word "unconscious" was first used in Germany in 1776 and in England, by Wordsworth, in 1800. By the time Freud received his education, the idea was relatively familiar to a well-educated German or Austrian; furthermore, it had already been directly linked to the discussion of the nature and significance of dreams.

The English view of the mind, however, was in marked contrast to the German. While romantic writers who had received a part of their education in Germany were talking in much the same language as Fichte, Schelling, and J. G. von Herder, most Englishmen inclined to a more matter-of-fact approach. It might be said that where the Germans moved from the abstract to the particular, the English inclination was to move from the particular to the abstract. From the time of John Locke onward, English philosophers and medical men started from the reality of the waking human being—his perceptions and his physiology—and sought to explain all mental phenomena, waking or sleeping, from the way the conscious mind appeared to behave.

In the middle of the 18th century, the pioneer physician David Hartley had written his *Observations on Man*—a book of considerable influence in which he set out a view of dreams that dominated most English writing on the subject for over a hundred years. For Hartley, there was little difficulty about the nature and causes of dreams.

" . . . dreams are nothing but the imaginations, fancies, or reveries of a sleeping man, and . . . are deducible from three causes, *viz.*: First, the impressions and ideas lately received, and particularly those of the preceding day. Secondly, the state of the body, particularly of the stomach and the brain. And thirdly, association. . . . A person may form a judgment of the state of his bodily health, and of his temperance, by the general pleasantness or unpleasantness of his dreams. There are also many hints relating to the strength of our passions deducible from them."

This concept of association—that one idea leads to another—was certainly a persistent one. A century after Hartley, the English author John Addington Symonds was still using it. "The phenomena of dreams," he wrote, "are regulated by the same laws of association or succession as those of waking thought, and the more closely we investigate the difference between these two classes of phenomena, the more clearly we shall perceive that many of the distinguishing characteristics are rather apparent than real." Hartley, moreover, had provided a reason why dreams should seem to be so different from the images and ideas of waking life, even though they were the product of the same process. "The wildness of our dreams," he observed, "seems to be of singular use to us by interrupting and breaking the course of our associations. For, if we were always awake, some accidental associations would be so much cemented by continuance, as that nothing could afterward disjoin them; which would be madness."

The German philosophers and the English physiologists were working from conflicting assumptions, and these differing assumptions inevitably led to contrasting conceptions of the dream. The German tradition pointed to the dream as a clue to a hidden aspect of man's personality; the English, much more prosaic, believed that at most it might indicate what had impressed a man's waking consciousness or, perhaps, his state of health. As early as 1808, Robert Gray had written in his *Theory of Dreams* that "the dream is the work of the mind . . . deriving its materials from experience." In other words, the difference between the German metaphysical approach to dreams and the English emphasis on their physiological aspect was that the Germans were more concerned with the *nature* of dreams—what they reveal about the problems and passions of a man's life—and the English more interested in their *cause*. In 1841, the Scottish author and physician Robert MacNish, in an important and influential book entitled *The Philosophy of Sleep*, took up Gray's point: "I believe that dreams are uniformly the resuscitation or reembodiment of thoughts which have formerly, in some shape or other, occupied the mind. They are old ideas revived either in an entire state, or heterogeneously mingled together."

Like other students of sleep, MacNish came to the conclusion that dreams emerged because logical control of consciousness was relaxed, and deeper and less well-organized feelings could emerge. But something was required to stimulate the dream. MacNish believed that there were four main kinds of stimuli: (a) the experience of the previous day; (b) indigestion; (c) illness, and especially fevers; (d) sensory impressions during sleep. In his book, which covered most of the characteristics of sleep, from nightmares and somnambulism to insomnia and trances, he recapitulated the medical knowledge of his time. Freud, who makes a brief reference to MacNish's book, seems only to have known of it indirectly through a passage quoted by the German author Jessen.

Freud, of course, could not read everything, and it is remarkable how much material he did manage to locate. The bibliographies in *The Interpretation of Dreams* are the first comprehensive survey of the literature in this field. But it is curious that besides omitting the significant work of MacNish, he made no reference at all to the fascinating book written by another Scottish physician, John Abercrombie. In *Inquiries Concerning the Intellectual Powers, and the Investigation of Truth* Abercrombie made three important points. First, the fact that dreams seem to have "a real and present existence" is due, he said, to the impossibility of comparing the dream experience "with the things of the external world." Secondly, dream images not only proceed "according to association . . . we cannot, as in the waking state, vary the series, or stop

The fact that some dream themes continually recur had already been noted by 19th-century observers. Left, the title page of a 19th-century novelette *Daniel O'Rouke* depicts the familiar dream situation of falling. Pre-Freudian work on dreams emphasized the role of internal and external stimuli. Right, an engraving called *Preparing for a Nightmare* (1878).

it at our will." Thirdly, it is possible to divide dreams into categories, each of which throws some light on the means by which dreams are produced.

With these propositions, Abercrombie reached a crucial point in the development of dream theory. Dreams were at last being treated as natural phenomena that were amenable to the scientific method of hypothesis-evidence-demonstration. Though almost another hundred years were to pass before effective experimental techniques could be developed, whereby the various hypotheses could be tested under anything like laboratory conditions, Abercrombie had at least indicated how this might be done. For this reason, it is worth looking more closely at his conclusions.

The first of his categories was the dream in which "recent events and recent mental emotions mingled up into one continuous series with each other, or with old events, by means of some feeling which had been in a greater or less degree allied to each of them...." He gave an example in which the dreamer hears unpleasant news of an absent friend, is concerned in some business that causes anxiety, and learns of a distressing accident. In the dream, all three events are linked, though "the only bond of union among these occurrences was that each of them gave rise to a similar kind of emotion." Abercrombie had not hit on the idea of reversing the process of association, so that the dreamer could be led back from the dream to a forgotten event or experience that caused deep emotion or anxiety—the essential psychoanalytical technique that Freud was to devise. But he had perceived

that the idea of association provided a vital clue to the structure of a dream precisely because it indicated how buried memories could well up in sleep.

Secondly, Abercrombie dealt with associations evoked by bodily sensations such as heat, cold, or noise: he records the dreams of a friend who noted several occasions of this type. A hot-water bottle made him dream that he was climbing Mount Etna; the falling of a pair of fire irons led to a dream of cannon firing as a warning against invasion; a poultice on his head was the cause of a dream of his being scalped. In each case the imagination seemed to have built a complete dream story around the single stimulus. Moreover, as Abercrombie noted, these dreams suggested a curious fact about the time scale of dreams. A loud noise awakened the dreamer, but it was also incorporated in what seemed a long dream. From this, Abercrombie concluded that there was a marked difference between the sense of elapsed time in dreams and in waking life. This conclusion, a reasonable one from the evidence, was long accepted, though modern research into the time sense in dreams has raised many objections to this view.

Abercrombie's third category led to problems that, understandably, he was unable to resolve; but, to his credit, he isolated exactly that aspect of dreams on which psychoanalysis was later to depend. It is worth quoting his definition in full:

When Freud wrote about dreams he was able to draw on a remarkable amount of previous work and thought on the subject: 19th-century writers, for instance, had tried to explain the problem-solving nature of dreams. Left, a humorous engraving from a book on dreams by Adolf von Menzel (1815-1905) illustrates an Austrian field marshal's dream that he will be victorious in the next day's battle only if he catches the marquis from the enemy camp. The nature of sleep as a whole, and it's associated phenomena—such as sleep-walking—were investigated. Right, a scene from a production of *La Somnambula* (1831) by the Italian composer Vincenzo Bellini.

"Dreams consisting of the revival of old associations respecting things which had entirely passed out of the mind, and which seemed to have been forgotten. It is often impossible to trace the manner in which these dreams arise; and some of the facts connected with them scarcely appear referable to any principle to which we are already acquainted."

The examples he gave, however, do not relate to "forgotten" emotional experiences, but rather to matters of fact which had become inaccessible to waking memory; most of them illustrate the way in which the dreamer may recall where to find a lost object or how to solve a difficult problem. Though some kind of "unconscious" is assumed in such cases, Abercrombie seems to have regarded this part of the mind more as some kind of filing system for waking experience than as a dynamic part of the personality.

Yet, in his fourth category, he sensed that some hidden process of reasoning, or even of intuition, could lie behind normal consciousness. He drew attention to dreams in which the dreamer seems to be aware of personality traits in another person of which he is unaware when awake. In the dream, the dreamer reads the character of another with such accuracy that he actually predicts what will happen. Thus, when the event occurs, the dream appears to have been prophetic, although all that has occurred is that the dreamer has projected some observed tendency to its conclusion. Typical examples quoted by Abercrombie include the case of a man who dreamed his children had set fire to his house, and returned home to find they had done so; and that of a mother who dissuaded her son from going on a boating expedition on which his friends were later drowned. Abercrombie argued that such dreams were reasonable extensions of known, if not consciously apprehended, possibilities—anxieties that had embodied themselves into a dream. The argument, he urged, was strengthened by the fact that many dreams of this sort are not fulfilled; they simply indicate a possibility.

This sensible reasoning is beautifully summarized in one of Abercrombie's examples, in which he tells of a clergyman who felt that a collection had fallen short of his hopes. The next night he dreamed that three pound notes had been stuck in the corner of a collecting box, or ladle. He went to the church and found three bank notes in the ladle. Abercrombie comments:

"It appears that on the evening preceding the day of collection, the clergyman had been amusing himself by calculating what sum his congregation would probably contribute, and that in doing so he had calculated on a certain number of families who would not give him less than one pound each. Let us then suppose that a particular ladle, which he knew had been presented to three of those families, had been emptied in his presence, and

Methods of inducing and directing dreams were demonstrated by the Marquis d'Hervey in *Les Rêves et Les Moyens de les Diriger* (1867). The frontispiece (below) depicts what Freud later called a "typical" dream—the appearance of a nude girl in a conventionally dressed group. D'Hervey explained the dream as the unconscious merging of two different memory images.

found to contain no pound notes. His first feeling would be that of disappointment; but in afterwards thinking of the subject, and connecting it with his former calculation, the possibility of the ladle not having been fully emptied might dart across his mind. This impression, which perhaps he did not himself recollect, might then be embodied into the dream, which by a natural coincidence was fulfilled."

Abercrombie's attempt to sort dream experience into four categories was sensible; only by some such systematic division could progress in analyzing the nature of dreams be made, and Freud himself found it necessary to build his own work around a structure of this kind. In order to see how the attitude to dreams during the half century that lay between Abercrombie and Freud demonstrates that there were distinct "lines of advance," it will be useful to make our own classification of dream studies here.

The first category consists of theories about the causes of dreams. We have already seen that the German philosophers and the English physicians differed in this respect; this distinction persisted right up to the time of Freud, and continues in modern research into dreams. The borderline between psychological and physiological theories has never been clearly defined, nor are the two types of theory necessarily incompatible. One can explain how a dream may occur without denying that it may have a psychic function or meaning for the dreamer. Conversely, though one regards dreams as a symbolic manifestation of unconscious thought, it may still be valuable to investigate the mechanism that produces them. But, in pre-Freudian controversies, before the concept of the unconscious was generally accepted, there seemed to be a conflict between these two points of view, and considerable emphasis was placed on the possibility that dreams were no more than random fantasies woven by the sleeping mind around some physical (or somatic) stimulus.

The second category includes various observed phenomena of sleep. Leaving aside visions, or the hallucinations of the insane—though the similarity between these waking fantasies and those of sleep had often been noted—there are various kinds of behavior in sleep that had attracted attention. There was, first, the curious fact of somnambulism; sleepwalking, talking, or simply movements in sleep, were common enough to be the subject of inquiry. There were, secondly, such curious things as the recollection of dreams under hypnosis, or the possibility of suggesting dreams to hypnotic subjects.

The third category covers the different types of dream experience that were a matter of common note in the pre-Freudian period.

When Abercrombie sought to classify dreams according to type he was making the kind of distinction that had been known since antiquity. But whereas classical dream interpreters had wrestled with the problem of distinguishing between divine and profane dreams, in the later part of the 19th century more emphasis was placed on typing dreams as a possible means of discovering what part the dream played in the mental or organic life of the dreamer. There were dreams that, as Abercrombie was aware, suggested that individuals might be able to solve problems or find lost objects that had eluded them in waking life. There was the creative dream, in which a writer or a scientist would hit on what seemed a completely new idea relevant to his work. There were dreams that seemed prophetic or prodromic, and others that related more to the past; dreams that dealt with the life of the dreamer, and those that appeared to be telepathic, offering knowledge of events at a distance. Finally, there were dreams that were apparently the result of toxic influences, such as those induced by opium in de Quincey.

The last of the four categories contains much material that Freud was to use as the basis of his theory of dream symbolism. It deals with the actual content of dreams. It had long been observed that despite the oddities and distortions of dreams that seemed peculiar to each dreamer, certain themes and structures recurred—as if the mind had a predilection for particular groups of images. The dream of flying is one example; dreams of imprisonment and trial, of having one's teeth pulled out, of swimming, being naked, running upstairs, or of the death of loved relatives, are other well-known examples of "typical" dreams. As the dream books of the ancients show, the assumption of "typical" or "recurrent" themes, structures, and symbols is the essential basis of systematic dream interpretation. Freud's analysis of dreams may have been far removed from that, say, of Artemidorus, but it rested on the same assumption. We should note, moreover, that when Jung came to break with Freud, the question of the universality of dreams played a vital part in their disagreement. Though Jung shared Freud's assumption that there were common and discoverable patterns in dreams, he took a different view of the origins and character of these patterns, believing that Freud's reduction of complex symbols to simple sexual forms was too limited a means of interpretation.

To work in this field, of course, one requires large numbers of dreams, dreamed by persons of different ages, conditions, and cultural backgrounds: scientific comparison can begin only when there is sufficient evidence on which to base it. But when Freud and Jung were doing their pioneering work, like all 19th-century investigators of dreams, they were hampered by lack of material. Enough dreams had been recorded, over the centuries, to indicate that there might indeed be "typical" themes and recurrent symbols, but it was only after Freud that psychoanalysts and others began to collect dreams in a sufficiently systematic way for this hypothesis to be open to any serious test.

In addition to our examination of pre-Freudian dream theories and experience, it is necessary to consider one other category of dreams—those of primitive peoples living outside the pale of civilization. Most of this material was collected after anthropologists had become familiar with Freud's main work, and the search for it was partly stimulated by the possibility that dreams drawn from a different cultural background might confirm or refute some of the Freudian hypotheses. Though the data is fragmentary and the value of some of it difficult to assess, much of it is relevant and suggestive.

In the 15th and 16th centuries, the European view of the world was transformed by great geographical discoveries; in the 19th century, the European attitude toward man and his habits of existence was comparably transformed by discoveries no less important in the fields of anthropology and ecology, resulting in the first systematic descriptions of pre-industrial and pre-historic communities in the Americas, Africa, Asia, and Oceania. Each of these communities had its own social structure, traditions, habits, and beliefs. The study of these differences gave rise to a number of vital questions. Were such peoples comparable to our own remote ancestors? Could we, by studying them, perceive the forms of society and the mental patterns from which modern cultures have evolved? The early anthropologists, strongly influenced by evolutionary ideas, usually gave a positive answer to such questions. Today, they are inclined to be less certain. They are not even sure that such communities were so sharply cut off from the experience of the rest of the human race as their geographical isolation suggests: they see evidence that, far back, whole groups of such peoples came from common ethnic stocks, and that ideas, techniques, even manufactured objects, may have been transmitted over long distances by the process that is now called "cultural diffusion."

The controversies that engaged the great anthropologists were directly relevant to the study of dreams. Take, for instance, the question whether all men have a similar psychic constitution. Does the Trobriand Islander of New Guinea think and behave differently from the French farmer merely because he has grown up in a different environment? Or is it that his mind is different, or less well developed? Have certain ideas that can be found among the Papuan tribes arisen spontaneously, because they are generic to human existence, or have they been derived—however indirectly—from some other source? Do the similarities of religious belief or social custom, found (as was the case with incubation) in societies scattered around the globe, develop from similar states of social or intellectual development, or do they reflect some lost common origin?

These issues had already been raised before Freud's theories about the nature of man gave a new turn to the controversy. As scholars studied the craftsmanship or social structure of tribes dotted around the world, they began to make comparisons between them, and also between these modern discoveries and the archaeological record. They noted that, in such things as ritual, myth, or folk tale, certain themes recurred—even that particular symbols were repeated. And soon dreams were also called in evidence.

The idea that there was a relation between myth and dream did not begin with Freud. He was certainly familiar with the work of the German writer

Ludwig Laistner, in whose book, *The Riddle of the Sphinx*, it is powerfully argued that dreams were related to myths. Freud's crucial contribution was the idea that both myth and dream were symbolic expressions of the same inner forces—the presentation in verbal and visual images of instinctual feelings or childhood experiences that, for a variety of reasons, could not be directly admitted to consciousness.

This theory of Freud's gave valuable impetus to the collection and study of dreams in pre-literate societies, and thereby led to new disputes among anthropologists about the implications of the evidence thus secured. And as more and more anthropological evidence of all kinds accumulated toward the end of the 19th century, new light was cast on the problem of symbolism. At the very moment, in fact, when the pioneer psychoanalysts were directing their attention to the symbols presented by modern man in his dreams and fantasies, they were being almost swamped by a flood of symbolic material pouring in from the corners of the earth.

The basic Freudian view has been well expressed by the English psycho-analyst and biographer of Freud, Dr. Ernest Jones:

"One of the most amazing features of true symbolism is the remarkable ubiquity of the same symbols, which are to be found, not only in different fields of thought, dreams, wit, insanity, poetry, etc., among a given class and at a given level of civilization, but among different races and at different epochs of the world's history. A symbol which today we find, for instance, in an obscene joke is also found in a mythical cult of Ancient Greece, and another that we come across only in dream analysis was used thousands of years ago in the sacred books of the East. The following examples may be quoted in illustration of this correspondence. The idea of teeth, in dreams, is often symbolically related to that of childbirth, a connection that is hardly ever found in consciousness; in the Song of Songs we read: 'Thy teeth are as a flock of sleep which go up from the washing, whereof everyone beareth twins, and there is not one barren among them.' The idea of the snake, which is never consciously associated with that of the phallus, is regularly so in dreams, being one of the most constant and invariable symbols in primitive religions; the two ideas are quite obviously interchangeable, so that it is often hard to distinguish phallic from ophitic (i.e. snake) worship; many traces of this are to be found even in the Old Testament."

It was on such recurrences that Jung, going far beyond Freud, eventually based his theory of the collective unconscious, from which he believed such fundamental symbols as the circle and the cross, the trinity, the hero, the wise old man, and the dragon-like devouring mother, ultimately sprang. The point here, however, is not how one explains such recurrences. It is simply that a belief in the universality of symbols is as crucial to the dream inter-pretations of the psychoanalyst as it was to Artemidorus, the compilers of dream books, or the oneiromancers of antiquity.

The sun is one of the most powerful and universal of all symbols, appearing in myths, religions, art, literature, and dreams. It generally represents life-giving qualities and the triumph of light over darkness. Its daily setting and rising have been associated symbolically with the theme of death and resurrection. The Babylonians personified the sun as Shamash, god of justice (below: ninth-century B.C. carving of Shamash in his shrine). Top right: a Bronze Age sun chariot from Trundholm in Denmark. Right: a sun carving on a bowl from the sun-worshiping Inca civilization. Bottom left: an 18th-century African drum decorated with suns. Bottom right: a Navajo sand-painting of the sun.

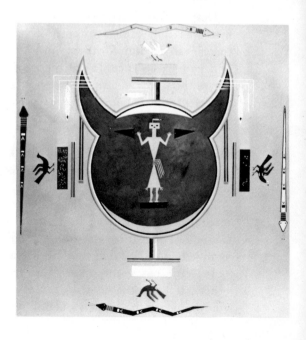

If the dream is a random phenomenon, peculiar to each individual and without any recognizable pattern or consistent content, then it speaks in a language no one but the dreamer can interpret. But if the dream follows certain definite patterns, and employs a relatively limited set of symbols, then dream interpretation of this symbolic language becomes conceivable. These patterns and symbols, moreover, must transcend a given time, place, and culture or, once again, they would not be amenable to common principles of interpretation. They may assume different forms, and combine the symbols differently, according to the personality of the dreamer and the nature of the culture in which he lives. But unless we assume that they rest upon a common human experience, any kind of systematic dream interpretation is impossible.

Thus, when the anthropologists began to investigate the dreams of distant peoples, this new evidence was closely scanned to see whether the hypothesis could be maintained. How did primitive people regard their dreams? What rituals and beliefs were associated with dreams? How were dreams interpreted, and what symbols and situations did they contain? Might one find the symbols emerging in the dreams of modern man repeated in the waking rituals of the primitive and in the legends of antiquity? Would the dividing line between the reality of waking life and the fantasies of sleep prove to be less sharp among peoples who were unaffected by the Cartesian revolution in thought? Would the symbols of sleep be closer to the experience of life where that experience was more simple and the society less complex than in advanced countries? Answers were offered to all such questions; but the further such answers move from fact and the nearer to speculation, the more controversial they become.

Despite the controversies, however, some facts did begin to emerge. The first was that almost all primitive people took note of their dreams, had theories to account for them, and frequently modified their behavior in the light of dream experience. It was reported that many tribes believed that the "soul" leaves the body in sleep (as we noted in Asian dream theory) and that dreams represent the experience of its wanderings. This belief, found from Greenland to the Gran Chaco and New Guinea, has various forms. Some West African tribes thought that the soul can meet another soul and fight it: a man waking with stiff bones would think another soul had thrashed him during his sleep. The Aru Islanders refrained from sleeping in a house after a death in case the dead soul still lingered, for they feared to meet it in a dream. And where there is a belief that the soul leaves the body there is always an anxiety about ensuring its return; in parts of India, the fear that the soul might not recognize its own body if the appearance of it was changed was signified by a law that made it a capital offense to paint the face of a sleeper.

In some cases, the dream was seen as the result of the soul traveling; in others, it was attributed to the visiting spirits of friends, the dead, or tribal guardians; or both views could be held, as they were by the Zulus, who

Right, the Gnawing-Squirrel totem, adopted, like many other totems, after the animal had been seen in a vision. An Indian tribe in British Columbia was so scared by a volcanic eruption in 1780 that for a long time after the event its members experienced frightful hallucinations: the country seemed to be infested with giant squirrels. The squirrel became their totem.

thought that an ancestor could visit them to warn of danger, or that the ancestor (the *itongo*) could take them to a distant place. Some West African tribes developed an interest in dreams that seems to have been almost obsessional. The missionary J. L. Wilson tells us that "all their dreams are construed into visits from the spirits of their deceased friends. The cautions, hints, and warnings which come to them through this source are received with the most serious and deferential attention, and are always acted upon in their waking hours. The habit of relating their dreams, which is universal, greatly promotes the habit of dreaming itself, and hence their sleeping hours are characterized by almost as much intercourse with the dead as their waking are with the living."

Such peoples understandably treat an event in a dream as if it were as real as in waking life; among the Ashanti—and the same is reported about the Kai people of New Guinea—a dream of adultery invokes the same penalty as actual adultery. Among the Cherokee Indians, a man who dreams of being bitten by a snake is treated as if he had been so bitten, and among American Indians there are many examples of a tribe attempting to satisfy the fantasies of its dreamers. We know, from the tales of early travelers, a good

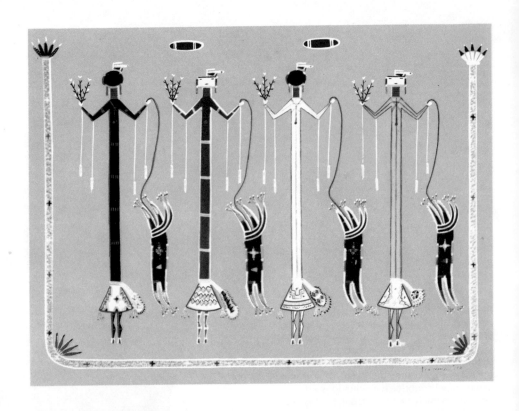

deal about these customs of the American Indian, and such accounts emphasize the important role that the dream played in the life of both the individual and his tribe. From the time of a boy's initiation into manhood, when he goes to a lonely place to fast and meditate, his attention is focused on dreams or visions—especially those relating to the animal that becomes his guardian spirit. And those whose fantasies are full of valuable revelations are regarded as prophets, inspired with wisdom and insight into the future. Dreams of this kind were even developed by some North American tribes into a form of therapy that strikingly resembles modern conceptions of the dream.

Many tribal societies made a distinction between personal and social dreams. those of the first type, ordinary dreams, often being lightly regarded, but great value being attached to the second type. Jung tells of a visit to an African tribe that, after the coming of the white man and the imposition of a new pattern of government, ceased to have the "official" dreams from which it previously drew inspiration in its tribal affairs. It might perhaps be more accurate to say that it ceased to "seek" such dreams, for the evidence suggests that the distinction between the personal and the social dream lay partly in the means by which the dream was induced (by normal sleep, or by fasting, ritual, and drugs), and partly in the nature of the dreamer (an ordinary member of the tribe, or a chief, medicine man, or shaman). In this respect the primitives do not greatly differ from the ancients.

J. S. Lincoln, in his book *The Dream in Primitive Society*, gives many examples of the "social" consequences of dreams. They affected the selection of personal or tribal totems, or the choice of guardian spirits and secret helpers; they often indicated when a sacrifice had to be made to propitiate an ancestor or an evil spirit; they indicated the necessary cures for illness or the magic ritual required to ensure success in war or hunting; they were embodied in dances, songs, and other ceremonies; they pointed out the lifepath for an individual; and were frequently responsible for acts of murder and cannibalism, for the activity of secret societies, and even for the migration of whole peoples. Lincoln summarized his findings in these words: "Much of primitive culture is derived from the dead father or ancestor spirit, who communicates through the culture pattern dream or vision, the dream image being

The Navajo Indians of North America counteract a bad dream by a protective ritual—above, a sandpainting from the Feather Chant depicts supernatural beings bringing healing herbs. In a ritual to cure illness (below) Navajos enact a legend about the Dreamer—a mythical forefather who, like other ancestors, acquired his supernatural status because of dreams in which he talked to the gods. Here, they show how the Dreamer foresaw in a dream the failure of a hunting expedition.

The North American Iroquois choose vivid
dreamers as medicine men. Some of the most
powerful belong to a society that guards
against the False Faces—forest demons that
cause illness. Above, a ritual mask.

accepted by the primitive as the real father or ancestor. It is important to
realize that this makes the totem or father the carrier of culture."

At the same time as anthropologists were providing such evidence about
the attitudes toward dreams, and their influence on the waking behavior of
primitive peoples, they were also providing data on the contents of these
dreams. It was found that some themes not only appeared in widely separated
cultures, but that they also evoked very similar responses. C. G. Seligman,
for instance, found that dreams about raw meat occurred in Ireland, Switzerland, China, Greece, the Ukraine, Nigeria, Tanganyika, Borneo, and
Achin in Sumatra—and that in all these places such a dream was associated
with some impending misfortune. In the Ukraine it presaged a burial; in
the Zungeru district of Nigeria, the death of a friend; in Tanganyika, it was
a symbol of a funeral feast. The origins of this common belief may be simple:
for many poor societies, the consumption of large quantities of meat would
be limited to funerals and similar occasions, and the association would therefore be direct.

Seligman suggested a further association—that raw meat symbolizes a
repressed cannibalism, that such thoughts are taboo, and that the "raw meat"
symbol has thus become linked to both death and misfortune. In recent years,

much has been done to analyze such symbolism in psychoanalytical terms; common dreams of tooth-pulling, flying, and other themes found in the clinical experience of psychoanalysts have been compared to those found among primitive peoples. But long before such Freudian or Jungian analyses could be made, it was evident that the dream interpretations of primitive peoples—like those of antiquity—were based upon the recurrence of symbols.

A striking example of this can be found in the comparison of certain interpretations by Artemidorus and by 10 headmen of a tribe in Nyasaland—reported in 1926 by A. G. O. Hodgson and H. J. Rose. In Artemidorus, *fire in the sky* meant war or famine; for the Africans a *bush fire* in a dream meant war. Artemidorus said that to dream of *losing a tooth* meant to lose a member of one's household; to the Africans such a dream showed that the dreamer would lose a wife or child. A *flood dream* in Artemidorus indicated misfortune in litigation or ill-tempered masters; and it had virtually the same meaning for the Africans. To them a *snake round the leg* signified slavery, while the dream of a *dragon round the body* is a symbol of bondage in Artemidorus. And, as with Artemidorus and many other interpreters, dreams often go by contraries. Both for the Africans and for Artemidorus, a dream of illness or of death, for instance, means recovery.

Such similarities in both symbols and interpretation provided Freud and his followers with the evidence on which it could be asserted—as, for example, by J. S. Lincoln—that "the human mind tends always and everywhere to think alike," and that the dreams or myths of primitives were amenable to precisely the same techniques of analysis as those of modern man.

This view is by no means universally held; but even if a strict Freudian view is not accepted, any comprehensive dream theory has to take account of the evidence on which Freud and Jung based their conclusions about universal symbols and must offer some better explanation of this universality than mere coincidence. If scores of scattered and seemingly quite unrelated tribes develop similar attitudes to dreams, have similar dreams, and embody their dream experience in essentially similar rituals, the evidence points strongly toward certain conclusions. First, that dreaming is not only a common human experience, but one that conforms to definite patterns. Second, that these patterns are more closely related to the structure of the human mind, and to certain fundamental human relationships and experiences, than they are to specific cultural situations; the latter provide the outer form rather than the inner nature of the dream. Thirdly, that the dream may be feared or sought, but is always valued. And, finally, that almost all human societies see some connection between dreams and waking behavior. What the anthropological evidence did, in fact, was to offer vital data on the significance of dreams, in all places and at all times, at the very moment when Freud was devising a theory of dreams that, if it was in any way valid, pointed to exactly this kind of universality.

5　The dream pioneers

Could anything be done to test theories about the cause of dreams? There had been ample speculation, argument by analogy, and conclusion by introspection. But could anyone devise experiments that would conform to the scientific rule that like cause should produce like result? Some experimenters in the 19th century believed such tests were possible and, in a simple fashion, began to attempt them.

Of these, the most famous are the experiments made by the Frenchman L. F. Alfred Maury, who reported them in his book *Le Sommeil et les Rêves*, published in 1861. Maury was convinced that dreams were caused by external stimulation, and his tests were designed to show that even in sleep the senses can convey messages to the brain, and that the brain responds with appropriate imagery. Nine of the tests were similar. The stimuli he used varied from the use of a feather for tickling the nose, to drops of water, speech, burning matches, and bright lights before the eyes. Each stimulus apparently produced a relevant dream. A burning match held beneath the nose, for instance, led Maury to dream that he was at sea—the wind was blowing through the window in his bedroom—and that the powder magazine of the ship had blown up. A pair of tweezers held close to the ear, and struck to make a slight ringing noise, caused him to dream of the sound of bells ringing out a tocsin that recalled the Paris revolution of June 1848. The smell of eau de

A painting by the Marquis d'Hervey, 19th-century author of a book on dreams, of his own hypnagogic images. He describes these as "wheels of light, tiny revolving suns, colored bubbles rising and falling ... bright lines that cross and interlace, that roll up and make circles, lozenges, and other geometric shapes." D'Hervey's investigations were paralleled by other writers during the 19th century who tried to explain the phenomena of dreams by analyzing retinal effects.

cologne prompted a dream of a perfumery in Cairo, from which Maury was led into a series of exotic adventures that he was unable to remember in detail. For years thereafter, Maury's tests were quoted in support of the theory that dreams had a physiological cause.

In the course of his book, Maury touched on many other aspects of dreaming that seem to lead toward contemporary concepts of the dream. He pointed out that the power of concentration and the judgment of the rational mind are diminished with the approach of sleep. As a man begins to doze, he said, his state is like that of senility, while in the actual state of sleeping he is like a person mentally deranged. In both conditions, moreover, there is a regression to childhood, as there is in dreams, for our earliest education and environment set the basic pattern of our instincts. "In dreaming," he said, "man reveals himself to himself in all his nakedness and native misery." Maury was also convinced, from his own experiences, that dreams could recall long-forgotten memories of names, places, and events, of which the conscious mind apparently knew nothing. But the main impact of his work was to focus attention on the sensations that might serve as a key to open the door of memory.

Many writers on dreams returned to this theme after Maury, but most of them did little more than add new examples of the same theme. Some remarked on the effect of the posture in sleep, pointing out that touching one leg against another might produce a dream of being manacled; pushing the leg down might lead to a dream of going downstairs; grasping one's own hand, numbed by sleeping on it, could explain a dream in which one dreams of touching the dead. A dream of being crushed might be due to the pressure of bedclothes, or a dream of the Arctic could arise when the sleeper is cold.

Into this "sensation" category fall all dreams that relate to touch, taste, sound, and smell, as well as those that arise from hunger and thirst. Starving explorers or shipwrecked seamen have often reported dreams of banquets or refreshing fountains. Other dreams of this sort have often been attributed to an upset stomach due to unwise or excessive eating—what the poet Robert Graves has called the "Pickled Walnut" school of dream theory. At the end of the 19th century, the English writer Havelock Ellis, whose work on dreams was of considerable importance, reported a case in which the "dreamer awoke from a disturbed sleep associated with indigestion, having the impression that burglars were tramping upstairs, but immediately realized that the tramp of the burglars' feet was really the beating of her own heart." (Edgar Allan Poe's story "The Tell-Tale Heart" is based on a similar illusion.) And Ellis added, in another context: "Most of the examples I have presented of the influence of emotion of visceral origin in suggesting dream theories have had the stomach as their source. Its easily and constantly varying state of repletion, its central position and liability to press on other organs, its important nervous associations, together with the fact that sleep

One famous dream—of the Frenchman Alfred Maury—seems to show that dreams are almost instantaneous. He saw himself, a victim of the French Revolution, being tried and sent to the guillotine. He felt the knife fall —and then awoke to find the bedrail had fallen on his neck. One explanation could be that the impact of the bedrail linked a series of vague images to make a coherent dream scene—in this case of the revolutionary tribunal.

sometimes tends to impede its activity and initiate disturbance, combine to impart to it a manifold and extensive influence over the emotional state of sleep, and at the same time render the source of that emotional state peculiarly difficult for sleeping consciousness to detect."

Much of the work that Ellis did was written and a good deal of it published before Freud, though his book *The World of Dreams* did not appear until 1911. His dream theory was far from being a straightforward stimulus-response concept of dreams. Yet, because of his early medical training, the theory had a strong physiological bias; without denying the psychic relevance of dreams, Ellis constantly looked for evidence in them of the way that the mind and body worked, and were related to one another. He could take, for instance, the "typical" dream of flying. To Freud—as he put it in his essay on Leonardo da Vinci—this signified "nothing else but the desire to be capable of sexual activities. It is a wish of early childhood." But to Ellis, it might signify this, or it might relate to other memories and feelings, possibly to an archaic and instinctive recollection of man's ancestry, of the labile movements of maritime creatures, or even of the child within the womb. Or could it be, he asked, the product of internal sensations—the rising and falling of respiratory muscles,

or the systole and diastole of the heart muscles, accompanied by the loss of internal equilibrium due to the horizontal position in which most men sleep? Cardiac and respiratory stimulation in children, he observed, is often caused by running up and down stairs, or by skipping and jumping, and there might well be a symbolic expression of this sensation in sleep. Even more, the loss of tactile pressure on the feet may also lead to some loss of the sense of balance or orientation. Many examples are known of believed levitation in states of hysteria or ecstasy. The French psychologist Pierre Janet had found a condition of temporary anesthesia on the soles of the feet of persons suffering from hysterical attacks. Ellis also remarked on the often-reported phenomenon that persons on the point of death feel themselves to be rising or flying—an experience not difficult to associate with the concept of angels.

The point here is not whether Freud or Ellis gives the most acceptable interpretation of the "flying" dream. It is simply to demonstrate the degree to which the physiological theory of dreams had been developed by the end of the century. From the crude explanation that certain images are associated with given physical sensations, common in the years between Hartley and Abercrombie, it had been extended to cover much more complex aspects of the dream. Ellis was able, moreover, to offer an explanation of the difference between the tiny stimulus and the large effect it appeared to have on the sleeping mind. He took as an example a dream by Leonard Guthrie of being tortured by savages (Guthrie sweated heavily in his sleep and thought that the under-arm rivulets of perspiration were the cause of tickling), and he suggested what might cause such an exaggeration:

". . . we have to remember the tendency to magnification in dream imagery, a tendency which rests upon the emotionality of dreams. Emotion is normally heightened in dreams. Every impression reaches sleeping consciousness through this emotional atmosphere, in an enlarged form, vaguer it may be, but more

An example of a "taste" dream from *Sleep and Its Derangements* (1869) by William Hammond. A girl who wanted to cure herself of thumb-sucking in her sleep covered her thumb with bitter aloes. She dreamed that she was in a ship made entirely of wormwood (far left): she could not breathe, eat, or drink without tasting its bitter flavor. Arriving at Le Havre, she asked for a drink of water but was given an infusion of wormwood (left) which made her feel sick. She went to Paris to consult a doctor called M. Sauve Moi (right), who told her that oxgall was the only remedy to remove the wormwood from her body. This she took in large doses and soon the wormwood was gone—only to be replaced by the equally unpleasant taste of oxgall.

Having been advised that only the pope could help her to get rid of the oxgall, she went to Rome and obtained an audience (above). He told her she must search for the statue of salt into which Lot's wife had been changed, break off from this statue a piece of salt, and put it in her mouth. When she eventually found the statue she decided to break off the statue's actual thumb and thus, she reasoned, cure herself not only of the oxgall but also of her habit of thumb-sucking. So she put the statue's thumb into her mouth—upon which she awoke to find herself sucking her own thumb. A psychoanalyst's interpretation would emphasize the "father" symbols of doctor and pope and the phallic significance of the thumb.

The psychologist Havelock Ellis (1859-1939) pointed out that the sense of rising and floating in the air has played a large part in the religious experiences of many Christian saints. He compared "flying" dreams to these experiences, suggesting that the rising sensation might be due to lack of tactile pressure on the feet. The feeling of floating he attributed to some "sensory obtuseness of the skin," a condition that has been found among people in a state of hysterical ecstasy.

The dances and exercises that play a large part in primitive ceremonies may both help to induce, and be a manifestation of, this ecstasy. Above, exercises being performed at a meeting of the Shakers, a 19th-century American religious sect. Below, left, a Smoki Indian (Arizona) taking part in a ceremonial dance. Below right, the climax of all Masai warriors' dances comes when the young men make a series of leaps into the air. This was the preliminary to going into battle.

massive.... The problem is to find an adequate cause, not for the actual impression, but for the transformed and enlarged impression. Under these circumstances, symbolism is quite inevitable. Even when the cause of the excitation is rightly perceived its quality cannot be rightly perceived."

What Havelock Ellis was seeking to do here was to find a means whereby the apparent contradiction between the physical cause of dreams and their emotional content could be resolved. He was also trying to explain how all kinds of memories could be caught up, by either the physical stimulus or the aroused emotion, and woven into the elaborate fabric of the dream. Emotions, he believed, welled up in dreams because "the fetters of civilization are loosened and we know the fearful joy of freedom": we no longer have to eliminate, choose, or concentrate to face the practical problems of life, but can allow our pains and pleasures release in the world of dreams.

Yet, in this dream world, we find associations linked together: we take a physical experience, a memory that has strong emotional value for us, an attitude to another person, maybe some external stimulus and, because they all evoke the same state of feeling, we run them together in the form of a dream. The dream, that is, may consist of clusters of feelings, each linked to other associations. Some of the oddity of dreams, indeed, may be explained by the fact that at an elementary level the mind does not easily discriminate between similar symbols, or between images drawn from different sense organs. This is called "synesthesia". Height, for example, may express both a physical fact and a moral idea. We can envisage, in our dreams as in ordinary speech, a "cold" or "deep" person, "bitter" remorse, "sweet" pleasure. Dreams are full of such visual and verbal puns, and they may even extend to motor imagery. The translation of symbols into music with strong motor impulses is wonderfully well demonstrated in the work of Bach—associations between light colors, high musical notes, and happiness, on the one hand, and between dark colors, low notes, and somber feelings on the other (a point ingeniously exploited by Walt Disney in his cartoon film *Fantasia*).

Ellis was searching for a means to synthesize feelings, memories, and physical sensations—thus anticipating a direction in which much modern dream research has moved—but, in studying the relation of the emotions and the senses in dreams, he paid relatively little attention to the most important though obvious fact about dreams: they are predominantly visual. True, he was interested by the visions that pass before the eyes on the threshold of sleep and often in moments of waking—what are technically called hypnagogic phenomena. But some of his contemporaries were looking for a clue to the nature of dreams in the most sensitive of all our perceptive faculties, the optical system. It had already been suggested by some neurologists that, when the eyes are closed in sleep, sensations and impressions coming from other parts of the organism are transferred, as it were, to the relatively dormant part of the brain that deals with visual impressions.

This idea had been taken up by the American George Trumbull Ladd, who was the founder of the American Psychological Association. In an issue of *Mind*, in April 1892, Ladd described his own experiments with "the phenomena of retinal *Eigenlicht*"—the colored spots and patterns that one sees if the eyes are closed in a darkened room. Ladd went so far as to insist that "I have never been subject to waking visual hallucinations, but I verily believe that there is nothing I hope to have known to me by perception or fancy, whether of things on earth or above the earth or in the water, that has not been stimulated by the retinal images under the influence of intra-organic stimulation."

Ladd trained himself to watch these images until he fell asleep, and then to wake at once—a method, he said, which "actually catches the retinal schemata as they are vanishing from the retinal field, and then compares them with the visual images they have already produced." He made a distinction between three types of visual, or light-induced, dreams. First, dreams that occur on going to sleep; second, dreams in the middle of the night, when both the retina and the visual centers of the brain might be the origin of the dream; and third, early morning dreams when light could penetrate to the retina through closed eyelids. All three types were essentially conversions of visual sensations. What puzzled Ladd was how retinal excitement could enable one "to see a page of printed words clearly spread out before one in a dream. How can so orderly a visual phenomenon owe its origin to chance arrangements of the 'retinal dust?' . . . The minute light and dark spots which the activity of the rods and cones [the nerve cells of the retina] occasions, had arranged themselves in parallel lines. . . across the retinal field."

The same point was made some years later by the French philosopher Henri Bergson in his book *Dreams*. Though published after Freud's book, it argues so strongly for the "optical" theory of dreams that it properly belongs to 19th-century concepts of the dream. It is possible that such "ocular spectra," causing or perhaps the result of stimulation of the optic nerve (though they may be the product of loose blood cells in the cornea), provide some of the visual patterns that are woven into dreams. But Bergson realized that, like the stimuli of sound or touch, these patterns explained no more than the mechanism by which a dream could be produced. They were, that is, a product of the biology of dreaming. But some further explanation was

The "Retinal Eigenlicht," which G. T. Ladd suggested was the framework for dream images, may have influenced some modern artists. For instance, *Woman in the Night*, a painting by Spanish artist Joan Miró, may represent the colored shapes that are seen when the eyes are shut.

needed of the psychic aspect of the dream images. Bergson believed that all past experiences and emotions are stored in the memory, that man forgets nothing; but the memories that rise to the surface are those that correspond to the immediate visual or tactile sensation and the mood of the dreamer— a concept that relies heavily on the old association theory of perception. When a man is asleep, he is essentially *disinterested:* Bergson used the word literally, meaning that the mind has nothing that particularly engages its interest or attention, or forces it to concentrate on an object, an idea, or a feeling. He speaks of his memories: having "raised the trapdoor which kept them below the floor of consciousness . . . they rise, they move, they perform in the night a great *danse macabre* . . . They all want to get through. But they cannot; there are too many of them. From the multitudes which are called, which will be chosen?" Bergson suggested that waking memories were related to present experience, and that in sleep more vague sensations were felt, many of which "arise from the deepest parts of the organism."

In the closing years of the last century, ideas such as those advanced by Bergson had become fairly well known and experiments were being made to verify some of the hypotheses involved. Such experiments were simple compared to modern research on dreams. But it is significant that they were being

Wilhelm Max Wundt (1832-1920), German physiologist and founder of the first institute for experimental psychology at Leipzig. He believed that dream-images were caused by slight sensory impressions—a theory that Freud examined and rejected.

undertaken. It was, after all, only in 1877 that a German physiologist, Dr. Wilhelm Wundt, had established the world's first psychological laboratory at Leipzig and laid the foundations of experimental psychology. Wundt, like Ellis and Bergson, inclined to a sensation-association view of dreams, and committed himself forcefully to the view that it was purely "a physiological problem to formulate a theory of sleep, dreams and hypnosis." The dream interpretations of this school had, before Freud, already reached a point where significant meanings could be found by meticulous analysis.

Wundt described, for instance, a dream in which he saw the funeral of a friend who had died long ago. The man's widow called on Wundt and another friend to join the funeral procession on the other side of the street. After she had gone, the friend said to Wundt: "She only said that because there is cholera raging over there, and she wants to keep this side of the street to herself." Wundt tried to flee from the cholera. When he returned to his house, the procession had gone, the street was strewn with nosegays, and crowds of men dressed in red, who seemed to be funeral attendants, were hurrying to catch up with the procession. Wundt remembered that he had forgotten to take a wreath for the coffin. He then woke up with a fast-beating heart.

What were the components of his dream? The day before it occurred, he had seen the funeral procession of a friend; he had read of cholera breaking out in a particular town; he had talked about the "bereaved wife" in the dream to the friend who appeared in it, and this friend had told him something which proved that the lady was extremely selfish. The anxiety to hurry from the neighborhood and overtake the funeral was, Wundt suggested, caused by the beating of his heart. Finally, he attributed the flowers and the gaily dressed mourners to visual sensations.

James Sully, the 19th-century English psychologist, carried the analysis of this dream still further. Discussing the way in which its various elements were fused together, he suggested that the dream rested on the foundation of "a gloomy tone of feeling," probably arising from some irregularity in the action of the heart. He also argued, as Havelock Ellis surmised as well, that emerging consciousness tends to impose some sort of order retrospectively on the apparent chaos of dream material. The dream begins with the funeral procession; the widow enters consciousness, bringing with her the associated ideas of her dead husband and the mutual acquaintance. The lady, moreover, raises the theme of selfish motives, which link to the funeral, the cholera, and the attempted flight. Thus, says Sully, there is clearly association; but there is also evidence of selection, since the mind picks out other images—the nosegays and the red-clothed attendants—and joins them to the apparently logical thread of the dream story.

A much more thorough interpretation of this dream could, of course, be made by Freud or any of his successors. But this example shows how far the physiological theorists had been able to carry the analysis of dreams in terms of the dreamer's own memories and wishes. Sully, especially, had reached a position very close to the general assumptions of Freud's theory, and had published his work earlier. In 1893, he noted that the higher and more recent centers of the brain control "*and in a measure repress*, the functional activities of the lower and earlier. Translated into psychological language, this means that *what is instinctive, primitive, elemental in our mental life is being continually overborne by the fruit of experience, by the regulative process of reflection....* In sleep, we have a reversion to a more primitive type of experience, an upwelling in vigorous pristine abundance of sensation and impulse." The italics in this remarkable passage are added, to indicate the crucial concept contained in it. Sully suggested also that the dream "strips the ego of its artificial wrappings and exposes it in its native nudity. It brings up from the dim depths of our subconscious life the primal, instinctive impulses, and discloses to us a side of ourselves which connects us with the great sentient world ... By noticing this aspect of our dreams, we may learn much concerning the organic substrata of our conscious personality which link us on to the animal series ... Sleep does for us temporarily what old age does permanently; it cuts us off from the fullness of the present, and so allows us to drift back into the past."

The English psychologist Havelock Ellis (1859-1939) believed that a dream is confused because each separate image contains several elements that are rearranged on waking to make a coherent story. For instance, a girl's single dream image (left) contains a clock, a cage, and a horse's head that she wears in a dance. Such elements, Ellis believed, might subsequently be combined in a dream "report" of this kind: "I was like Cinderella, dancing against time, only somehow I was like Bottom in Shakespeare's *Midsummer Night's Dream*— a kind of prancing horse. Then the spell was broken. I fell exhausted, the dance was over, and the magic slipper was shut away

To compare Sully's ideas with those of Freud is not to minimize the latter's work, which was original, courageous, and enormously influential. It is to show how Freud underestimated the way in which dream theory had developed in the 19th century, to demonstrate that his book was a climax toward which several "lines of advance" had moved. The point becomes even clearer if one weaves in the influence of German romanticism and metaphysics. In words that remind one of Freud's own style, German philosophers had consistently maintained the idealist conception of an immanent soul in man—a conception that required little modification to make it square with the emerging idea of the unconscious—and had seen the dream as one of the means by which this soul expressed itself. A characteristic passage occurs in the work of F. W. Hildebrandt, writing in Leipzig in 1875:

"The dream sometimes allows us to look into the depths and folds of our very being—mainly a closed book in states of consciousness. It gives us such valuable insights into ourselves, such instructive revelations of our half-hidden tendencies and powers that, were we awake, we should have good reason to stand in awe of the demon. . . peering at our cards. . . ."

Even more relevant, perhaps, was Eduard von Hartmann's book, published 10 years before Freud's. In *The Philosophy of the Unconscious* Hartmann observed

that: ". . . unconscious sleep is the relatively happiest condition, because it is the only *painless* one known to us in normal life . . . As for dreams, all the troubles of the waking state are prolonged into the dormant condition . . ." The clues, in short, were fast accumulating; the young Freud was soon to piece them together. But all the clues so far examined belong to a single category—the origin and nature of dreams.

Studies of somnambulism were not uncommon in the 19th century, and the apparent similarity between sleepwalking or sleeptalking and the state of hypnosis had already been observed. The use of mesmerism, or "animal magnetism," was widespread, partly as a form of entertainment, but increasingly as an aid to medical and psychological work. Both Freud and Jung were trained in the use of hypnosis for the treatment of mentally disturbed patients; and the case with which Freud's career really began was the famous one of Anna O., a hysteric who, under hypnosis, could describe the origins of her symptoms in the most minute detail, yet on waking was unable to see any connection between these symptoms and long-past experiences or repressed memories.

Even before Freud, it had been realized that somnambulism, in all its forms—walking, talking, and other motor actions—was closely related to dreaming. Yet even though they are asleep, many somnambulists are able to speak as well as move, to hear, and obviously to see—how, otherwise, could they perform such actions or negotiate such hazards as are sometimes overcome by sleepwalkers? They appear not only to see the scenery of their dreams, but at another level of perception to be aware also of their actual environment.

A similar duality has been observed in the speech of somnambulists. They ignore spoken words, or refrain from speaking, if normally addressed. But if the conversation fits into the fantasy—if, that is, a doctor or other bystander assumes the role of one of the dream characters—direct contact may be made without waking the sleeper from his trance-like condition.

After several notorious cases of sleepwalkers committing serious crimes, the question arose of whether they could be held responsible for their acts. One such case occurred in London, in January 1859. A woman had dreamed that her house was on fire and had thrown a child through a window into the street. A police officer, called as a witness, said that the woman had taken about five minutes to come to her waking senses. Despite pleas for clemency, the magistrate considered "that it would be a most dangerous doctrine to say, that because a person was dreaming while committing an offence, they were not culpable for their acts." In the superior court the judge took a more charitable view: "If the prisoner really did act under the idea that it was the best mode of ensuring the safety of the child," an acquittal was permissible. A somewhat similar attitude has been taken in other cases where the accused was clearly acting under the influence of a dream.

Yet, though a person may not be legally culpable or consciously responsible in such cases—any more than a deranged person—subsequent studies of somnambulism suggest that the dream that is acted out may reflect a deep if unconscious wish on the part of the sleeper. Most modern psychoanalysts feel, as Emil Gutheil puts it, "that in acts of somnambulism it is the dreamer's repressed anti-moral and anti-social ego that drives the sleeper out of bed." The impulses are so strong that they break through the customary safeguards of sleep and compel the dreamer to perform the desired acts in pantomime: indeed, the acting-out seems to provide such an effective means of discharging the repressed impulse through the motor apparatus that on waking all recollection of the sleepwalking is lost. There may be some form of reversal of the normal dream process. In ordinary dreams, the impulse to make some sort of movement is generally completed, but only in the imagination. In somnambulism, as in hypnosis and drugged conditions, the reverse may be true: muscular and other motions are accomplished, but many of the other characteristics of dreaming sleep are absent. Muscular actions, which may be compulsive, actually seem to promote the fantasy, rather than be promoted by it.

This hypothesis, simply stated here, derives some further support from the fact that a person who regularly sleepwalks goes through the same cycle, repeating words and gestures with the accuracy of an actor. The same phenomenon is found in persons affected by hallucinogenic drugs, and even in certain forms of psychosis. Pierre Janet, a specialist in hysteria, studied many such cases. In one of them, a girl who had tried to revive her dead mother "had the habit of acting again all the events which took place at her mother's death, without forgetting the least detail.... Not only are the different attacks always exactly alike . . . but in the course of the same attack, when it has lasted a certain time, the same scene may be repeated again exactly in the same way five or ten times." In this respect, the sleepwalking trance seems more akin to a recurrent dream. It is as if a particular episode or emotion has so imprinted itself upon the dreamer's mind that, in fantasy, it wells up again and again without any of the sense of relief that, in psychoanalysis, often ensues after a person has rediscovered a lost and painful experience and, in technical terms, "abreacted" to it by reliving the buried feelings it aroused.

Up to the time of Freud, the relevance of hypnosis to the study of dreams was slight. All that knowledge of hypnotism did was to provide clinical confirmation of the belief that powerful memories might be lost to consciousness yet, under certain circumstances, remain accessible—thus pointing to the existence of the unconscious and, as Freud realized, indicating a way in which the symptoms caused by such memories might be treated therapeutically. After Freud several attempts were made to employ hypnosis experimentally to test Freudian theories about the symbolism of the dream and its relation to the problems and passions of waking life.

The scientific history of hypnotism dates from the 18th century, when the Austrian doctor Franz Anton Mesmer treated patients by what he called "Animal Magnetism." Above, an engraving of *Mesmer's Tub*: the iron hooks on the tub "conducted" the mesmeric power to the patients' limbs.

Both popular and scientific interest in hypnotism continued after Mesmer had been discredited. Below, a comedy scene and, above right, an engraving of a hypnotised woman from a medical paper. Hypnotism is today sometimes used instead of drugs in surgical operations like that below, right.

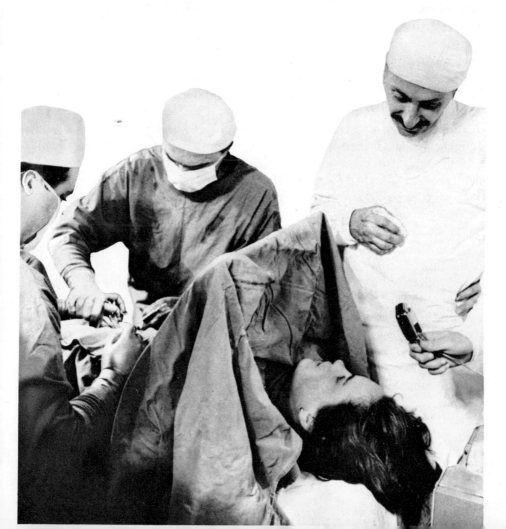

125

One of Freud's best-known dicta is: "The dream is the guardian of sleep." Following attempts to explain the origins and mechanism of the dream, and to relate it to other phenomena of sleep, it was a logical step to investigate its function. What does the dream do, physiologically or psychologically, for the human organism? With this question, which stems from the study of types of dreams, begins the modern phase of dream studies.

Some attention had already been paid to this question. A hundred years before Freud, the German romantic poet Novalis had seen what Freud was to call the compensating functions of the dream, the part it might play in permitting what, in waking life, proved inaccessible. "The dream," Novalis wrote, "is a protection against the regularity and the routine of life. It is the release of our much-restricted fantasy, it produces a kaleidoscope of all the pictures of life, and it interrupts, with its happy childishness, our adult seriousness." The element of play that is found in dreams may prove to be an important, if symbolic, means of discharging tensions of personality.

It is arguable that certain types of person feel such tensions more strongly than others and desire to release them more symbolically, as for instance the creative artist-poet, writer, painter, musician, and possibly the mathematician and the scientist as well. "Especially do creative dreams have this function," the famous Czech physiologist J. E. Purkinje observed in 1846. "They are plays of the imagination which have no connection with the data of daily life. The soul does not want to continue the tensions of waking life, but rather to resolve them, to recuperate from them. First and foremost, the dream creates conditions which are the very opposite of waking life—it heals sadness through love and friendship, fear through courage and confidence." Though Purkinje seems to be repeating the old idea that dreams go by contraries, his suggestion is rather more subtle; the dream is seen more as a release, an escape into a world where conventional time, space, and even moral imperatives no longer operate. And he is implying that this may be one of the keys to the creative process.

Dreams had long been associated with the idea of creativeness. Synesius, in the fifth century A.D., left a detailed account of the way his dreams had helped him to write, or to devise answers to problems. And many of the dreams that, in antiquity, were regarded as divine inspirations may more reasonably be classified as dreams of a creative type. Voltaire, a rationalist and skeptic about dreams, was said to have dreamed a whole canto of his *La Henriade;* the composer Giuseppe Tartini composed the "Devil's Trill" for an abandoned sonata after a dream in which the devil appeared and played the violin to him; and Edgar Allan Poe drew heavily on his dreams, for both the macabre mood of his stories and the theme of some of his poems. The English novelist Mrs. Gaskell gives an interesting case in her biography of Charlotte Brontë. Asked if she has ever taken opium, because she gave such a precise description of its effects in one of her novels, Charlotte Brontë replied:

The Italian composer Giuseppe Tartini
(1692-1770) called one of his sonatas *The
Devil's Trill* because when he was unable
to complete it he dreamed he heard the
devil play it. The trill was all he was
able to remember of the dream music.

". . . that she had followed the process she always adopted when she had
to describe anything which had not fallen within her own experience; she
had thought intently on it for many and many a night before falling to sleep—
wondering what it was like, or how it would be—till at length, sometimes
after the progress of her story had been arrested at this one point for weeks,
she awakened in the morning with all clear before her, as if she had in reality
gone through the experience, and then could describe it, word for word, as
it happened."

Mrs. Gaskell did not say in so many words that Charlotte Brontë had
dreamed the sought-for experience, but the process she reports is so similar
to that employed by Robert Louis Stevenson that we can reasonably classify
it as a dream inspiration. As we shall see, Stevenson interwove his dreams
into his waking life in order to devise his stories; he was well aware how
much he owed to the fantasies of sleep. Other writers, such as William Hazlitt
and Charles Lamb, realized that the mind was creatively active in sleep,
but did not rely on such activity so consciously or so fully as Stevenson. Hazlitt,

Dream Palace, constructed by Ferdinand
Cheval (1836-1924), a postman in the
French province of Drôme. Whether the
original idea of this building began as
dream or daydream is uncertain, but
Cheval's diaries record that, years before he
started to build, he had daydreamed of the
fantasy palace while he made his rounds.
One day Cheval stumbled across some
strangely shaped rocks, and realized he
could build his palace from them.

for instance, suggested that in sleep, "as in madness," there was "the same tyranny of the imagination over the judgment . . . single images meet, and jostle, and unite together, without any power to compare them with others, with which they are connected in the world of reality. . . . There is, however, a sort of profundity in sleep; and it may usefully be consulted as an oracle in this way. It might be said, that the voluntary power is suspended, and things come upon us as unexpected revelations, which we keep out of our thoughts at other times. . . . We are not hypocrites in our sleep . . . we may repress any feelings of this sort that we disapprove of in their incipient state, and detect, ere it be too late, an unwarrantable antipathy or fatal passion." In this passage, Hazlitt is observing the phenomenon that Freud was later to describe as "the censor"—a function of the mind that prevents seemingly dangerous or unpalatable thoughts from reaching consciousness. Much the same view was taken by the American writer Ralph Waldo Emerson, who commented that "a skillful man reads his dreams for his self-knowledge; yet not the details but the quality . . . However monstrous and grotesque their apparitions, they have a substantial truth" because "dreams retain the infirmities of our character."

Self-knowledge, or creative inspiration, may come in the form of dreams, or through waking introspection. How it comes, and what part dreams play in its coming, seems to vary from one person to another. Some merely dream, some hear voices or see visions; some can read off their work, as it were, from their minds, as if it were inscribed complete in some hinterland of consciousness; some sink almost into a trance when about to write or compose. All, however, seem to be tapping some source of creative energy not directly accessible to waking consciousness in order to release images and thoughts that whirl in the darker reaches of the mind.

It is now common knowledge that certain drugs or even some physical conditions, such as fevers, carry man into the twilight zone that lies between creative ecstasy and delirium, between genius and madness. The best-known example of this in English literature is Thomas De Quincey's *Confessions of an English Opium Eater*. De Quincey started to take opium as a sedative, and from early manhood his dream life became more elaborate and, indeed, painful for him. He first noticed an increase in hypnagogic illusions, a recovery of the child's knack "of painting, as it were, upon the darkness all sorts of phantoms. . . . In the middle of 1817, this faculty became increasingly distressing to me; at night, when I lay awake in bed, vast processions moved along continually in mournful pomp . . . concurrently with this, a corresponding change took place in my dreams; a theatre seemed suddenly opened and lighted within my brain, which presented nightly spectacles of more than earthly splendour." De Quincey's condition was also one of "deep-seated anxiety and funereal melancholy"; his "sense of space, and in the end the sense of time, were both powerfully affected . . . sometimes I seemed

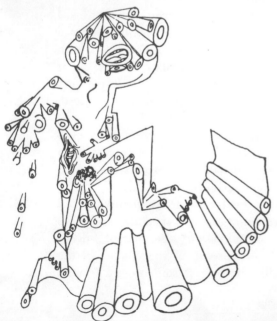

Above, an engraving from a series called
Le Carceri d'invenzione by the Italian artist
Giovanni Battista Piranesi (1720-1778).
These engravings—which were inspired by
the visions of a high fever—fascinated the
poet Samuel Taylor Coleridge, who
described them to the British writer Thomas
De Quincey. They depict scenes of towering
buildings and elaborate machinery, which
De Quincey said were similar to those of
his own dreams. Left, a drawing by Jean
Cocteau (1891-1963), French artist and
poet, from his book *Opium—The Journal
of a Cure*. These notes and drawings—
made while Cocteau was undergoing a
cure in a French clinic—record his struggle
to free himself from opium, and
convey both the good and evil aspects of
the drug. "It is hard to know," Cocteau
wrote, "that this magic carpet exists and
that one will no longer fly on it."

to have lived for seventy or a hundred years in one night"; the "minutest incidents of childhood, or forgotten scenes of later years, were often revived." Here De Quincey makes a significant point: "I could not be said to recollect them; for, if I had been told of them waking, I should not have been able to acknowledge them as parts of my past experience. But ... I *recognized* them instantaneously ... I feel assured that there is no such thing as an ultimate *forgetting*." It is precisely this shock of recognition that proves so valuable in the psychoanalytical use of dreams. It is the point where the waking consciousness makes contact with the buried experience that lies behind the symbols of the dream.

The horrific, yet dazzling, complexity of De Quincey's dreams may no doubt be attributed largely to opium. No one else has left such an elaborate record of his dreams over a period of years as De Quincey, nor described them so vividly. Yet, had he not made his dream experience the basis of his most significant work, one would scarcely categorize such narcotic fantasies as an example of dream creativeness. He was writing *about* his dreams, not using the contents of his dreams as the source of his writing. The distinction can be made clear by the well-known story of the way in which Coleridge wrote the uncompleted *Kubla Khan*, the poem about the "stately pleasure dome" in Xanadu. Curiously, Coleridge—who was also taking opium at the time as a sedative—not only knew De Quincey, but had talked with him about the theme of *Kubla Khan* in a conversation that arose from a discussion of dreams. De Quincey tells us:

"Many years ago, when I was looking over Piranesi's *Antiquities of Rome*, Coleridge, then standing by, described to me a set of plates from that artist, called his "Dreams," and which recorded the scenery of his own visions during the delirium of a fever. Some of these (I describe only from memory of Coleridge's account) represented vast Gothic halls; on the floor of which stood mighty engines and machinery ... With the same power of endless growth and self-reproduction did my architecture proceed in dreams. In the early stages of the malady, the splendours of my dreams were indeed chiefly architectural. ..."

So, too, was the poetic vision of Coleridge, dozing in his West Country cottage in the summer of 1797, after reading the words, "Here the Khan Kubla commanded a palace to be built. ..." Three hours later, he woke from his opium-induced doze, with the complete poem in his head. All the images rose up before him, "as things, with a parallel production of the correspondent expressions, without any sensations or consciousness of effort." After writing down part of the poem thus created, he was interrupted "by a person on business from Porlock," and returning to write an hour later found that he "still retained some vague and dim recollection of the general purport of the vision, yet ... all the rest had passed away like the images on the surface of a stream."

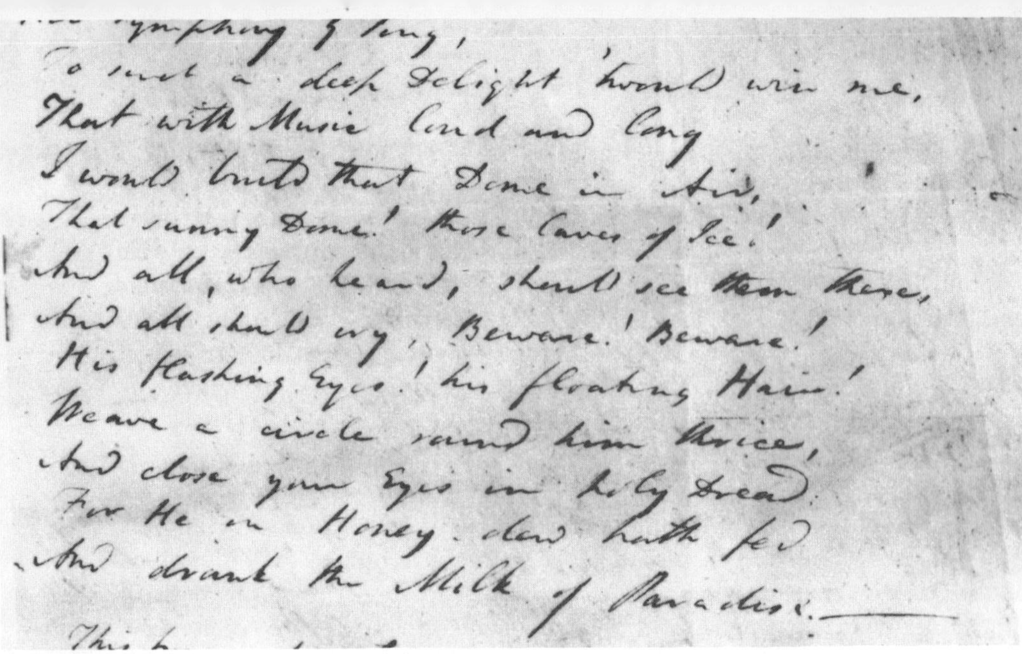

[handwritten manuscript fragment]

symphony & song,
To such a deep delight 'twould win me,
That with Music loud and long
I would build that Dome in Air,
That sunny Dome! those caves of Ice!
And all, who heard, should see them there,
And all should cry, "Beware! Beware!
His flashing Eyes! his floating Hair!
Weave a circle round him thrice,
And close your Eyes in holy dread:
For He on Honey-dew hath fed
And drank the Milk of Paradise.——
This ——

Above, part of the original manuscript of *Kubla Khan*, a poem composed in a dream by the British poet Samuel Taylor Coleridge (1772-1834). On awaking he began to write down the poem, which was two to three hundred lines long, but an interruption caused him to forget all but a fragment. Left, a Persian miniature painting (about A.D. 1600) of Kubla Khan's palace. Coleridge's dream description of Kubla's palace is oddly similar to that given by Rashid ed-Din, 16th-century author of *General History of the World*, a book that was not translated until after Coleridge's death. Rashid notes that Kubla himself dreamed of the palace and its location.

Unlike Coleridge, Stevenson trained himself to remember and then to use the rich storehouse of his dreams. Though these were not narcotically induced he did suffer from chronic ill-health and fevers from the tuberculosis that killed him. Indeed, it is possible that the fevers may explain why he dreamed so much and so coherently. Apart from the mild delirium they may have induced in sleep, they probably kept his sleep at the shallow level that later research has shown to be very productive of dreams. In his book *Across the Plains*, Stevenson described the evolution of his dreams. He tells how, in early life, they often came in the form of nightmares; these (like those of Charles Lamb and De Quincey) were succeeded by scenery and travels. The third phase started when he began to dream complete stories and, while still a student, to dream in sequence. Each night he could take up the fantasy life envisaged in his dreams at the point at which he had quitted it; each morning he returned to reality. At this time, the alternating experience— later to be reflected in his story "Dr. Jekyll and Mr. Hyde"—was so terrifying, and the dream life so hard to shake off, that he had to consult a doctor.

Stevenson had now begun to write for money, and his dreams were gradually reduced to two main types. He could still read entire and imaginary books in his sleep, and travel to distant places; but for the most part his dreams were concerned with "making stories for the market." What he described as the "Little People" not only set before him "truncheons of tales upon their lighted theatre," but also seemed to know when to perform for the dreamer. "They share in his financial worries and have an eye to the bankbook; they share plainly in his training; they have plainly learned like him to build the scheme of a considerable story in progressive order . . . they can tell him a story piece by piece, like a serial, and keep him all the while in ignorance of where they aim." Stevenson thus had the knack of putting the demand for saleable stories to his sleeping self. He actually regarded his conscious self simply as a kind of agent, writing down and doing the general mechanical work of authorship—as well as enjoying its material rewards— while the "Little People" did the creative part.

This sense of double identity in Stevenson found its classic expression in "Dr. Jekyll and Mr. Hyde"—the story of the distinguished doctor who was capable of changing into a murderous villain. Even here, Stevenson turned to his dreams for help:

"I had long been trying to write a story on this subject, to find a body, a vehicle, for that strong sense of man's double being which must at times come in upon and overwhelm the mind of every thinking creature. . . . Then came one of those financial fluctuations. . . . For two days I went about racking my brains for a plot of any sort; and on the second night I dreamed the scene at the window, and a scene afterwards split in two, in which Hyde, pursued for some crime, took the powder and underwent the change in the presence of his pursuers. All the rest was made awake, and consciously."

The Strange Case of Dr. Jekyll and Mr. Hyde (1886) by the Scots author Robert Louis Stevenson, is a story of a split personality. The drawing by Mervyn Peake, modern British artist, is of the monstrous Mr. Hyde—the distinguished Dr. Jekyll's "other half" into whom Jekyll can change himself by taking a powder. Stevenson was given the idea by a dream in which such a transformation occurred.

The implications of "Dr. Jekyll and Mr. Hyde" are profound. The story seems, symbolically, to dramatize the contrast between the conscious man, with the veneer of civilization, and the instinctive and destructive man within him—precisely the contrast on which Freud was to build his theory of human nature. Stevenson seems to have sensed this contrast, and to have been aware that the conscious mind is actually struggling with the instincts. He described how his dreams haunted him: "the gloom of these fancied experiences clouded the day."

We find precisely the same point in the writing of Stevenson's American contemporary, William Dean Howells, who believed that the dreamer was, in sleep, "purely unmoral" and "reduced to the state of the merely natural man," that he had "shameful dreams ... whose infamy often lingers until about lunch time ... the victim goes about with the dim question whether he is not really that kind of man harassing him, and a sort of remote fear that he may be. I fancy that as to his nature and as to his mind he is so, and that but for the supernal criticism, but for his soul, he might be that kind of man in very act and deed." The apparent absence of a moral sense in dreams, the revelation of secret and even potentially criminal wishes, was noted by others besides W. D. Howells—and we shall see later what use Freud made of this fact. It is relevant here because it demonstrates yet again the growing awareness that, behind the conscious self, there lay another and largely unknown part of the personality, capable—so it seemed—of thoughts and feelings that were independent of consciousness and might even seem to conflict with cherished values in waking life.

The unconscious, more and more people were coming to realize, was capable of feats which proved beyond the capacity of conscious thought, and the dream might be one vehicle through which such "creative" efforts might find expression. For the act of creation is not confined solely to the imagination of poets and storytellers. It can well be a striking scientific (or philosophical) insight, or the discovery of a solution to a problem. We are told, for instance, that the French philosopher Condorcet was able, in a dream, to solve a mathematical equation that had proved beyond his waking powers; and that William Blake, searching for a means of engraving his designs, dreamed that his dead brother Robert indicated how this could be done and then, awake, found that this dreamed process actually worked.

All such examples indicate the way in which a symbolic solution can be found to an elusive problem. All the elements of the solution exist in the dreamer's conscious knowledge, but he has been unable to combine them correctly. One of the most significant of such discoveries was the dream which revealed the ring structure of benzene to the German chemist F. A. Kekulé. He had tried for years to find a graphic means of representing the molecular structure of trimethyl benzene, and eventually in a dream found that:

"Again the atoms were juggling before my eyes . . . my mind's eye, sharpened by repeated sights of a similar kind, could now distinguish larger structures of different forms and in long chains, many of them close together; everything was moving in a snake-like and twisting manner. Suddenly, what was this? One of the snakes got hold of its own tail and the whole structure was mockingly twisting in front of my eyes. As if struck by lightning, I awoke. . . ." Reporting this to a scientific convention in 1890, Kekulé concluded: "Let us learn to dream, gentlemen, and then we may perhaps find the truth."

Another case of this kind, dating from 1893, is the fascinating dream of Dr. H. V. Hilprecht, a professor of Assyrian at the University of Pennsylvania. He was endeavoring to decipher two small fragments of agate presumed to be Babylonian finger rings; from the scraps of cuneiform characters on them, he was inclined to date the rings to the period of King Kurigalzu, about 1300 B.C., but he was unable to decide exactly what these rings were. He then had a long and complex dream, in which a priest of Nippur appeared, led him into a treasure chamber, and explained that the objects were not finger rings but parts of an agate votive cylinder cut into three parts to make earrings for the statue of the god Ninib. The next morning he examined the fragments again, found that they did fit together, and that the inscription named both King Kurigalzu and the god Ninib.

At this time, Professor Hilprecht had been working from drawings of fragments; later that year he went to Constantinople, where the actual pieces of agate were kept in a museum—though separately, because it was not realized that they were related. Putting them together, Hilprecht found that they were indeed two parts of a single votive cylinder; in this, as in several other respects, the dream-priest had precisely indicated the facts. Yet, even though Hilprecht either was aware of the facts, or was capable of reaching them by deduction, his conscious mind had failed to solve the problem. It had been the dream that had combined evidence and logical thought in a symbolic package.

How much, indeed, does the unconscious mind know, and how far can it make combinations of the evidence available to anticipate what is as yet unknown? These two questions become increasingly relevant when one moves beyond the "creative" or "problem-solving" dream. It is relatively easy to understand such dreams, as it is to explain the common dream that reveals where a lost object may be found. All kinds of clues are available that conscious thought has overlooked. But when one turns to "prognostic" dreams about individuals, or "clairvoyant" dreams about future events, the question of the forward projection of known tendencies becomes crucial.

The apparently prophetic character of some dreams is so striking that, from antiquity, this class of dream has always attracted great attention. Sometimes such dreams seem to forecast quite trivial but unusual happenings; sometimes they refer to great public events. Yet the question is whether dreams of this kind go beyond what could be expected by coincidence, or more precisely, the random combinations of dream and event which follow from the immense number of dreams that occur each night, and the even greater number of events that follow in life. Millions of dreams, in infinite permutations with uncountable events, must fairly often produce apparent correspondence between dream and subsequent event. And where, as was commonly the case in pre-scientific cultures, the concept of dreams embodied the idea of prophecy or warning, there would inevitably be a tendency to emphasize the prognostic rather than the coincidental explanation. At the end of the 19th century, the British Society for Psychical Research examined hundreds of "telepathic" or "prophetic" dreams—published in an enormous volume called *Phantasms of the Living*—and came to the conclusion that the evidence was indecisive.

In the pre-Freudian period, however, large numbers of apparently prophetic dreams were noted and known, without much care being taken to verify them by checking, when they were told, how closely the dream was related to the event, the general veracity of the dreamer, and the form in which the dream was recorded. Little effort was made, moreover, to identify those dreams that apparently predicted events that were the obvious extension of known or knowable facts.

At what we may call the "folk story" level there is, for instance, the 15th-century Swaffham tinker, John Chapman, who dreamed that he must go to London and meet on London Bridge a stranger who would give him news of great fortune. He went to London and then met a man who told him that he had dreamed that a pedlar in Swaffham had a pot of money buried in his garden. Chapman went home, found the money, and used part of it to pay for building the church of St. Peter and St. Paul, in which carvings and stained glass commemorate the story.

The dream that foretells the death either of the dreamer or of someone else is the most frequent of all premonitory dreams. We should here note the distinction between dreaming of someone else's death and the "diagnostic" prophecy, in which the dream may reveal to the dreamer a physical condition of which he is unaware. A famous example of this kind is that of the French actor, Champmeslé, who died in August 1701. Two days before his death, his deceased mother and wife appeared in a dream, and his mother beckoned him. He not only told his friends of this dream, but actually paid in advance for a funeral mass, heard it sung, went out of the church, met some friends, and while talking to them, dropped dead.

Champmeslé may, for all we know, have been subliminally aware of a fatal illness. In the same way, Abraham Lincoln must surely have had in mind the possibility that he would be shot. A few days before he was murdered, he remarked to a friend that he had been greatly impressed by the number of dream prophecies and warnings in the Bible. "If we believe the Bible, we must accept the fact that in the old days God and his angels came to men in their sleep and made themselves known in dreams. Nowadays dreams are regarded as very foolish, and are seldom told, except by old women and young men and maidens in love." Asked by Mrs. Lincoln why he had raised the subject, Lincoln then described a dream in which, wandering through

While researching into the molecular structure of benzene the chemist Kekulé (1829-96) dreamed of a snake with its tail in its mouth—an age-old symbol, here depicted in a third-century B.C. Greek manuscript. This dream revealed to him the ring structure of benzene.

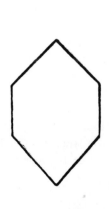

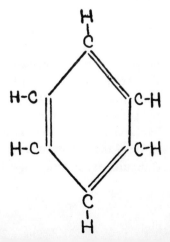

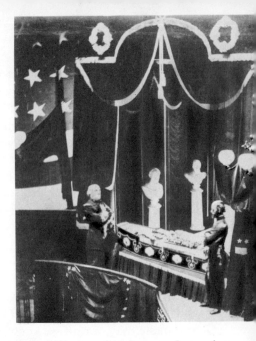

the White House, he saw a coffin guarded by soldiers, and a throng of weeping people. "Who is dead?" he asked in the dream. The answer was: "The president, killed by an assassin."

As a final example of many more that could be quoted, there is the extraordinary case of Bishop Joseph Lanyi, tutor to the Archduke Franz Ferdinand, who dreamed of the archduke's assassination at Sarajevo in June 1914. He was so impressed by the dream that he not only wrote it down and drew a sketch of the incident, but even attempted to warn the archduke. When he failed, at an early hour in the morning, he celebrated a mass for him.

Many different explanations of such phenomena have been offered. In antiquity, it was this aspect of dreaming that attracted most attention and led to theories of divine prophecy or warning; in more modern times, such dreams are part of the stock-in-trade of occult theorists. The author Henri de Maeterlinck, for instance, expressed this point of view in *The Unknown Guest*. He suggested that "every event, past, present, or future, in any point of space, exists now somewhere, in an eternal present, and being existent, it is possible for us in certain states to become conscious of events in what we term the future, that is to say, which we in our passage through time have not yet arrived at.... According to the theory, every dream is a partial consciousness of some scenes or events in this eternal present, events, that is, which may be past, present, or future." The English writer J. W. Dunne produced a similar theory of dreams in *An Experiment with Time*, published in 1927. Such concepts, like the metaphysical time theories of Asia, open an enormous field for speculation. But, before one turns too easily to supernatural explanations, it is desirable to exhaust possible psychological causes for dreams of this kind, or even to call in the mathematical theory of probability. The difficulty is that no aspect of dreams is more intriguing and less amenable to

Far left, the figure of John Chapman—the 15th-century English pedlar whose dream led him to buried treasure—carved on a pew in the Suffolk church he helped to build with the money he found. Left, the body of Abraham Lincoln lying in state in the White House—a scene that he himself saw in a dream, and described to friends, a few days before his death. Above, the assassin of the Archduke Franz Ferdinand is seized in Sarajevo in 1914. The assassination had been foreseen in a dream by the Archduke's tutor.

Below, a scene from the 1955 British film *The Night My Number Came Up* based on the true experience of Air Marshal Sir Victor Goddard. The night before he was due to fly from Shanghai to Tokyo, Goddard overheard an acquaintance describing a dream in which Goddard's plane crashed. Goddard noted with relief that the dream was at least inaccurate in giving the number of passengers as seven—but next day other passengers came to make up the required number. The plane did crash but all the passengers escaped alive.

systematic inquiry. It may not be impossible to set up significant experiments to test the extent and character of such dreams, but it is very hard—and such experiments are still in the earliest stages.

Research of this kind, moreover, demands the regular collection and analysis of dreams on a large scale—a study both of their contents and of the subsequent life experience of the dreamers. Such work is now proceeding, but at the time when Freud was writing virtually no material of this sort was available. It was possible only to collect examples ranging from antiquity to contemporary writers that suggested that certain themes and symbols used in dreams might crop up again and again. These themes and symbols were then compared by some students of the dream to those occurring in mythology.

How little was being done, beyond the introspective reports that have been noted in this chapter, is emphasized by the fact that one of the earliest scientific attempts to present statistics on dreams appeared only in 1892, when an American student, Mary W. Calkins, published an article in the *Journal of Psychology*, reporting the dreams of two persons over a period of six weeks. Analyzing 375 dreams noted in this period, she observed that dream images had verbal or visual associations to waking life, that the persons appearing in them were mostly relatives or close friends, that problems causing concern in the ordinary thoughts of the dreamer were seldom directly represented in the dream—and rashly concluded (only a year or so before Freud began to write) that "the importance of a dream as a revelation of character is not a suggestive topic."

In the 1890s, that is, scientific investigators were dealing merely with hundreds of dreams drawn from small numbers of people; within a few years, thousands of dreams were to become available. Freud's work, and the profession of psychoanalysis that grew up after it, put the remembering, reporting, and study of dreams on a regular basis. Where there had once been a dearth of material with which to work, there was now a plethora. One analyst, Dr. Medard Boss, has stated that in 25 years of practice he had reported to him 25,000 dreams by about 500 patients; C. G. Jung, at the end of his life, put the number he had listened to at over 80,000.

So far in this book we have seen the changes in men's attitude to dreams over the centuries between the soothsayers of Assyria and the psychoanalysts of Vienna. We have also seen how, in the last of those centuries, dramatic developments in philosophy, psychology, medicine, and science had prepared the way for a new view of dreams—and for a new form of an old art: healing by means of dreams. Finally, we have come to see how studies of sleep began to yield fresh ideas and to point toward modern scientific investigations.

The stage was now set for Freud's work, which was to make a slow but ultimately decisive change in the attitude to dreams. The Freudian revolution, as we shall see in the next chapter, made possible the final transition from superstitious to scientific concepts of dreaming.

Certain symbols are "universal": they appear in the dreams of individuals today, in the rituals of primitive societies, and in the myths of antiquity. The box is a familiar dream symbol, referring either to the mother's body, or to the destructive potentialities of the unconscious—as in the myth of Pandora's Box. Right, a sculpture of Pandora opening the box to let loose on earth all its afflictions.

Dream books of all ages have recognized flying to be a symbol of escape or transcendence. The Greek myth tells how Daedalus and Icarus escaped from the labyrinth of Minos by flying with the wings Daedalus had made. But Icarus flew too near the sun: the wax attaching his wings melted and he fell into the sea. Below, *Daedalus Winged* (1959), a pen and ink drawing by British artist Michael Ayrton.

141

6 Freud and the dream

Success often comes slowly to a book of major importance, for if its ideas are truly revolutionary it will have to make headway against the prejudice as well as the ignorance of its times. Today, when the name of Sigmund Freud is a household word, it is difficult to realize that just over 60 years ago he was an ambitious but undistinguished Viennese doctor. Many of those who knew of his pioneering work in psychoanalysis dismissed it as pretentious and even as somewhat disreputable. His first important book, *The Interpretation of Dreams*, was published, in an edition of 600 copies, on November 4, 1899 (though it was dated 1900). Freud received the equivalent of $209 for it, and it took eight years to exhaust the first small edition. Since then, there have been innumerable editions, and it has been translated into several languages.

Freud himself commented on the belated recognition of this book in his preface to the second edition: "The fact that this very difficult book required the publication of a second edition, even before the end of one decade, is by no means thanks to the interest of the specialist circle for whom the book was originally intended. My psychiatric colleagues do not seem to have taken any trouble to overcome the initial suspicions which my new conceptions of the dream produced in them." Freud, in fact, felt that he was having to fight every inch of the way, to establish not simply his theory of the dream, but more importantly his new ideas about the nature and treatment of mental

In 1899 Sigmund Freud published *The Interpretation of Dreams*. Until this book dreams had, for the most part, received little scientific attention, but for Freud they were "the royal road to the unconscious." His work on them marks not only the beginning of a new approach to mental illness, but also a new epoch in man's awareness of himself. Right, the frontispiece of the first edition superimposed upon a mental patient's painting.

DIE

TRAUMDEUTUNG

VON

Dᴿ· SIGM. FREUD.

»FLECTERE SI NEQUEO SUPEROS, ACHERONTA MOVEBO.«

LEIPZIG UND WIEN.
FRANZ DEUTICKE.
1900.

Left, Dr. Joseph Breuer, co-author with Freud of *Studies in Hysteria* (1895), which at the time provoked scathing criticism, but which today is acknowledged as one of the starting points of psychoanalysis. In 1885 Freud studied under Jean Martin Charcot, a French neurologist who used hypnotism to study hysterical patients. Freud said of him: "No other human being has ever affected me in such a way." Below one of Charcot's patients under hypnosis in a scene from the 1964 American film of Freud's work, *The Secret Passion*. Right, Freud, photographed in 1900 after *The Interpretation of Dreams* was published.

John Houston's   Freud—The Secret Passion

illness, which rested on the arguments set out in *The Interpretation of Dreams*—the book that was the real starting point of psychoanalysis. "Insights such as this," Freud remarked, "fall to one's lot but once in a lifetime." And his biographer, Ernest Jones, reported that this book remained his favorite among his many writings, and that Freud took pride in keeping new editions of it up-to-date.

It was a book born out of personal suffering, as well as clinical experience. In 1890, Freud was 34 years old. He was avid for recognition, but professional success was slow in coming and he had a growing family to support. He had developed new and unorthodox ideas, and he seemed unable to find a suitable framework for them. He was already drawn to the study of mental disorders, and especially of hysteria, but he was dissatisfied with both the psychological and the medical concepts then current in the two centers in which he had studied—Vienna and Paris. He called himself a neurologist, and he was slowly building up a practice dealing with organic disorders and with a class of patients who were extremely difficult to treat. Though they showed symptoms of various diseases, pains, ocular disturbances, and even physical paralysis, they appeared to have nothing organically wrong with them; nor did the standard teachings of anatomy and physiology help to explain their conditions or offer effective means of treating them.

With a Viennese colleague, Dr. Joseph Breuer, to whom he owed much, Freud began to study hysterical symptoms in detail. Freud and Breuer treated such patients by hypnosis; the results of their work were reported in a book called *Studies of Hysteria*. They had come to the conclusion that their hysterical patients were suffering from the persistence of painful memories that, even

A patient dreams that his wife will kill his sister Peggy on Sunday, March 12th. His associations to this date—which is, in fact, a Thursday—lead from Caesar's murder on the Ides of *March*, to a crossword he and his fiancée Lucy did one *Sunday* involving a question about Columbus Day (October 12th) which Lucy could not answer. The patient's critical attitude to Lucy in the dream reveals the cause of his neurosis—a conflict between his love for his sister and his love for Lucy. He knows that when he is married Lucy will "kill" the love he feels for his sister.

20 years after a psychic shock, were capable of dramatically modifying their attitudes and consequently their behavior. Freud, in fact, soon saw that hysterical paralysis, phobias, obsessions, delusions, and hallucinations all appeared to have something in common. They were defenses whereby the patients warded off unbearable feelings. These feelings or buried experiences seemed so dangerous to them that they could not be consciously recognized; they were "repressed," and so found expression—as well as relief for the powerful emotional charge they carried—in the form of physical or mental symptoms. Very often, Freud suggested, these emotional charges were sexual in character, and it was the resistance to them by the conscious mind that led to conditions ranging from paralysis to the characteristic patterns of anxiety—dizziness, heart spasms, vague apprehension, or actual panic.

By 1890, Freud had turned his attention to the problem of neurosis. "My tyrant is psychology," he wrote to his good friend Wilhelm Fliess, an ear, nose, and throat specialist in Berlin; "it has always been my distant, beckoning goal and now, since I have hit the neuroses, it has come so much nearer." But Freud was plagued by his inability to find the crucial link between the mind and the body. While he was puzzling over this psychological problem, he was also passing through a period of intense anxiety himself. Besides studying his patients, he also tried to understand what was happening within his own mind, to investigate and explain his own feelings and reactions. "No matter what I start with," he wrote to Fliess in 1897, "I always find myself back again with the neuroses and the psychical apparatus.... Inside me there is a seething ferment, and I am only waiting for the next surge forward ... I have felt impelled to start writing about dreams, with which I feel on firm ground."

Why did dreams seem to offer "firm ground"? Freud had already found that his patients were led toward the origin of their neurosis if he let them talk freely—a technique which later became known as "free association." The more freedom he allowed them, the more often he found them introducing

a dream into their association of ideas; the dream, moreover, usually proved to be the starting point of a new and fruitful chain of memories and ideas. Having already begun to pay attention to his own dreams, Freud realized that he would have to undertake a scrupulous and searching examination of himself; as he would say, to treat his own neurosis. He had not only to become the first patient of modern psychoanalysis, but to be his own analyst as well. "I have been through some kind of neurotic experience, with odd states of mind not intelligible to consciousness—cloudy thoughts and veiled doubts, with barely here and there a ray of light."

Through his dreams, Freud found himself recapturing lost memories of his own childhood, and through his associations to the dreams he aroused feelings and thoughts of which he had not previously been aware. "Being entirely honest with oneself is a good exercise," he declared, but it was painful to a degree. "Some sad secrets of life are being traced back to their first roots, the humble origins of much pride and precedence are being laid bare," he wrote. "I am now experiencing myself all the things that, as a third party, I have witnessed going on in my patients—days when I slink about depressed because I have understood nothing of the day's dreams, fantasies, or moods."

It is important to understand this personal background to Freud's theory of dreams. Without this intense self-examination he would not have come to believe so passionately in his discoveries, nor would he have had the wealth of material drawn from his own life that, in the end, he chose to make the basis of his book. But it is equally important to appreciate the manner in which all his subjective experience was being set in the context of a general psychological theory. As we have seen, the idea of an unconscious aspect of the mind was fairly widely accepted by the time Freud was educated. But where his predecessors and contemporaries saw the unconscious as a counterpart to consciousness, Freud was coming to believe that consciousness was the least part of the mental processes, and that most of the psychic processes that dominated man's life were concealed from consciousness. Within a few

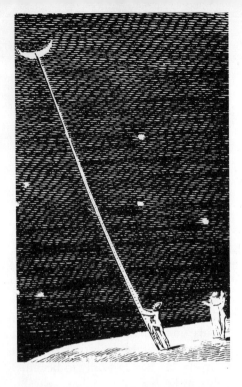

William Blake's engraving *I Want! I Want!* represents pictorially the phrase "crying for the moon"—a common way of expressing the desire to reach the unattainable.

In dreams the unattainable may sometimes be achieved. In Albrecht Dürer's engraving *The Doctor's Dream* the old man dreams of a nude woman in place of the warm stove.

years, he had come to the conclusion that the unconscious was the source of all motivation of thought and behavior—whether one considered dreams or insanity, gestures, slips of the tongue, jokes, compulsive actions or obsessional thoughts, artistic creation or the solution of problems. In the unconscious, moreover, the mental processes took archaic forms, were patterned by infantile and pre-logical experience, and were dominated by instinctive and predominantly sexual drives.

This concept was not fully worked out by 1895, the year in which Freud made his dramatic entry into the field of dream theory. But much of it had been sketched out, and more existed in Freud's work in an embryonic form. Enough, at least, had been done for him to have reached the crucial hypotheses on which he could build *The Interpretation of Dreams*. His interest in dreams was not a by-product of his general concern with the normal and abnormal functioning of the mind. It was central to his whole argument, the means whereby the entire range of mental phenomena and their relation to conscious or waking life could be brought into focus. Others before him had anticipated many of his insights, or provided clues that he had followed up. But he was the first to attempt a comprehensive explanation of the dream, of its function, and of the means whereby it could be interpreted.

In order to understand the full significance of *The Interpretation of Dreams* it is necessary to examine what Freud was trying to do and how he set about doing it—but for the moment we must do so without the benefit of hindsight. It is only in this way that the profound significance of his work can be seen in proper perspective.

The effort that went into the book extended over almost a decade. All through the 1890s, Freud was pressing on with his self-analysis, using the new techniques he had developed, toward the point where he hit on what he conceived to be the essential feature of the dream. And on July 24, 1895, he succeeded. He was sitting on the terrace of the Bellevue Restaurant in Vienna, thinking about the dream that in his book he calls "Irma's Injection," when it struck him that this dream was the fulfillment of a hidden wish—the gratification during sleep, and in a disguised form, of some unexpressed and unacknowledged desire. From that moment he believed that he held the key that would unlock the door to the unconscious. The book which was to be the foundation of his own career, as well as of a new theory of human motivation and a technique of healing mental illness, could now be written.

In the very first paragraph Freud boldly set out his claim to have solved the puzzle that had baffled men for millennia.

"In the pages that follow I shall bring forward proof that there is a psychological technique which makes it possible to interpret dreams, and that, if that procedure is employed, every dream reveals itself as a psychical structure which has a meaning and which can be inserted at an assignable point in the mental activities of waking life. I shall further endeavour to elucidate the processes to which the strangeness and obscurity of dreams are due and to deduce from those processes the nature of psychical forces by whose concurrent or mutually opposing action dreams are generated."

In the 600 pages that followed, Freud set out, with a definite plan, to substantiate his claim. This plan, he had told his friend Fliess, was modeled on "an imaginary walk." First comes "the dark wood of the authorities (who cannot see the trees), where there is no clear view and it is very easy to go astray. Then there is a cavernous defile through which I lead my readers— my specimens with all its peculiarities, its details, its indiscretions, and its bad jokes—and then, all at once, the high ground and the prospect, and the question: 'Which way do you want to go?' " (The curious syntax indicates the tension under which Freud was then laboring.)

We can now come directly to Freud's ideas; and the best way to grasp his concepts (short of reading *The Interpretation of Dreams*) is to accompany him along the path he sketched for Wilhelm Fliess.

Freud's first purpose was to emphasize the role of memory in dreams. All dream material must be based on memory traces in the brain, though not necessarily on conscious memories. This point was proved by hypermnesia, or the appearance of recollections beyond the reach of conscious memory—

a phenomenon to which Maury had devoted much attention. Many people can dream in languages they do not consciously know but have heard spoken in infancy, or can recall persons and places from long-forgotten childhood. The days of childhood, indeed, were already seen as an important source of the dream—a conviction that Freud had carried over from his experience with hysterical patients. But recent events, too, could play their part. Given all the available sources of the dream images, however, there remained a basic question—one that 20 years earlier the German philosopher F. W. Hildebrandt had raised in his book on dreams.

"For the remarkable thing," Hildebrandt had written, "is that dreams derive their elements not from major and stirring events, nor the powerful and compelling interests of the preceding day, but from incidental details, from the worthless fragments, one might say, of what has been recently experienced or of the remoter past." What mechanism of the mind lay behind the selection of dream material, making it so bizarre that many sensible men shrugged off dreams as collections of foolish images? Freud could not offer a simple or direct answer. There were other questions to be asked along the road of discovery. All he could do was to insist on his belief that dreams had some meaning, that the process by which their material was selected had some purpose, and that to trace back this meaning and this purpose would lead ultimately to the innermost secrets of the personality.

He next reviewed the various suggestions put forward to explain the origin of dreams—suggestions we have examined in earlier chapters. His main conclusion was that whatever *caused* a dream—a stimulus to the senses or a physiological condition—the *nature* of the dream was the important fact. To attribute the cause of a dream to a given stimulus was useful, but it explained nothing about the psychic significance of the dream.

In the dimly lit world of sleep, however, the dream emerges in images, while waking thought is expressed in concepts. These images, incoherent, unrestricted by normal limitations of time and place, free from the influence

All dream material draws on past experiences —even though these may consciously be forgotten. Freud quoted a dream of the French philosopher Delbœuf. He saw a plant that he did not know in waking life, but in his dream he knew it was called *Asplenium ruta muralis*. Sixteen years later Delbœuf found an album of dried plants, their names written in his own handwriting and dating from two years before the dream. Among them was the Asplenium. Dream thoughts are expressed in images, like the drawings of children and the picture language of simple societies. Right, a petition sent in 1859 by the Chippewa Indians to the American Government. The lines from eye to eye and heart to heart express the message that all the tribes, represented by different totems (crane, bear, etc.), are unanimous in their views and feelings.

of critical and reasoning judgments, usually seem remote from and irrelevant to everyday experience. They are, as Freud and others had noted, much more like something from man's past rather than man's present—some archaic form of psychic function that has survived the emergence of human consciousness and finds an outlet in sleep. One could say, perhaps, that dream images are childish or primitive means of expressing what the modern adult conceives and describes in more sophisticated fashion.

Such a primitive mode of expression, moreover, could well be used as the vehicle for the most primitive or infantile feelings. As we have seen, several significant writers on dreams, Plato among them, had put forward this idea. Freud took as his example the French writer Alfred Maury, who had spoken of "yielding" to "faults" and "vicious impulses" in dreams, "without fear or remorse." Maury had gone on to say:

"Thus in dreams a man stands revealed in all his native nakedness and poverty. As soon as he suspends the exercise of his will, he becomes the plaything of all the passions against which he is defended while he is awake by his conscience, his sense of honor, and his fears.... What is revealed in dreams is primarily the man of instinct.... Man may be said to return in his dreams to a state of nature."

If, however, the dream is a series of images drawn from memory and animated by instinctual drives—and this is the point that Freud's argument had so far reached—how and why does the mind produce the dream in sleep? Does it have some special function, possibly related to the process of sleep, whereby the imagination and deep associated feelings are released from the constrictions of conscious judgment? And can one find any means of explaining the patently symbolic character of the images that are conjured up in the dream? All three questions were vital to Freud's theory.

Before Freud completed his study of previous dream theories, he explicitly noticed the work of three of his predecessors in the same field—Scherner, Griesinger, and Radestock.

An engraving, *The Dream of Reason Produces Monsters* (1799) by Francisco Goya expresses the irrational nature of dreams as the counterpart of rational consciousness.

Karl Albrecht Scherner's book, *The Life of Dreams*, was published in 1861: Freud called it "the most original and far-reaching attempt to explain dreaming as a special activity of the mind, capable of free expansion only in the state of sleep." This was somewhat extravagant praise in comparison with Freud's grudging recognition of other authors whose insight was at least as profound as Scherner's. But Scherner had made a couple of important points. One was to stress the weakening of the ego, or self-control, in sleep, so that "the activity of the soul which we call fantasy is free from all the rules of reason and is also free from all restrictive factors, and thus rises to unlimited heights. . . . It shows a bias in favor of the immoderate, the exaggerated, the grotesque. At the same time, freeing itself from the hindrances of the categories of thought, it gains a greater elasticity, a greater adroitness, a greater versatility. It is extremely sensitive to the most delicate and the most passionate emotional stimuli, and it immediately changes the inner life into pictures of the outer world. The dream fantasy lacks a conceptual language— what it wants to say it must paint pictorially, and, since there are no concepts to exercise an attenuating influence, it makes full use of all the power and splendor of the pictorial form. Thus, however forceful its speech may be, it is diffuse and clumsy. The clarity of its language is impaired by the fact that it has a dislike of representing an object by its proper image, and prefers some extraneous image which will express only that one attribute of the object which it is seeking to describe. Here we have the symbolizing activity of fantasy."

Freud was quick to seize on and develop the ideas in this passage, especially the last of them. The fact that a symbolic image represented one aspect of an object, possibly a quality, provided a vital clue to its interpretation. He had already noted that the dream seemed to contain verbal and visual puns. The image of a man standing in the snow might be the dream's way of saying that he was a *cold* person. And he had picked up from Artemidorus the famous dream in which Alexander the Great saw a satyr, which Aristander interpreted to him as *sa tyros*, meaning in Greek, "Tyre is thine."

The second contribution Scherner made was possibly an even more important hint to Freud. Scherner inclined to the physiological explanation of the cause of dreams, but he believed that the original stimulus prompted the flights of imagination that, on analysis, would indicate their source. Thus his theory of symbolism placed great emphasis on the body and its parts. A dream caused by a headache, he suggested, might take the form of an image of a ceiling covered with loathsome spiders; a breathing lung might be represented by a blazing furnace. In a passage that was pregnant with significance for Freud, Scherner pointed out that a clarinet or tobacco-pipe in a dream might symbolize the male sex organ. "In the case of sexual dreams in a woman, the narrow space where the thighs come together may be represented by a narrow courtyard surrounded by houses."

Almost all the materials Freud needed to embark on his new form of dream interpretation were now to hand; there remained only one other crucial contribution for him to weave into the fabric of his argument. He quickly ran over the works of various medical authorities, especially that of the pioneer psychiatrist Wilhelm Griesinger, whose book had been published in 1845, and of P. Radestock, who had written *Sleep and Dreams* in 1879. Not only had both noted the similarity between the phenomena of dreams and those of mental illness, but both had shown—as Freud puts it—"quite clearly that ideas in dreams and in psychoses have in common the characteristics of being *fulfilments of wishes.*"

The italics indicate Freud's own impatience. He was no longer able to withhold from the reader what he considered to be the crux of his argument, and he added these words. "My own researches have taught me that in this fact lies the key of a psychological theory of both dreams and psychoses." But, he hastened to remark, "it is not to be expected that we shall find the ultimate explanation of dreams in the direction of mental disorders.... It is quite likely, on the contrary, that a modification of our attitude towards dreams will at the same time affect our views upon the internal mechanism of mental disorders and that we shall be working towards an explanation of the psychoses while we are endeavouring to throw some light on the mystery of dreams."

Freud was here describing much more than his dream theory. These sentences were a preview of his whole subsequent career. He was now ready to show how one of his dreams could be interpreted.

It is difficult, today, when the use of dream interpretation in psychoanalysis has been common practice for a generation, to realize what was involved for Freud—to understand just why the day on which he unraveled the dream of "Irma's Injection" was one of those moments of what is commonly called invention, when the knowledge of the past confronts the problem of the present and, through the insight of genius, gives a novel answer. For Freud was literally taking a step in the dark, abandoning conventional medical concepts and practices in favor of the unorthodox, apparently reverting to ideas that smacked of superstition and the occult. He made no secret of this. "I have been driven to realize," he wrote, "that here we have one of those not infrequent cases in which an ancient and jealously held popular belief seems to be nearer the truth than the judgment of the prevalent science of today."

The technique Freud was to employ was one that he had learned from his clinical experience. He had found, in dealing with patients suffering from hysteria, phobias, and obsessions, that if a pathological idea could be "traced back to the elements in the patient's mental life from which it originated, it simultaneously crumbles away and the patient is freed from it." This is the fundamental assumption underlying all psychoanalytic treatment. In order to do this, however, the patient must be fully relaxed and willing to turn attention inward, so that the critical faculty does not inhibit the flow of ideas that can eventually lead to the hidden or repressed ideas that are the source of his difficulties.

Freud placed great emphasis on the relaxation of the normal critical faculty. He illustrated his point by a quotation from the German poet, Friedrich von Schiller, who in 1788 had described the process by which creative ideas came to him:

"It seems a bad thing and detrimental to the creative work of the mind if Reason makes too close an examination of the ideas as they come pouring in—at the very gateway, as it were. Looked at in isolation, a thought may seem very trivial or very fantastic; but it may be made important by another thought that comes after it, and, in conjunction with other thoughts that may seem equally absurd, it may turn out a most effective link."

The 1964 film about Freud's work depicts his investigation of the role of the unconscious by a symbolic dream in which he sees himself entering a deep tunnel.

John Houston's   Freud—The Secret Passion

It was by such reasoning that Freud came to his first rule of dream interpretation. The dream must be set in the context of the ideas that, as Schiller once put it, could "rush in pell-mell" once the dreamer permitted himself free association. No matter how foolish or extravagant the dream—or the trains of thought it evoked—everything must be admitted to consciousness and reported. Only by letting the ideas well up could the dreamer (or his analyst) hope to trace back the tortuous path of dream thoughts.

This conviction led to Freud's second rule. All the elements in a dream must be treated in detail, and association found for every idea, image, and turn of phrase. For Freud (though this is a point on which important differences of opinion later arose between him and other psychoanalysts) the dream had to be broken down into all its component parts. The dream as it was remembered was, for him, only the superficial form in which the underlying thoughts were symbolically expressed—what he called the "manifest" dream; his purpose was, as we shall see, to break up the dream and, with the aid of the associations secured, to reconstruct or reassemble it in its "true" or "latent" form.

By the time Freud came to complete his book he had already analyzed over one thousand of his patients' dreams, but for several reasons—not the least being the crucial importance of his dream about Irma in the evolution of this technique—he chose one of his own as the "specimen" by which his technique of dream dissection could be best demonstrated. But (as he insisted throughout his professional career) with rare exceptions a dream does not stand alone, and cannot properly be interpreted except in the context of the dreamer's personality and problems.

The couch that Freud used when analyzing
his patients during his practice in
Vienna at the end of the 19th century.

The dream of "Irma's Injection" therefore must be set against the background of Freud's own life at that time. He was 39 and aware that as he grew older he would be faced by a vital decision—whether to continue an orthodox medical career or risk striking out in an altogether new direction. He was well aware that, in the Vienna of his day, the fact that he was a Jew would be an obstacle to his professional advancement and a possible point of attack on his reputation. He was, in short, in a state of anxiety, induced by both the environment and the inner forces that were compelling him to push on with his pioneer work in psychotherapy.

The evening before he had this dream about Irma, an old friend and colleague (called Otto) had come back from a holiday, during which he had visited one of Freud's patients (a young widow called Irma) whom Freud had cured of hysterical anxiety but who continued to have certain somatic symptoms, notably spasms of retching. Before the holiday, Freud had reached deadlock in his treatment of Irma. He had become impatient and she had become resistant to the insights he had offered her. When Otto reported that Irma seemed "better, but not well," Freud detected a note of reproach, which seemed to him to reflect the attitude of "Dr. M.," a physician who was "the leading figure in our circle"; he had, in fact, written a report to "Dr. M." after hearing Otto's comments on Irma, and then gone to bed, feeling that for the moment the matter was settled. Yet his anxieties were carried over into sleep. In the dream that followed the main characters were Irma, Otto, Dr. M., and another physician, Dr. Leopold.

"A large hall—numerous guests, whom we were receiving—among them Irma, whom I at once took on one side, as though to answer her letter and to reproach her for not having accepted my 'solution' yet. I say to her: 'If you still have pains, its really only your own fault.' She replies: 'If you only knew what pains I've now got in my throat, stomach, and abdomen—I'm being choked by them.' I am alarmed and look at her. She looks pale and puffy. I think that after all I must be overlooking some organic trouble. I take her to the window and look into her throat. She shows signs of recalcitrance, like a woman with false teeth. I think that there is really no need for her to do that. She then opens her mouth properly and on the right I find a large white spot: elsewhere I see extensive grey-white scabs upon some remarkable curly structures which are evidently modelled on the turbinal bones of the nose. I at once call in Dr. M., who repeats the examination and confirms it. Dr. M. looks quite unlike his usual self; he is very pale, he limps, and his chin is clean shaven ... Now my friend Otto is also standing beside her, and my friend Leopold is percussing her through her bodice and saying: She has a dull area low down on the left. He also calls attention to an infiltrated portion of skin on the left shoulder. (I noticed this, just as he did, in spite of her dress.) Dr. M. says: There is no doubt that it's an infection, but no matter: dysentery will follow and the poison will be eliminated ...

We were directly aware, too, of the origin of the infection. Not long before, when she was feeling unwell, my friend Otto had given her an injection of a preparation of propyl, propyls . . . propionic acid . . . trimethylamin (the formula of which I see before me printed in heavy type). . . . One ought not to give such injections so thoughtlessly. . . . Probably, too, the syringe was not clean."

Where could one begin to make sense of this dream—except to note that it was clearly concerned with Freud's worries about his professional position? He himself confessed that "no one who had only read the preamble and the content of the dream itself could have the slightest notion of what the dream meant. I myself had no notion." He therefore set to work to break up the dream into its elements, and to find associations with each—a process that takes up more than 10 pages of his book. Even so, he confessed, several important aspects of the dream were omitted, some because their implications would seem too gross a violation of privacy, some because he wished to use them as illustrations later in the book.

Freud began with the hall and the reception. He concluded that the occasion was a party for his wife's birthday at their summer house, at which a number of guests—including Irma—were expected. Next, he dealt with his reproach of Irma. This "showed I was specially anxious not to be responsible for the pains which she still had. If they were her fault they could not be mine. Could it be that the purpose of the dream lay in this direction?" Then the difference between Irma's "pale and puffy" appearance in the dream and her normally rosy complexion led Freud to suspect that one or more other patients were being substituted for her—and a series of associations followed about cases in which he had not been notably successful.

Freud then turned to the idea that he must be "overlooking some organic trouble." For "if Irma's pains had an organic basis, once again I could not be responsible for curing them. It occurred to me, in fact, that I was actually *wishing* that there had been a wrong diagnosis; for if so, the blame for my lack of success would also have been got rid of."

A series of memories related to previous patients was aroused by the phrases in the dream that describe the examination of Irma's mouth. They all pointed toward the same state of anxiety. In particular, the scabs on the turbinal bones "recalled a worry about my own state of health. I was making frequent use of cocaine at that time to reduce some troublesome nasal swellings, and I had heard a few days earlier that one of my women patients who had followed my example had developed an extensive necrosis of the nasal mucous membrane. I had been the first to recommend the use of cocaine, in 1885, and this recommendation had brought down serious reproaches upon me. The misuse of that drug had hastened the death of a dear friend of mine." Freud also recalled—in an association to the sentence where he calls in Dr. M.—that he had once prescribed "what was at that time regarded as a

harmless remedy" (suphonal) for a woman patient who was poisoned by it.
"It seemed as if I had been collecting all the occasions which I could bring
up against myself as evidence of lack of medical conscientiousness."

By this time a pattern was beginning to emerge from the dream. As Freud
continued to press the associations, reasons came up for the appearance of
Otto and Leopold in the dream, for the diagnosis that Leopold made, for Dr.
M.'s remark about dysentery, for the injection that Otto gave in the dream,
and for the nature of the injection. The last—the groping for the word
"propyl ... propyls ... proprionic acid"—Freud attributed to a bottle of
liqueur that Otto had given him the previous evening, which had given
off such a strong smell of fusel oil (amyl . . .) that Freud refused to drink it in
case it poisoned him. The word "amyl," he believed, led to "propyl" and then
to "trimethylamin." He then saw the chemical formula for this substance,
emphasized by its being printed in heavy type. "What was it, then," he asked,
"to which my attention was to be directed in this way by trimethylamin?"
Once more the associations provided a clue. Freud recalled that a friend
had suggested that trimethylamin was a chemical product of sexual metabolism.

Freud had already reached the conclusion that sexual factors were of the
greatest importance in the origin of the nervous disorders he was treating.
He now linked these thoughts to the single word "trimethylamin."

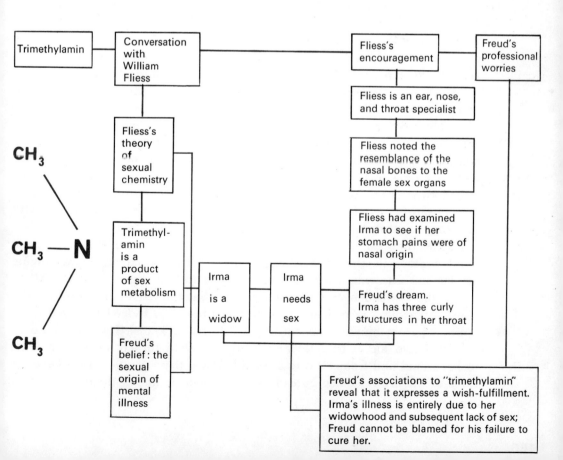

Freud did not make a complete analysis of the sexual implications of this dream. At one stage, when he discusses the phrase, "in spite of her dress," he remarks: "Frankly, I had no desire to penetrate further at this point." And later, in a footnote, he added these words: "I have not reported everything that occurred to me during the process of interpretation." But, from the abbreviated version of this interpretation, it is possible to see how his mind was moving toward the major conclusion from this crucial dream. It is essentially a defense against self-reproach (and criticism by colleagues) of his professional competence. In the dream he is asserting that his treatment of Irma has been correct both medically and socially, and that unlike other physicians he was free from fault.

What, then, was the "meaning" of the dream as he interpreted it? Since the passage in which he summarizes the meaning may be regarded as the foundation of all subsequent psychoanalytical work built on the basis of dream interpretation, it must be quoted at length:

"The dream fulfilled certain wishes which were started in me by the events of the previous evening (the news given me by Otto and my writing out of the case history). The conclusion of the dream, that is to say, was that I was not responsible for the persistence of Irma's pains, but that Otto was. Otto had in fact annoyed me by his remarks about Irma's incomplete cure, and the dream gave me my revenge by throwing back the reproach on him. The dream acquitted me of the responsibility for Irma's condition by showing that it was due to other factors—it produced a whole series of reasons. The dream represented a particular state of affairs as I should have wished it to be. *Thus its content was the fulfilment of a wish and its motive was a wish.*

"Thus much leaped to the eyes. But many of the details of the dream also became intelligible to me from the point of view of wish-fulfilment. Not only did I revenge myself on Otto for being too hasty in taking sides against me by representing him as being too hasty (in giving the injection); but I had also revenged myself on him for giving me the bad liquor which had an aroma of fusel oil. And in the dream I found an expression which united two reproaches: the injection was of a preparation of propyl. This did not satisfy me and I pursued my revenge further by contrasting him with his more trustworthy competitor (Leopold). I seemed to be saying: 'I like *him* better than *you*.' But Otto was not the only person to suffer from the vials of my wrath. I took revenge as well on my disobedient patient by exchanging her for one who was wiser and less recalcitrant. Nor did I allow Dr. M. to escape the consequence of his contradiction but showed by means of a clear allusion that he was an ignoramus on the subject.... Indeed I seemed to be appealing from him to someone else with greater knowledge (to my friend who had told me of trimethylamin) just as I had turned away from Irma to her friend and from Otto to Leopold. 'Take these people away! Give me three others of my choice instead! Then I shall be free of these undeserved reproaches!' The groundlessness of the reproaches was proved for me in the dream in the most elaborate fashion. *I* was not to blame for Irma's pains, since she herself was to blame for them by refusing to accept my solution. *I* was not concerned with Irma's pains, since they were of an organic nature and quite incurable by psychological treatment. Irma's pains could be satisfactorily explained by her widowhood (cf. the trimethylamin). This cryptic reference was to Irma's lack of a satisfactory sex life. Irma's pains had been caused by Otto giving her an incautious injection of an unsuitable drug—a thing *I* should never have done. Irma's pains were the result of an injection with a dirty needle . . . whereas I never did any harm with my injections. I noticed, it is true, that these explanations of Irma's pains (which agreed in exculpating me) were not entirely consistent with one another, and indeed they were mutually exclusive . . . .

"Certain other themes played a part in the dream, which were not so obviously connected with Irma's illness. . . . But when I came to consider all of these, they could all be collected into a single group of ideas and labelled, as it were, 'concern about my own and other peoples' health—professional conscientiousness.' I called to mind the obscure, disagreeable impression I had had when Otto brought me the news of Irma's condition. This group of thoughts that played a part in the dream enabled me retrospectively to put this transient impression into words. It was as though he had said to me: 'You don't take your medical duties seriously enough. You're not conscientious; you don't carry out what you've undertaken.' Thereupon, this group of thoughts seemed to put themselves at my disposal, so that I could produce evidence of how conscientious I was, of how deeply I was concerned about the health of my relations, my friends, and my patients. It was a noteworthy fact that this material also included some disagreeable memories, which supported my friend Otto's accusation rather than my own vindication. The material was, as one might say, impartial; but nevertheless there was an unmistakable connection between this more extensive group of thoughts which underlay the dream and the narrower subject of the dream which gave rise to the wish to be innocent of Irma's illness."

In this long passage we have Freud's first public attempt at dream analysis. There are many levels, and many directions, in which one can mine the raw material of the dream, but Freud was not yet ready to follow other trains of thought. He could, for instance, have pursued the double meanings of many of the phrases he used. The fact that Dr. M. is *bartlos* or beardless, clean-shaven, has implications of interest. An important professional man of that time would generally be bearded, as was Dr. M. in real life. To deprive him of the beard is to diminish him, to suggest that he is immature or insignificant, possibly even to hint at emasculation of this father figure.

In the dream moreover, Otto is given a syringe, but in the German original the word is *Spritze*, a colloquial word meaning "squirter"—an instrument to which many associations can be attached. As Dr. Erik H. Erikson, the noted American psychoanalyst, points out in his penetrating comments on this dream, this makes Otto "a dirty squirter," for he used a dirty syringe, and this raises a whole range of phallic-urinary connotations, from the infantile to the adult sex level. Even the words "birthday reception" will bear close analysis, because "numerous guests" are all being "received": the German word used by Freud is *empfangen*, which can also mean "conception." From the association of this thought with that of a birthday, it would be easy to probe further into Freud's money worries about the growth of his family.

By these, and many other clues in the dream and in what we know of Freud's life, it is indeed possible to trace out ideas and experiences that carry one far beyond Freud's original purpose in presenting this dream "specimen." But, as he himself said, when he had finished interpreting it, "for the moment I am satisfied with the achievement of this one piece of fresh knowledge. If we adopt the method of interpreting dreams which I have indicated here, we shall find that dreams really have a meaning, and are far from being a fragmentary activity of the brain, as the authorities have claimed. *When the work of interpretation has been completed, we perceive that a dream is the fulfilment of a wish.*"

The idea that a dream is an attempt to fulfill a wish was Freud's central theme. It provided him with an answer to the vital question: What is the motive for a dream? As Freud demonstrated the way in which sexual impulses —often dating back to a period in childhood at which sexual desires were presumed not to exist—emerge in dreams, it was assumed that he was arguing that all dreams can ultimately be traced back to some sexual feeling or mood. But, as he was at pains to point out, there are many other powerful wishes that remain ungratified and find expression in fantasy. Children, as he had observed them in his own family, often dream that desires denied them in daytime are granted in sleep, just as explorers starving in the desert sometimes dream of running water and huge banquets. He felt it essential to stress that "there are countless dreams which satisfy other than sexual needs, such as hunger, thirst, comfort, etc., even if we take the widest possible view of the term 'sexual'." But the more a dream deals with feelings or situations that have been repressed, because they seem unacceptable to the individual's consciousness, the more peculiar and indirect they become: they are distorted, so that the "manifest" dream bears little apparent resemblance to the "latent" dream. Such distortion was Freud's explanation of the fact that dreams often seem nonsensical; it also explains why Freud believed that horrifying and terrifying dreams could still be regarded as wish-fulfillments, even though no one could rationally wish for the horrors they expressed. Beneath them, he insisted, lay a wish so contradictory to the dreamer's "normal" personality that it could not be recognized or admitted to consciousness without distortion—without what he called "censorship."

It was, therefore, to the problem of distortion that Freud next turned his attention. In doing so, he believed, he could also show why most of his predecessors in dream interpretation had run into a dead end. They had concerned themselves with the manifest dream, and had overlooked the fact that it had a double lock on its secret—the symbolism of its images, and the concealment of the latent dream because its hidden theme had been translated into this symbolism. This was a complex conception, and one that some of his colleagues (notably Jung) and many of his successors were skeptical about. They continued to insist that the manifest dream had significance in its own right, and could not be regarded as a mere disguise for something else.

To Freud, the distinction was crucial, and he never abandoned it. It provided him with the essential structure of a dream, built up in this fashion. An instinctive wish or, at least, some very powerful desire, attempts to find expression; some part of the mind—what he had named the "censor"—changes the wish (let us say, a repressed infantile desire to kill one's father) into something less dangerous (say, a dream of being in a waxwork museum and knocking the head off one of the figures) and this then appears in the manifest dream. To interpret the dream, the process would have to be reversed—as we saw in the dream about Irma—by breaking up the manifest dream into its parts, finding the associations, and then reassembling them so that they would reveal the hidden desire.

Whether or not one accepts Freud's argument at this point, it is necessary to understand it, because it provides the link with his next conclusion—though this conclusion is now open to even more damaging criticism than

Our Christmas Dream (1845), a drawing by Phiz, the artist of *Pickwick Papers*. When the glutton dreams of Christmas Day he sees scenes of dancing, drinking, and eating. Freud recognized that food fantasies of this kind are common forms of wish-fulfillment.

A boy's dream that he is cutting off his teddy bear's head exemplifies Freud's distinction between the "manifest" and the "latent" dream. The dream reveals the boy's repressed wish to attack his father, but the "manifest" dream substitutes the harmless toy for the powerful father.

his insistence on distinguishing between the manifest and the latent dream. Why should the dream disguise the hidden wish? Why could it not present the cause of anxiety or fear directly, without the intervention of the censor?

To answer these two questions Freud went back to the old physiological theories of the dream, with their emphasis on somatic stimuli. He noted the way in which a sound, a smell, a touch, or light falling on the eyes was often woven into a dream immediately before the stimulus in question aroused the sleeper. Why should this be so? It was because the dreamer was trying to stay asleep, to resist the disturbing stimulus, and his dreaming mind was therefore endeavoring to give an explanation of the sensation. In the same way, if the dreaming fantasy was confronted by disturbing impulses, welling up from within the mind, it would attempt to make them palatable in dream form, for otherwise the uncomfortable feeling would wake the sleeper and cause him considerable distress. Thus, Freud concluded, "*the wish to sleep (which the conscious ego is concentrated upon, and which, together with the dream-censorship and the 'secondary revision,' which I shall mention later, constitute the conscious ego's share in dreaming) must in every case be reckoned as one of the motives for the formation of dreams, and every successful dream is a fulfilment of that wish.*" The italics are Freud's; and nothing in his book is stated with more categorical force. "All dreams," for Freud, "are in a sense dreams of convenience: they serve the purpose of prolonging sleep instead of waking up. *Dreams are the GUARDIANS of sleep and not its disturbers.*" Here, too, the capitals and the italics are Freud's.

How could these ideas be applied to the practical interpretation of dreams? Once again it was necessary for Freud to dissect "specimens" to establish his case, and he did so by reviewing a series of "typical" dreams—the dream in which one is embarrassingly naked, the dream of the death of a near relative, dreams of flying and falling, or taking an examination.

In each of these examples Freud was able to expand his conception of childhood experience, and its decisive role in determining both "normal" and "abnormal" psychic patterns in the adult—in this respect, he believed that the difference between the mentally "healthy" and the "neurotic" person lay in the manner in which the first had been able to grow through the experiences of childhood, while the latter had been unable to assimilate certain of these experiences and had repressed them. Social controls, such as the influence of parents, the scolding and threats that shape a child's behavior, had driven instinctive and irrational forces below the surface, to emerge later in physical symptoms or in dreams.

The point is clearly illustrated by the type of dream in which one is naked in the presence of strangers, who seem indifferent to the fact. Freud cites Hans Andersen's story of "The Emperor's New Clothes" as a comparable situation to those that appeared in the dreams of his patients. His experience, he said, proved "beyond a doubt that a memory of the dreamer's earliest childhood lies at the foundation of the dream. Only in our childhood was there a time when we were seen by our relatives, as well as by strange nurses, servants, and visitors, in a state of insufficient clothing, and at the same time we were not ashamed of our nakedness . . . One of my patients has retained in his conscious memory a scene from his eighth year, in which, after undressing for bed, he wanted to dance into his little sister's room in his shirt, but was prevented by the servant. In the history of the childhood of neurotics, exposure before children of the opposite sex plays a prominent part; in paranoia the delusion of being observed while dressing or undressing may be directly traced to these experiences; and among those who have remained perverse there is a class in which the childish impulse is exaggerated into a symptom: the class of *exhibitionists*."

In a famous passage, with far-reaching implications, Freud went on:

"This age of childhood, in which the sense of shame is unknown, seems a paradise when we look back upon it later, and paradise itself is nothing but the mass-fantasy of the childhood of the individual. This is why in paradise men are naked and unashamed, until the moment arrives when shame and fear awaken; expulsion follows, and sexual life and cultural development begin. Into this paradise dreams can take us back every night; we have already ventured the conjecture that the impressions of our earliest childhood . . . crave reproduction for their own sake, perhaps without further reference to their content, so that their repetition is a wish-fulfilment. Dreams of nakedness, then, are exhibition dreams."

Freud believed the flying dream (above) repeats the rhythms of childish games—like seesawing—to which erotic sensations are often attached. Dreams of being undressed in a crowd of people (below) are based on childhood memories of a similar state.

Another "typical" dream analyzed by Freud is that of missing trains (right). He called it a consolation dream. The departing train is a symbol of death: when the train is lost the dream is saying: "Compose yourself, you are not going to die (depart)."

Similar arguments were used by Freud in unraveling childhood patterns in other "typical" dreams, such as "those in which the dreamer imagines the death of a loved relative and is at the same time painfully affected." In this case, again, he was quite dogmatic. "The meaning of such dreams, as their content indicates, is a wish that the person in question may die." He realized, of course, that the feelings of his readers would "rebel" against this assertion, but he insisted that the rivalry and hatred between brothers and sisters was deep-rooted though unconscious and, in adult life, concealed by apparent warm affection. One reason for this, he suggested, was that for the child the idea of death meant no more than being "gone": to wish another dead, in early childhood, is simply a way of wishing him removed from the scene.

But could the same relatively innocent explanation serve for the death-wish against parents who have cherished a child from infancy? Freud not only believed that such hostile attitudes toward one or both parents could be found in most individuals—"wrong" or "unjustified" though they might seem. He was also convinced that such hostility was the clue to much neurosis in later life. Hostility, moreover, was often (as he discovered in the analysis of his patients) directed toward the parent of the same sex, while an excessive affection was shown to the parent of the opposite sex. It was this observation that led Freud to the conviction that, in infancy, there was sexual rivalry between, say, a boy and his father, and sexual attraction between the boy and his mother—a situation pregnant with many infantile fantasies, and one to which (taking the story of the famous Greek legend) he gave the name "Oedipus complex."

This hypothesis of Freud's has been subject to more critical scrutiny than any other. As he himself said in 1914, nothing he wrote "has provoked such embittered denials, such fierce opposition—or such amusing contortions—on the part of critics as this indication of the childhood impulses towards incest which persist in the unconscious." Whether the hypothesis is valid or not, and whether it can be found as a universal theme in the dreams and myths of almost all peoples, is not an immediately relevant issue. The point here is simply that Freudian dream interpretation and Freudian psychotherapy take the Oedipus (or, in the case of a girl, the Electra) complex as a basic assumption, and neither can be understood without a recognition of this fact.

As we can now see, in every case Freud tried to search out an infantile base for the latent meaning of a dream. Unlike those writers who attributed dreams of flying to the movement of the lungs in sleep, he asserted his belief that the sensations of flying, falling, giddiness, and so on were recollections of erotic feelings in childhood.

Such ideas, however, merely helped to explain the source or motive of dreams. It was still necessary for Freud to offer an explanation of the form of dreams—why, for instance, the manifest dream should appear to be such a strange muddle when, on analysis, the basic dream thought turned out to be relatively simple. He therefore turned to what he called the "dream-work," in which he discerned four basic processes. The first was *condensation*. One person, one event, even one word contained many levels of meaning telescoped together. The second was *displacement*. Painful or otherwise disagreeable feelings were displaced from the true to a substitute object, thus escaping the watchful "censor." The example of the child who dreamed of breaking the wax figure is a case in which its hostile attitude to its father was safely displaced on to the apparently harmless waxwork. Thirdly, the dream images were not merely symbolic, being images they also had to represent ideas specifically, rather than in the abstract. The dream cannot provide conjunctions, as if to say "this happened and therefore that happened"; it can only show the causality by presenting the two events together. Similarly, it cannot say "as if," "perhaps," "either/or." In the manner

Freud suggested that "condensation"—the process whereby dream thoughts become bizarre combinations—was an important part of the dream-work, and that it most frequently applied to words and names. A man dreamed he recognized everyone at a party except one woman who was wearing military uniform with burns on it. On waking he remembered the woman's real name, which was Marshall-Byrnes (marshal plus burns or martial plus burns).

of some medieval paintings, the dream picture presents related events all at once without apparent order or perspective. Thus Freud's third category was the *means of representation* for the dream thought. Finally, he drew attention to the phenomenon of *secondary revision*—that is, what is added to the dream as the waking mind recalls, attempts to order, and finally reports it. He found significant differences in the way a dream was told for the second or third time, and these differences in the report would, by emphasis or omission, indicate sensitive aspects of the dream at which the patient and analyst should look with special care.

Two of the examples of condensation that Freud gave illustrate the point clearly. The first was in the "Irma" dream, in which he had conjured up an image of Dr. M., a figure that spoke and acted like his senior colleague, though "his physical characteristics and his malady belonged to someone else, namely my elder brother." Once Freud had made this distinction, it was possible for him to make fresh associations to both aspects of this figure and thus shed additional light on the dream. His second example came from a woman patient who dreamed she was with her husband at a peasant festivity. In the dream she uttered the apparently meaningless remark: "This will end in a general *Maistollmütz.*" All of us are familiar with the introduction of seeming gibberish into dreams, and it is instructive to watch how Freud managed to deal with this "verbal hotch-potch."

"In the dream she had a vague feeling that it was some kind of pudding made with maize—a sort of polenta. Analysis divided the word into *Mais* (maize), *toll* (mad), *mannstoll* (man-mad, or nymphomaniac), and *Olmütz* (a town in Moravia). All these fragments were found to be remnants of a conversation she had had at table with her relatives. The following words lay behind *Mais* (in addition to a reference to the recently opened Jubilee Exhibition): *Meissen* (Dresden) a porcelain figure representing a bird; *Miss* (her relatives' English governess had just gone to Olmütz); and *mies* (a Jewish slang term, used jokingly to mean "disgusting"). A long chain of thoughts and associations led off from each syllable. . ."

Similar techniques of dissection can, as Freud went on to show, be applied to displacement—notably the search for identification between persons and places that appear in the fantasy and those of real life concealed behind them. In some cases, Freud pointed out, two persons may appear linked by a common element. Two men, let us say, are chasing a wild horse. In this instance, one should search for another common element, not represented but repressed. Both men may have sexual aspirations toward the same woman, though the dreamer is reluctant to admit this. Or a dream may present a real situation in reverse, as if it were a mirror image of reality. A man dreamed that his father was scolding him for coming home late. Analysis revealed that this man had intensely disliked his father, and that this dream was expressing his anger with his father because he came home *too soon*—it would have been better if the father had never come home *at all*. The dream was based on a wish to have things different from what they were, and the reversal was a clue to this wish.

Freud insisted that great caution is necessary in interpreting dream symbols. But from his research and clinical experience he listed and offered explanations of some of the commoner symbols. A king and a queen are usually symbols of the dreamer's parents, while a prince or a princess may represent the dreamer, according to sex. The act of walking up stairs or ladders may be a representation of the sexual act: "It is not hard to discover the basis of the comparison: we come to the top in a series of rhythmical movements and with increasing breathlessness and then with a few rapid leaps, we can get to the bottom again." Freud's list is long, and later studies of dream interpretation have added to it.

Much of the controversy in the psychoanalytical movement was caused by differences of opinion on what certain symbols represent and how they should be interpreted. But Freud's view, essentially reductive, was hostile to most of the modifications or alternatives offered by his colleagues and successors. He even offered an explanation of the feeling (in waking life and in dreams) of "I have seen this before," or what is called *déjà vu*—a fascinating though often disturbing experience. It was, Freud said, simply that the locality suddenly perceived was a symbolic way of recalling "the genitals of the dreamer's mother; there is indeed no other place about which one can assert with such conviction that one has been there once before."

It was examples such as this that led both to criticism of Freud on grounds of "indecency" and—even from those who were prepared to accept much of his argument—to charges that he pressed his interpretations too far.

A number of similar symbolic situations were used by Freud to sustain this part of his analysis—the way in which dreams of water symbolized birth or dreams of nocturnal visitors were based on forgotten childhood nights, when a father (in the dream, usually a robber) or a mother (usually a ghost) had entered the bedroom, possibly to lift and change a sleeping child.

With "secondary revision," the last of the four factors that Freud believed shaped the content of dreams, we come to a phenomenon noted by many others besides Freud: the fact that we cannot directly *know* a dream, but can only recollect it. Into the dream as remembered, therefore, ideas close to waking consciousness may be inserted as we wake, possibly in an attempt to make sense of the dream story or (as in the case of external stimuli) to account for sensations at the moment of waking. Freud claimed that it was possible to recognize such "alien" elements in a dream report, because they were qualitatively different from the rest of the dream. Be that as it may, it is clear that such elements lie much closer to what we commonly call daydreams or waking fantasies than to the deeper thoughts of the dream proper. They appear, so to speak, as prepackaged images, more logical, more direct, less disguised, as if the mind had already conceived them and now attached them to some suitable point in the dream.

This is an interesting idea that Freud more or less tossed into his argument as a bonus—but one that may prove to have more validity than some other conceptions to which he attached greater importance. For, in discussing Maury's famous dream of being tried and guillotined during the French Revolution, Freud sought to find an explanation for the apparent speed of this long dream, how it was that it could all be composed between the head-rail of the bed hitting Maury's neck and his almost immediate awakening. One suggestion could be that Maury was having such a dream and the rail provided a final lucky stimulus. But it is better to follow Freud's idea that Maury's dream "represents a fantasy which had been stored up in his memory for many years and which was roused . . . at the moment he became aware of the stimulus which woke him." The story was clearly one that any Frenchman of Maury's age could have imagined (or heard as a tale in childhood) not once, but many times, and have, as it were, held "available" for discharge under a suitable stimulus.

Such a hypothesis fits into the general conception of dreaming as a fantasy-function, to which modern psychology and physiology have been directing renewed attention. It is, in fact, a conception that—though Freud employs it only as a possible explanation of *some* arousal dreams—may be capable of explaining many dream phenomena that he deals with entirely differently.

Freud believed that a dream is modified and made intelligible to waking thought by a process that he called "secondary elaboration." A man may dream of hearing a snatch of music from Mozart's opera *The Marriage of Figaro* but on waking he retrospectively imposes a *visual* element that elaborates the dream fragment.

It is now possible to see the main outlines of Freud's theory, and to appreciate the scale, thoroughness, and consistency of outlook that characterized his work. Since no one summarized it better than he himself, and we have now reached the stage in his argument when he felt recapitulation necessary, his own account remains the best:

"Dreams are psychical acts of as much significance as any others; their motive force is in every instance a wish seeking fulfilment; the fact of their not being recognizable as wishes and their many peculiarities and absurdities are due to the influence of the psychical censorship to which they have been subjected during the process of their formation; apart from the necessity of evading this censorship, other factors which have contributed to their formation are a necessity for the condensation of their psychical material, a regard for the possibility of its being represented in sensory images and—though not invariably—a demand that the structure of the dream shall have a rational and intelligible exterior."

We should add two other considerations. The first is Freud's insistence on the significance of unfulfilled childhood wishes; the second is his suggestion that the dream not only regresses to the dreamer's "earliest condition," a revival of his childhood, "of the instinctual impulses which dominated it and of the methods of expression which were then available to him"; it also

Freud believed that unresolved childhood conflicts can unconsciously influence behavior in waking life, and that dreams often point the way to discovering the origin of neurotic attitudes. For example, a girl walking along the street sees, by chance, a funeral hearse (right) that provokes memories of her father's funeral and her lack of sorrow at his death. She recalls incidents during childhood when her father displayed a characteristic bullying and dominating attitude (center right). Her aggressive attitudes toward any form of authority—stemming from the father-child relationship—are aroused: that night she dreams she is driving a car and runs a policemen down (top). At work she dislikes her boss, whose dominating attitude makes her associate him with her father, and next morning she oversleeps and arrives late at the office (far right).

gives, he suggested, a picture of a phylogenetic childhood—"a picture of the development of the human race, of which the individual's development is in fact an abbreviated recapitulation influenced by the chance of circumstances of life."

This proposition, prompted by Freud's own recognition of similar patterns in dreams, folktales, and mythology, and by Nietzsche's assertion that in dreams "some primeval relic of humanity is at work which we can now scarcely reach any longer by a direct path," seemed to promise that "the analysis of dreams will lead us to a knowledge of man's archaic heritage, of what is psychically innate in him." This hint was later taken up by C. G. Jung and expanded in a way that became unacceptable to Freud. But, once again, it fitted consistently into Freud's overall theory. It was quite logical for him to argue that "dreams and neuroses seem to have preserved more mental antiquities than we could have imagined possible; so that psychoanalysis may claim a high place among the sciences which are concerned with the reconstruction of the earliest and most obscure periods of the beginnings of the human race."

Why does the dream take place at all? To this Freud had given a partial answer in his insistence that the dream is the guardian of sleep, but he needed to elaborate the idea in terms of his general description of mental processes.

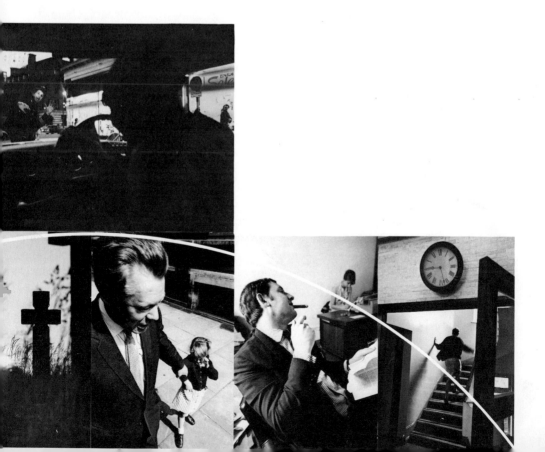

Freud's dream interpretations are often criticized as dogmatic but ingenious. Here is a typical example. A patient whom Freud was treating at her summer resort dreamed that she dived into the water at this resort "just where the pale moon is mirrored." The dream, Freud said, was a birth dream and such dreams must be interpreted by reversing their events: the patient is really coming *out* of the water. The word *lune* (moon) is French slang for "bottom" from where, children believe, babies come. The dream replaces "bottom" by "moon." On being asked why she should wish to be reborn at the summer resort, the patient replied: "Isn't it just like being reborn during treatment?" For Freud, this confirmed his interpretation. He concluded that the dream expressed the patient's wish that he should continue treating her at the resort.

He was well aware that the terms in which he sought to describe mental processes were unsatisfactory—that he had to draw upon physics, chemistry, and anatomy for both technical phrases and analogies or models that would approximate to what he wanted. He was equally aware that to make his system intelligible he had to describe what he could only assume happened within the mind, to create a topography for functions to which no definite location could be described. Hence the use of such nebulous concepts as the "unconscious"; the "preconscious" (the threshold of consciousness, where information lost to sight was not "out of mind" but still available to consciousness, and where the symbolic images of the unconscious were translated into forms in which consciousness could comprehend them); and "consciousness" itself, the state of being with which we are most familiar but which represents the least part of our complex mental activities.

In Freud's view, it was "more expedient and economical" for the unconscious wish to take its course and construct a dream, during sleep, than for the preconscious to exercise continual supervision over the unconscious and block off the wishes that welled up. Indeed, consciousness is virtually extinguished in sleep, and it must be presumed that the preconscious also has diminished power. If the wish appears in dream form, the preconscious need not work so hard to deal with the uncomfortable thought as it would if the wish were directly expressed; it can "bind and dispose of it with a small expenditure of preconscious work." In waking hours, the preconscious represses fresh but unacceptable impressions; in sleep it is busy keeping already repressed material from invading consciousness and thus waking the dreamer. The preconscious, Freud suggested, is the bridge between thought and fantasy. The unconscious might continuously attempt to gratify infantile wishes, and hallucinate such gratification indefinitely—as it does with a psychosis. Consciousness, on the other hand, retains contact with reality through the evidence of the senses as well as by the organization of such perceptions in thought. Here, in short, are two distinct psychic systems, which seem to meet in the no-man's-land of the preconscious. One seems to produce "dream" thoughts that are "perfectly rational" and "of no less validity than normal thinking"; the other is an apparently chaotic, bewildering, and irrational system capable of providing an unlimited supply of images from the furthest recesses of the mind.

To understand this conflict, or merging of opposites, Freud went back to his studies in hysteria. In his patients, he said, "we come across a series of perfectly rational thoughts, equal in validity to our conscious thoughts, but to begin with we know nothing of their existence in this form and we can only reconstruct them subsequently.... We accordingly borrow the following thesis from the theory of hysteria: *a normal train of thought is only submitted to abnormal psychical treatment of the sort we have been describing if an unconscious wish, derived from infancy and in a state of repression, has been transferred on to it.*" What Freud was suggesting here is that current impressions, from the thoughts and experience of everyday life, are woven into dreams, where they serve the purpose of an unconscious and emotionally charged wish.

In his play *Six Characters in Search of an Author*, Pirandello poses the problem of six people, conceived by the mind of a dead playwright who was unable to work out their drama to its conclusion before his death. They are doomed to wander in a kind of theatrical limbo, trying to come to life and bring their tragedy to a climax—and they search for an author and a set of actors who can serve their end, to allow them to resolve their hatreds and passions once and for all and release them from their endless and repetitive cycle.

The unresolved conflicts and the ungratified impulses of infancy, Freud was arguing, similarly wander through the human mind, always seeking material drawn from contemporary life in which they can live again, look once more for the denied gratification, and even influence our waking behavior.

In extreme cases, they can come to dominate our lives: the result is mental illness, neurotic symptoms, delusions, and hallucinations. But in all of this, the dream reveals what we have been and what we have wanted to be. "For dreams are derived from the past in every sense. Nevertheless, the ancient belief that dreams foretell the future is not wholly devoid of truth. By picturing our wishes as fulfilled, dreams are after all leading us into the future. But this future, which the dreamer pictures as the present, has been molded by his indestructible wish into a perfect likeness of the past."

7 The dream debate

Between 1900 and 1914, educated Europeans became aware that new ideas about psychology were being developed in Vienna and to a lesser extent in Zurich. A group of doctors calling themselves "psychoanalysts" were experimenting with new methods of treating mental disorders and advancing new theories about the way in which the hidden processes of the mind affected attitudes and behavior. In particular, they were insisting (as many had believed in antiquity) that dreams not only contained important clues to the unknown but were also a means of healing the sick. Working on the very frontiers of medical knowledge, they were attempting to draw sketch maps of what might lie beyond; confronted by the skepticism and hostility of more conventional colleagues, they had to endure the resentment that is often directed at those who challenge established opinions.

Their new conceptions of human behavior helped to confirm their conviction that they were moving in the right direction. For just as Freud's work showed that the conscious mind resists the pressure of uncomfortable ideas, so the objections of other physicians and psychologists indicated that the pioneer psychoanalysts were exposing aspects of the human personality that it would be more comfortable to ignore. For no one likes to have his secret wishes revealed, or to be told that beneath apparently orderly adult behavior there lurk unresolved sexual conflicts, or even infantile incestuous aspirations.

Jung attached special importance to the circle as a symbol of psychic integration, and discerned such "mandala" designs (above, a Tibetan mandala) in dreams, myths, art, and architecture. The emergence of these symbols during the course of therapy was for him a sign of recovery, indicating that the patient was beginning to move toward an integrated personality. Another example, similar to this one, is to be found on page 281.

177

Just when psychoanalysis was coming to be reluctantly accepted as a means of treating the mentally disturbed, the small group of pioneer psychoanalysts was increasingly disrupted by internal disagreements. For all of them Freud's work was the point of departure; and for all of them Freud was a teacher as well as a colleague. Yet his authority, on matters of theory as well as practice, was challenged almost from the outset. By 1914 several of Freud's closest collaborators—including Carl Gustav Jung, whom he had regarded as the "crown prince" of the psychoanalytic movement—had broken away in order to set up dissenting schools of therapeutic psychology. Jung was the most important; but Alfred Adler, Wilhelm Stekel, Otto Rank, and other early associates of Freud had all differed with him profoundly and had formulated new versions of what was, originally, classified simply as psychoanalysis. Personal difficulties between Freud and these men undoubtedly played some part in the rift that had occurred; but the differences of opinion about Freud's theories went deeper than this. In disagreeing with Freud's view of the human mind, and of the best ways of treating its derangements, they necessarily came to conflicting conclusions about the nature and significance of dreaming.

None of the dissenters challenged Freud's fundamental assumption that dreams were meaningful psychic phenomena; but all of them disputed to some extent the meaning he ascribed to dreams and the techniques he employed to interpret them. Some were dissatisfied with the emphasis he placed on the element of wish-fulfillment; some with his implication that dreams are essentially neurotic symptoms, reflecting archaic memories and experiences that the individual has been unable to integrate into his adult personality; some (notably Jung) criticized his emphasis on the sexual component of the unconscious. Almost all of them in one way or another challenged his attitude toward dreams.

Freud had set great store by his distinction between the manifest and the latent dream, and had emphasized that all previous dream interpretation had mistakenly concentrated on the manifest dream. The heretical Freudians, however, were unwilling to abandon entirely the dream in its manifest form. To them it seemed that Freud had first reaffirmed the importance of dreaming and then cut the ground from under his own feet by arguing that dreams were significant only as clues to something else, that they were merely the visible part of a psychic process that could be inferred but not directly observed. Freud, in short, had moved away from an interest in dream phenomena to a preoccupation with the forces that produced dreams. Almost all those who came into dispute with him attached much more value than he did to the dream itself—its structure, its symbolism, its contents, and its overall "message" in relation to the dreamer's personality and problems.

Such dissent led rapidly and inevitably to different types of dream interpretation, so that while Freud and his followers were evolving the "Freudian" style of interpretation, adding detail to the symbolism of the dream and refinement to the techniques of using it in therapy, Jung, Stekel, Rank, and Adler were beginning to develop quite different theories of interpretation. This diversity of opinions led, for obvious reasons, to such situations as that described by Stekel in his book *The Interpretation of Dreams*. Stekel was visited by a young doctor (ostensibly a patient) who was trying to make a comparative study of psychoanalysts by asking several of them in turn to interpret the same dream. Naturally, each one offered a different reading of the dream. Stekel adds: "He cherished the idea of publishing a book which would prove to all and sundry how arbitrary and undependable is the art of dream interpretation." The book, it seems, never appeared. But precisely this line of criticism has been employed against all forms of dream interpretation—that it is arbitrary and inconsistent, and therefore valueless.

As a matter of fact, the interpretations offered by different schools of psychotherapy often vary less in substance than might be imagined from any summary of their theoretical differences. Only by a detailed comparison of many interpretations, together with case studies of the patients producing the dreams, would anyone be able to estimate just how widely the substance of the interpretations does differ, or how much these differences really matter. In terms of therapeutic practice—as we shall see in the next chapter—the detailed differences in interpretative techniques, or in the methods generally employed in psychotherapy, appear less important than would seem sometimes to be suggested by the fierce controversies about theoretical assumptions. But before we can consider the significance of dream interpretation in

The founders of psychoanalysis at a conference in Weimar, Germany, in 1911. Among them are (1) Otto Rank, (2) Eugen Bleuler, (3) Sigmund Freud, (4) C. G. Jung, (5) Ernest Jones, and (6) Wilhelm Stekel.

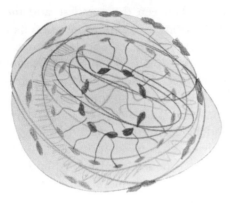

For Jung the circle (or mandala) was the symbol of psychic integration and in this patient's painting the flower emphasizes the theme of recovery, though the scribble suggests continuing destructive feelings. A Freudian, however, would regard the recurring lip motif as oral symbolism.

Freud thought such symbols as the serpent and the lighthouse were essentially sexual. But Jung regarded them as "healing" symbols—the serpent symbolizes medicine and the lighthouse gives a guiding light over the stormy sea of life. The cross is a sign that the patient feels himself to be at a crucial point in his development.

dealing with mental disorders—or indeed in everyday life—it is necessary to understand what some of Freud's distinguished contemporaries made of the dream world to which he had introduced them.

Of these, Jung was undoubtedly the most important, as regards both his original contribution to psychotherapy and his dream studies. For Jung, even before he had read Freud or met him, which he did in Vienna in 1907, had moved independently toward the new methods of treating mental illness. He always regarded dreams as a vital aspect of the human psyche and as an essential part of its balancing mechanism. In Jung's view the dream was not a neurotic symptom, and it was a mistake to think that it could be understood simply in terms of psychopathology. It was as necessary and as valuable to the functioning of the mind of the so-called "normal" person as it was to the mentally disturbed. And as it was an integral part of the emotional life of every individual it could not be explained or dealt with simply as a messenger of one or two powerful instinctive impulses. In a passage criticizing Freud's arguments Jung wrote:

"Just as human life as such is not limited to this or that basic instinct but is built up of a multiplicity of instincts, needs ... and physical and psychic conditioning factors, so dreams cannot be explained from this or that element, however attractively simple such an explanation may seem ... no simple theory of instincts will ever be capable of comprehending that powerful and mysterious thing, the human psyche, nor yet the dream which is its expression.... It is true that there are dreams which embody suppressed wishes and fears, but what is there which the dream cannot on occasion embody? Dreams may give expression to ineluctable truths, to philosophical pronouncements, illusions, wild fantasies, . . . anticipations, irrational experiences, even telepathic visions, and heaven knows what besides."

In these words Jung was offering a view of dreams that was in marked contrast to Freud's—more comprehensive, more elusive, one might say more metaphysical, since Jung's emphasis was as much on man's "spiritual" orientation as on his organic impulses or his social environment. He saw dreaming as one of the ways in which man tried to confront and explain the mystery of his life and the meaning of his existence, as well as a recapitulation of the unsolved problems of his past. He saw the moment at which the dream occurred as the meeting point between the future and the past, between all that an individual might be and all that he had been.

This view has been described as Jung's "respectful" attitude toward dreams. He himself wrote:

"I have no theory about dreams; I do not know how dreams arise. I am altogether in doubt as to whether my way of handling dreams even deserves the name 'method.' I share all my readers' prejudices against dream interpretation as being the quintessence of uncertainty and arbitrariness. But, on the other hand, I know that if we meditate on a dream sufficiently long and thoroughly—if we take it about with us and turn it over and over—something almost always comes of it. This something is not of a kind that means we can boast of its scientific nature or rationalize it, but it is a practical and important hint which shows the patient in what direction the unconscious is leading him."

This idea of direction—what Jung called the "prospective" aspect of the dream—was not wholly absent in Freud's theory; but Jung put special emphasis on it because he believed that the unconscious embodied a larger and more far-reaching view of a person's true situation in life than the conscious mind. It can draw on more data and is better able to arrange our perceptions, thoughts, and feelings together in new and unexpected combinations than the concentrated and limited form of thought that we consciously employ when we are awake. The dream was for Jung an "involuntary psychic process not controlled by the conscious outlook." It could therefore reflect the wide range of unconscious mental activities, all the permutations of fantasy that go on within us whether we are asleep or awake, and "present the subjective state as it really is. It has no respect," said Jung, "for my conjectures or for the patient's view as to how things should be, but simply tells *how the matter stands.*"

An example that Jung often cited concerned a woman whose dreams expressed the difficulties she was about to encounter with three psychoanalysts whom she was to consult. Each of the following dreams occurred at the moment when she began treatment.

The dream that coincided with her first visit to the first analyst was described in these words: "I must cross the frontier to the next country, but no one can tell me where the boundary lies, and I cannot find it." The analyst concluded from this dream that the patient unconsciously realized he could give her little help, and he therefore referred her to a colleague. To the second doctor the patient reported a second dream: "I must cross the frontier. It is a black night, and I cannot find the customs house. After a long search, I notice a small light far away and suppose that the frontier lies over there. But in order to reach it, I must cross a valley and go through a dark wood, in which I lose my sense of direction. Then I notice that someone is with me. This person suddenly clings to me like a madman and I awake in terror."

Once again the treatment had to be broken off because of the patient's failure to make progress and her marked disorientation—due, Jung suggested, to her unconscious identification of the analyst with the stranger in her dream, the person who suddenly clung to her like a madman. Finally the woman came to Jung as a patient. Again she described a dream, but this time with marked differences: "I must cross a frontier, or rather, I have already crossed it, and find myself in a Swiss customs house. I have only a handbag, and believe that I have nothing to declare. But the customs official dives into my bag and, to my astonishment, pulls out two full-sized mattresses."

Jung insisted that the symbolism of crossing the frontier in all three dreams was obvious. It was the decisive step that indicated the patient's will to recover. The customs house and the customs official were equally clear representations of the analytical situation and the analyst. The mattresses, Jung suggested, referred to a marriage that the patient was at first unwilling to contract and only entered into after overcoming a severe resistance during her analysis with him. But the relevance of these three dreams to Jung's essential hypothesis is that through them the patient was anticipating the difficulties she would meet with each of the doctors to whom she went for treatment.

Dreams, for Jung, were one way in which the unconscious bridges the gap between an individual's past and his future. This is one clue to his conception of the psyche. He saw the psychic constitution of man as a self-balancing system that attempts to establish an equilibrium in the same way as the body maintains a physical balance with built-in devices for the control of temperature, circulation, glandular activity, ingestion, digestion, and excretion. The dream, therefore, also has a *compensating* function, focusing attention on aspects of a situation—or of a personality—that have been overlooked or undervalued in waking life. Just as we sweat when we become too hot, or pant when we run, so the unconscious has to compensate for the excesses of consciousness. This process occurs at all levels, from the trivial to the profound. The man who has been concentrating on a problem during the day may find in his dream that his attention is drawn to some aspects of the problem he had neglected, and—as in the "problem-solving" dreams we considered

Jung believed that in dreams the individual is compensated for the frustrations of everyday life, and that these fantasies reveal what he would truly like to be. An example of this process comes from the British film *Billy Liar*, in which a young man escapes from his dreary surroundings into a fantasy world where he plays many dominant roles—such as the leader of a liberating army and a great lover.

earlier—come forward in the dream or next day with a solution that had previously evaded him. Or he may find that his dream is about some domestic or emotional matter that he had put out of his mind.

It is this kind of compensation (which bears resemblances to wish-fulfillment, but is more closely linked to present reality than to infantile aspirations) that leads, for instance, to the man who feels small and inferior dreaming of his meeting Napoleon or the queen of England, or playing some heroic role—a concept to which Adler also attached great importance. Or it might indicate the true feelings of one person about another person. Jung described the case of a young man who dreamed that his father was a drunkard. The father's behavior in real life was exemplary, but being something of a paragon, he made his son feel unworthy and cramped his emotional development. Jung suggested that the dream seemed to be saying to the son: "He is not so marvelous after all, and can behave in a quite irresponsible manner. So there is no need for you to have such a feeling of inferiority."

Conversely, a person whose worth we normally underrate may be elevated in a dream. A man who took his wife very much for granted, and was consciously unaware of all she did to make his life pleasant and easy, dreamed of being caught in a heavy sea and being buoyed up and carried to shore by a sturdy woman lifeguard. Similar compensating feelings can be found, for example, in the case of the timid man who was unable to make advances

C. G. Jung used the word "anima" to describe the feminine component within every man—the hidden aspect of male personality that can be a guiding force in the search for self-fulfillment, or a source of negative impulses. Left: an engraving by the French artist Gustave Doré (1833-83) of the Sleeping Beauty—a fairy tale which expresses the awakening of the capacities for love. The "animus," or the masculine aspect of feminine personality, often appears in dreams or folk-myths as an attractive but rather disreputable figure —such as (right) the reckless and vain highwayman Macheath in *The Beggar's Opera* by the 18th-century poet John Gay. In the search for an integrated personality a woman must come to terms with this disregarded component of her psyche.

to women, but dreamed of nights in a harem of his own; or among persons of gentle disposition who have dreams that reveal a capacity for cruelty.

In the idea of compensation Jung was providing a possible explanation of the traditional belief that events in dreams run contrary to their meaning. True, he did not offer quite the same interpretation of these apparent contradictions, but he was describing a dream characteristic long known to be significant. He also carried this idea of opposites (complementarity) in dreams much further. For in this, as in much else, his thinking was more dialectical than Freud's—a fact that makes it more difficult both to expound and to comprehend his ideas. He believed that the person who was in waking life an "extravert"—the term was coined by him to describe the outgoing, sociable type of personality—was unconsciously introverted; and vice versa. The individual whose external relations were governed by his sensations was, in his unconscious, a deeply feeling person, though such feelings remained beyond the direct access of consciousness; while a highly intellectualized man concealed within himself a profoundly intuitive, although unconscious, manner of evaluating his life.

Though Jung's overall psychological theory is too complex to describe in detail, it is important to note two further aspects of it. The first was Jung's belief that in every man there is a feminine component—the *anima*—and in every woman there is an equivalent element of masculinity—the *animus*. It

Jung believed that each man presents to the world the aspects of his personality that he thinks attractive. He called this the "persona." At the same time, he conceals his "shadow"—the negative and unacceptable aspects of himself. In Oscar Wilde's story *The Picture of Dorian Gray* (1891), a handsome young man is driven to fearful deeds by the destructive forces within him. In this scene, from a British film of Wilde's story, Dorian Gray sees his own "shadow" in a painting.

is from these converse aspects of identity that a wealth of symbols arises, from the angel-like guardian female figure that appears in many myths and dreams, to the wise old man, the tutelary image of masculine wisdom. Each individual, moreover, possesses what Jung called the *persona*, the face that he presents to the world, and wishes others to see. Composed of all the roles a man plays in his relations with others, it is a protective mask that hides the weaknesses or personal traits he does not wish to be recognized—even by himself. The opposite of the *persona* is the *shadow*, that part of the personality that is "the devil within us," the suppressed and unacceptable aspects of the personality, which are not consciously admitted. Thus the shadow of the mild-mannered man may be aggressive and destructive while that of the bully will probably be timid and anxious. It is our "shadow" qualities that we attribute to others, because we cannot accept them in ourselves. We "project" them and fail to recognize, as Jung once put it, that it is our own face that peers back at us. In dreams, "shadow" qualities usually appear as characteristics of persons of the same sex whereas the symbolic aspects of the *anima* in a man are always associated with female figures and the *animus* in women with male figures.

It may seem that this description of the components of the psyche does not provide much direct help in the interpretation of dreams and still less perhaps in the treatment of mental illness. Yet to begin to appreciate the complex forms of dream interpretation that Jung developed after his breach with Freud, and the ever-widening distance between their two conceptions of the nature and role of dreams, it is necessary to understand the main conceptions Jung employed until his death in 1961.

To Jung, the unconscious was the larger aspect of the self, and a source of wisdom equal to or even greater than anything found in consciousness. From this source, he wrote, come "dream-images and thought-associations that we cannot create with conscious intention. They develop spontaneously . . . hence they represent a mental activity that is withdrawn from voluntary direction. Essentially, therefore, the dream is a highly objective and, in a sense, natural product of the psyche. Accordingly, we might with reason expect from it some indications, or suggestions at least, about the fundamental tendencies of the psychic process." And the more an individual could "tune in" to the signals of the unconscious, the more integrated his personality, the less the conflicts that might disturb his mental equilibrium, and the more fully he could realize all his potentialities and live a rich and mature life.

How could such conceptions be applied to the practice of dream interpretation? Jung, in the anthropomorphic terms that he often used to describe psychological phenomena (just as Freud frequently introduced analogies and figures of speech from physics and anatomy), once put his view of dreams in a few sentences. "Within each of us," he said, "there is another we do not know. He speaks to us in dreams and tells us how differently *he* sees us from how *we* see ourselves. When we find ourselves in an insolubly difficult situation, this stranger in us can sometimes show us a light which is more suited than anything else to change our attitude fundamentally; namely, just that attitude which had led us into the difficult situation." The problem, however, is to understand what that "stranger" is saying, to trace the connection between his message (symbolically phrased) and the reality of the "difficult situation."

The first and most important assumption that Jung made was that the dream *as it stands* is meaningful, and is not, as Freud argued, a disguise that conceals its "true" meaning.

"There is no doubt that neurotics hide disagreeable things, probably just as much as normal people do. But it is a serious question whether this category can be applied to such a normal and world-wide phenomenon as the dream. I am doubtful whether we can assume that the dream is something else than it appears to be. I am rather inclined to quote another Jewish authority, the Talmud, which says: 'The dream is its own interpretation.' In other words, I take the dream for granted. The dream is such a difficult and intricate subject that I do not dare to make any assumptions about its possible cunning. The dream is a natural event, and there is no reason under the sun why we should assume that it is a crafty device to lead us astray.

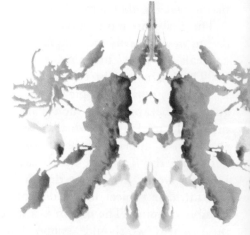

Two ways of eliciting free associations—
one ancient, one modern. Gazing into a
clear object, like the crystal ball (above),
induces visual images that a fortune
teller will relate to his client's life.
The Rorschach test (right)—named for the
Swiss psychiatrist Hermann Rorschach
(1884-1922)—is a psychological test in
which a subject is asked to describe what
he sees in different inkblot designs.

The dream occurs when consciousness and will are to a great extent extinguished. It seems to be a natural product which is also found in people who are not neurotic. Moreover, we know so little about the psychology of the dream process that we must be more than careful when we introduce elements foreign to the dream itself into the interpretation."

Two important conclusions follow from this assumption. The first is that every dream is unique to the dreamer, and that no mechanical technique of interpretation will serve to discover its meaning—even though common or universal symbols may appear in it. The second is that to break up the dream into fragments, and pursue the "free" associations to each fragment will lead away from the dream itself. Such trains of thought may well, as Freud believed, point to what lies behind the dream; the hidden impulse and the way it has been distorted can then be revealed. But, Jung insisted, such a technique tells us nothing about the dream as such—and to reach hidden impulses or complexes other methods will serve just as well. Free association can begin with a crystal ball, a postage stamp, or a Rorschach projection test, and disclose just as much about the traits that a person wishes to conceal. But if that is the case, why bother about the dream at all? Thus, for Jung, it was essential to keep returning to the actual dream, working over it as a whole and also in detail, to puzzle out a meaning from its form as well as its contents, to recognize the richness and complexity of each symbolic image.

Jung also believed strongly that dreams are best understood in series rather than in isolation. Over a number of dreams, certain themes will recur, underlining a point by repetition; certain omissions or "blind spots" will equally become apparent; above all, later dreams will often include comments on those preceding them or even upon the interpretations offered—as if the unconscious is saying, "No, you have not understood the point, so I will show you again in a different way." Finally, for the analyst or the dreamer to understand the dream images fully, a wide knowledge is required of the symbolism of the myth as well as of the dream—for Jung believed that both sprang from deep in the human unconscious and were attempts to express the same fundamental ideas. The classical story of Sisyphus, for instance, is of a man who is doomed to perform the same task over and over again, only to be confronted each time by failure. This idea can occur in a myriad of ways in the dreams of people who have never heard of Sisyphus. Similarly, fairy or folk tales seem to be a way of making points so common to human experience that we refer to them in dreams in all sorts of oblique and condensed forms.

Let us now consider an example of the way in which Jung's interpretation of dreams differed from that of Freud. Here is a dream: "I was going up a flight of stairs with my mother and sister. When we reached the top I was told that my sister was going to have a child."

From what we have already seen of Freudian techniques, it is easy to interpret this dream in a Freudian sense. To go up a flight of stairs in a dream is, according to Freud, a "censored" version of sexual intercourse. The reference to the mother and sister is, in the same way, the distortion by the censor of an incestuous wish. The expected child could be either a form of displacement—the sexual aspiration being shifted from the mother to the sister—or an expression of brother-sister sexuality.

Yet, Jung remarks, "if I say that the stairs are a symbol for the sexual act, whence do I obtain the right to regard the mother, the sister, and the child as concrete, that is, as not symbolic?" Perhaps the whole dream, which was that of a young man who had finished his studies but was unable to choose an occupation, should be treated differently—bearing in mind that the young man had homosexual inclinations.

On his associations to his mother the young man reported: "I have not seen her for a long time, a very long time. I really ought to reproach myself for this. It is wrong of me to neglect her so." On this Jung comments that "mother" in this dream context stands for something that had been inexcusably neglected. He then asked the young man what it was that was actually so neglected, and he replied, with considerable embarrassment, "My work."

Referring to his sister the young man said: "It is years since I have seen her. I long to see her again. Whenever I think of her I recall the time when I took leave of her. I kissed her with real affection; and at that moment I understood for the first time what love for a woman can mean." Jung thought that it was "at once clear to the patient that his sister represents 'love for woman'."

The stairs had a fairly straightforward association: "Climbing upward; getting to the top; making a success of life; being grown up; being great;" and the idea of the child led to the association: "New born; a revival; a regeneration; to become a new man."

"One has only to hear this material," Jung remarks, "in order to understand at once that the patient's dream is not so much the fulfillment of infantile desires, as it is the expression of biological duties which he has hitherto neglected because of his infantilism. Biological justice, which is inexorable, sometimes compels the human being to atone in his dreams for the duties which he has neglected in real life."

This relatively simple example illustrates the contrasting assumptions and conclusions of Freud and Jung, but it is not meant to suggest that either is "correct." The gap between the two becomes wider once the concept of the "collective unconscious" is introduced. Jung believed that at a deeper level of the psyche than the personal unconscious—which contained the individual's specific experience and his unique though often hidden characteristics—lay another part of it which contained elements common to all men, the universal psychic inheritance of the human race. Within the collective unconscious (the most disputed of all Jung's propositions) lies the wisdom, the accumulated history, the common predispositions of man, the source of his highest aspirations and his lowest propensities. It is this aspect of the psyche that concerns itself with the ultimates of existence, birth, life and death, the conflicts of growing up to a mature independence (which Jung calls the "individuation" process), hunger and heroism, marriage and murder. Each of us contains a predisposition to express these indescribable experiences in a symbolic form, because their very nature defies precise definition or articulation. These symbolic patterns, common to all men, are charged with great power and are capable of evoking images that transcend the limitations of language. Jung called these universal symbols "archetypes." Such symbols play a vital energizing part in the formation of dreams and an equally vital part of dream interpretation consists in identifying them.

In order to show how Jung looked for archetypes in a dream, let us take an abbreviated case. It is an interesting example because it also illustrates a phenomenon that often appears in dream interpretation—the "prodromic" dream that seems to point to a physical illness as yet undiagnosed. The dreamer was a girl of 17 who suffered from a muscular inhibition. Doctors had disagreed about the cause of her condition and, as one of them thought it might be a case of hysteria, she was referred to Jung. He believed that the girl might have an organic disease, but as she also showed some hysterical symptoms

Like dreams, folk-tales often contain symbolic material. Tom Thumb (right, an etching by George Cruickshank) may be seen as symbolizing male potency—the thumb often appears in dreams as a phallic symbol. The character of Cinderella, below expresses the hidden feminine potential.

he asked if she dreamed. "Yes, I have terrible dreams," she said. "Just recently I dreamed I was coming home at night. Everything is as quiet as death. The door into the living room is half open, and I see my mother hanging from the chandelier and swinging to and fro in a cold wind that blows in through the open windows. At another time I dreamed that a terrible noise breaks out in the house at night. I go to see what has happened, and find that a frightened horse is tearing through the rooms. At last it finds the door into the hall, and jumps through the hall window from the fourth floor down into the street. I was terrified to see it lying below, all mangled."

How did Jung explain the symbolism underlying these two dreams, both concerned with the theme of death? It is best to let him offer his own explanation: "We must . . . look more closely into the meaning of the outstanding symbols 'mother' and 'horse.' The figures must be equivalent one to the other, for they both do the same thing: they commit suicide. The mother symbol is archetypal and refers to a place of origin, to nature, that which passively creates, hence to substance and matter, to material nature, the lower body (womb), and the vegetative functions. It connotes also the unconscious, natural, and instinctive life, the physiological realm, the body in which we dwell or are contained, for the 'mother' is also a vessel, the hollow form (uterus) that carries and nourishes, and it thus stands for the foundation of consciousness. Being within something or contained suggests darkness, the nocturnal, a state of anxiety. With these allusions I am presenting the idea of the mother in many of its mythological and etymological formations. I am also giving an important part of the *yin* concept of Chinese philosophy. All this is dream content, but it is not something which the seventeen-year-old girl has acquired in her individual existence; it is rather a bequest from the past. On the one hand, it has been kept alive by the language, and on the other hand, it is inherited with the structure of the psyche and is therefore to be found at all times and among all peoples."

This passage is difficult to understand at first glance; it is extremely characteristic, however, of Jung's style and ideas. For this reason it deserves to be read again with special care. Few other passages in Jung's voluminous writings demonstrate both his faults (forced and extended interpretation) and his virtues (depth and flexibility of thought) so strikingly. Much of what is hinted at can be comprehensible only to someone familiar with Jung's writings, with mythology, and with Chinese philosophy. Jungian dream interpretation is one of the most erudite exercises in psychology, though it is precisely the need for this erudition that is challenged by Jung's critics.

This passage must raise a number of questions in the mind of anyone to whom Jung's ideas are unfamiliar. How, for instance, did Jung give the girl's dream a meaningful interpretation.

"The familiar word 'mother' refers apparently to the best-known of mothers in particular—to 'my mother.' But the mother symbol points to a darker

The horse symbolizes powerful instinctual feelings. The sea is often a symbol of the unconscious from which such feelings emerge. In the painting, which resembles a dream situation, a woman patient shows herself beginning, with reluctance, to turn towards previously unrecognized emotions.

meaning which eludes conceptual formulation and can only be vaguely apprehended as the hidden, nature-bound life of the body. Yet even this expression is too narrow and excludes too many side meanings. The psychic reality which underlies this symbol is so inconceivably complex that we can only discern it from afar off, and then but very dimly. It is such realities that call for symbolic expression.

"If we apply our findings to the dream, its meaning will be: the unconscious life destroys itself. That is the dream's message to the conscious mind of the dreamer and to everyone who has ears to hear.

" 'Horse' is an archetype that is widely current in mythology and folklore. As an animal it represents the non-human psyche, the sub-human, animal side, and therefore the unconscious. That is why the horse in folklore sometimes sees visions, hears voices, and speaks. As a beast of burden it is closely related to the mother-archetype; the Valkyries bear the dead hero to Valhalla and the Trojan horse encloses the Greeks. As an animal lower than man it represents the lower part of the body and the animal drives that take their rise from there. The horse is dynamic power and a means of locomotion; it carries one away like a surge or instinct. It is subject to panics like all instinctive creatures which lack higher consciousness. Also it has to do with sorcery and magic spells, especially the black, night horse which heralds death.

"It is evident, then, that 'horse' is the equivalent of 'mother' with a slight shift of meaning. The mother stands for life at its origin and the horse for the merely animal life of the body. If we apply this meaning to the dream it says: 'the animal life destroys itself'."

Both dreams, Jung concluded, make the same assertion but, as is usually the case, the second is more specific. The peculiar subtlety of the dream is brought out in both instances. There is no mention of the dreamer's death.

"It is notorious that one often dreams of one's own death but that it is no serious matter. When it is really a question of death, the dream speaks another language." Both these dreams, Jung concluded, pointed toward an organic and fatal disease in the young girl.

A well-known English follower of Jung, Dr. H. G. Baynes, once advanced an objection to Freud's theory that the true content of the dream is disguised. The argument was similar, he said, to that of the English visitor to Paris who assumed that the Parisians were talking gibberish in order to make a fool of him. Anyone unfamiliar with the larger framework of Jung's ideas might conclude from the interpretation of the young girl's dream that the language of the dream is unintelligible to anyone except a professional ethnographer and cultural historian. And it is true that almost any passage in Jung's writings is full of abstruse scholarship, just as his dream interpretations seem to go far beyond normal experience into concepts that his readers—let alone an ordinary dreamer—may feel they are meeting for the first time.

In practice, Jung's attitude to dreams was more down-to-earth than his writings suggest, for his interpretations were always based on one simple question: what is the *purpose* of the dream? His own assumption was that it was a frank, spontaneous, and profoundly informed statement of some current problem or situation, of special authority because it was independent of conscious control. In the unknown regions of the mind, from which dreams well up, lay the source of true individuality, the forces that guide man's growth toward self-realization. Part biological, part psychic, these regions tend toward integration, toward the fulfillment of the original promise of the whole personality.

The circumstances in which we live, however, force us to deny much of that original promise, to make compromises, and to distort our true nature. To the extent that we deny this essential humanity within each of us, we deny the meaning of our own lives; and it is from such denials that neurosis springs. This is where Jung's view of the determining power of infantile experience differed so strongly from Freud's. He agreed that it was valuable to search for the childhood origins of neurosis, but insisted that the objective was to discover what had been lost—that the purpose of analysis was to dig up buried treasure, rather than to purge oneself of past sexual or other instinctive frustrations.

Thus, for Jung, a dream always points forward to what is to be done to redirect life into the proper path toward maturity and fulfillment. The dream may stress "objective" elements, as when the images in it signify an actual object or person and reveal the dreamer's relationship to it or him. Alternatively, it may emphasize "subjective" aspects, as when the dream figures are personifications of feelings or characteristics of the dreamer himself. But invariably it expresses a tendency to redress an imbalance in the dreamer's life or to correct an error of consciousness.

194

Jung regarded the dream as the end product of many unconscious processes. It expresses ideas from the non-conscious experience of life that flows on, whether we are asleep or awake, and provides its own commentaries on that limited segment of our existence which, in our over-evaluation of consciousness, we consider to be the major part. It is, one might say, consciousness that interrupts that state we call dreaming—or depresses it to the level of reverie and fantasy in waking life—rather than dreaming that is the temporary relapse from normal reason.

This point of view (which has far-reaching philosophical as well as physiological implications) was also advanced by Henri Bergson in his book *Dreams*. "You ask me what it is I do when I dream? I will tell you what you do when you are awake. You take me, the me of dreams, me the totality of your past, and you force me, by making me smaller and smaller, to fit into the little circle that you trace around your present action. That is what it is to be awake. That is what it is to live the normal psychical life. It is to battle. It is to will. As for the dream, have you really any need that I should explain it? It is the state into which you naturally fall when you let yourself go, when you no longer have the power to concentrate yourself upon a single point, when you have ceased to will, for willing and waking are one and the same thing."

It was such a sense of the immensity of the psyche as a whole—of the extent and power of the unconscious as against consciousness—that led Jung to believe that behind conscious thought lay the land of dreams in which the pattern of one's thoughts, though non-verbal, was nonetheless meaningful; that this pattern was dominated by feeling, rather than intellect and the formal logic of consciousness; and that the language in which it was expressed was the richer-than-words language of imagery. The dream is experienced only by the dreamer, and can be only inadequately, and often with difficulty, articulated by him—in the first place to himself and then to others. But if one is aware of its symbols, one can understand such language by empathy as much as by formal understanding and analysis.

This intuitive approach to dreams (which Freud himself employed but distrusted because it seemed to hinder his attempt to establish psychoanalysis as a scientific discipline) plays a vital role when one moves from dream theory to the actual use of dreams in psychoanalysis. But because this approach cannot be exactly defined and depends so much on the subjective aspects of the relationship between the analyst and the patient, it cannot be reduced to a neat formula. It is, indeed, one of the chief obstacles to any attempt at scientific verification of psychoanalytic techniques.

If, however, one takes the manifest dream as a significant set of images, intuition can clearly be assigned a larger role than if one assumes—as did Freud—that the images are merely a facade. To Freud, such interest in the presented images was "a simple misunderstanding," but it was a misunder-

standing that was important enough to separate him from such distinguished collaborators as Silberer, Maeder, Adler, and Stekel, as well as Jung. Each of these psychologists had his own views about the interpretation of dreams, but each of them agreed that in some way the dream *in the form it appears* has a definite purpose. This, as we have already seen, was Jung's view. For Adler the dream was "a tentative feeler toward the future"; for Stekel it was "the signpost which shows the way to the life-conflict"; for Maeder, dreams were "a preparatory exercise for the ensuing activity of waking life. They seek and reach attempts at solutions of current conflicts."

Alfred Adler, founder of the school of Individual Psychology, and a colleague of Freud's in Vienna, believed strongly that the dream had such an anticipatory function. It was, he said, "a dress-rehearsal for life," in which the dreamer reveals his hopes, fears, and plans for the future. The thought processes underlying such planning—review of the evidence, a testing of the evidence in the light of past experience, and the formulation of a number of possible courses of action—do not greatly differ whether one is asleep or awake. The difference lies in the fact that the dream presents in symbolic form the problems, and the evidence relating to them, that the individual neglects in waking life because they are too threatening or because he does not want to face their practical consequences. Thus, like Jung, Adler saw the dream as a compensation for the selective partiality of consciousness. Like Freud too, he saw the distortion of the dream as a protective device— though for him it protected the dreamer's ego against life situations, while for Freud the distortion was the work of the moral censor who refused to pass the raw instinctive impulses of infancy.

Adler believed that his patients came to him because they were unable to cope with the conflicts of everyday life, because the patient's "life-style"

An individual who suffers from personal disabilities will, Alfred Adler suggested, try to offset them by a different form of achievement. Napoleon's drive to power was thus a compensation for his short stature, Beethoven's musical genius made up for his deafness and other physical defects, while Byron's flights of poetic fantasy might have been due to his attempt to overcome the handicap of a club foot.

did not fit his actual situation, and he therefore suffered from a sense of inferiority. In attempting to overcome this inferiority, which might arise from some psychic or organic defect—Napoleon's short stature, Byron's clubfoot, and Beethoven's deafness are examples of this—the patient would overcompensate, in behavior, attitude, neurotic symptoms, and dreams. Every individual has a wish for power, that, if obstructed, turns his need for self-assertion into neurotic maladjustment. Thus, in his dreams, he continually experiments with situations that compensate for his failures or humiliations, picturing himself as successful or admired. Where, in childhood, the inevitable feelings of smallness and inferiority are used by the infant to evade the challenges of growing up, the adult will develop an inferiority complex that prevents him from realizing the goals toward which his personality should move if it is to achieve full maturity. It is significant that Adler, who placed much greater emphasis on the influence of the social setting than was allotted to it by orthodox Freudians or the Zurich school led by Jung and Maeder, believed that psychotherapy was a matter more of building up a patient's capacity for living a full life than of analyzing the past in order to discharge repressed tensions. He accordingly attached much less importance to dreams as a technique of analysis, believing that they merely revealed what could in any case be deduced from the patient's conscious attitudes and behavior.

Wilhelm Stekel broke with Freud in 1912, primarily because he attached so much importance to dreams that he thought the analyst should not allow the patient to reach the stage of partial interpretation, but should "intervene" by offering his own reading of the patient's dreams. This technique he called "active psychoanalysis," and argued that it produced quicker and more effective treatment than the drawn-out process of Freudian analysis. Stekel was thus reverting to the oldest form of dream interpretation, that of antiquity,

This painting by a patient in an English mental hospital dramatically emphasizes three "archetypal" motifs—the tree, the serpent, and the egg—which Jung believed symbolized an individual's potential for growth.

in which the skilled interpreter revealed to the unperceptive dreamer the significance of his dream. "I am able," Stekel wrote, "from the manifest content to draw important inferences as to the secret thoughts of the dreamer, and I hope that in a few years I shall do better still." The note of self-satisfaction in this statement is echoed elsewhere in Stekel's work. He was convinced, for instance, that the patient always sought to deceive his analyst, and much of his book—to which he gave the same title as Freud's work, *The Interpretation of Dreams*—is devoted to case histories that give the impression that Stekel wished to show his superiority to his patients and to other analysts. The patient, one sometimes feels, was a passive creature whose task it was to produce dreams which Stekel's talent alone could unravel. The speed with which he worked enabled him to analyze more than 10,000 patients—probably more than any other analyst has ever attempted. For one thing, he was basically uninterested in the patient's associations to his dreams, and it is the laborious analysis of such associations that takes so much time in Freudian therapy. "There is no trustworthy standard of values," Stekel wrote, "whereby we can decide which of the patient's associations are to be regarded as important, and which can be ignored as irrelevant. I am firmly convinced that dream interpretation will not become a teachable and learnable science until our technique of interpretation has grown independent of associations and other remarks of the patient, except for trifling items of information about persons and things."

What, then, did Stekel consider "trustworthy"? Mainly his own catalogue of symbols, ingeniously developed and applied, which enabled him to discern the essential conflict which the neurotic individual seeks to solve in a dream. Every dream, in Stekel's view, demonstrates the conflict in two distinct forms—one "material" and the other "functional." He cited this dream as an example: "I break open a locked door, and in doing so I destroy the lock, so that the door can no longer be closed properly." Seen in its "material" aspect, this means that the dreamer desires to seduce a virgin, and this is symbolized by breaking the door and destroying the lock (the hymen). But a "functional" interpretation would be that the dreamer is opening the door to an awareness of his own sexuality, breaking the lock of ignorance or disregard that had previously protected him from a consciousness of this powerful but unacknowledged tendency within himself.

Stekel, like most analysts, attached great importance to the first dream recounted by a patient starting a course of treatment, for he considered that this provided a kind of summary of the patient's problems and an anticipation of the course the treatment would take. Here is an example of such a dream, with Stekel's own comments on it, which shows how he employed his own type of symbolic interpretation:

"I am standing upon a lofty, well-wooded hilltop. It is warm up here. In the valley I see a torrent, which is carrying down a thick tree trunk. Descending the mountain side, I pass through a current of cold air. Below, upon a dancing floor in the open, I see a couple dancing to the strains of jazz that is being sent (not received) by wireless. The dispatching station is quite a little place, which I cannot see. It is called St. Andra. I am surprised that so small a place should be a dispatching station."

In spite of Stekel's limited regard for associations, they are of some value here. The patient tells him that the dream recalls Davos, Switzerland, where he had been treated for a tubercular infection that had changed the course of his life. "His high demands, his ideals, remained unfulfilled. He is the felled tree trunk which is being swept downstream. At these lower levels it is cold." Because he is impotent, the man has an unhappy marriage, though he loves his wife. Stekel continues:

" 'Down below' people are amusing themselves. A couple is dancing: jealousy of the wife, and reminiscences of his student days. St. Andra would be inexplicable, did he not mention, as an association, that on the night following St. Andrew's Day one can foresee one's future. A different future had awaited him, but now he is bound to the new path. That is the little place which he cannot see, but which dispatches music to him. The relationship to the impotence: the felled tree and the cold current of air. A fixation from childhood (the little place) induces him to make a sister image out of his wife. Further, we notice relationships to his masochistic impulse. Andrew was a martyr, crucified on a cross of a peculiar shape. The patient, like St. Andrew, has to bear a cross. Andrew means 'manly.' He is impotent, but the other man, who is dancing with his wife, is doubtless fully potent. His wife is a musician. The conflict between himself and his wife—the triangle, etc. It is all given in the first dream."

So it may be, but the interpretation seems both slipshod and superficial when compared to the meanings that could have been given to this dream by several of Stekel's colleagues. It also raises the question whether interpretation at this level—especially when it is provided by the analyst—has much value for the patient. The patient seems to be sitting there just to be told what his troubles are. The impression is not greatly changed by Stekel's attempt to develop his interpretation.

"But the dream contains something more, a disappointment in love, which comes to our knowledge later. In the little town where his factory is, he made the acquaintance of a girl who represented his ideal. He had always been a man with serious tastes, striving to attain the heights of knowledge, wanting to make a fine art of life. He was not a dancer, and did not like jazz, preferring Mozart and Beethoven. His first great love ended unhappily. She married another. This induced depression, and as a result of the depression he became tubercular. (Depression was the mental factor which reduced his resistance to infection.) It was she, his predestined bride, whom he had seen on St. Andrew's night. Strains of music from this little place still rang in his ears, and the wound had not yet healed. I ignore certain other determinants of the dream.... Gloomy is the image of the felled tree, which the current is carrying down the valley. Thus life ebbs away, and he is drawing near to the tomb, where it is cold. In his brain a ferment is at work, and passion conjures up deceptive pictures; but down below, in the valley, it is cool. (An allusion to the central problem, that of his impotence.)"

Stekel's ingenuity was applied to a great mass of case material, and it is this that accounts for his continuing influence. Because his concept of symbolism could be applied to situations almost by rote—as in the dream-book interpretations—he became a significant source on whom subsequent analysts have drawn freely.

In particular, Stekel's ideas were developed by the eminent American psychotherapist Dr. Emil Gutheil, in *The Handbook of Dream Analysis*, a monumental work designed to show the value of Stekel's methods of dream interpretation in "brief" psychoanalysis—a technique that shortens the treatment and is therefore assumed to avoid some of the complications that develop from the prolonged involvement of analyst and patient. But the symbols that Gutheil interprets show how far concepts of symbolism have changed from those originally advanced by Freud.

Today most analysts would accept, as images representing the father, such figures as kings, teachers, policemen, or officials of any kind, just as the mother may be symbolized by queens, nurses, housekeepers, (or even such impersonal symbols as a city, an island, or the earth), or sisters as nuns and brothers as priests. Gutheil considers that such actions in dreams as telephoning, dancing, writing a letter, eating a meal, traveling or walking with a member of the opposite sex, stoking a fire, sewing, weaving, rescuing someone, riding in a car or on a horse, are all *contact* symbols representing sexual intercourse. Like Freud, Gutheil adds, "we usually consider water as a symbol of birth. Yet we know it is also a symbol of life. We speak of a "stormy life," a "smooth sailing," a "shipwrecked individual," etc. Water is also a symbol of the psyche of instinctual cravings (which sometimes can, like a flood, break through moral barriers), a symbol of the treatment, particularly if bathing or cleansing is involved. It is also an ancient symbol of the unconscious. We speak of dark, turbid waters. Particularly the dark, mystery-bearing waters are understandable symbols of the unconscious."

Stekel had given special attention to symbols of life and death, and the dream of one of his patients, a woman painter, provides an excellent example of his treatment of such symbols.

"In a primitive forest there stands a tall, spreading tree. From a far-spreading branch of the tree there hangs a long, sharp sword. Before me stands

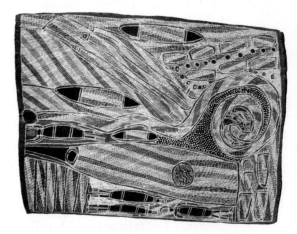

Left, an Australian aborigine, a member of the Wulamba tribe, painting on bark a scene from a Creation myth. Parts of this myth are enacted by the tribe at times of trouble or change, a fantasy outlet that may be compared to an individual's "rebirth" dream. Above, the artist is telling how two women of the tribe and their children were swallowed by the Great Python.

a man whom I am unable to distinguish clearly. The sword hangs between us, and therefore we cannot see and recognize one another. Stronger and warmer grows our mutual longing for each other; with a powerful grip the man seizes the sword with the determination to bring it down. I shout exultantly, and throw both arms into the air. He has seized the sword too hastily, and it slips from his hand and pierces my heart. I sink to the ground with the sword sticking in my breast. The figure of the man dissolves like a shadow and I am alone, lying on the ground, mortally wounded.''

Stekel's comment is this: "Does this dream really portray nothing more than death caused by an accident resulting from a man's lack of adroitness? Not at all; this is not a death-dream—*this is a dream of life.* The 'tall, spreading tree' in the primitive forest is the phallus. The erection is represented as a long, sharp sword." It is, in fact, fairly obvious that the whole of this dream is a fantasy of sexual intercourse, culminating in orgasm (which in French is called *le petit mort*) and ending with the detumescent male figure dissolving "like a shadow." Of special interest is the symbol of the Tree of Life, found in the Bible and in the symbolism of many religions, and the symbol of the sword, sharp, penetrating, painful, and transfiguring.

The sword, moreover, pierces the breast—an example of what Freud called "displacement from below upward," whereby the dream substitutes a more acceptable image for an idea that is overtly sexual. But displacement, according to Stekel and others, need not only be a disguise for sexual themes. "Above" and "below" may also be symbols of the spiritual and the carnal, of the intellect and the physical senses, of consciousness and the unconscious. In much the same way—according to a reasoning too complex to summarize here—"left" and "right" can be assigned profound symbolic significance. The "left" usually indicates the taboo or "sinister" impulses such as criminality, incest, homosexuality, or (in common usage) illegitimacy; the "right" represents law and order, respectability, and heterosexuality.

Another type of dream, which has not been mentioned so far, is the birth dream. The following is a typical example: "I am crawling through a long, narrow, muddy, dark tube which has in it a large number of curves. Whenever I think I am approaching the end, I discover that what I believed to be the exit was in reality another curve. I am uncomfortable and anxious. After much strain, I come to a narrow opening on the upper part of the tube and am free. I feel relieved and breathe freely. I have had this dream repeatedly."

Among psychoanalysts there is profound disagreement on the extent to which one's memory can retain the experience of birth or, in the extreme view, prenatal and intra-uterine experience. Certain drugs (as we shall see in Chapter 10) seem to induce some remembrance of birth; a great many dreams can be made to carry such a conception; and some established schools of psychoanalysis (notably those founded by Melanie Klein and Otto Rank) focus considerable attention on the so-called "birth trauma."

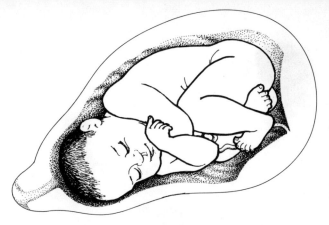

Freud likened sleep to intra-uterine existence, pointing out that many sleepers lie in the fetal position—right, a drawing of the baby in the womb.

Freud had already suggested that "sleep is an act which reproduces intra-uterine existence, fulfilling the conditions of repose, warmth, and absence of stimulus; indeed, in sleep many people resume a foetal position. I have learned to value the significance of fancies and unconscious thoughts about life in the womb. They contain the explanation of the curious fear felt by so many people about being buried alive, as well as the profoundest unconscious reason for the belief in a life after death which represents nothing but the projection into the future of this mysterious life before birth."

Freud had offered an explanation for the fact that many birth dreams seem to contain references to water. This, he suggested, could be a race memory, since all mammals are descended from amphibious creatures, or a prenatal memory, since all human beings began life in the amniotic fluid in the womb. He also raised the possibility that all anxiety stimulated unconscious memories of birth, the earliest of all anxieties. Such anxieties, as in the dream that has just been quoted, may well involve breathing difficulties, or claustrophobia. As Freud pointed out, anxiety often involves physical constriction, and may be accompanied by panting, an overwhelming sense of fear, or even an apprehension of imminent death.

It was such considerations that led Otto Rank to argue (in *The Trauma of Birth*) that the primal anxiety of being born forms a mental barrier between the conditions of life and the "pleasurable state" before birth. It is, he said, "the first repression." Every impulse is directed toward regaining that prenatal state of union with the mother, and every dream reveals this deep desire.

Birth dreams, however, may have a different symbolism—as they had for Jung and his followers, and have for many modern analysts. They can be regarded as an expression of the individual's desire to be born again, to achieve a new orientation in life, or to abandon a long-standing neurosis or other mental disorder. The symbolism of death and rebirth is a theme found repeatedly in mythology—in the story of Jonah and the whale, for instance—and in the rituals of primitive societies.

One follower of Jung, Dr. Maurice Nicoll, argued that at critical stages in life—such as puberty, or middle age, the menopause, and the coming of old age and then death—the individual has to make fundamental psychic

A 15th-century French painting shows the expulsion of Adam and Eve from a walled (and womb-shaped) Garden of Eden.

as well as physiological adjustments. At such times, Nicoll found that "rebirth symbolism is regularly found in the dream." All such symbols refer in some way to the entrance into the womb: Jonah enters the whale's belly; the initiate lies in a cave or in a chapel; the knight lies naked before the altar; the hero is temporarily swallowed by the earth. Like Otto Rank, Dr. Nicoll suggested that each of these symbols (and the many other different forms taken by the same theme) represents a movement of return to the mother. But, unlike Rank, he believed that this regression may have a healing or regenerative effect, so long as it does not become a fixed state. Such a fixation in an infantile attitude causes neurosis—the inability to meet a challenge and to grow toward maturity by overcoming it. Thus the appearance of a baby in a dream may indicate either the birth of a new individuality or the psychological bondage of infantility.

An illustration of this theory occurs in the following dream recorded by Dr. Nicoll. The dreamer was a young officer in his early thirties, who developed neurotic symptoms.

"He dreamt that he was on a steamer with a crowd of people. He suddenly dived over the side of the steamer and plunged into the sea. As he went down, the water became warmer and warmer. At length he turned and began to come up. He reached the surface, almost bumping his head against a little empty boat. There was now no steamer, but only a little boat."

A full analysis of this dream would take many pages, but Dr. Nicoll has selected the essential elements. After telling us that the young man, in his associations, felt the water to be at blood-heat, he continues:

"The idea of going into the water as a symbol of rebirth is found in the ritual of baptism. Baptism means birth. But why should going into the water mean rebirth? Rebirth, concretely expressed, means a return to the womb. The sea is a symbol of the Great Mother. The water is of *blood-heat*. This is a mythological expression used by the unconscious to indicate the idea of returning to the maternal depths. The unconscious in its aspect of the recreative mother. You will see by the manifest content of the dream, which is always of the utmost importance, the motif of rebirth comes between two symbols, that of the steamer crowded with people and the little boat. Broadly speaking, this means that the dreamer must leave collective values, which are represented by the crowd on the steamer, and go through a process of rebirth whereby he comes to the little boat; that is, to something individual."

All analysts are familiar with dreams of this type, but among them Nandor Fodor has placed special emphasis on the interlocking concepts of birth and death. The fear of dying, or of a madness equivalent to death, is a common defense mechanism against feelings which, if released, may lead to a new birth of personal freedom. In his book *New Approaches to Dream Interpretation* Fodor argued that the transition from prenatal to postnatal existence is an ordeal as severe as dying. Thus the fear of death and the fear of life begin at the same cataclysmic moment of entry into the world—a moment which, protected by amnesia in the conscious state, emerges in dreams, nightmares, and mental illness. Fodor, in fact, believed that even attempts at abortion or acts of intercourse during the mother's pregnancy can be detected as memory traces in some dreams. He wrote:

"At least in one instance in my experience, the genesis of a schizoid personality was traced back by the voices which the patient heard, to the prenatal fright which he experienced in the womb. I am also inclined to think that the well-known dream fantasy that the mother has a male organ may originate in memories of ante-natal aggression in which the male organ is conceived to be part of the maternal environment."

Fodor's explanation of the "falling" dream also differs profoundly from that given by Freud. It is, he suggests, "an acquired fear, acquired in falling from the uterine heaven to the terrestrial abyss. The legend of the Fall of Man in the Garden of Eden is a mythological record of our biological origin." And he cites the following dream as a typical example:

"I was in an orchard surrounded by a hedge. Both the orchard and the hedge were unkempt. I passed through a hole in the hedge and fell into a canal. There I was sucked down into a hole under the water where everything was peaceful. I knew that water was above me and that someone was calling my name, but I experienced no distress."

It is, of course, easy to offer alternative interpretations of such a dream, or to suggest reasons why such extreme views are unnecessarily elaborate. But here we are concerned only to point out the wide range of dream interpretation that has emerged since Freud, and the way in which different psychoanalytic assumptions led to contrasting explanations of the same symbolism. Apart from those symbolic patterns that have engaged the attention of many analysts, there is one to which Fodor devoted a significant and stimulating section of his book—the symbolism of numbers.

Consider, for example, a dream that consists of no more than these words: "Three on two makes five." There are many such dreams in which there is a curious emphasis on numbers or some numerical pattern. "The source material behind our number dreams," said Fodor, "is as abundant as behind any other symbolic expressions." There is an almost infinite choice in ways of arranging numbers—which are, in any case, highly abstract and condensed symbols. Since antiquity, numbers have been endowed with magical (that is, emotionally charged) properties.

Let us take two relatively simple dreams as an illustration. The first is the one we have just mentioned: "Three on two makes five." There is one

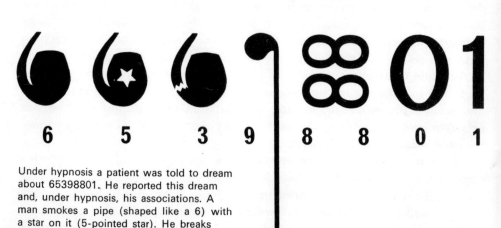

6   5   3   9   8   8   0   1

Under hypnosis a patient was told to dream about 65398801. He reported this dream and, under hypnosis, his associations. A man smokes a pipe (shaped like a 6) with a star on it (5-pointed star). He breaks the pipe in half (half of 6 is 3) and turns it up to become a golf-club (6 becomes 9). He speaks of two impressions of infinity and twice draws the infinity sign ∞ (vertically 88). He says: "the whole thing is nothing (0). There is nothing except one thing, which is unity (1)."

immediate meaning. "Three" is a symbol of masculinity—either male genitals, or the genitals added as a "third leg." "Two" can symbolize the legs of a woman. Thus the first part of a dream in which these figures appear could be held to represent an act of intercourse. "Three *on* two makes five" could, in this case, refer to the size of the family. The dreamer already had two daughters: another child would make the family five in all. But deeper associations lie beyond this manifest interpretation. There are the many emotive and symbolic meanings of "three": the father, mother, and child; the unity of the family; the first perfect number in Pythagorean philosophy, and also the first "male" or odd number; and, for the Pythagoreans, the peace of happy marriages springs from the Triad. As for "two", it is a "female" or even number. It can also represent the sense of the opposites or the polarities of life; the idea of one added to one, making two; the concepts of irrationality and rationality; the beginning of a hierarchy of numbers—the symbol of something more than one. Two also means, in English, a "couple", and "to couple" is a vernacular expression for sexual intercourse. Finally, "five" is the last of the elementary numbers; it completes a group. Five (as in the hand) is an organic unit; it is the Pythagorean Pentad, the nuptial number, symbol of generation and life. It is unnecessary to continue the associations or to complete the analysis of the dream. The preoccupation (one might say the hope) of the dreamer has been clearly revealed.

The second example was the work of a professor of mathematics who dreamed of reading of heavy rains and floods in California. Next, he found himself there with the sun shining but the grass full of water. Finally, he was on a train heading home. His ticket cost $ 576. This is how Nandor Fodor interpreted this dream.

"In view of the fact that this patient frequently associated numbers with the power or cube, I asked him if 576 was the power of any number. He thought so and suggested 24. Indeed, 24 times 24 yields 576.... He was surprised when I suggested that the most obvious meaning of 24 would be the hours of the day. I queried, could 24 by 24 stand for day by day? He said, no, it would stand for 24 days (24 hours by 24). The date of the day of the dream was February 25th. By adding 24 days, we reach March 21st, the first day of Spring. The rains and floods of California correspond to the winter season.... The patient arrived there in the dream after the rains and flood. The sunshine, the water in the grass and the 576 dollars all merged into one significant statement: SPRING IS COMING. The worst part of the patient's analytical ordeal was over.... now he was coming to life."

Ingenuity, at least, is not lacking in the interpretation techniques that have been developed since Freud redirected attention to the dream. The next question to consider is the relevance of such ingenious oneirology to the treatment, or even the diagnosis, of mental illness. It is therefore necessary to turn to the actual use of dreams in analysis.

8 Dreams and psychotherapy

Freud not only focused attention on dreams as one means of discovering the hidden emotional conflicts that lead to mental and even physical disorders; he also demonstrated, through the techniques of psychoanalysis, how dreams might be used in the treatment of such conditions. For orthodox psychoanalysts, Freud's essential ideas and the methods he developed remain the classic teaching, even though strict adherence to his teachings inhibited both studies of dreams and experiments in ways of using them—as he himself recognized in 1932. New ideas and new therapeutic practices were developed by the dissenters from formal psychoanalysis, whose views we briefly examined in the previous chapter, as well as by modern psychotherapists who realized how much they owed to Freud but who went on to treat their patients in ways far removed from the conditions he laid down in Vienna in the first years of the present century.

There is a popular stereotype of psychoanalysis, found in countless jokes and cartoons: the patient lying on the couch, with the analyst sitting behind him, notebook in hand, recording the dreams, childhood recollections, and current anxieties that the patient recounts. The hourly session is repeated daily, perhaps for months, possibly for years, and almost invariably at great expense. That situation can indeed be found today in many consulting rooms from San Francisco to Athens, from London to Sydney. But within the general

Most mental hospitals today have a special art therapy department—like this one, right, in a British mental hospital. For the patient, drawing, painting, or modeling may be a way of releasing tensions, but art may also become a form of communication between patient and therapist. For the therapist a patient's creations may be as revealing as his words, actions, and dreams.

framework of psychotherapy there is now a bewildering variety of theories and practices. Therapy sessions may take place daily, weekly, or monthly; the patient may receive individual treatment or participate in group therapy; he may receive "intensive," "active," or "brief" psychoanalysis; his therapist may be a physician with special psychological training, a clinical psychologist, or a lay counsellor; he may undergo hypnosis, or chemotherapy with drugs ranging from sodium amytal and pentathol to the hallucinogens such as LSD 25; he may receive his treatment in an institution, privately at his own expense, or free from a clinic or welfare organization. Yet, in almost all such therapeutic situations, some use will be made of dreams.

The difficulty about making any general statement on dreams and psychotherapy thus becomes apparent. There are really no common assumptions about dreams, or about the ways in which they may be used in therapy, beyond the basic (but now rather vague and unhelpful) proposition that they reveal unconscious mental processes. There is not even any means of collecting comprehensive data on the use different therapists make of dreams or of evaluating the degree to which they help analyst and patient pursue the course of treatment.

A few years ago, Dr. Werner Wolff interviewed a number of distinguished American therapists and reported (in his book *Contemporary Psychotherapists Examine Themselves*) that there was no agreement among them on the significance of dreams and the technique of using them:

"To some, a lack of dreams is just as much an indication of resistance and defence as an overwhelming production of dreams. Dreams are considered a diagnostic tool in evaluating the transference situation, the patient's degree of activity, his relationship to other people, his moods: they are used as prognostic indicators suggesting the patient's development; by acting out dreams through drawings, plays or psychodramatic action, their value as a means

"You said a moment ago that everybody you look at seems to be a rabbit. Now just what do you mean by that, Mrs. Sprague?"

Left, drawing by James Thurber (d. 1961). Right, beauty treatment helps to restore a patient's confidence: a photograph taken at a psychiatric hospital in Manila. Far right, doctors—nicknamed locally "Les Demoiselles de Nerfs"—of a remarkable child medical service provide psychiatric help for children in the Swiss state of Valais.

of relief is emphasized and further developed. The technique in the use of dreams varies. Some follow the Freudian scheme of ready-made symbols and offer fixed interpretations; others focus upon the dream from certain points of view; some use only the manifest dream, others only the symbolic layer and the hidden meanings; some let the patient associate to the total dream, some to its elements, some to drawings or fantasies related to it."

A statement of this kind is, of course, taken by the critics of psychoanalysis as evidence that it is an unsystematic branch of medicine, working by hit or miss methods from unverifiable assumptions to untestable conclusions. In particular, the critics have fastened on the manifold concepts of the dream: all cannot be right, possibly none are right. Such criticisms have a good deal of force, and the layman may well incline to agree with them after reading Dr. Wolff's account of the apparent confusion that prevails. Yet they are not wholly to the point. For many reasons, therapists of different views have stressed their conflict of theories and methods. After half a century of experience, however, there seems to be an increasing amount of evidence that the degree of success achieved in therapy depends less upon the concepts of the therapist than upon his own personality—expecially his intuitive or empathic capacity for establishing a truly therapeutic relationship with his patient.

This is not the place to describe such a relationship in detail, nor to discuss the technical problems of psychoanalysis or psychotherapy in general: there are many books on such themes. But without some understanding of the roles of patient and therapist, it is impossible to perceive how and why dreams can be used to further their dynamic relationship. Though Freud was the first to demonstrate at length how this could be done, and to study the intricate and demanding emotional process of therapy, it had long been recognized that even in the formal medical relationship of doctor and patient (let alone

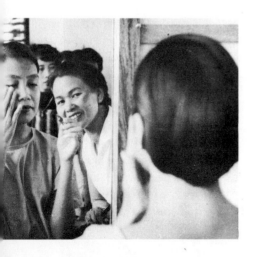

in the sphere of mental illness) a warm human concern might make a remarkable contribution to the patient's recovery.

There is a fascinating passage in Nathaniel Hawthorne's novel *The Scarlet Letter*, published in America in 1850, which puts the point as well as it could be put by any present-day writer on psychotherapy.

"He deemed it essential, it would seem, to know the man, before attempting to do him good. Wherever there is a heart and an intellect, the diseases of the physical frame are tinged with the peculiarities of these. In Arthur Dimmesdale, thought and imagination were so active, and sensibility so intense, that the bodily infirmity would be likely to have its ground work there. So Roger Chillingworth—the man of skill, the kind and friendly physician—strove to go deep in to his patient's bosom, delving among his principles, prying into his recollections, and probing everything with a cautious touch, like a treasure-seeker in a dark cavern. Few secrets can escape an investigator who has opportunity and licence to undertake such a quest, and skill to follow it up. A man burdened with a secret should especially avoid the intimacy of his physician. If the latter possess native sagacity, and a nameless something more—let us call it intuition; if he show no intrusive egotism, nor disagreeably prominent characteristics of his own; if he have the power, which must be born with him, to bring his mind into affinity with his patient's, that this last shall unawares have spoken what he imagines himself only to have thought; if such revelations be received without tumult, and acknowledged not so often by an uttered sympathy as by silence, an inarticulate breath, and here and there a word, to indicate that all is understood; if to these qualifications of a confidant be joined the advantages afforded by his recognized character as a physician—then, at some inevitable moment, will the soul of the sufferer be dissolved, and flow forth in a dark, but transparent stream, bringing all its mystery into the daylight."

Nowhere, even in the forceful precision of Freud's own prose, can one find a more revealing summary of what actually happens in a therapeutic relationship. The consulting-room techniques devised by Freud and refined in a generation of use are a valuable asset to the therapist. The libraries of theoretical literature and years of professional experience provide the modern therapist with a wealth of information and practical skill. The therapist himself, through training in analysis and continual scrutiny of his own personality, may slowly learn how better to understand and help those who come to him. Yet he still could not improve (even as to the hints on behavior) on Hawthorne's insight into the way the physician can "bring his mind into affinity with his patient's, that this last shall unawares have spoken what he imagines himself only to have thought." It is essentially the same concept that Jung was expressing when he said: "The man in the patient confronts the man in the doctor on equal terms to reach a mutual agreement which is the fruit of joint reflection."

We have here, in fact, the crucial characteristic of all forms of psychotherapy: the search for insight as the result of cooperative endeavor on the part of both patient and therapist. In order to achieve this insight, moreover, what Hawthorne called "a nameless something more—let us call it intuition" is needed. Both the patient and the therapist are striving to discover and initially comprehend emotions that cannot easily be identified (since they are beyond the reach of normal consciousness) and even less easily understood (since they are often too elusive for conscious language and logic). It is one thing to diagnose a patient's condition and attach to it a label from a medical textbook. It is, however, quite another matter patiently to explore what is hidden away because it has once seemed painful, shameful, dangerous, or downright destructive to the individual's sense of identity, and slowly to find forms of speech and states of feeling that enable the patient to communicate to himself (as well as to the therapist) hopes and fears of which he had no previous conscious knowledge.

Such an exploration can be conducted only by an alliance of intuition and intellect. "The patient," Dr. Frieda Fromm-Reichmann once observed, "is in need of an experience, not an explanation": he needs to be able to confront what comes from within himself, and by recognizing it for what it truly is, diminish the fears that prevent him living as a full personality. The patient is rather like Alice, in Lewis Carroll's *Alice in Wonderland*. "Alice knew it was the Rabbit coming to look for her, and she trembled until she shook the house, quite forgetting that she was now about a thousand times as large as the Rabbit and had no reason to be afraid of it."

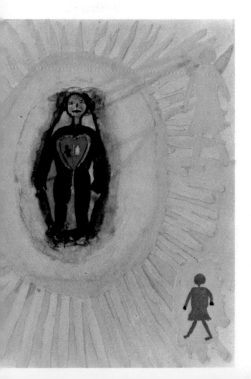

This painting by a patient in a British mental hospital expresses the way he sees himself and his relationship with the therapist. Lines from the eyes, ears, mouth, and hands of the patient—who is enclosed in a sun-like womb—connect him with the therapist (top right). The patient feels imprisoned, but the links with the therapist are signs that the channels of communication (sight, hearing, speech, touch) are beginning to be reopened.

The purpose of psychotherapy is to repair the damage done by inadequate or harmful personal relationships in early childhood, partly by aiding the individual to see the magnified anxieties and conflicts of childhood in less terrifying dimensions, partly by enabling him to learn new methods of relating himself to others from the intimate and demanding experience of his relationship to the therapist. He will, of course, resist this process. All the motives that have caused his neurosis will be powerfully present, even though part of his personality wishes to struggle against them and overcome them. Growing to maturity will inevitably be a painful struggle for the patient; he will offer manifold resistances and resort to a hundred tricks and evasions to defeat the enterprise on which he and the therapist are engaged. He will, moreover, recreate infantile relationships in his attitude to the analyst, seeing him as a father, a mother, a sister, a brother, a rival, a teacher, or a friend, as the case may be; unknowingly (and usually symbolically) he will seek to live out the unfinished business of his childhood. He will attempt to involve the therapist in his neurotic attitudes to others, to manipulate him, to test him out, to attack, conciliate, confuse, or seduce him.

It would be wrong, however, to see this situation as one in which the individual's "good" or "healthy" consciousness is opposed to a "bad" or "unhealthy" unconscious, and to regard the process of therapy as one in which the patient is helped to dredge up the negative aspects of himself that are the cause of his neurosis. This, it is true, is the emphasis that Freudian therapy tends to give; but, as we have seen in the previous chapter, it is an emphasis that is widely challenged both in psychotherapeutic theory and in practice.

As Jung once put it, why should we behave "as if all that is good, reasonable, beautiful and worth living for had taken up its abode in consciousness?" The unconscious, he suggested, "is not a demonic monster, but a thing of nature that is perfectly neutral so far as moral sense, aesthetic taste and intellectual judgment go. It is dangerous only when our conscious attitude towards it becomes hopelessly false . . . as soon as the patient begins to assimilate the contents that were previously unconscious, the danger from the side of the unconscious diminishes. As the process of assimilation goes on, it puts an end to the dissociation of the personality. . . ."

The aim of therapy, therefore, is integration, to enable a person to be a whole personality, rather than a divided, conflict-torn individual, much of whose energy is devoted to holding down both negative and positive aspects of himself that, for one reason or another, he chooses not to accept. He can distort his personality, connive at his own defeats, and even actively pursue his own destruction. The technique of therapy, whatever methods are employed, is essentially the cooperative attempt to loosen the bonds by which both the experience of the past and the potential for the future are held in thrall.

Before we see how dreams are used in psychotherapy, three qualifications must be made. The first is a warning against the trivial or irresponsible use of dream interpretation. Simply to take the information in this or any other book and apply it, like a form of fortune telling, is to overlook the fact that the unskilled use of dreams outside the therapeutic situation is invariably misleading and may be actually harmful.

The second is a distinction between the diagnostic and the therapeutic analysis of dreams. In the former, the dream may indicate quite clearly a patient's condition; many dreams may be studied to gain insight into the mental processes of man (as Freud studied them in *The Interpretation of Dreams*); and great care may be taken to explore all the possible meanings and associations a single dream may have (as Jung was doing in his efforts to establish the relationship of dreams and myths in the collective unconscious). But such activities may not be helpful to the patient; much more may be achieved by singling out some particular aspect or aspects of the dream, by concentrating on its immediate relevance, or the light it sheds on a problem that is already part of the transactions between the patient and the therapist. If the dream is treated as an end in itself, rather than as one of the doors through which the patient and therapist may pass together, it will interfere with the

A child expresses itself more clearly in play than in words. The child playing with a doll's house in this photograph—taken at a child guidance clinic in Bangkok, Thailand—may re-enact a painful and, to the psychiatrist, revealing memory.

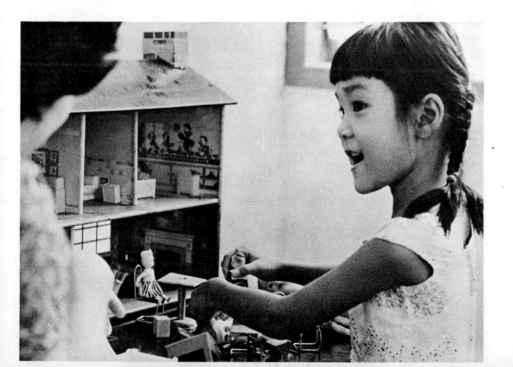

therapy, not assist it. If, as Jung said, the doctor should "prejudge the dream from the standpoint of a certain doctrine . . . make a pronouncement which may be theoretically sound, but does not win the patient's assent . . . it is incorrect in the practical sense; and it may also be incorrect in the sense that it anticipates and thereby cripples the actual development of the patient. We appeal only to the patient's brain if we try to inculcate a truth; but if we help him to grow up to this truth in the course of his own development, we have reached his heart, and this appeal goes deeper and acts with greater force."

The third qualification is one that has been implicit throughout this book. The central mystery of the dream, as we confront it in waking life, is the symbolic nature of dream language. It is an essentially pictorial language, usually illogical, and seemingly irrelevant to our ordinary lives

This painting, which was done by a
British woman patient at an early stage of
therapy, has many significant themes—
especially the diagonal division, the
strange positioning of the eyes, the masks,
and the floating cosmic circles. But at
that stage of the treatment the therapist
concentrated on the dominant symbol of the
draped figure, which expressed the patient's
special difficulties in her relationship
with her mother, who had been a nurse.

—indeed, may be in marked contrast to the way in which we customarily see ourselves. Yet it is precisely these special qualities of the dream that make it most valuable in therapy. Whatever may be the ultimate physiological or neurological function of the dream (and it is a *natural* function, of which therapy simply makes what use it can) it is an emotionally charged mental process that is different from conscious thought; when we think in waking life, we order thoughts according to the structure of our language and the rules of logic. In sleep, our thoughts are non-verbal and pre-logical. Words in themselves always have some meaning, but they rarely express the full meaning we wish to express, for behind each word lies a range of non-verbal meanings or inarticulate feelings.

Man, in fact, is endowed with at least two forms of thinking. The abstracted and conceptual thinking that is the product of consciousness, and a deeper, less coherent level of thought that finds expression in dreams, religious experiences, poetry, music, neurotic symptoms, and the ultimate delusions of insanity. Such thought, coming from the world of fantasy, can never be properly expressed in the language of consciousness, and cannot therefore be fully communicated. It is experienced, rather than formulated; and, to understand another person at this level, one must rely on empathy rather than speech, on the whole range of symbolism available to human beings—inflections of the voice, facial expressions, the posture and gestures of the body, the patterns of behavior, the hints, analogies, images that must be expressed symbolically because they represent more than can ever be fully apprehended by consciousness. Freud expressed this in the form of an analogy. The analyst, he said, " . . . must turn his unconscious like a receptive organ towards the transmitting unconscious of the patient. He must adjust himself to the patient as a telephone receiver is adjusted to the transmitting microphone. Just as the receiver converts back into sound waves the electric oscillations in the telephone line which were set up by sound waves, so is the doctor's unconscious able to reconstruct the patient's unconscious."

In this process of empathic communication the dream plays a vital role: it is not the only vehicle by which our deepest feelings may be carried across the chasm that divides any individual from another, but it is one of the most effective and economical. It is possible to conduct a successful course of therapy without the use of a single dream, or an analysis may rely heavily upon dreams and their associated material. The skilled and intuitive therapist will range between these extremes as circumstances and his own sense of his relationship with the patient dictate.

Since the dream—even in the partial, fragmentary form in which it can be recollected and told to the therapist—so richly conveys what a person is unconsciously feeling or creating in his imagination, and since it will evoke a resonance in the mind and feelings of the therapist that goes far beyond the reduced and inadequate language in which it is told, it is understandably regarded as the most consistent and universal form in which the individual reveals what he truly feels. The dream has, moreover, one further advantage that stems from its very obscurity. Because the dreamer normally does not understand the dream, he is less likely to censor it when he reports it. Attitudes or feelings that, especially in the early stages of therapy, he could not bring himself to relate to the therapist in words, may be presented in the form of dreams: he feels it safer to report them in such a code than to state them directly.

The patient, that is to say, can tell the therapist in dream form of aggressive or sexual feelings that would be withheld if he were aware of what he was really saying: he can present murderous or lascivious fantasies, petty meanness or overweening ambition, images of what he has been or what he hopes to become. The symbolism of his dream indicates more than he can possibly say and, at the same time, offers him a means of communicating what he does not consciously know. But in order to derive the maximum advantage from this empathic form of communication the therapist must try to detach himself from his own preconceptions: he must, as it were, allow the dream to flow over him, permit himself to feel it as well as strive to understand it. Deep thinking about a dream, indeed, can only follow from deep feeling about it—and the feeling must stem from the therapist's recognition that the dream is *his* experience as well as the patient's. To the extent that either the therapist, or the patient, or both, indulge in excessive intellectualization about any dream, so do they erect defenses against the full awareness of what the patient is feeling, what the therapist is feeling, and the state of the relations between them.

For this reason, dreams may be introduced into the transaction between therapist and patient in a number of ways. In formal psychoanalysis, for instance, the patient may already know that dreams will be expected of him and arrive prepared: he may, almost at once, offer a recent dream or one of the previous night, or he may bring notebooks filled with series of dreams and even his auto-analysis of them. Conversely, the analyst may ask for dreams as a means of quickly involving the patient, enabling him to show the varied facets of his personal relations, offering him a first glimpse into the methods of free association, indicating to him the role dreams can play in his therapy, showing him how the therapy will require cooperative effort, and demonstrating the manner in which the techniques of dream interpretation can be used to illuminate both his past and present experience. With other forms of therapy, nothing may be said about dreams at first. The therapist will wait until the patient spontaneously introduces a reference to a dream, or if this fails happen—if the patient seems to have run into a blind alley and is unable to produce material—a request for a dream may provide a new point of departure, leading to the uncovering of some problem previously ignored or repressed.

In all forms of therapy in which the dream is used, however, great importance is attached to the first or introductory dream—not least because it usually seems to sum up a life-problem that confronts the patient and may even indicate the course his therapy will take. It is, in a special sense, both diagnostic and prognostic. The initial dream, moreover, may not be immediately intelligible either to patient or analyst; its meaning—or its many meanings—may not fully emerge until much later, as more details about the individual's history and problems amplify the cryptic message. The therapist, nevertheless, will try to elicit the patient's own associations and (depending on the school of psychotherapy to which he belongs) will refrain from suggesting any interpretation, will offer a tentative reading of the dream, or will "try out" an elaborate analysis of the dream on the patient.

Many examples of first dreams are available in the literature of psychotherapy: we shall take some from a recent work by Dr. Walter Bonime (*The Clinical Use of Dreams*), which is one of the most helpful and discerning studies of dreams in psychotherapy that has yet been published.

Dr. Bonime, reporting on a patient—an intellectual businessman of 37, married, a father, much engaged in community work—who suffered from a coolness and strain in his marriage, gives the dreams the patient reported in his first three analytic sessions. This was the first: "I was at an ice-skating rink. All the skaters were going around in a circle. I was skating in a circle, too, but I was going in the opposite direction. I was having a good time." Dr. Bonime suggested that the dream (circling a round a skating rink) reflected the fact that the patient had entered into analysis like many of his friends (though he assumed he needed therapy less than they did) but was "still trying to maintain his special status, as represented by his skating in a different direction from the rest of the crowd.... The discovery of this trait was extremely surprising to him, because he had always felt himself to be notably modest." At the next session, the patient reported: "I was at a beach and in the water, bathing. The waves were small, and I waded in deeper and was enjoying myself. Then the waves began to get bigger and bigger and I kept bathing, but I was worried. I wasn't sure I'd be able to keep from being overwhelmed."

It is immediately plain that much of this dream refers to both the attraction and the fears of therapy: the patient is aware of rising emotions, but is anxious lest he be "overwhelmed" by them. In the course of the next hour he was able to explore his attitude toward his emotions, and it became plain that he in fact despised emotion, feeling superior to those who succumbed to their feelings. Already, in two sessions, the dreams were forcing him to look more realistically at himself and to discard illusions—and the unconscious anxieties aroused by such insight were to find expression in the third dream. "I was on a large tank like a swimming pool. There was also a shark in the water. I was swimming frantically to get away from him."

The patient could see no meaning at all in this dream, but his very first association to it was that the tank was about the shape of Dr. Bonime's office. From skating above the ice, to gradual and rather fearful immersion in the waves, he had come to complete involvement—he was now caught in an enclosed space with the analyst (shark) who seemed both more familiar with this new environment and potentially dangerous. Taken together, the three dreams reveal, first, the patient's concealed sense of superiority, secondly, his desire to avoid being overwhelmed by deep emotions, and thirdly, his fear that the analyst might "kill" the neurotic aspects of his personality that had so long served him as a crucial defence against his deep feelings.

Another example is that of a spinster social worker, aged 30, who felt she was "getting old," had no close relationships, and "went around feeling angry all the time." Here is her first dream. "A young woman is lying face down on the beach. There is no one else there. There is one barren tree. The water is still; everything is still and quiet. There is just one thing that moves in the picture, the clouds in the sky. They keep on moving constantly. The young woman is hopeless and depressed. I couldn't stand the clouds keeping on moving. I wanted them to stop. I was angry that they kept moving. I wanted them to stop."

The patient was aware that the dream depicted her feelings about her own life: hopeless and barren of emotional experience. She was, however, puzzled by the movement of the clouds. Yet the very feeling of passivity that she had was an indication of her failure to accept responsibility for herself. Life "happened" to her; she felt no capacity to get up and do something about it, merely a deep anger and resentment that, above her, motion and life were going on. She wanted life (the moving clouds) to stop; it seemed easier to deny life to others than to go out and make it for herself.

Both these examples show the use that can be made of the situation described by the dream as a whole: that is, the therapist is inducing the patient to respond to the manifest dream, rather than to break it up by free association and then reassemble its latent content. This latter process (as we saw in examining Freud's technique) uses the associations to the dream as a means of delving below its immediate and overall symbolism. But associations are not used merely in this Freudian manner. Whether one believes, with Freud, that the manifest dream is only the starting point from which by free association one may eventually come to the latent and truly significant dream material, or whether one has a more flexible attitude to the dream, almost all therapists agree that the next step after the report of the dream is to elicit the patient's associations to it.

These, however, are not simply the verbal chains of association that lead away from particular images or words in the dream. As we have seen in earlier chapters, the notion that a train of thought would lead to hidden ideas, feelings, and memories, was well established in philosophy and in

A patient's dreams may reveal more than
his words, and the first dream in therapy
may guide a therapist in the treatment he
adopts. Therapists, in fact, attach great
significance to the initial dream, which
may reveal the central theme of a neurosis.
In *The Golden Notebook* (1962) by the
modern author Doris Lessing, the central
figure, Anna, enters psychoanalysis: the
first dream that she reports depicts her
inability to feel. She dreams of a concert
in which she is the pianist. Dressed in
Edwardian clothes she sits at a grand
piano. The doll-like audience waits but
she is paralyzed and unable to play.

psychology long before Freud. The German philosophers Leibniz and Kant, the English historian William Lecky and, above all, the great English scientist Sir Francis Galton, were only a few of those who realized that the free play of associations would lead to what Lecky referred to as the "reappearance of opinions, modes of thought, and emotions belonging to a former stage of our intellectual history." What has happened since psychoanalysis attached the associational process to the interpretation of dreams is the discovery that verbal or intellectual associations may be almost the least of those aroused. Feelings, often inexpressible, will also be awakened; and with the feelings, related to some past or present experience, can come something much more than the spoken recollection.

This phenomenon was, of course, known from cases of somnambulism and hysteria. In this century, experience has taught psychotherapists that almost any action contains a hidden meaning and may unconsciously be used by the patient as a means of communication. From the manner in which the patient enters, addresses the analyst or sits in the room, to movements of the hands, restlessness, coughs, sneezes, or the manner of speaking (or, indeed, not speaking), whether he keeps appointments (or even whether he pays his bills on time), the therapist can draw significant clues. All such aspects of the patient's behavior are as associational as the words he uses and the ideas

Outpatients at a London hospital taking part in group therapy: a 1964 drawing by British artist Paul Hogarth.

he conveys. Even the moment at which an idea or a phrase is offered as an association—what we may call the dynamic context of the association—or the fact that a digression commences after a given word or movement are indicative of the underlying structure of the patient's personality. All these types of association to the dream, we must assume, are the product of processes integrally related to those that caused the original dream.

The therapist, all the same, cannot directly recognize all the hidden relationships, for much material is produced that may be intended to mislead, or that is related to associated but still hidden aspects of the patient's problems —aspects that will emerge only later in the treatment. The ability to identify what is immediately relevant is one mark of the really skilled therapist; another is the capacity to remember material that previously appeared obscure and has later become significant. The point has been well put by Dr. Bonime:

" ... the associations to a dream often do not illuminate but merely aggregate as a collection of items without apparent connection. The collecting of these items, however, the search for associations, is the beginning of a process. Every associative exploration is like Darwin's voyage on *The Beagle*, during which he collected specimens of all types and studied them for their relationships; many specimens were not immediately relateable, but none was discarded as irrelevant."

Even in the very first interviews, the patient is providing a wealth of evidence. The therapist will not normally do more than pick up a few leading points that may enable his patient to extend his insight: to offer elaborate comments on a patient's dream is worse than useless in a process of treatment that aims essentially at self-discovery. As Dr. Bonime observes, "unhappily, dreams offer a great arena for therapeutic exhibitionism . . . in response to the therapist's flair for interpretation, patients may feed dreams and readily accept interpretation, and thus unwittingly avoid involvement in their own treatment processes." It is always difficult to strike a good balance between, on the one hand, frightening or dazzling the patient and, on the other, teaching him what is best regarded as a working technique for approaching and then experiencing his own irrationality.

It must, moreover, never be forgotten that the therapist is not confronting the written record of a dream—as one does in the pages of a book. He confronts a living, suffering person, much of whose life history he has come to know; at the same time, he himself is living and feeling, and he must take account of his attitudes toward his patient, including his own dreams and fantasies. Jung has recorded many occasions on which his dreams provided him with insight about a patient, or about his relationship to a patient, that proved helpful in the course of the treatment. A sudden hunch may be even more valuable than hours of puzzling over a peculiarly esoteric dream. One analyst, for instance, had this dream:

"The patient and I are sitting at a small table in a sidewalk cafe, perhaps in Paris. The patient is saying very little, but has a troubled expression on his face. He appears worried. I say to him: 'Why not try to tell me what is the matter?'"

In this case, it appears, the analyst had a markedly ambivalent attitude toward his patient, though he had not consciously appreciated this fact. Intuitively, he had sensed that the patient was very fearful of his emotional involvement with his mother, but he had avoided probing into this fear lest it provoked a panic reaction by the patient.

Such examples confirm a general point. No therapist can help a patient beyond the limits to which his own self-discovery has carried him, enable the patient to bear fears or feelings that the therapist himself cannot bear, or assist him to understand things beyond the therapist's own comprehension. This is why dream interpretation is so intimately related to the inner life of each specific patient and his therapist, and why run-of-the-mill interpretation by the use of fixed symbols can so easily degenerate into a kind of parlor game.

A patient reported, for instance, that he dreamed he was riding in an automobile. Here are his associations, noted verbatim:

"It is rather a large and old-fashioned car—very shiny—a large crowd of people—waving—an old film—George Arliss—very dignified—apparently—in top hat—like a politician—hole in the floor—his feet coming through—he has to walk—perhaps it is Charlie Chaplin—a tramp dressed up—he isn't what he pretends to be—in fact he is a criminal—it seems more like a tumbril—a cart going to the place of execution—Tyburn Tree, or something like that—the man in *The Beggar's Opera*—a sort of carousing highwayman."

Every phrase here is rich with indicators. The patient's first association expresses a sense of self-importance, a desire to have people admire and applaud him. He may be referring to himself; the therapist can conclude that this is the case, from his direct knowledge of the patient and his life-problems. But he may be referring to some other person he sees in this way—possibly his father; conceivably the analyst. At the subjective level, he in fact describes himself as an actor (George Arliss) who appears (the upper part of his body: possibly his intellect) to be an important person, but who is actually a sham. He seems to be carried along in style, but in fact he has to walk; the vehicle in which he is traveling is a sham. And he too is a sham. He is a pathetic, tramp-like figure (Charlie Chaplin) "dressed up," and he "isn't what he pretends to be." In fact, he sees himself as something worse than a fraud: he "is a criminal." His triumphal progress has turned into something disreputable—a progress to the gallows. And then because he is beginning to release this inner image of himself, he doesn't feel so bad. The hero of *The Beggar's Opera* is indeed a carousing, jolly highwayman—and the important fact about the film (which the patient recalls seeing) is that Macheath is given a last-minute reprieve and escapes the hangman. There is ample material here (none of which would have emerged if there had been an obsessive concern with the original symbol of the automobile) for therapist and patient to explore for more than one session.

The therapist, however, was well-advised to remember that the dream had an objective as well as a subjective level. While the patient used the linking thought of "George Arliss" to introduce the image of himself as an actor, the same thought concealed a reference to the therapist. Not only did the patient see the therapist as an older man riding in his "old-fashioned car" (the patient's view of orthodox psychoanalysis) to popular acclaim, he also had hidden an aggressive feeling against the therapist in selecting the image of a *dead* actor. He was wishing the therapist was dead; and he is at the same time insisting that, living, the therapist was not what he seemed to be. He appeared to be riding, but was actually being forced to walk.

It was this double meaning of the fantasy association that attracted the therapist's own attention, and led him to a train of associations of his own. He too began his associations from the automobile, and realized that the patient was hinting at the whole process of therapy. He also had the advantage of the cue given by the stumbling feet. The "George Arliss" figure was a condensation—a symbol standing for both analyst and patient. The therapist's association continued:

"The top half—the head—myself—imposing—to impose means both to impress and to dominate—I am being dominating—I am imposing—imposing can also mean being a fraud, not what I seem—the patient and I are both frauds—we are concentrating on the impressive appearance and the public acclaim—we appear to be making progress—but what is really happening? —the feet are stumbling—while we are superficially getting on with the treatment we are actually dragging our feet—why?—we are not really going on a triumphal parade, but to execute a criminal—I am making the patient feel his own worthlessness—I am driving him to feel judged and condemned— I will 'see him hanged'—that means, I can't be bothered with him—I regard him as an outcast—I've 'put him in the cart'—I am in some way responsible for his troubles—he is trying to revenge himself—a highwayman—he holds people up to ransom—'your money or your life!'—another condensation— he sees himself as the highwayman but he also sees me as one—I am extracting money from him by threatening his life—he feels I will take this part of his identity away—yet he hopes for a reprieve—he feels that at the end of his trials he will be set free . . ."

The question here is not whether the patient's view of his associations or the therapist's parallel associations are correct. Nor does it greatly matter whether the therapist is right in concluding that the associations to the original dream can bear at least a double interpretation. The fact is that the have evoked a double interpretation, that there is a mutual stimulus from the original dream. This has led both patient and therapist to explore within themselves varied aspects of their relationship that had not previously been evident. In particular, the therapist (by not seeking to force an interpretation) has received an important hint about the therapeutic relationship. He has been led to realize that he is, in some way, judging the patient, diminishing his worth rather than wholly accepting him. The short dream and its rich associations have clearly revealed a resistance to the therapy by the patient and a somewhat dishonest and dominating attitude to the patient on the part of the therapist.

A short, but dramatic example of the same kind is given by Dr. Bonime to indicate the manner in which the simple report of a dream can convey a wealth of information about the relationship of patient and therapist. "For another patient," he writes, " 'resistance' is a very bookish word indeed to describe her resentful, passive role in analysis, as compared with her own vivid dream-picture of a wrenching, induced labor, which was painful and productive of nothing but a 'bloody mess.' Here was represented her determinedly passive resistance, her pain in the process, the consequent lack of therapeutic fruitfulness, and her associated hatred for the obstetrician-analyst."

Many dreams—possibly most of them—will reveal some aspect of resistance on the patient's part. In fact, the identification and overcoming of resistances is one of the most crucial functions of therapy. For the defense system that a patient has created (and which he may regard, at first, as his "real" self which is threatened with destruction) is serving a valuable purpose; it is the means by which he has adapted himself, or "kept going," and he is understandably reluctant to abandon neurotic habits that have protected him against seemingly dangerous feelings. They are the means by which, in fantasy, he has set up pseudo-reality for himself because it seems less painful than reality itself. In this fantasy world, it is not merely his wish-fulfillment for satisfactions denied in childhood—possibly the craving for love, ungratified aggressive feelings, and so on—that the neurotic symptoms attempt to achieve for him. His symptoms (as an expression of his whole personality disturbance) are a means by which he pursues present satisfactions that are denied him. No matter that his life is potentially rich, rewarding, and successful—if he has learned to prefer the pseudo-gratifications of fantasy to those of real life, he cannot let himself enter fully into his human heritage. He squanders his human assets and may even seek his own self-destruction rather than give up the neurotic means of escaping from responsibility for himself.

It is precisely the therapist's task to eliminate such means of escape, by forcing the patient to confront his resistances, because in them he will also confront the negative aspects of himself. As the therapy proceeds, this can become an increasingly cooperative endeavor, and the patient will ultimately become capable of recognizing—in dream, daydream, and behavior—the indicators of his own infantile demands on life.

One of Dr. Bonime's patients, who was moving toward a more positive attitude to herself and to him, had the dream presented—together with its first associations—on the following pages.

The way a patient sees her relationship with her psychiatrist is dramatically expressed in the drawing of a woman patient at an English mental hospital. The picture's caption reads: "All I want to do is give him flowers, but look at him!"

227

"I am driving with someone; he was vague but it was a man."

ASSOCIATIONS

"My first association with the man next to me in the car is you. I know that it is you."

"I drive past some shops with ugly old furniture and bric-à-brac in the windows. I tell my companion that my mother has that kind of junk in her house, and that I don't like it."

ASSOCIATIONS

"I seem to be showing him my past. In a casual, generally vague kind of way, I can accept and let him see that there are things like that *in the shop windows.*"

"Then driving on, I point to a spot and say that my mother's house is there—but it is not there and I feel quite dismayed not to see it. Then I see that the house is there after all, though it had not been visible from the road, as it used to be."

ASSOCIATIONS

'The modern houses surrounding my mother's house are, I think, the *newer ideas and attitudes I have acquired in order to avoid looking directly at my real feelings and at my past—but they are there when I look hard enough.*"

"I want to show my companion the inside of the house. When we go inside I am very much ashamed to see that the house is dark and old-fashioned, and filled with crude ugly things. The feeling is surprise and dismay, though I had said that this was the kind of thing that was in the house."

ASSOCIATIONS

"My feelings about the inside of the house are feelings I have had in talking in the analysis about my experiences and relationships of the past. Even though I had said in *general* that there was ugliness there, *I am surprised and ashamed when I really* find *specific examples of it*—and I know that it was this way.

"For instance, facing the fact that my mother never really loved me the way I wanted her to, and not just because she was busy or worried about other things; or looking at the really intense rivalry I had, and still have, with my brother— not *just dismissing it casually* with the assumption that 'of course I had some sibling rivalry.'"

The italics added by Dr. Bonime are useful guides to the resistances of the patient. She is trying to cooperate in the analysis, and superficially ("in the shop windows") she will show him things from her past. But she would rather he looked at the "new apartment houses" than witness her "surprise and shame" at discovering she has crude and ugly things in her life. Indeed, the patient hints that she would like to distract him, to slow up the treatment—a state of mind underlined by the next dream she told. In this she is the only passenger in a bus whose driver refuses to stop, ultimately taking her to his house and introducing her to his large family. Once again, she is describing her reluctance to continue, but her uneasiness is overcome and she admits her willingness to join the doctor's circle of patients—the large family at his house.

Dreams are not all of equal intensity, at least as the patient recalls and reports them—some appear to be much more emotionally charged than others, some seem to refer more directly to present situations, and others to much more infantile experiences. The differences between them are hard to clarify, but it has been suggested that the "depth" of the dream may relate to the point at which it occurs in the sleep cycle, to the particular somatic stimuli to which the dreamer is subject, or to the inner evolution of dream patterns. This last point is especially relevant to dream analysis in therapy, for it draws attention to two types of dream for which the therapist must always be watchful: the repetitive dream and the "serial" dream.

The first of these is familiar to anyone who has recalled his own dreams over a period. Sometimes over a period of months, sometimes over a period of years, almost precisely the same dream is repeated—usually one containing a strong element of anxiety, such as a trial, imprisonment, a task that can never be properly completed. Such a dream points to a profound problem confronting the dreamer. The actual setting of the situation may refer back to some frightening experience in infancy: the small child criticized by a parent *(the trial)* or locked in a room as punishment *(the imprisonment)* or even forced to attempt bowel control through rigid toilet training *(the task)*. But the experience has accreted to itself some larger problem. The dreamer's inability to grow through it, his continual harking back to it, indicate that this situation dramatizes his position in life and some of his vital relationships so forcefully that he literally cannot dismiss it from his mind.

For this reason, the therapist will devote much time and cave to analyzing such a dream and all its associations. He will observe, moreover, that a dream of this type will change in the course of therapy, retaining many of the same symbols but presenting the dreamer's situation differently. We can see two examples of such a change. The first (on page 232) is the case of the man who dreamed of his attempts to get out of prison: the second (in Chapter 7) is the case cited by Jung of the woman who, going from one analyst to another, presented each of them with the "crossing the frontier" dream in a different form. By studying the manner in which a repetitive dream evolves, important clues about the unconscious evolution of the personality can be obtained. Such a series often culminates in a dream of this kind: "Somebody was enclosed in walls. No one knew about it. He was closed in, and couldn't break out. I was the one inside, suffering in this closed area—and I was on the outside, too, struggling to let me out. I finally did, and it felt so good."

Here, in fact, is a retrospective dream, describing the course of successful therapy, and just as significant as the introductory dreams in summarizing the overall pattern of a neurosis.

It is often fairly easy to interpret repetitive dreams. It is more difficult to comprehend the "serial" dream because, in the absence of systematic record keeping, it is rare that the serial pattern draws attention to itself. Freud took the view that all the dreams of a single night were in fact the remembered fragments of a single dream, and that it should be possible to find a relationship between these parts. This view has been extended to the discovery of continuing dream themes. That is, a dreamer may revert to a dream (come back to the same setting, the same characters, perhaps the same problem or mood) the following night, then two weeks later, then a month later. If the links between these parts can be found, much more effective diagnosis and therapeutic analysis is possible. Jung was one of the first to stress the value of analyzing dreams in series, and this is now an established part of dream interpretation techniques. The process (though not the theoretical assumption) is similar to Freud's method of breaking down the manifest dream into its components and then assembling the latent dream from them. By careful identification of components in a number of dreams over a period of time, new and fruitful inner relationships can be established.

Such components may be references to real or symbolic individuals (e.g., *father and mother, policeman and politician*); to objects *(house, automobile, knife)*; to settings *(beach, prison, hospital)*; actions *(beating, embracing, running)*; or feelings *(loving, hating, fearing)*. Or they may be recurring references to the patient's ambitions or depressions, to his relationships with employers, friends, people he loves, and so forth. It is quite feasible to index references of this kind in case notes so that, over a long series of dreams, the dynamic evolution of the dreams and their interpretations can be traced. Various methods of classification can be employed; the method chosen will depend on the analyst's theoretical orientation—the kind of symbols or concepts that he chooses to emphasize and the use he makes of them. It is obvious that a series thus classified by a Jungian analyst would look entirely different from one classified by a Freudian.

Since it is not practical to present an extended interpretation of a series in these pages, the nature of such "linked" dreams may perhaps be more briefly demonstrated by three dreams of one patient, a 30-year-old artist, whose mother suffered from epilepsy:

"I dreamed about Hamlet. I was identical with him, or I had the feeling I had met him somewhere."

"My father eats soup and says that he is poisoned, as has happened once before."

"My father talks to a prostitute in my presence. I am astonished."

In this (and in other dreams in the series) the patient is accusing his mother of adultery and making clear references to what we may call a "Hamlet complex." Though we are not concerned here with a detailed analysis of these dreams, it is important to point out that the patient's mother had confessed in a post-epileptic delirium to incestuous relations with her brother. Not only was this "dangerous" confession the "target" of the dream series but it

In his book *The Forgotten Language* (1952) American psychoanalyst Erich Fromm gives a series of dreams that express the change in a dreamer's attitude over a long period of therapy. In the first dream he sees himself in prison, unable to get out; he is the prisoner of his neurosis. In a later dream he is trying to cross a frontier but has no passport; he lacks the means of eastablishing his true identity to strangers. The third shows him at a port unable to leave because there are no boats; as yet he is unable to find a way out of his problems. In the last dream he is in his home, trying to open a door. After some difficulty, he opens it. The theme running through the dreams is: "I am shut in, though I wish to be free," which the dream expresses by different symbolic devices.

seemed to have a direct relation to the extremely bad stammer from which the patient suffered: he apparently feared lest his secret thoughts should also pop out unawares.

If it can be established that dreams do have coherent themes running through them substantial support will be provided for the thesis that dreams reflect a definite though unconscious thought process and are not simply a succession of random and essentially meaningless images. One effort to establish precisely this fact has been made by the American clinical psychologist, Dr. Calvin S. Hall. His book *The Meaning of Dreams*, published in 1953, was based upon the systematic analysis of 10,000 dreams. Dr. Hall is far from uncritical about the dream concepts used in psychoanalysis, and his criticisms are the basis upon which Professor H. J. Eysenck, the outstanding British critic of psychoanalysis, has argued that Freudian and post-Freudian dream interpretation has no scientific standing whatsoever:

"Psychoanalysts have poured forth an opulent array of hypotheses and theories. Their speculations are shrewd, sophisticated and, to the uninitiated, often esoteric. At their best, the psychoanalytic theories appear impressively insightful; at their worst, they appear impressively fraudulent. Good or bad, they are rarely dull.... The principal deficiency to be found in the psychoanalytical writings is that they fail to meet the standards of the scientific method...."

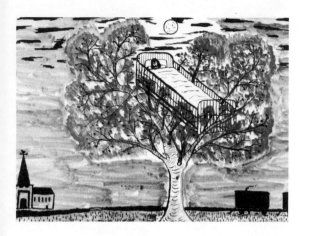

These paintings by a 36-year-old epileptic patient in a British mental hospital are of dreams that occurred over a period of years. All three dreams point to the patient's feelings of power. He associates himself with Christ—a feeling he bases on his dream, at eight years old, of Christ asleep in an apple tree (left). He thinks he has magic powers over other people and sees himself as a witch in one dream (right). He admits to feeling some kind of "cosmic" sense and in all his paintings the moon, Saturn, and the sun appear in prominent positions (far right).

Dr. Hall's book describes his own work in seeking to remedy this deficiency. He places the greatest possible emphasis on the collection of dream series, saying: "The larger the sample of dreams collected from a person the more accurate and comprehensive the picture of the person becomes." He bases his analysis upon the classification of the dream contents into four categories: (i) The Setting, (ii) The Characters, (iii) The Action, and (iv) The Emotions. Using this method, he argues, dream interpretation can in fact be undertaken by applying what (by Freudian standards) are very simple rules. He, in fact, shares the underlying assumptions of psychoanalysis, despite his criticisms, for he believes that:

"... dreams reveal what we really think of ourselves, how we regard others; they do not describe external reality, but a psychic reality—the ideas and attitudes that a person has in mind, whether true or false, whether acceptable or unacceptable in terms of his moral system. They show us his picture of the world around him and his relation to it, cut through all the rationalizations and illusions of ordinary life and bring us face to face with our true inner problems. And while the conscious mind is preoccupied with the outer world, ignoring what comes from within, so the unconscious pays relatively little attention to the outer world and is preoccupied with its own affairs."

This conception is so similar to those we have been examining that we may wonder how Dr. Hall's method of "diagnosing personality" in fact differs from those he criticizes in psychotherapy. The difference lies in the manner in which he insists that "anyone who is able to follow a few simple rules can interpret dreams.... They are pictures of what the mind is thinking. Anyone who can look at a picture and say what it means ought to be able to look at his dream pictures and say what they mean. The meaning of a dream will not be found in some theory about dreams; it is right there in the dream itself." To understand such pictures, however, Dr. Hall suggests that we regard the

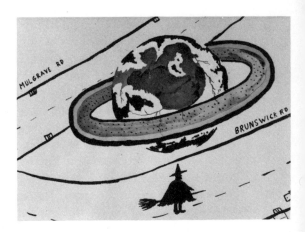

contents of the mind as a five-fold system of conceptions by which the mind endeavors to organize its inner and outer reality.

1. The system that contains a person's self-conceptions: it answers the question "How do I see myself?"

2. The group of interconnected systems that describe the way the individual sees other persons.

3. The system that contains the individual's view of the world—his ideology, values, his relation to his material and social environment.

4. The system that consists of "the conceptions of one's impulses or driving forces, the ways and means by which they are to be gratified, the obstacles which stand in the way of their fulfillment, and the penalties exacted when the rules governing the control of impulses are broken."

5. The system of conceptions that locate the inner conflicts confronting the individual and his attempts to solve them.

It is evident that Dr. Hall is offering a simplified model of the human personality that is not greatly at variance with the one underlying most psychotherapeutic practices. He claims, however, that each one of these five systems can be identified in any individual and, when applied to a large number of his dreams, used to build up a cumulative portrait of his personality and of its relation to external reality. But once this is done, a vital question remains. How do we deal with the system of conceptions that stem from the individual's conflicts? Once again, Dr. Hall offers a relatively simple model. He reduces the conflicts to five fundamental patterns.

The first of these is the earliest in life: the struggle each child goes through to separate himself from his parents, to distinguish their feelings toward him from his feeling toward them. From this the second follows: how can the opposing desires for security and freedom be reconciled? The third relates to sexuality—for, "since bisexuality is the biological norm and uni-sexuality the social norm, it is easily understandable why man is tormented by conflicting conceptions regarding his sex role." Man, moreover, is torn between the demands of nature and those of society, between his instinctual impulses and the restrictions his culture imposes upon them; the fourth, and a most important series of conflicts, thus besets him. Finally, there is the conflict of life and death, the essentially biological drama of man, the struggle between the constructive, synthesizing, and assimilating processes and those that are destructive, disintegrative, and decomposing.

The more closely one examines these personality patterns, of course, the more the difference of principle between them and the psychoanalytical theories seem to turn into one of degree. In the end Dr. Hall's theory begins to look like a simplification, an insistence that analysts are sometimes too clever by half; but, on the positive side, he does make a valuable attempt to demonstrate by a large-scale analysis of dream material that, behind our conscious thoughts, the mind is continually at work trying to organize our total experience into forms that are sufficiently meaningful to allow us to feel and behave coherently.

The last of these conclusions, and, indeed, Dr. Hall's work as a whole, thus focuses our attention on what seems to be an increasingly widespread theory of the dream—one to which much clinical and laboratory evidence seems to point. *The dream is simultaneously a reflection of the ways in which the mind is attempting to formulate the conflicts and problems of our lives and one of the means by which we attempt unconsciously to solve them.*

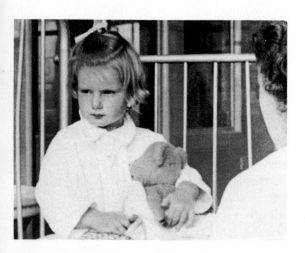

A child's first reactions to a stay in hospital. Separation has made her feel rejected, and she is unable to distinguish between being rejected and rejecting others. When her mother visits her this uncertainty leads her to show mistrust and hostility (above). The child's effort to disentangle rejection and affection, love and hate, is, Dr. Hall suggests, one of the most basic human conflicts.

A fuller consideration of this theory must wait until we have considered whether modern psysiological research into the nature of sleep, and contemporary discussions of the nature of thinking, perception, and behavior, support or modify the conclusions that can be drawn from more than 60 years of psychological inquiry into and experience of dreams in the treatment of mental disorders. But it is useful at this stage to consider a little more closely the idea that the dream is fundamentally a problem-solving function of the mind.

A most important and much neglected suggestion of this kind was made soon after World War I by the noted British physiologist and anthropologist Dr. W. H. Rivers, who had founded the school of experimental psychology at Cambridge University and then, during the war, specialized in treating shellshocked soldiers. Dr. Rivers found himself unable to explain the nightmares and recurrent battle dreams of soldiers in terms of Freudian theory, and came to the conclusion that far from being wish-fulfillments such dreams were "the attempted solution of a conflict" between the tendency of a painful experience to recur and an attempt to prevent it recurring. That is, the wish to repress the memory of the painful experience is operative only in consciousness, and in sleep successful repression cannot occur. But, as Dr. Rivers suggested in his book *Conflict and Dream* (1923), the attempted solution is often a failure; it is only as the patient moves toward mental health that he becomes more successful in solving his conflicts in sleep. The degree of

Conflicting desires for freedom and security are apparent in teenage "gang" behavior. Left, British "Mods" and "Rockers," whose negative behavior toward society as a whole contrasts with their positive group solidarity. Right, a man leaves for the Spanish Civil War (photograph by Robert Capa)—a scene that illustrates the most profound of all conflicts, that between life and death.

emotional feeling or distress accompanying the dream is, for him, the measure of the dream's success in problem solving: a successful, symbolic solution leaves no emotional traces; the unsuccessful, directly perceived solution leaves all the marks of a nightmare. To this idea Dr. Rivers added the suggestion that the fantasy solutions of sleep were invariably of an infantile or regressive character, dating from the "period of life in which the human being is liable to affective disturbances of a very intense kind with the crude explosive nature which is characteristic of the effect of the nightmare or war-dream."

Any suggestion that dreams are an attempt to solve problems, however, must be based on the assumption to which we have come back several times in these last three chapters—that dream thoughts make sense, but that they are "thoughts" of a different order from those of consciousness. That assumption has now much more evidence to support it than it had when Freud was first attempting to translate the language in which these thoughts appear to consciousness. Despite the differences in techniques of dream interpretation and the conflict of views among interpreters, it now seems reasonable to argue that the assumption seems to work in practice—that the picture of a person's personality and problems that can be deduced from his dreams is congruent with the picture that can be obtained by other means.

An argument of this kind is advanced in detail in a number of recent books, notably *Prelogical Experience* by E. S. Tauber and Maurice S. R. Green and *Dream Interpretation* by Erika Fromm and Thomas French. In both books it is argued that "prelogical" or "practical" thinking is a form of thought which operates below the level of consciousness, a mental process to which we commonly give the name of "intuition". Thoughts of this kind cannot be directly communicated because they are experienced rather than verbalized: they can, however, be transmitted by empathy—that is, by precisely the form of interpersonal communication that exists in the effective therapeutic relationship. Part of the process of therapy is to find ways (which are only partly verbal) whereby the patient is slowly able to bring what has previously existed in his mind as pre-verbal or pre-logical thought (the feeling or experience) into forms identifiable to consciousness, which can then confront the inner and hitherto inarticulate reality. That is the reason why, for instance, the transcript of an analytic session may seem trivial and boring: the verbal record cannot show either what is happening between analyst and patient or, even more, the changes of feeling (the reorganization of responses to present reality) that are taking place at a deep level within each of them. It accounts, moreover, for the sudden and apparently inexplicable changes of mood in a patient in the course of one session of therapy and for the striking and often painful moments when a flash of insight occurs.

At the very beginning of this book we laid stress on the symbolic form in which these buried feelings or experiences express themselves. The modern view is that symbolism is much less the product of "censorship"—which

British soldiers believed their success in halting the advance of the superior German army at Mons (Belgium) in 1914 was due to the appearance of angels encouraging them to fight—depicted by Marcel Gillis in a painting *The Legend of the Angels of Mons*. Such a myth is an example of mass wish-fulfillment in an unpleasant situation.

disguises unacceptable or dangerous thoughts so that they may enter consciousness without too much psychic disturbance—than the result of a process whereby the unconscious is endeavoring to formulate attitudes that are at that moment beyond verbal definition. The rich, multiple-meaning language of imagery actually is more capable of encompassing our deepest thoughts and experiences than the imperfect language of words. That is to say, the dream images do not conceal or limit the experiences of the unconscious; they reveal and amplify the unconscious material in a manner superior to the logical and restrictive medium of speech.

If the individual was capable of comprehending all the external reality to which he is exposed, and all the reality which he has experienced, he would have no conflicts and every problem arising in his life would be understandable and soluble. But that is not the case. His life is an on-going process whereby he both discovers the world and explores his own relation to it, and in this process he must continually encounter difficulties. To the extent that he surmounts them, he grows; to the extent that they defeat him, he regresses to an earlier life-situation which was more tolerable. If he grows, he is healthy; those parts of his personality that fail to grow are the causes of his neurosis or even more serious mental disorders.

As each problem arises (and, in fact, as problems are anticipated) the whole of the resources of the mind seem to be available for the attempt to deal with it. Freud's opinion was that, rather than attack the problem if it seems too difficult or dangerous, the unconscious takes refuge in wish-fulfillment—that is, it hallucinates a solution. He thought that such hallucinations were the underlying cause of dreams, daydreams, and fantasy phenomena of all kinds. Yet this emphasis on the wish-fulfillment element is far too exclusive, in the light of subsequent evidence. In Freud's view, all the wishes that sought fulfillment were infantile wishes, and they merely took rational material from the dreamer's present and past in order to rework it as part of a highly irrational purpose. The purpose of all therapy, for Freud, was to discover, and thus release the fixated wishes (largely instinctual) of early childhood.

But why should one so limit the process, or regard it as basically pathological, or separate the deep thought processes that emerge in the dream from similar processes that are taking place, waking or sleeping, continuously in all of us? Might it not be better to regard the pre-verbal, pre-logical, or practical thought patterns of the unconscious as a continuing psychic function; to accept that we become more acutely aware of them, or that access to them becomes easier, in sleep (when consciousness is depressed), but that they are accessible in other ways? We can reach them by daydreaming, by using fantasy as a projective device, seeing images in the fire, the clouds, the water, or in the ink-blots of the Rorschach test. We have access to them in the creative process of writing poetry, painting, or sculpting, or in the hypnotic illusions that precede sleep. True, the imagery is then less clear because it is dimmed by the light of waking consciousness, but it is nonetheless there.

This is the conclusion to which psychotherapy—whether or not it relies on dream interpretation—points with growing emphasis. The fantasy life of each individual is the means by which he organizes innumerable and transient answers to problems he has met (but failed to solve), to those he is currently meeting, and to some at least of those he may meet in the future. The dream life of the individual, however, often focuses on a particular problem that has, for a longer or shorter period of time, assumed special importance. This is what Erika Fromm and Thomas French, the distinguished psychoanalysts from Chicago, have termed the "focal problem." The analogy is an apt one. For it is as if a problem acts as a lens through which the potential solutions offered by the unconscious pass into consciousness and are directed in attitude or behavior at reality. When we suddenly "change our minds," or abruptly "do something unexpected," we are in fact adopting a new (possibly "illogical" or "unpremeditated") solution to the situation we confront. Conversely, our experience of people and things is focused by the dominant problem or problems at the threshold of consciousness and transmitted to memory in a form determined by the nature of the focal problem.

The theory that a "focal problem" may provide the basic structure of a dream is illustrated in the three diagrams (right). The man referred to in the text has difficulties in his relations with his father; his infantile fears of his father's explosive anger are projected into his fears of nuclear war, while his genuine anxieties about a nuclear conflict reactivate his childhood terrors at the prospect of his father "blowing up". The fantasy and reality elements mingle in the focal area. When this happens, what Freud called "condensation" occurs. The bomb and the father become a condensed symbol (1); death and loss of identity are similarly merged (2). When the dream occurs, therefore, some recent reality material is fused with infantile and even instinctual feelings. On waking (3), the dreamer attempts to reconstruct a coherent dream story. In this case, he might report: "I was with my father, and I was very frightened. He shouted at me, and then he disappeared, and there was a terrible explosion and I felt I was dying in a nuclear war." This is only a schematic explanation, but it is compatible with Freud's description of the "dream-work," which produces a fusion of real and fantasy elements in symbolic form, and indicates what may determine the selection of these components and the relative weight given to them in different parts of the dream. The dream story connects the nodal points of the dream material, while the associations to past and present experience lead off from them. The dream story (the manifest dream) and its associations (the latent content) are thus a product of the focal problem.

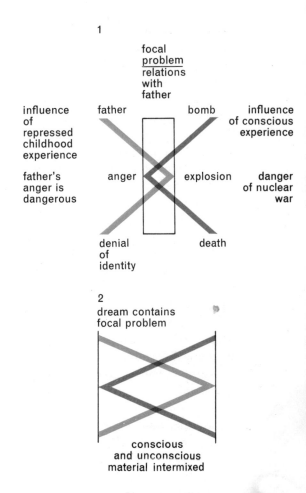

1

focal problem relations with father

influence of repressed childhood experience

father   bomb   influence of conscious experience

father's anger is dangerous

anger   explosion   danger of nuclear war

denial of identity   death

2
dream contains focal problem

conscious and unconscious material intermixed

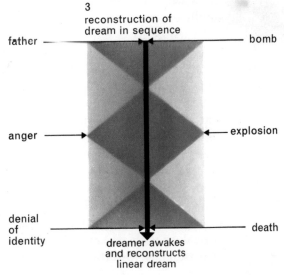

3
reconstruction of dream in sequence

father — bomb

anger → ← explosion

denial of identity — death

dreamer awakes and reconstructs linear dream

This two-way process can be illustrated by an example. An intelligent professional man of 40 has never resolved the problem of his relationship with his father. All his life he has feared his father "blowing up" in a destructive manner. The fear, though unacknowledged, is such that it seems to threaten him with loss of his identity—with extinction. He is thus afraid of his father, views him as immensely powerful, and is deeply hostile to him. This is a "focal problem" for him. In his political activities he is a strong opponent of nuclear weapons, and this is a position which, in reality, is logically tenable. But his attitude toward nuclear weapons is emotionally loaded: he is given to panics and to an obsessional concern with the prospect of annihilation. While he has a genuine reality problem—how to secure the banning of nuclear arms—he is also continually attempting the solution of the dominant problem: that is, how to prevent his father "blowing up." His view of the possibilities and dangers of nuclear war is distorted by his unconscious assessment of the chances of "avoiding a showdown" or "achieving a compromise" with his father. In his attitude to the possessors of nuclear weapons who threaten him he will try to be as conciliatory as he has always been to his father. Similarly, the real nuclear situation will be distorted as it is transmitted to the unconscious and will provide rich material for the fantasy-forming function to play with in formulating solutions to other problems. (The degree of distortion is proportional to the neurosis of the individual. The more neurotic a person becomes, the greater the role of the focal problems at the threshold of consciousness, the more elaborate his fantasy life, and the less realistic and responsible his behavior.)

Such a case illustrates only the more simple aspects of this process, which is immensely complicated. But the theory that underlies it offers a better explanation of the role of fantasy than merely to sum up all fantasy activity as wish-fulfillment. Everyone undoubtedly has unresolved problems from childhood, infantile needs or aggressions that have never been satisfied. But each of us is living in the present, and drawing continually upon our fantasy life as a kind of computer, receiving data on our life situation and, from the store of knowledge and experience acquired over a lifetime, endeavoring to offer answers to the problems life is posing. Many of those problems will re-awaken long-lost impulses or disturbing wishes—and it is these that appear in our fantasies, along with material drawn from the immediate present. They are integrally related, whether they emerge in dreams, daydreams, or in actual relationships with others.

The function of psychotherapy, seen in this context, is to identify those elements in a person's past that thus distort his ability to face reality and react maturely to it. Thus the concept of the focal problem (whether it is so expressed or not is unimportant compared to the practical consequences of dealing with it) can play a decisive role in singling out the major causes of personality distortion or disturbance. What are generally called resistances are, indeed, found at this threshold point; as they are confronted and overcome, a new problem or a different aspect of the old one will reach the threshold and the patient must again be assisted, first to delineate it and then to gain insight both into its origins and its consequences in his relationship to other persons.

This is why the dream is so valuable, whatever the theoretical assumptions one makes about it or the techniques by which it is interpreted. Both the assumptions and the techniques are subordinate to the fact that the dream describes the focal problem, and thus directs the attention of both therapist and patient to it. They may deal with it well, or less well, but in the imagery of the dream—when consciousness can no longer easily repress the urgent claim of a problem for a solution that may involve painful reconsideration of one's position in life or one's self-conceptions—they confront a constellation of interlocked meanings, all of which point to the decisive issues in the hidden life of the dreamer. When the dreams refuse to change (repetitive dreams) it is a sign that the individual is refusing to change: but as they change, they mirror in their complex and meaning-loaded imagery the evolution that is taking place in the dreamer's total personality. This evolution may be concealed from the dreamer himself—often he will be unable to understand the imagery because it relates to what is to come as well as to what has already been. For the dream, to recall one point that Jung often emphasized, is prospective as well as retrospective, and in ordinary life as well as in therapy it can indicate the direction in which the dreamer's life will move if he is to progress toward self-fulfillment.

This may be the reason why dreams can seem to forecast the future, at least so far as the progress of therapy goes—and, presumably, on much wider aspects of a person's life. For they scan the possible solutions to each of life's dilemmas. To the extent that these solutions are harmonizing with reality, the dreamer is making progress toward an integrated personality capable of facing life: to the extent that the solutions are distorted, the more "fantastic" and removed from reality they are, the greater the evidence of mental illness.

This is a valuable idea in considering the role of the dream in therapy. Indeed, the manner in which dreams indicate a dreamer's approach to his life problems—we may recall Adler's phrase that they are a kind of "dress reharsal" —may be more important in therapy than are the specific interpretations given to them by either the patient or the therapist. But we must now go on to examine other evidence on the nature of dreaming than that derived essentially from clinical psychology. We must ask whether the dream seems to have functions or characteristics that relate to the body as well as the mind, in other words, we must see whether in treating the dream as Jung suggested, as a "thing of nature," we must recognize that it has a role in human physiology as well as in psychology.

9   Sleep and science

Waking and sleeping, Aristotle believed, "are opposites, and sleep is evidently a privation of waking." This is the traditional attitude toward sleep—and most of us still accept it. It seems sensible to regard sleep as a period of oblivion, apparently necessary for rest but nonetheless an interruption to our daily lives. After all, a man who has slept reasonably well throughout 70 years of his life will have spent more than 22 of them asleep. Though the time thus spent has been both physically and psychologically beneficial to him—as he can realize whenever he has been deprived of sleep—he still does not know why the human organism needs to spend such a substantial part of its life insensible to the world in which it lives. Scientists cannot yet give him an explanation, any more than they can answer the specific riddle of sleep that is the concern of this book—why, in our sleep, we dream.

In both respects, however, great progress has been made in recent years. Using modern research techniques, from neuro-surgery to the use of complex electrical apparatus, scientists have been steadily extending their knowledge of the human brain, of the central nervous system, and of the biochemistry of the body. They cannot so far tell us for certain why we sleep, or dream, but they can describe much of what happens when we do; and they are already able to challenge some long-accepted ideas about sleep and dreams, and answer certain age-old questions about them.

The girl in the photograph (bottom) is one of many volunteers who have spent hundreds of nights asleep in laboratories while their brain waves are recorded by a machine called an electroencephalograph (top). This machine has opened up a new era of sleep and dream research—for instance, it enables a trained observer to tell when a sleeper is dreaming.

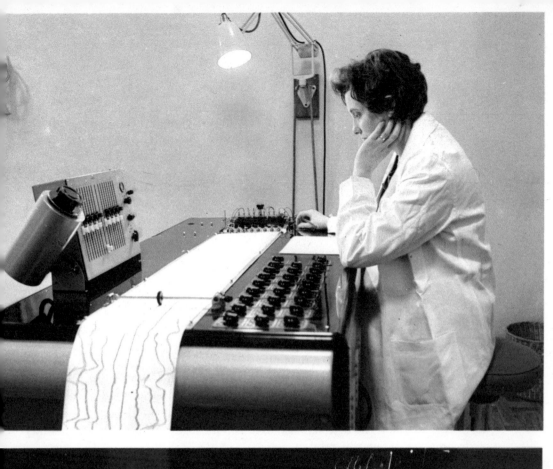
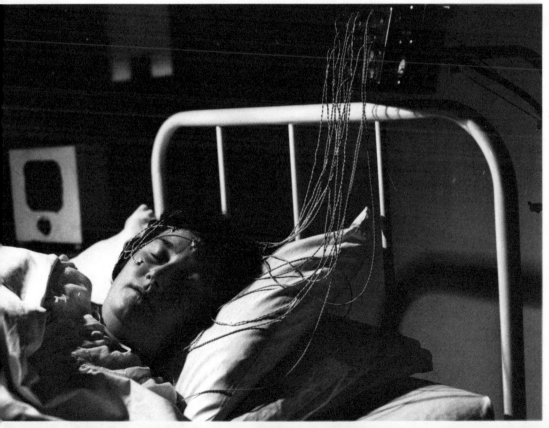

Much of their work lies beyond the immediate scope of this book. The physiology of sleep is a highly technical subject, and one that involves many branches of science and medicine. It is, moreover, a subject in which our knowledge and ideas are changing so fast that they may be revolutionized in the next decade. In 1939, Professor Nathaniel Kleitman, of the University of Chicago, published the first edition of *Sleep and Wakefulness*. This important book, internationally recognized as the standard work on the subject, appeared in a revised edition in 1963. But, as Professor Kleitman has said, so much had changed that the need for revision was urgent: "The bibliography was hopelessly out of date, the text itself obsolete." The superb new bibliography provides a measure of the work now being done in many countries: it lists 4337 books and learned articles on the nature and problems of sleep.

With so much research in progress or completed, contemporary scientists and psychologists are in an immeasurably better position to study the relationship of sleep to dreams than were their predecessors at the beginning of this century. In earlier chapters of this book we saw how the physiological, philosophical, and psychological theories of dreams developed more or less independently, and were often in conflict. Freud himself, attempting something of a synthesis, still concentrated almost wholly on the dream. In *The Interpretation of Dreams* he wrote: "I have had little occasion to deal with the problem of sleep, for that is essentially a problem of physiology." It would be foolish to make such a remark today. The study of sleep and the study of dreams are integrally related.

We are now witnessing the transformation of dream theory from an art to a science, with an inevitable shift of emphasis from the nature of dreams to the nature of dreaming. Until recently, every theory about dreams had to rest ultimately upon introspection—what we remembered and thought about our own dreams and what we could deduce from the similarly subjective reports of others. Under such conditions it was almost impossible to distinguish fact from fancy, or to secure data on which any comparative or statistical work could rely. True, remarkable progress was made once the dream had been recognized as a natural phenomenon, rather than the work of gods and demons. But the logic of that recognition demanded a unified theory of dreams: the traditional antithesis between mind and body (expressed as a conflict between psychological and physiological theories of the dream) had become an obstacle to knowledge. It could be overcome only by searching for objective evidence about the nature of sleep and dreams.

Sleep, like dreams, has always been a matter for speculation. Like dreams, again, it has been explained since antiquity by theories that range from the ludicrous to the shrewd, from the primitive conception that it was due to the flight of the soul to the complex concepts of modern neurology and biochemistry. There is a third and related similarity to dreams; despite the fact that sleep is common to all men, it is only in relatively modern times that

Above, a fourth-century BC sculpture of Hypnos, the Greek god of sleep. It was thought that Hypnos brought sleep by touching men with his magic wand or by fanning them with his wings. Left, the Russian physiologist Ivan Petrovich Pavlov, who showed that a dog held in harness in a sound-proof room will repeatedly fall asleep. He concluded from his experiments that monotony induces sleep by diminishing sensitivity to the environment.

any systematic effort has been made to study it. How much sleep does man really need? Does he need regular sleep? How does the physical state of sleep differ from that of waking? What is happening to the organism when it is asleep? What makes a man go to sleep, and what wakes him? Are the senses immobilized, or does a man hear and feel without responding? What is the relation between sleep and other states of diminished consciousness?

It is not necessary to rehearse in detail the responses that have been offered to such questions since men like Aristotle and Galen were first attempting to deal with them rationally. Some, as yet, remain unanswerable; some are beyond the limits of this book; some we shall return to in the last chapter. Libraries are full of books based on theories that have been wholly discarded, modified, or incorporated into new conceptions. There was the theory of circulation, held by Hartley among others, which was that sleep was due to the pressure of blood on the brain, or conversely, the draining of blood away from it. There were many chemical theories, which suggested that sleep might be due to toxic conditions caused by a decline in oxygen intake, or to the accumulation of acids in the system; biological theories, such as that advanced by the French savant, Édouard Claparède, in the early part of this century, which defined sleep as an active instinct, characteristic of the rhythms of animal life; and neurological theories, which attribute sleep to causes that range from the need of the brain cells to restore themselves to the interruption of signals between the cerebral cortex and other parts of the brain.

Each of such theories had its own explanation of the causes and nature of sleep; each made valuable contributions in concept and in clinical and experimental evidence; each has helped us toward a deeper understanding of the subtle mechanisms of the human brain. But the more we know, the more difficult it has become—in the cautious words of Dr. Ian Oswald, of the University of Edinburgh—"to arrive at a definition of sleep or a definition of consciousness which will satisfy everyone." In his invaluable book, *Sleeping and Waking*, Dr. Oswald is unwilling to go much beyond this statement:

"Sleep is a recurrent, healthy condition of inertia and unresponsiveness. In the normal individual the unresponsiveness is manifested not only by a decrease of overt responses to stimuli, but also by a decrease of covert responses. Signals reaching the central nervous system from the sense organs may no longer bring about those responses within the brain that we believe must underlie perception."

What may cause such a lack of response? It could be that there is something that inhibits the customary responses we make to the signals we receive from our senses. Conversely, something that is usually present in waking life to help the brain send the appropriate response signals to the body may be missing in sleep. Oswald, Kleitman, and other specialists in the field now incline to the latter view, partly because they consider that the cerebral cortex is essential to consciousness.

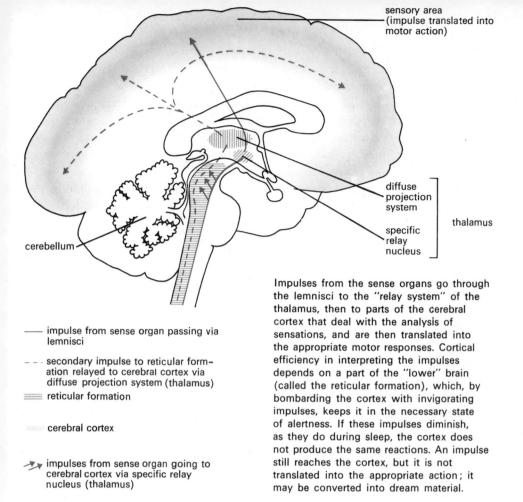

sensory area (impulse translated into motor action)

diffuse projection system

specific relay nucleus

thalamus

cerebellum

—— impulse from sense organ passing via lemnisci

- - - secondary impulse to reticular form-ation relayed to cerebral cortex via diffuse projection system (thalamus)

▨▨ reticular formation

cerebral cortex

➤➤ impulses from sense organ going to cerebral cortex via specific relay nucleus (thalamus)

Impulses from the sense organs go through the lemnisci to the "relay system" of the thalamus, then to parts of the cerebral cortex that deal with the analysis of sensations, and are then translated into the appropriate motor responses. Cortical efficiency in interpreting the impulses depends on a part of the "lower" brain (called the reticular formation), which, by bombarding the cortex with invigorating impulses, keeps it in the necessary state of alertness. If these impulses diminish, as they do during sleep, the cortex does not produce the same reactions. An impulse still reaches the cortex, but it is not translated into the appropriate action; it may be converted into dream material.

This reduction in the "feed-back" from the cerebral cortex may explain why we fail to respond to the stimulation of any of our senses in sleep (unless we are thereby wholly or partially aroused), and it also has particular relevance to the study of dreams. It seems that in sleep the forebrain may behave as if we are awake, but that its activities are not translated into positive responses by the motor mechanism. The ability to respond does, it is true, seem to be selective: a mother will waken to her child's cry but sleep through a thunderstorm. But normally we "switch off": we may dream that we are frightened and run away, but we do not actually run unless it is the type of dream we call a "nightmare": at most we may twitch. It is when this normal inhibitory process is seriously impaired that the phenomenon of somnambulism occurs.

There is, moreover, the significant fact that our eyes are the first of the sense organs to switch off when we go to sleep and the last to switch on when we awake. But as long ago as 1892 the American psychologist Professor George Trumbull Ladd suggested on the basis of his own experience that it is possible that the brain has "a psycho-physical mechanism for the production of visual images" and that what we called "retinal fantasies" may be the raw material of dreams. The brain, to put it simply, no longer "sees" in sleep; the eyes—a million nerve centers, each carrying hundreds of impulses per second—have stopped transmitting significant signals. But, in some way, the part of the brain that operates and interprets this elaborate and delicate mechanism continues to behave as if it were "seeing"—even though the sensory perception of reality has ceased to work.

Professor Ladd's theory seemed, at the time, to belong with other introspective attempts to explain the nature of dreams by physiological causes. It has become clear only recently that he had hit on a vital clue: the activity of the eyes in sleep appears to be closely related to what we call "dreaming." It is odd that this link should have been generally overlooked when the visual character of dreams has been recognized for so long. But it is difficult to study the eye movements of a person in sleep.

A few investigators had raised the point in a tentative way. For example, an American named Jacobson, who had realized as early as 1930 that eye movements occurred when a man was recollecting some visual memory, suggested in a book published in 1938 that "when a person dreams . . . most often his eyes are active. Watch the sleeper whose eyes move under his closed lids. . . . Awaken him . . . you are likely to find . . . that he had seen something in a dream." If Jacobson had been able systematically to follow up this clue, he might have inaugurated a phase of dream investigation potentially as significant as that which began with Freud's sentence: "The dream is the royal road to the unconscious."

As it happened, the first crucial step was taken by one of Professor Kleitman's assistants in a study of rest and waking in newborn infants. Professor Kleitman has described what happened:

"As so often happens in research, the objective indicator of dreaming was discovered by accident. During a study of the cyclic variations of sleep in infants, a graduate student named Eugene Aserinsky observed that the infant's eyes continued to move under its closed lids for some time after all major body movements had ceased with the onset of sleep. The eye movements would stop and then begin again from time to time, and were the first movements to be seen as the infant woke up. Aserinsky found that eye movements provided a more reliable means of distinguishing between the active and quiescent phases of sleep than did gross body movements."

What use could be made of Aserinsky's observation? It was an obvious step to investigate the eye movements of adults in sleep, in order to test whether they similarly indicated a distinct cycle. But a more reliable indicator of these movements was needed than even the most painstaking visual observation could provide. Such an instrument existed in the electroencephalograph (EEG) machine, a device that can record "brain waves"—the very weak electric currents generated continuously by the brain.

The EEG machine has been developed in the last 40 years from the work in Germany of Dr. Hans Berger, of the University of Jena, who found that electrodes placed on the scalp could detect these electric currents; amplified a million times, they could be fed into a machine in which automatic pens traced the variations in the signals on a slow-turning drum of graph paper. Dr. Berger had shown that the patterns that were traced varied according to the state of the subject: in sleep, at rest, or responding to a waking stimulus, the individual's brain gives off rhythms characteristic of the given state. Over the years so much experience has been acquired in the use of EEG recordings that a trained interpreter can read off a tracing and detect from it the variations that show how the brain is working—and whether some of its vital functions are impaired.

Professor Kleitman and Dr. Aserinsky decided to use this machine to monitor the sleep of adults, but to add an extra channel (or circuit) to the tracings to show eye movements. By pasting electrodes to the skin above and below the eyes and on either side of each eye it is possible to measure the changes in electric potential that occur when the eye moves up and down or

The brain is composed of at least ten thousand million electrical cells: when a million or so repeatedly discharge their energies, a definite rhythm can be measured. Electrodes placed on the scalp relay the frequencies and amplitudes of electrical changes in different parts of the brain for recording by the pens of the electroencephalograph (EEG) machine.

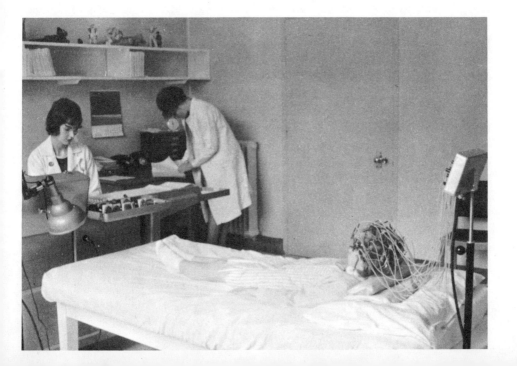

from side to side (Figure 1). They also set out to measure the sleeper's breathing rate and body movements. They would thus see the relationship between the electric currents in the brain, the movements of the eyes, the respiration, and the movements of the sleeper. For the first time, they were about to secure experimental evidence about sleeping and dreaming that did not primarily depend upon subjective impressions and inspired guesswork.

Volunteers came to the laboratory and, as they slept, the EEG recorded their sleep patterns and the movements of their eyes. Very soon, Aserinsky and Kleitman found that their records were showing two types of eye movements—the slow, rolling movements they had observed in infants and bursts of very fast movements that might last from a few minutes to more than half an hour. At intervals through the night, each sleeper was producing these groups of rapid eye movements (which are now generally known as REMs). What could be the cause of them? And with what other characteristics of sleep were they associated? Looking over the EEG tracings, Kleitman found that just before the sleeper began to produce REMs there was a distinct change in the brain-wave patterns recorded by the EEG and an increase in the pulse rate. Could it be that the sleeper was dreaming at this point?

The only way to find out was to wake the sleeper and ask. As soon as the REMs were detected, the sleeper was awakened. The first 27 wakenings produced 20 dreams. As a control, 23 sleepers were then awakened when the record showed no sign of REMs; and 19 of them failed to recollect a dream. Encouraged by this success, Kleitman and Aserinsky tested out their theory on larger numbers. In the first 190 arousals during the REM bursts, 152 yielded dream reports.

Even from this limited evidence, published for the first time in September 1953, it seemed probable that what we loosely call "dreaming" was associated with the REMs; with increased pulse and respiration rates; and with some kind of sleep rhythm. It appeared, moreover, that dreaming might be a regular and systematic process; that everyone might have more or less the same amount of dreams; and, not least, that a technique had now been found whereby the process, if not the content, of dreaming could be measured. It was no longer necessary, in short, to rely upon the individual's own recollection of his dreams in order to arrive at estimates of how much and when he dreamed.

It was necessary, however, to continue and extend the range of these experiments, both to secure additional confirmation of the Aserinsky-Kleitman findings and to exploit the breakthrough they had made. In the next few years the work went on, slowly, though other experimenters had begun to work along the same lines and to produce results that supported the pioneer work done in Chicago. In 1964, Dr. Charles Fisher, one of the leading investigators in this field, could write that the cyclic pattern of dreaming is "universally present in the thousands of subjects that have by now been investigated in numerous laboratories."

The next significant development also came accidentally. A new assistant to Professor Kleitman, Dr. William Dement (now at the University of Stanford in California, and another outstanding contributor to dream theory and experiments), was studying the EEG tracings of a group of schizophrenics. While in previous dream studies the EEG was turned on and off at intervals throughout the night, thus saving expense, Dement turned it on every fifth minute. He found some interesting differences between the dreams schizophrenics reported when aroused during an REM period, and those produced by the ordinary volunteers. But the most important result of this experiment was found in scrutinizing the much greater quantity of EEG tracings yielded by Dement's decision to run the machine more often. The REMs invariably began when a quite distinct pattern appeared in the EEG tracings—a fast brain wave much more like that of a waking person. When this pattern came to an end, the REMs also stopped.

The next step was obvious—there had to be an experiment in which the EEG machines were run all night. It was made on a group of volunteers at the University of Chicago. From this work it became plain that there was a relationship between the REMs and the special EEG rhythm, and that both the REMs and this rhythm appeared at fairly regular intervals throughout the night, occupying a definite place in the pattern of sleep. Moreover the pattern itself began to look very different from the traditional view.

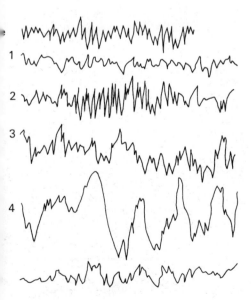

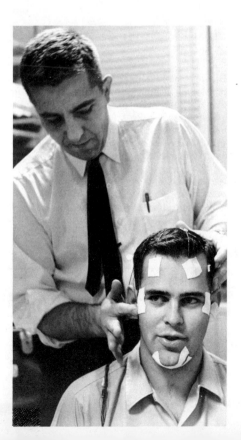

The American researcher Dr. William Dement preparing a subject for a night-long dream experiment. Above, the brain waves in sleep recorded by the EEG machine.

Dr. Nathaniel Kleitman, former professor of physiology at Chicago University, has shown that the adult cycle of sleep and wakefulness in a 24-hour day is an acquired habit. Kleitman proved that the cycle could be broken when he and a colleague spent a month in Monmouth cave, Kentucky, in 1938 (above). With no light, constant temperature, and no communication from outside, Kleitman's colleague—a younger man—soon developed a 28-hour cycle of 9 hours' sleep and 19 hours' wakefulness.

A newborn child alternates between sleep and wakefulness in periods of 50-60 minutes duration. These periods (shown in the diagrams by the undulations) lengthen in the four-year-old child to 60-70 minutes and in the adult to 80-90 minutes. As the child adapts to family and community life its sleep is consolidated into one period of approximately eight hours; in old age a waking-dozing cycle appears— similar to that of infancy (see diagram below: red areas represent sleep).

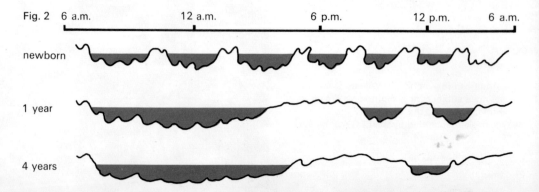

Fig. 2   6 a.m.   12 a.m.   6 p.m.   12 p.m.   6 a.m.

newborn

1 year

4 years

For one thing, Kleitman and Dement were well aware by this time that what we call a "normal" night's sleep is not inborn: it is an acquired habit. As early as June 1938, Kleitman and one of his assistants had spent a month in Monmouth Cave, Kentucky, where no light penetrated, temperature was constant, and no distractions from the outside world were permitted. The younger man soon found that he could break the standard 24-hour cycle and shift to a new one that consisted of 19 waking hours of work and exercise, and nine of sleep. Dr. Oswald also reports an experiment in which one of his colleagues was able to get along on a 48-hour schedule, taking about 11 to 12 hours of sleep every alternate night.

Could an explanation of this fact be found in studying the evolution of the sleep cycle from infancy onward? Kleitman already had valuable data about this. He knew that very small infants had a natural sleep rhythm of about 50-60 minutes, that they were more liable to wake at the end of such a cycle, and that their longer sleeps of three to four hours tended to be multiples of the basic rhythm. This hour-long rhythm was not merely one of sleep and wakefulness in the conventional sense; it could be demonstrated by studying the EEG pattern, by measuring respiration, heartbeat, blood circulation, and the electrical conductivity of the skin. By making such measurements at various ages Kleitman had found that, as children grow older, two things happen. First, the 60-minute cycles tend to stretch out, becoming something like a 90-minute cycle in adults. Secondly, for people who live in temperate zones and do not take siestas, actual sleep becomes consolidated in a single period. Up to the age of four the child may still take an afternoon nap: then, for most of one's life, sleep is taken in a single stretch at night, until in old age there is a regression, beginning with afternoon naps and then tending to revert to a waking-dozing cycle not unlike that of infancy. The pattern is indicated in Figures 2 and 3.

Even though sleep is consolidated, however, the underlying 90-minute rhythms seem to remain; underlying our wakefulness is the basic biological cycle. The overall control of sleep and waking in healthy adults seems to be conscious—we decide when to go to sleep, so long as we are getting regular and sufficient sleep—but the 90-minute rhythms appear to be beyond the control of consciousness and to be much more closely linked to the autonomic

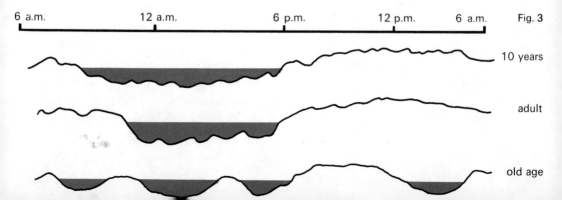

6 a.m.   12 a.m.   6 p.m.   12 p.m.   6 a.m.   Fig. 3

10 years

adult

old age

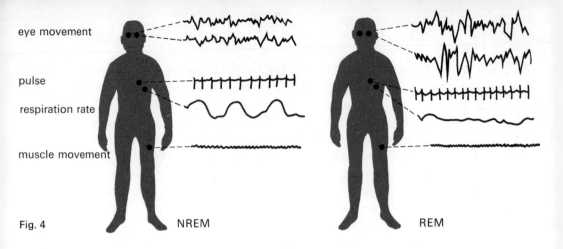

Fig. 4   NREM   REM

nervous system that regulates the basic metabolism of the body. Wakefulness, it seems, is a function of the cerebral cortex, but the pattern of sleep is not.

Could the rhythm detected in the REMs and the EEG tracings of sleep be related to continuous 90-minute cycles? It seemed a more than reasonable hypothesis. To test it, and to draw a chart of the sleep process, it was necessary to make night-long records of the EEG responses, the eye movements, respiration, pulse, and body movements of the sleeper. The shape of the recordings is shown in Figure 4, which compares a characteristic set of tracings for a period when REMs are occurring with a set for a period of sleep with no REMs. By plotting such contrasts throughout the night, it is possible to draw a chart showing the entire sleep rhythm of any individual.

Such a chart is shown in Figure 5. The sleep scientists have broken down sleep, as registered by the EEG, into four stages, ranging from Stage 1 (light sleep) to Stage 4 (deep sleep), each of which produces a characteristic and recognizable type of EEG tracing. Our example shows that, with the first onset of sleep, the sleeper plunges down to Stage 4, and that after about 80 or 90 minutes his sleep rhythm rises toward Stage 1. It is at this point that the particular waves associated with REMs begin: the solid dark line at the top shows the duration of the REM period. At the end of it, the sleep cycle dips down again, then up toward a new Stage 1 and a new burst of REMs. Thus the REMs occur only after the sleeper has reached Stage 1 sleep. Below the graph are a series of vertical lines. These show significant muscle movements in sleep. The example shows that these also occur throughout the night and at various stages of sleep; that they are often associated with the transition from one stage of sleep to another; and that they are less in evidence during the Stage 1—REM period.

An even more striking piece of evidence can be found by relating changes in breathing (and thus in heartbeats) during the stages of sleep. Dr. Dement found that, during the REM period, we begin to breathe more rapidly, and that the respiration rate drops as we slide back into the deeper stages of sleep. A characteristic example of this rhythm is shown in Figure 6. Something is clearly happening to the whole of our nervous and physical systems during

All-night EEG recordings reveal several stages of sleep—usually classified in four stages—which are defined by different EEG patterns. Fig. 5 charts the sleep pattern of a typical night showing how, in terms of brain waves, the depth of sleep fluctuates regularly. The sleeper first sinks into Stage 4 of sleep but after some 80-90 minutes his sleep lightens; Stage 1 emerges and he begins to dream. Dreaming always occurs during the emergent Stage 1 period (shaded areas) and is accompanied by REMs. As the night progresses the REM periods lengthen.

Physiological changes accompany the REM (Stage 1) period. These include changes in the heart and respiration rate, in the pulse, and in muscular tension. Fig. 4 contrasts non-REM sleep with REM sleep. Fig. 6 depicts the striking changes in the breathing rate during the REM period. The top graph plots the appearance of the EEG stages: dark bars indicate eye movement periods. The vertical lines (representing five-minute periods) indicate rate and regularity of the respiration. The longer, higher lines show more rapid irregular breathing during REM periods.

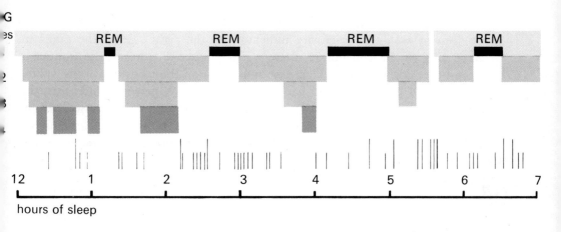

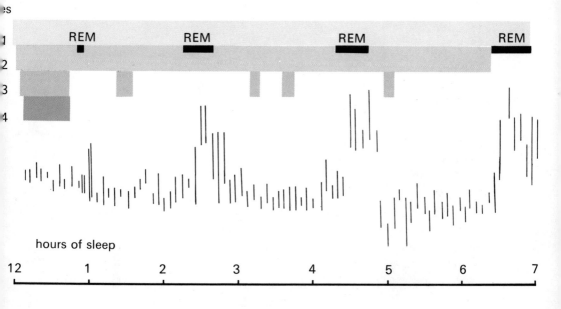

these highly significant REM periods: they are so unlike the rest of sleep that the difference raises the question whether they can be regarded in the same way. Whether, that is, sleep is a single or a complex state of being.

It had long been realized that there were depths of sleep as well as peaks of wakefulness. People often say they have "slept heavily," or feel "alert and excited"; they are aware when they feel drowsy before sleep or dopey when waking up. But, for many reasons, it seemed as if the range of sleep and waking was a continuous scale along which, for somewhat mysterious causes, man customarily moved. Such a scale, from the hyper-excitement of mania to the insensibility of a clinical coma, could be indicated in the manner shown in the left half of Figure 7. It could, moreover, be given some empirical verification by the study of EEG patterns associated with some of these levels of sleep or waking, which are indicated on the right side of the diagram. According to this conception, there was a "hypnoid" state at the frontier of sleep—a region through which man must pass on the transition from waking to sleep and on the passage back to wakefulness. A person could enter this twilight zone in the normal fashion, as sleep approached or passed off; he could enter it by hypnosis; he could enter it in fevered or mentally disturbed states; or he could enter it by taking drugs that sedated or hallucinated him.

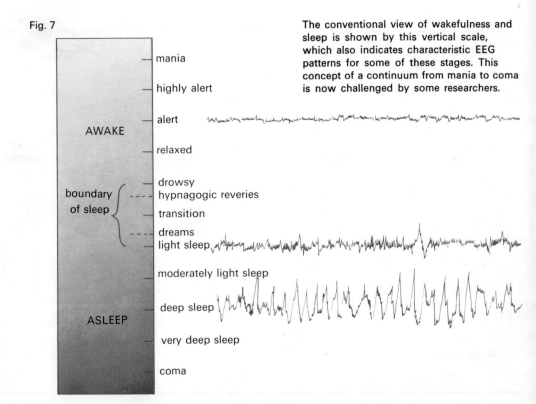

Fig. 7

The conventional view of wakefulness and sleep is shown by this vertical scale, which also indicates characteristic EEG patterns for some of these stages. This concept of a continuum from mania to coma is now challenged by some researchers.

mania

highly alert

alert

AWAKE

relaxed

drowsy
hypnagogic reveries

boundary
of sleep

transition

dreams
light sleep

moderately light sleep

deep sleep

ASLEEP

very deep sleep

coma

This conception served well enough as a model which seemed to explain several interrelated facts. We are not so much concerned here with the neuro-physiological evidence advanced for it, as with its relevance to hallucinatory states of mind. First of all, it was topographic. That is, it seemed to locate the onset of all hallucinatory states at the same point on the sleep-waking frontier: it looked as though the psychoanalytical idea that there was a "threshold" of consciousness conformed to the physiological facts. The Freudian view that consciousness repressed or suppressed the contents of the unconscious, but that these unconscious elements began to well up as the control of consciousness was diminished, fitted very well into the concept of a physiological threshold. Many psychoanalysts, indeed, tend to interpret the dream symbolism of frontiers and customs houses as a disguised reference to such a crossing-point between the unconscious and the conscious. Figuratively, one could say, the repression-barrier was opened.

If, secondly, there was a remarkable similarity between the imagery produced by dreams, drugs, and the delusions of hypnosis and insanity, this could also be explained by attributing them all to the confused functioning of the brain at the transition point: something seemed to be happening at this point to the relation between the cerebral cortex and the rest of the brain. In a healthy person, the process of transition merely produced dreams; but if the functioning of the nervous system was impaired by drugs, by brain injury, or by severe psychological disturbance, other types of hallucination ensued. Where the function was seriously impaired, a person could be regarded as psychotic.

This view was reinforced by the fact that hallucinations seemed to be associated with this transitional stage from consciousness to unconsciousness, rather than with a state of deep sleep. Those who studied dreams in the period before Kleitman, Aserinsky, Dement, and others made their discoveries were aware of this fact. Much evidence had been collected, beginning especially with the studies by the Frenchman Alfred Maury a century ago, about "hypnagogic illusions"—the dream-like state which arises immediately before true sleep supervenes. It was also well known that dreams frequently occurred immediately before waking—indeed, that the only dreams we appear to remember are those that precede arousal, whether this has happened earlier in the night, or in the morning. This third fact about the twilight zone lay behind much of the interest in the role of external and internal stimuli in causing or at least influencing the content of dreams. All the studies of dreams that, like Maury's "French Revolution" dream (see Chapter 5), had linked them with noises, heat, cold, the pressure of bedclothes, physical aches, pains, and digestive processes, had assumed that "coming out" of sleep was the time when we were most likely to have dreams.

According to this belief, however, it was the stimulus that led both to the dream and to the arousal: simply by ringing a bell, or physically disturbing a sleeper *at any time of the night*, one could start a dream and waken the sleeper. If sleep were a constant state and dreaming could occur at any time, it should be possible for this theory to be demonstrated experimentally. As a matter of fact, it cannot. On the contrary, Dr. Dement has shown that external stimuli and such internal physical factors as bladder pressure do not create dreams to order, and that arousal may actually be more difficult in the "light sleep" of the REM period than in what is regarded as "deep sleep." Other investigators, moreover, have found that waking a sleeper from "deep sleep" does not usually produce dreams: it is when waking occurs immediately after an REM period that the dream seems to have preceded arousal.

How does this affect Freud's argument that the dream is "the guardian of sleep"? What Freud did was to take the known fact that dreams occurred in "light sleep," and that they appeared to be connected with a certain restlessness and even partial arousal, deducing from this that the dreamer would actually have awoken if the dream had not absorbed the disturbing stimulus. He also paid considerable attention in *The Interpretation of Dreams* to dream theories that dealt with the seeming effects of physical stimuli. He did not wholly accept the physiological view. But neither did he reject it out of hand. As a model, it was too close to his own concept of psychic stimuli to be dismissed as arbitrarily as some other theories. He considered that the instinctual wishes sought to reach consciousness in sleep, thereby disturbing the sleeper physically and psychologically. The dream, however, served as a fantasy outlet for the instinctive drive, which was further disguised both by its symbolic nature and the activities of the "censor." Since the human organism has a physiological need and possibly a psychological wish for sleep, the dream has thus (in Freud's view) done what was needed. The disturbing psychic stimulus has been absorbed and sleep can continue.

Freud and other dream theorists in the earlier part of this century realized that this dreaming process took place several times a night. What they did not realize was how systematically it took place, and how unrelated its onset seems to be to the causes that they believed promoted it. Freud never appeared to offer any explanation of the dream rhythm—why, for instance,

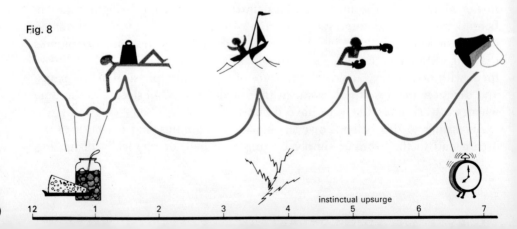

Fig. 8

instinctual upsurge

dreams should start at all, whether they occurred at random or at definite intervals, and why a psychic stimulus should strive to reach consciousness at one point in the night, while at other times no such potential disturbance was apparent.

Psychoanalysts and others, therefore, have long been working with a sleep-dream model that explained a good deal, but left some crucial points unexplained—or at best, indicated some tortuous reasons for them. Their model of a night's sleep would look something like that shown in figure 8. Such a model, as Dr. Dement has pointed out, left no way of telling the frequency or duration of dreams. Nor did it offer any means, except guessing, of knowing when they were likely to occur. Clearly, if one sets out to explain the cause of dreams by the emergence of disturbing wishes (or by the influence of external stimuli to the senses) it is somewhat disquieting to be confronted by the fact that this appears to happen at about 90-minute intervals throughout each night!

Let us compare this *a priori* model of a sleep-dream pattern with something more than the example shown in Figure 5. This, it is true, showed three or four distinct Stage 1 and REM periods (or dream-peaks) during the night. Nonetheless it would provide far more powerful evidence if these patterns proved to be relatively stable night after night for the same person, or comparatively similar for different persons. Professor Kleitman and other researchers have obtained such evidence, which is presented in Figure 9 in the form of histograms—or profiles of a person's dream-sleep rhythm over a period of two weeks.

Such profiles show that there are usually three REM periods per night. The later they occur, the longer the average duration. The intervals between them each night are approximately the same. On nights 5, 11, and 13, for instance, the first REMs came earlier than on other nights, but so too did the ensuing periods. Such diagrams, which can be repeated for any person in normal health, show a remarkable consistency—so remarkable, in fact, that in conjunction with other evidence it points to a physiological mechanism at work rather than the random influence of psychic and physical stimuli.

Fig. 8 represents a typical night's sleep in terms of traditional ideas, which assumed that dreams were a random experience evoked by physical stimuli. As sensory impressions diminish, sleep sets in, but at intervals different stimuli—such as indigestion—nearly wake the sleeper. In each case, until the alarm clock finally arouses him, a dream assimilates the disturbance and he is able to sleep on. Fig. 9 plots the appearance of REMs (horizontal bars) during 14 nights of sleep: each horizontal line of bars represents a single night's sleep. The graph below (a histogram) shows the overall dream habits of the sleeper over this period of time.

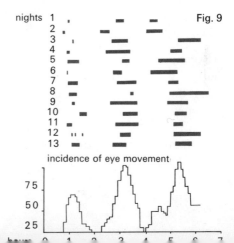

Some of this other evidence comes from the study of changes in the state of the body at the time such REM bursts are punctuating sleep. Such changes are illustrated by the tracings shown in Figure 6 on page 257. The heart beats faster, we breathe more quickly and irregularly, the electrical conductivity of the skin changes, and there is a degree of muscular relaxation. The last of these changes is an interesting one. In point of time, it occurs first: a skilled observer of EEG tracings can, in fact, note the change in the muscular tension (electromyographic potential) before the characteristic "saw-tooth" EEG waves or the REMs appear. Experimentally, as we shall see, this has great importance, for it means that the sleep scientists can actually awaken someone before that person starts to dream. This relaxation gives the impression that the body is somehow settling down before the dream begins, like a spectator at the theatre who makes himself comfortable before the curtain goes up.

By 1960, Dr. Dement and others were already being led to vital questions. Was it possible any longer to regard sleep as a single state of being? Was sleep, that is, to be understood as a unitary mechanism of the human body? Were there, within sleep, quite distinct conditions due to something much more than differences in the "depth" of sleep?

At first, it seemed that something of the old conception of sleep could be saved despite the contrast between the condition of the body and brain during the REM periods and the rest of sleep. For the REM periods always seemed to come at the end of a cycle of non-REM sleep—the sleeper having passed through EEG stages 1, 2, 3, and 4, and beginning the REM phases as Stage 1 approached again. Thus the dreams apparently emerged when the sleeper was in a "light sleep" that was close to consciousness. But there were certain difficulties about this. Non-REM sleep is very different from the REM periods; although the EEG varies in the other stages of sleep, the heart beat, breathing, body temperature, muscle tone, and muscular tension do not alter as they do in the REM bursts. And, despite the similarity between the EEG tracings for Stage 1 at the onset of sleep and the Stage 1 tracings that accompany the REMs, in normal circumstances, there are no REMs in the period immediately after sleep has started. This "onset" Stage 2 must therefore differ in some significant way from the other Stage 1 periods during the night, even though the EEG does not reveal what this difference may be. Conversely, it is possible for human beings in certain circumstances to pass directly from waking into REM sleep, without ever passing through the preliminary period normally noted. This has been observed in infants and in persons suffering from the condition known as narcolepsy, in which one suddenly and unexpectedly falls asleep. This type of REM sleep, it seems, is "light sleep" only in terms of its EEG tracing: it is in practice often more difficult to arouse the infant or narcoleptic in this condition than from what seems like a normal deep sleep.

Such developments have led to what Dr. Dement calls the "new concept"; and though it has to be stated in fairly technical language, Dr. Dement himself has summarized it quite clearly.

"First of all, we have the waking state in which the organism is attentive to external stimuli, in which the brain is more or less active depending on what the organism is doing, and in which there are no signs of complete suppression of motor output. In other words, movements are seen, muscle tone is maintained, and reflexes may be elicited. Then we have *sleep* with four EEG stages in which there is a relative quiescence of the organism. The EEG synchrony is coupled with the maintenance of motor excitability in terms of the excitability of reflexes and the continued presence of tonic muscular activity. Finally, we have the REM state, in which, again, we see brain activation often to a point above that of the waking state, coupled with suppression of skeletal motor outflow; and this state is, of course, associated with heightened dream recall."

This paragraph may one day be a landmark in our understanding of the human mind and its dream-making function. For the first time, an empirical and objective distinction can be made between the dreaming and non-dreaming phases of sleep. Dreams no longer seem like a haphazard phenomenon, scattered at random through a state of sleep. They begin to seem like a regular and identifiable process, which is distinct from what has traditionally been regarded as sleep. We might even go a step further and suggest, tentatively, that dreams punctuate sleep just as daydreams and other hallucinatory effects can punctuate waking—and that, in both cases, what we call the dream or the fantasy is arising from a part of the brain that is relatively unaffected by the alteration of sleep and wakefulness.

It is still too soon, however, to pursue such a hypothesis very far. Most of the experimental work on which it is based has been done only in the last five years, and the theory of the "third state" is far from being fully worked out or verified. We can, however, notice that, in addition to the substantial part of the life of the adult human that is spent in this "third state" (as distinct from "normal" sleep and "normal" wakefulness) an even larger part of the life of infants seems to be of this character. Long before the child has achieved full development of its brain, or control over its conscious behavior, it is experiencing the REM state that, in adults, we now associate with dreams. From this fact, again, we may conclude that some fundamental biological mechanism is at work.

Some fascinating new evidence in support of this belief was produced in 1964 by Dr. Charles Fisher, working at Mount Sinai Hospital in New York. Dr. Fisher, who had collaborated with Dr. Dement in earlier researches, picked up two clues which both led him to a novel series of experiments. The first was provided by three German investigators, P. Ohlmeyer, H. Brilmayer, and H. Hullstrung, who noticed—more than 20 years ago—that sleeping men seemed to have penile erections at regular intervals throughout the night. They reported, moreover, that the interval between these periods of tumescence seemed to be about 85 minutes and that the average duration of each period was 25 minutes. The similarity of this rhythm to that of the sleep cycle (subsequently discovered by Aserinsky and Kleitman) was so marked that Dr. Ian Oswald attempted to discover whether the erections in fact occurred during the REM or dream periods. His work was inconclusive, but it gave Dr. Fisher his second hint and led him to devise experimental methods of testing the theory that were superior to those available to Dr. Oswald.

The technical difficulties were, for obvious reasons, very great. It was necessary to devise apparatus that would not itself be a physical stimulus, and it was also desirable that the volunteer subjects should as far as possible be ignorant of the object of the experiment. As the experiments proceeded, improvements were made both in the apparatus used and in observation techniques; the more sensitive the equipment employed, the more striking the results became. Each erection, moreover, began a few seconds before the EEG tracings showed the Stage 1 pattern or the first eye movements; they appeared to coincide with the loss of muscle tone which, we have already noted, seems to be the prelude to a dream period. And the erection is generally sustained throughout the REM period, however long it may be. Conversely, no erections were observed outside the REM period except for the diminishing tumescence carried over from each REM into the following Stage 2 sleep (Figure 10). From this evidence Dr. Fisher concluded: "There is approximately as much erection during the night as there is dreaming." Though further experimental confirmation of this revolutionary statement is needed, and research work is continuing, Dr. Fisher's discovery fits in so remarkably with all that we now know about the "third state" that it opens up great new possibilities for that future research.

The implications of this fact are far-reaching, physiologically and psychologically. Has Dr. Fisher provided some experimental evidence of a link between sexuality and dreams? Do we have some clues here as to the link between instinctual drives and emotional discharge? Dr. Fisher believes there may be a link between the erections and dream content. He claims that, in a quite early stage of his research, it has been possible to show that certain types of dream seem to have an inhibitory effect on the accompanying erection. He suggests, moreover, that the erections may perhaps be regarded as an index of "limbic activation"—that is, the activity of those parts of the mid-brain which are involved in sexual, oral, and aggressive behavior. If Dr. Fisher is right—and his experiments are continuing—he may be indicating the point at which psychological drives and physiological mechanisms connect. It is clearly becoming possible to devise experiments in which at least some part of the dream content can be checked against physical changes, from penile erections, to respiration and eye movements. Such progress reinforces the physiological

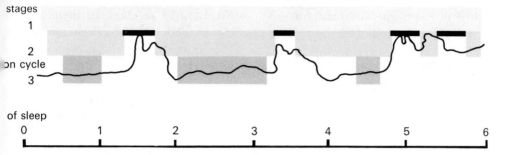

0

stages

1

2

on cycle

3

of sleep

0   1   2   3   4   5   6

The American psychiatrist Dr. Charles Fisher links the dreaming cycle to a nightly recurrence of penile erections. Fig. 10 shows how increases in penile circumference coincide with the REM periods (dark horizontal lines).

evidence for a regular dream cycle and for regarding the REM period as the "third state" produced by some fundamental mechanism.

Such a mechanism, moreover, does not seem to be confined to the human species. While it is clearly impossible to know whether an animal is "dreaming," because it cannot report its experience as a human can, there has long been speculation about the "dreams" of dogs, cats, and other mammals that were observed in different phases of sleep. Now that objective studies can be made of the EEG and other physiological responses of animals in sleep, of the same type as those we have been describing in humans, a basis of comparison exists. There is the additional fact that, in the laboratory, surgical and other experiments that are not possible with human beings can be performed on animals. From these it is clear that, despite certain differences, what we call "dreaming sleep" or REM sleep can be noticed in all the species yet studied— monkey, sheep, dog, and cat.

The most important work in this field has been done by Professor M. Jouvet and his colleagues at the University of Lyons. Their elaborate experiments have shown, among other things, that what they call "rapid sleep" is, as Dr. Dement argues, a different organismal state from ordinary sleep. They have further found that this type of sleep is not dependent upon the functioning of the cerebral cortex—that, in a decorticated cat, all the manifestations of REM sleep continue and appear to stem from the most primitive portions of the brain. If by surgical or chemical means cats are deprived of such periods of rapid sleep, various behavioral abnormalities ensue—abnormalities that seem comparable to psychotic or hallucinatory behavior in human beings.

The direction in which such findings point is clear. The "third state" apparently has a vital role to play in the functioning of the human organism. It is a state in which, for adults, what we call dreaming either occurs, or—to put it in the most cautious terms—is most likely to be recalled. If, therefore, an adult is deprived of the periods we may call either REM sleep or dreaming, his physical and psychic functioning will be impaired. In short, we could say that there is a need to dream that is as vital to our life as the need to eat or sleep.

It had been known for many years that individuals who were deprived of sleep developed serious psychological disturbances, varying in intensity from irritability and increase of appetite to the extreme forms of hallucination. Both torture and, in a more sophisticated form, distortion of personality by "brain-washing" have been based on this known fact. To keep a person awake for long periods, to permit only broken and irregular periods of sleep, is to disrupt all established patterns of thought and behavior. When this is coupled with prolonged isolation from the outside world and other persons, as in solitary confinement, the results are even more dramatic.

It had similarly been found, by many experiments in sensory deprivation, that states similar to psychosis could very rapidly be induced in persons who were shut off in sound-proof rooms, wrapped in special clothing to prevent sensations of touch, heat, and cold, blindfolded, or otherwise cut off from normal reality. In one of these experiments, Dr. John Lilly, of the United States National Institute of Mental Health, immersed himself in a tank of water kept at blood heat; he was naked except for a breathing mask. He experienced fantasies of a kind generally associated with serious mental illness. In other experiments, personality disturbance was equally marked—the volunteer subjects found themselves unable to concentrate, liable to daydreams and visions, given to confusion, headaches, nausea, and outbreaks of anger and despair. When similar experiments, or those involving the deprivation of sleep, were tried with patients in mental institutions, it was found that acute symptoms reappeared. Healthy persons usually recover after a good night's sleep, but anyone who suffers from nervous disorder of any kind may well find that loss of sleep or sensory deprivation produces a pathological reaction: both mental functioning and behavior become much more like that occurring both in schizophrenic conditions and in dreams.

In 1959, Dr. Dement and Dr. Charles Fisher, working at the Mount Sinai Hospital in New York, began to investigate the problem of what would happen if a man were deprived of his dreams. Such a question would have been meaningless before the discovery of REM sleep and, with it, a means of using the EEG machine to discover when a sleeper was about to dream. If the sleeper could be disturbed, either as the eye movements began, as the "sawtooth" EEG waves appeared, or—best of all—as soon as the loss of muscle tone heralded an REM period, then something of interest might be observed.

In September 1962 a young Frenchman, Michel Siffre, emerged from the subterranean cave in which he had spent two months alone; he lost all sense of time, had to receive medical attention for his eyes, and collapsed on reaching the outer world.

A year after the experiment began, the first results were published in *Science*. They indicated two conclusions. First, that just as a man seems to need to "catch up" on lost sleep, so he needs also to make up for dreaming time that he has lost. On the "recovery nights", when the sleeper could dream as much as he needed, the amount of REM sleep substantially increased. Secondly, as the experiment progressed, the subjects showed marked signs of psychological disturbance, showing anxiety, irritation, and a noticeable increase in appetite.

Dr. Dement and others continued to make such dream-deprivation experiments, improving their technique each time—among other things, arranging "control" nights on which the subjects were disturbed just as frequently but not in REM periods. By this means, they were able to test whether the observed results were the result of loss of dreams or loss of sleep. The "control" awakenings showed clearly that it was the loss of the REM periods rather than the awakenings that led to the observed results. The experiments also revealed that not only did more REM sleep occur on the recovery nights, but that as the experiment went on over a period of days, the sleepers attempted more and more REM periods. It therefore became necessary to wake them more and more often each night, until the experiment had to be abandoned both because it was virtually impossible to stop REM sleep occurring and because the subjects were becoming seriously affected.

The easiest means of demonstrating what was happening is to show diagramatically what happened to an individual who was not only prevented, as far as possible, from having his REM sleep for 15 consecutive nights, but

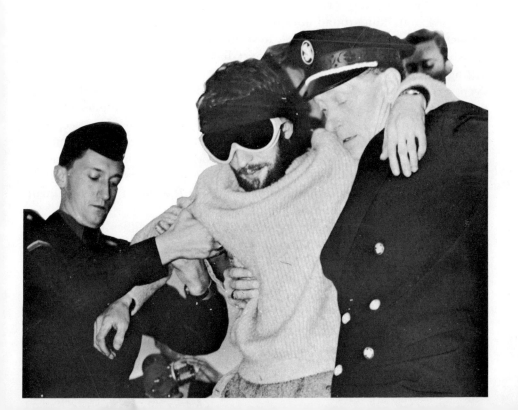

who was also watched day and night to ensure that he was not taking "bootleg" sleep when he was not in the laboratory. The first diagram (Figure 11) is a chart showing the increasing number of awakenings necessary on successive nights to prevent REM sleep. It indicates that even with the aid of a drug (without the use of Dexedrine to help the awakenings, the experiment could not have gone on so long) there was a steadily rising number of attempts at REM sleep. The sleeper was doing all he could to make up for what had been lost on previous nights.

The second diagram (Figure 12) is even more striking. This is the EEG tracing for the 15th and last night. By this time the need to dream was so compelling that REM sleep was beginning immediately the sleeper dropped off—something that is never seen in adults under normal circumstances. (The dots on the bottom line indicate moments when the subject was wakened.) In the first two hours, 20 awakenings were necessary and, as the EEG tracing shows, the subject was continually returning to Stage 1 sleep. After 4 A.M. the situation was becoming desperate. Thirty-six awakenings were needed, and the subject never got past Stage 2 sleep. By this time the subject was reduced to the condition Dr. Dement has described:

"... the experiment had to be halted because it had become absolutely impossible to awaken the subject and interrupt the dream periods. Eye-movements could be temporarily halted by struggling with the subject hoisting him upright, shouting in his ear, etc. (though this never produced a waking EEG), but as soon as the stimulation ceased, the eye-movements resumed. The only way dreaming could be stopped was to drag the subject out of bed, walk him around until he was awake, and then keep him awake."

Once allowed, on the next night, to sleep undisturbed, the volunteer began quickly to make up for lost time. In the next diagram (Figure 13), we see his EEG tracing for that "recovery" night. Once again, he plunged straight into REM sleep, and then throughout the night registered long REM periods. By the time he awoke at 7 A.M., he had recorded 4 hours and 52 minutes of REM sleep in 7 hours and 20 minutes total sleep; over 60 per cent of his sleep time had been given to compensating for lost REM time, or nearly four times as much as usual. Similar results were found in other experiments, one subject achieving an uninterrupted REM period of over three hours: in this case the subject showed marked psychotic characteristics at the end of the experiment, before he had taken his recovery night.

The experimenters, however, have run into technical difficulties. It seems, at the present state of knowledge, to be impossible to carry an experiment to the point where a draconian reduction of dreaming can occur—even if volunteers could be found to run the risks and accept the very considerable discomfort involved. For the accumulating pressure to relapse in REM sleep becomes so strong that, before marked physiological or pathological consequences ensue, the organism insists on having its dreams. But even

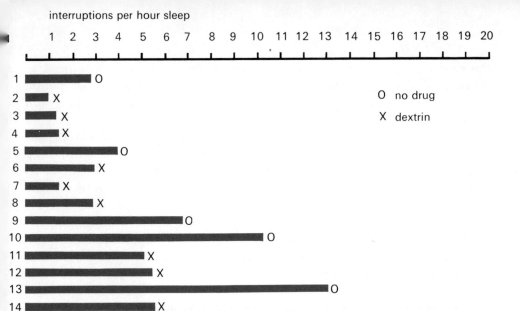

interruptions per hour sleep

O no drug

X dextrin

Dr. Dement has prevented sleepers from dreaming by arousing them at the start of an REM period. The experiment in Fig. 11 shows that the loss of dream time increases the need to dream. In this case dexedrine was given on some nights (marked by a cross). The drug helps the subject to sleep but does not affect the need to dream. On the 15th night 19.3 awakenings per hour were made.

Fig. 12 plots the EEG stages of the final REM deprivation night (see text). The experiment had to be abandoned because of the difficulty of waking the subject. The lines under the chart indicate the times when the sleeper was awakened on the emergence of REM sleep. After 4 a.m. almost no non-REM sleep occurred. On the first recovery night (Fig. 13) 60.2 per cent of total sleep time was spent in dreaming.

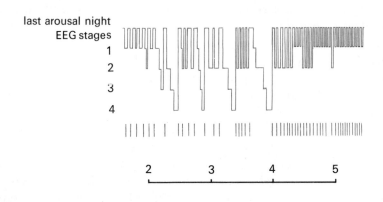

last arousal night
EEG stages

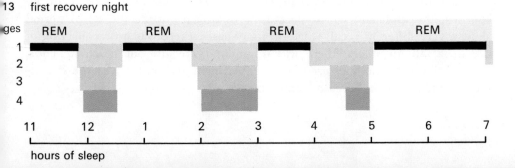

first recovery night

hours of sleep

this negative fact is valuable. For it demonstrates that there is a need to dream and that the human being is equipped with so strong a mechanism to meet that need that it can break all the normal rules about sleeping and waking and have its way.

This mechanism may be physiological—some sort of biochemical process that, in its operation, produces the condition that we record as REM sleep and experience as dreaming. It may also be a process so vital that, in its absence, we would die. Professor Jouvet, indeed, has shown this to be the case with cats that were denied REM sleep for over 20 days and then died for reasons otherwise inexplicable. And it may be this process (rather than the need for sleep in a conventional sense) that is interrupted when we are deprived of sleep. The psychotic-type experiences of the sleep-deprived, that is to say, may be more properly ascribed to their loss of dreams than to their lack of sleep.

This hypothesis has revolutionary implications for the study of mental processes and mental disorders: it raises some fundamental questions about psychological theories of the causes and contents of dreams. But before considering such implications it is desirable first to examine some of the other conclusions reached by dream investigators who have used the new tools of research and the new concepts developed in the last 15 years.

Is there any additional evidence, for instance, that what we call "dreaming" is taking place during the REM sleep? Do we know any more about the relative speed at which a dream tells its fantastic story? Can we divide sleepers into those who dream and those who do not? What is the relation of the eye movements to the contents of a dream? To such questions at least tentative answers can be given—answers, moreover, that are the first scientifically based attempts to deal with some questions that have puzzled men ever since they sought to unravel the mystery of dreams.

Consider, first, the evidence of a link between REM sleep and dreaming. Work with EEG machines is expensive and time-consuming: the tracing for one person for one night could be as long as 700 yards. Yet, despite this limitation, many research studies are now available. The first 15, covering a total of 214 persons for an average of four nights each, or a total of 885 nights of sleep, confirmed the original experiments in a remarkable manner, for they were made by different scientists, at different times and places, and with subject who themselves differed. We can summarize their findings. There were 2240 awakenings during periods of REM sleep. Of these, 1864 awakenings were accompanied by vivid dream recall—a recall rate of 83.3 per cent. By contrast, the studies in which sleepers were woken outside the REM period show a very different recall rate. In many cases, there was no recollection of dreams at all: in others, there was fragmentary recall. But much depends, here, both on the methods used in the experiment and on the way the experimenter defines both "dream" and "recall."

The scientists who report the highest recall from outside REM sleep have used a very generous definition of both: their evidence that dreaming may occur outside the REM sleep is disputed by Dr. Dement and others, who argue that the sleeper who is woken outside the REM period may actually be recalling a memory of a dream within the last REM sleep. This matter is unsettled. But what is not in doubt is that *the ability to recall dreams is greatest during the REM period.* Whether one considers that the dream is then taking place, or that the state of the mind is such as to make recollection of it more easy, there is no doubt that the link between maximum dream recall and the REM period is now established.

One of the complicating factors here is the speed at which we forget our dreams. All of us know how, on waking, we struggle to retain the fast-evaporating memory of a dream; how, unless we write down some notes at once, even its main outlines can be lost in an hour or so; and how, on some mornings, we have the sense of having had two or three dreams without being able to recall their order. Conversely, most people have had the experience of suddenly remembering a dream several days, weeks, or even months later because something has reminded them of it. The memory trace seems to be there, but to be subject to a powerful amnesic process. How much of our dreams is erased is obvious if we compare the amount of dreaming shown by the EEG tracings with the fragments we normally remember.

The ability to recall dreams clearly varies: in some people, recall is rare or seemingly non-existent and they will insist that they "seldom dream" or "never dream." Until the objective test of dreaming was discovered by the Chicago researchers, and until the possibility of awakening sleepers at the precise moment when they were likely to be dreaming was created by the use of EEG tracings, there was no systematic means by which the difference between "dreamers" and "non-dreamers" could be investigated. But the Chicago experiments led two doctors in New York, Arthur Shapiro and Donald R. Goodenough, to attempt such an inquiry in 1957. Taking two groups of students from Brooklyn College, divided into those who professed to dream regularly and those who believed that they did not dream, they not only showed that the patterns of REM sleep were similar in both groups but that if the non-dreamers were awakened in REM periods they also reported dreams.

There were, however, significant differences between the two groups. The non-dreamers seemed to have greater difficulty in knowing whether they were dreaming; sometimes they said, on being awakened, that they were "just thinking." They also revealed differences in sleep characteristics. For one thing, it was harder to wake them, and it was only when a stronger waking stimulus was applied to them that their recall rate improved in relation to that of regular dreamers. For another, the eye movements appeared at a slightly different stage of sleep, and some of these non-dreamers at least seem to belong to that small section of the population (about 15 per cent of all adults, according to the brain specialist, Professor Grey Walter) that is more visually-minded. Such people often have a surplus of visual material, think visually in dealing with problems, and may have very elaborate visual images in the hypnagogic state just before falling asleep. They will, in fact, call such imagery "thinking," and when it appears in sleep it is usually less bizarre than the dreams of most people because it is closer to normal patterns of thought. Just how such natural characteristics are related to the propensity to dream, or to recall dreams, is far from clear: the evidence does suggest that non-dreaming has both physiological and psychological aspects.

Yet the question remains: are the "lost" dreams really lost, or do they remain accessible? The question is important because R. M. Whitman, M. Kramer, and B. Baldridge reported in 1963 that they had found a discrepancy between the dreams that a patient reported when awakened from REM sleep and those subsequently told to the analyst. When were the "analyst" dreams being dreamed, and why were they remembered, while those produced in REM sleep awakenings were not?

The "forgetting" of dreams is an interesting and mysterious process. We do not know why it happens. Most dreams are not remembered at all, and even those we recall on waking vanish so quickly that they are lost unless we tell them or write them down. It has been found that dream recall drops with great rapidity. The sooner a dreamer is awakened after the end of the REM period, the more comprehensive and detailed the dream report he gives. Even so, there appears to be an upper limit on the dream report. An individual

"Non-dreamers" may belong to a small group of people who think visually. A person may solve the following problem using either visual imagery, abstract reasoning, or a mixture of the two. If a painted cube is cut in half across one side, the halves cut in half, and the resulting halves cut again at right angles, how many sides of the small cubes are unpainted?

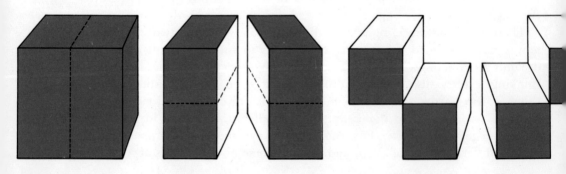

aroused in the first few minutes of an REM period will give a report that is proportional in length to the time that has elapsed since the dream state began. But, after about five minutes, the length of the dream report does not increase with the duration of the dream. The dream may last up to 30 minutes, but the dreamer will be able to recall no more than he could after five minutes of dreaming. It could be that forgetting begins while the dream is in progress, so that any dream report deals only with the most recent part of a dream. Or this inability to remember more than a limited amount of a dream may be due to the failure of conscious thought to preserve and order more than a certain quantity of dream material.

What the recent experiments have done, however, is to demonstrate how little of our dreams is normally available for study. This fact, as Dr. Whitman and his colleagues suggested, has important implications—above all for psychotherapy. Since we now know that the dreamer is actually remembering mere fragments of his total dream experience, we cannot properly talk of a "dream" as if it were a complete well-rounded anecdote—the form in which it is usually presented in case reports. It is no more than a piece of a dream experience, and the dream as it is recalled and reported may be a kind of collage made up of fragments that were quite differently ordered during the dream state. The remembered pattern of the dream, that is, may be partly the work of conscious thought, which is endeavoring to reduce the dream material to a more logical and coherent shape.

This view, put forward by Havelock Ellis and other writers before Freud, and actually underlying Freud's own distinction between the manifest and latent contents of the dream, does not mean that the dream indicates nothing about the psychic state of the dreamer. But it does mean that the dream *as we know it* is probably very different from the dream *as we actually experience it*. It follows that, in using the dream in therapy, the analyst must be continually aware that his patient is unavoidably if unconsciously selecting his dream material for presentation. That selection is itself an indicator of his psychological processes and, in particular, of his relation with the therapist.

Research has shown not only that much of the night's dreaming is forgotten, but also that there seems to be some relationship between the fragments we do remember—and that, too, is relevant to psychotherapy. In 1957, Dr. Dement and Dr. Wolpert set out to study the content of dreams obtained during an REM period. The sleepers were awakened about 10 minutes after an REM period had begun. A tape-recorder was provided for the sleeper to dictate his dreams to before going back to sleep, and a series of dreams were recorded each night. There are obvious limitations to this method, of which the investigators were aware. If the dreamer is awakened 10 minutes after the start of each REM period, material will be missed that might have been part of a longer and interrupted dream. The very act of being aroused might affect the dream pattern. The fact that a dream has been reported might serve as a kind of cue to the next one. And, if a particular dream theme is strongly in the sleeper's mind, he may simply go back to it when he returns to sleep. Yet, given these considerable qualifications, the experiment did suggest that there was a relationship between the successive dreams of one night. Each dream was a self-contained episode, but linked to others either by a common theme or common details in the material. This excellent example shows how a distinct attitude is emerging through a series of dreams:

"In the first dream, the dreamer was attending a lecture. He asked a question of the professor, who rebuffed him with a sneering remark. He became very angry, but managed to control himself. In the second dream, he was talking to a male acquaintance. He made some remark to which his friend took exception. Again he became very angry, and this time he called his friend

Dr. Dement suggests there may be a direct correspondence between eye movements and dream content. When one subject was awakened immediately after an REM period that showed marked vertical movements, she told the experimenter—who had not seen the EEG tracings—that she had dreamed she walked up some stairs glancing at every step she took, and at the top walked over to a group of people. The experimenter correctly concluded that the EEG tracing would show a series of five vertical upward movements followed by a horizontal movement.

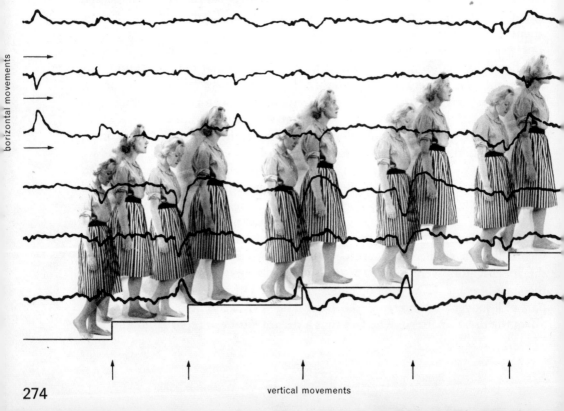

horizontal movements

vertical movements

a few uncomplimentary names before walking away. In the third dream he was working in a hospital and a nurse began to criticise him severely for some minor ineptitude in his work. Again, he experienced anger, but controlled it and confined himself to thinking: 'What an old hag she is.' The fourth and final dream found the dreamer eating dinner with his family. His mother wanted him to eat some leg of lamb, which he refused. She began pleading with him and he began to get angry. Then: 'She kept kissing me like a little kid and fishing for compliments on her cooking. I got absolutely burned up, and walked out of the house.'"

Here is a constant theme, in which the targets of anger change from a professor into a friend, from friend into nurse, and nurse into mother. The whole process is an example of what Freud was describing when he talked about interpreting dreams in the same night. "The possibility should not be overlooked," he said, "that separate and successive dreams of this kind may have the same meaning, and may be giving expression to the same impulses in different material. If so, the first of these homologous dreams to occur is often more distorted and timid, while the succeeding one will be more confident and distinct."

Obviously, there is no other way of knowing what an individual experiences in a dream than by asking him what he dreamed. But it may be possible to devise experiments that provide some check on what he says, and thus to discover something more about the content of dreams and the order in which dream material occurs. This work, again based upon the research of Dr. Dement and his colleagues, is still in an early stage, and it is much more controversial than their basic findings about the physical rhythm of dreaming. But, even if the provisional conclusions are not generally accepted, the manner in which they have been reached at least indicates the type of experiment that can now be devised.

Dr. Dement has argued that the eye movements in the dream state are directly related to the images of the dream, as if the eyes are actually seeing the scene that is dreamed. Using the EEG machine, he has obtained tracings which record the amount of vertical and horizontal eye movement. The dreamer is then wakened and asked to report his dream, and the action of the dream is compared to the eye movements. A dream of watching a tennis match, for example, would be accompanied by much movement from right to left and back again; a dream of watching firemen on a ladder would have a high proportion of up and down movements. This is a logical assumption to make, especially since it seems that the optical system is working as if it were actually receiving visual impressions.

Dr. Dement believes that, whatever types of "dreaming or visual thought may occur in other states of sleep, in the REM sleep the evidence all points to a relationship between the eye movements and what is apparently witnessed by the moving eyes. For some reason, the oculomotor apparatus is behaving *as if* it were watching real scenes." Within the brain, that is, what is going on is similar to what would be going on if one were awake. "The nervous system," Dement says, "would be behaving as if it were receiving a sensory input appropriate to the dream imagery." In this respect, therefore, dreaming is similar to active wakefulness (and possibly different from unconscious mental processes occurring outside the visual dream period). Somewhere in the nervous system, dream imagery is replacing normal retinal stimulation from the world beyond the eyes.

We can draw attention to only two of the possible implications of this idea. Whatever may be the cause of these visual signals (reality-substitutes), so far as some parts of the brain are concerned they are equivalent to reality; no distinction is made between the visual imagery of a dream and the visual imagery of waking life. The distinction lies in what the brain does about it. There is clearly some mechanism that prevents the body acting on the sensory information—that tells the body, so to speak, that "this is only a dream, and action is unnecessary." When this motor-inhibiting mechanism does not work properly, we will twitch, move restlessly, or even break into sleepwalking and sleep-talking. But if it is working efficiently our dreams may indeed enable us to gratify ourselves in fantasy without the risks involved in acting on the feelings we dream.

The second implication follows from this. A psychological as well as a physiological cause may exist for the images that appear before the eye—the first writing the scenario for the performance, in a manner of speaking, and the second putting on the show. Such a division of labor might well account for the fact that psychologists and physiologists have hitherto concentrated on different aspects of the dream.

Dr. Dement's experiments have also been used to test whether the passage of time in dreams is similar to the time scale of waking life. Many dreamers have reported long dreams—sometimes, like the dreams of de Quincey, covering a span of centuries in mere minutes that seem to occur in brief snatches of sleep. But Dr. Dement suggests that, if a man dreams of walking across a room and opening a door, it will take just as long as the real actions. He found that if, in the REM period, a physical stimulus was given to the sleeper, it was usually incorporated in his dream. He therefore sprayed water on the sleeper's face, or rang a bell. Soon afterwards, the sleeper was wakened and asked to report his dream. The dream events that occurred after the water spray or the ringing of the bell were noted, and timed. They were then compared to the time they would normally take. From the evidence thus secured, Dr. Dement concludes that dream images succeed each other at approximately the same speed as waking sensory impressions of the same actions or experiences.

This view is challenged by other specialists in this field, notably Dr. Oswald, of the University of Edinburgh, who argues that "normal" time is not a characteristic of all dreams, and insists that the case for rapid or recapitulatory dreams is a strong one. One difficulty about Dr. Dement's present experiments is that they all involve waking the sleeper, and it is more than possible that arousal-dreams may be different from the continuing dream. We have no means of knowing, but it is at least possible that different types of dream may have different types of time scale.

One reason for suspecting this is the fact that in other fantasy states, such as we find in psychotic persons or in individuals with chemically induced hallucinations, marked disruption of the time sense is common. The feeling that much time has elapsed may provide an important clue. We know that in ordinary life our estimates of time will vary with our mood or our occupation. In a bad temper, waiting for someone to arrive for a rendezvous, we feel that time drags; in an exciting situation, doing something which interests us, we feel that the hours have rushed away. It is conceivable that much greater fluctuations in our sense of time can occur outside consciousness and that the *feeling* of time may be very different from the *actual* time of a series of events.

If we thus separate the feeling from the action, we can carry the argument a stage further. We saw, in the discussion of dream symbolism, that many complex emotions are evoked by a single image; an altered sense of time could well be one of these feeling-responses.

A man, for example, has a single dream image that he is running away from enemies; the whole of that situation can be depicted in a single picture. But the image also evokes intense feelings that cannot be represented pictorially; the *act* of running away from enemies may be such a powerful symbol for the dreamer that he could well *feel* that he has been running for hours.

It is not necessary for an action to take the full time in order to give the impression that much time has passed. Every movie demonstrates this fact; a series of shots lasting no more than a few seconds suggests to the audience that a man has taken a long journey, or even that a boy has grown into a man. We are thus making a distinction between the fleeting action in dreams and the enduring situations they imply. It may be true, as Dr. Dement has tried to show experimentally, that the actions occur at the same speed, whether we see them in a dream or in real life. But why should the actions and the associated emotional situations be measured on the same time scale? We all know how we can intuitively comprehend a relationship or a situation that spans a great deal of space.

If we think of painting a wall in all its detail, brush-stroke by brush-stroke, it will take as long as it would to do it. It only takes an instant, however, to think of painting a wall as a completed experience—and, at the same time, to feel that it has been a slow and wearying business.

This seems to be what happens in our dreams. There is no need to conclude from Dr. Dement's experiments that, because dream actions appear to move

18th Nov 1812   -5th [

historical time

viewing time 7 min —7 sec

The discrepancy between the dreamer's estimate of the time elapsed in a dream and its actual time may be analogous to the way the passage of time is conveyed in films. In the film *War and Peace* images lasting seven minutes seven seconds suffice to show Napoleon's troops retreating from Moscow (left) to an encampment in the snow (right) they really reached 17 days later.

at the same speed as their waking counterparts, the dream as a whole is confined to a "normal" time-scale. Dream analysis since Freud has been based on the idea of condensation; the dream images are seen as a kind of shorthand notation for memories, feelings, and conflicts that can range over a whole lifetime. All such experiences exist simultaneously in the memory; but the images that express (or summarize) them can emerge into consciousness only in some sort of order.

Once again, the world of the cinema provides a helpful analogy. The entire content of a movie, which records many relationships and a variety of situations, is stored on the film spooled up in the projector. But it is not available in that form. Its story, which seems as continuous and as convincing as real life, actually has to be told by a succession of single images. Each group of images—a man walking, a plane flying—must show these movements taking place at what looks like a normal speed. When, however, these groups are put together, much is omitted; we do not have to watch a man walk the whole length of a street or see a plane fly all the way from Paris to New York.

We instantaneously supply the missing links because we know what has happened. To say that the time element in a dream must be limited by the "true" time of its component images is like saying that the time span of a movie can be no greater than the sum of all the individual actions it portrays.

In any case, the actions of a dream that we remember are only a fragment of its visual material. We describe a scene in a film quite simply—a man takes a drink in a bar. There are innumerable details in that scene we omit to describe, from the man's appearance to the furniture of the bar. We must presume that dream images, as we recall them, are also gross simplifications of what we have "seen" in the dream. We must presume this because we know that in waking life we actually notice relatively few of the hundreds of sights, sounds, smells, and other impressions that are registered by our senses at every moment of the day. The remainder become part of our total experience, but they are perceived "subliminally," and unconsciously become part of our accumulating stock of memories. We draw on this stock to produce the images of our dreams—and other hallucinations. These images, however, seem to be unfamiliar because they are made up of sensory impressions that were never consciously recorded; and such impressions have been run together in new combinations that radically distort our original perceptions. In a dream, as Freud showed, we take a face from one person, clothes from another, a personal quirk from a third, and fuse all three into a new and seemingly unrecognizable character. This is one reason why dreams seem to be so bizarre. The process by which we select the significant memories for the purpose of condensation is complex and still obscure. But here psychoanalysis—especially Freud's technique of free assocation—has been useful in unraveling the tangle of emotions and images that we observe in our dreams. It enables us to tease out the emotional connections of apparently irrelevant aspects of the dream material and see how they are fused by what Freud called the "dream work."

Much more investigation of the kind done by Dr. Dement and others is clearly needed before it will be possible to speak with more conviction about such matters. What is important, however, is that the new techniques do seem to provide a much better means than any formerly available for testing dream theories of all kinds. Now we are able to awaken sleepers at the time of maximum recall, much more can be done than when the recovery of dream material was haphazard and fragmentary. A whole range of new and monitored interventions in dreaming can now be made—from the use of stimuli, drugs, hypnosis, and dream deprivation to the analysis of the rich psychological material provided by arousals in REM sleep.

In this chapter, we have examined some of the implications of these developments. But others must be set in a wider context of dream theory and, indeed, of theories of the nature and functioning of the human mind. It is therefore necessary to see what light modern research in drugs and chemotherapy may shed upon fantasies of all kinds, waking and sleeping.

10   Drugs and dreaming

"There is undoubtedly one common psycho-biological law explaining the activities of the brain cells." This sentence, which reads like an extract from a report on modern dream research, was written in 1888, some 12 years before Freud published *The Interpretation of Dreams*. The author was Julius Nelson, who wrote in one of the first issues of the *American Journal of Psychology* an article suggesting that such a general law must govern perception, volition, excitement, desire, and all man's other responses to the outer world and the promptings of his inner nature. Once such a law has been formulated, Nelson argued, "we shall then see why there is such a marked similarity among the different sorts of abnormal manifestations, such as the hallucinations of insanity, the delusions of hypnotism, the experiences of the dreamer, the fancies of reverie, and still other facts in anthropology."

This was an unusual prediction for its day, for it strikingly anticipated the direction in which recent research has been moving—and Nelson, it is interesting to note, arrived at this opinion by a method that foreshadowed the experiments we examined in the previous chapter. He lacked the apparatus now available, and had to depend upon the recall of dreams, whereas Professor Kleitman, Dr Dement, Dr Fisher, and others have been able to record the electrical rhythms of dreaming. But Nelson did have the ingenious notion of looking for a definite pattern in his own dreams. He had always been a vivid

This painting by a woman patient done after treatment with LSD 25 marks a transitional phase in her recovery. A phobia of spiders, which revealed strong destructive feelings, persists, but the spiders are giving way to the mandala design—which C. G. Jung regarded as a sign of the healing powers of the Self. The patient still sees herself (the square at the center) as imprisoned by her fantasies, but the imagery shows she is beginning to realize her inner potential.

dreamer, and between 1884 and 1887 he kept a detailed note of over 1000 dreams a year. On some nights, he realized, he dreamed much more than on others; and this increase seemed to come at regular intervals—a fluctuation that intrigued him, for he believed that "the fact that a person dreams much or little is of more significance than *what* one dreams. A curve representing the variations from day to day in the amount of dreaming has scientific interest, while the hobgoblins that we saw are of interest to children." He therefore sought to draw such a curve by examining both his own dream habits and those of other people.

Nelson soon came to the conclusion that it was the total time spent on dreaming each night that was significant, rather than the number of dreams. He thought—another notable anticipation of recent work—that the amount of dreaming varied with changes in physical state, especially alterations in blood pressure, pulse, and respiration. Since he lacked the means to take night-long observations, and thus was unable to detect the special characteristics of what we now call the REM period, he sought for other correlations. He first tried to check the vacillation in dreaming time with the phases of the moon. This test gave no useful result. But he then compared his curve with the "sexual month" of 28 days and came to the conclusion that, in women, dreaming varied with the time of menstruation and ovulation. It therefore seemed to him that some glandular process, linked to sexual metabolism, was responsible for the production of dreams.

Most contemporary experiments, using material provided by the EEG apparatus, have been concerned with the daily rhythm of dreaming; the usual assumption is that the number and duration of REM periods is relatively constant from one day to another. No one, apparently, has yet taken such recordings over a long enough period to indicate whether Nelson's idea of a monthly rhythm was based on fact or on a mere statistical coincidence. But whether he was right or wrong he deserves credit for putting forward a theory that there was a definite and measurable rhythm in dreaming and that this rhythm might be part of a psycho-biological process.

Nelson was a curious and obscure writer, whose theory has been overlooked for 70 years. Yet an idea of this kind does provide one possible means of reconciling the physiological and psychological concepts of the dream—indeed, as he himself remarked, it may indicate a vital link between "the different sorts of abnormal manifestations." There was nothing new in the proposal that all such phenomena, from hallucinations to the fantasies of the starving, from mental illness to the visions of the opium-eater, might have much in common. But Nelson seems to have been the first person to suggest that they might all be the outcome of regular biochemical processes that have psychic consequences, and are in turn liable to be affected by psychic experience.

For most of this century, an important and unresolved debate has gone on among psychiatrists about the causes of psychotic conditions—especially the

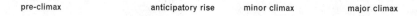

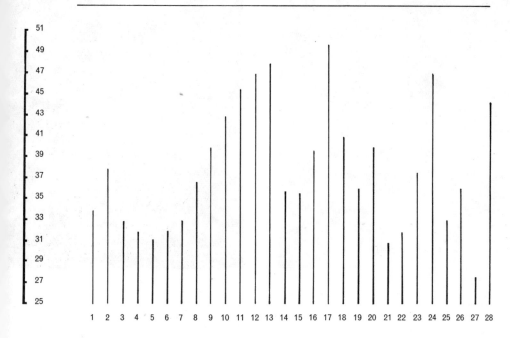

Julius Nelson tried to relate dream recollection to the menstrual cycle. He recorded the number and length of women's dreams from November 24 1884 to March 13 1887, giving a numerical value to the dreams. He then plotted this as a monthly average, suggesting the amount of dreaming recalled might be related to the sexual rhythm.

group of mental illnesses that are generally classified as schizophrenia. Since Freud, much progress has been made in psychotherapy as a means of diagnosing and treating severe mental disorders. But Freud himself once said that "behind the psychiatrist stands the man with the syringe." He never excluded the possibility that a physical cause (and possibly chemical cures) might eventually be found for at least some forms of psychosis. Conversely, many doctors and scientists recognize that even if, one day, a genetic or biochemical cause of schizophrenia is found, the insights of therapeutic psychology will still be indispensable in treating mentally disturbed people.

Thus there have been two different attitudes toward the disorders of human personality—one emphasizing the dislocation of "mental" processes, and the other the impaired functioning of the neuro-chemical systems of the body. But these two approaches are not mutually exclusive; indeed, modern science

A 20th-century artist, Louis Wain, who was fascinated by cats, painted these pictures over a period of time in which he developed schizophrenia. The pictures mark progressive stages in the illness.

and medicine have shown that they are increasingly complementary. As we shall see in this chapter, remarkable discoveries in the field of psycho-pharmacology—the use of drugs that affect the mental processes that govern perception of ourselves and our atitudes to others—hold out the hope that in the next few years we shall learn much more about the relation of mind and body and be able to treat effectively many "abnormal manifestations" once thought to be beyond cure.

The more we learn, the clearer it becomes that "abnormal" is a question-begging term. Early in this century, C. G. Jung found that the dreams and the free associations of apparently "normal" people were very like the thought patterns of his schizophrenic patients. It has since been realized that an immense range of feeling and psychic experience is open to all men, and that "abnormal manifestations" are not in themselves a sign of mental illness. The vague frontier between mental health and psychological disturbance is crossed when unconscious fantasies are no longer confined to sleep (or to brief periods when consciousness is otherwise diminished by fatigue or drugs) but break out continuously and powerfully in ordinary waking life. As Professor Manfred Bleuler of Zurich has put it, the schizophrenic "lives mainly

in a world which, in the everyday life of the healthy, is concealed... the schizophrenic openly demonstrates what is hidden in the healthy... he has surrendered to his unconscious."

It is important to stress this point because it is often assumed that there is a clear dividing line between the sane and the insane. This is not the case. Each of us has within us the whirling fantasies that dominate the life of the mentally disturbed, just as the schizophrenic has the potential to live a "realistic" life. What has happened to the psychotic person is that he has become incapable of distinguishing his inner experience from his external reality. "This inner life," Professor Bleuler wrote in 1963, "creates a fantastic world according to our inner needs, it pays no attention to experience and logic or to the real world outside us." We do not yet know why this happens. The balance of mind and body may be upset by some congenital defect, or by taking alcohol or drugs to excess, or by undue psychological stress in infancy or terror in war. Any one of these factors, or all of them in combination, may contribute to schizophrenia. Surveying 50 years of research on this vital problem, Professor Bleuler concluded that "nature and nurture... are pathogenic forces which are closely interwoven and not to be artificially separated."

As we saw in Chapters 6, 7, and 8, one reason why psychotherapy has hitherto placed such emphasis on the study of dreams is that it regards them as the common form in which we can observe at least some fragments of our rich but hidden fantasy life. If a healthy dreamer could speak and act while asleep, Jung once said, nobody could distinguish him from a schizophrenic patient. But it is now possible, with the aid of hallucinogenic drugs, to enable the healthy person to experience states that are very similar to those of the dreamer and the psychotic, to give him temporary access to the inner world that contrasts so dramatically with the outer reality he sees, hears, smells, tastes, and touches. To put matters simply, such drugs enable a man to enter a dream-like state without losing consciousness.

The discovery and systematic use of these drugs thus provide additional evidence that within all of us there are a host of mental states of which we are usually unaware—fantasies that powerfully affect our experience of outer reality and organize that experience. They also make it seem more probable that all forms of fantasy are different expressions of the same fundamental process, whether they manifest themselves as dreams or waking reveries, as hallucinations, hypnagogic imagery, the visions of saints, or the delusions of the schizophrenic. As many writers had noted—long before Jung produced his theory of the "collective unconscious" to account for the similarity of symbols in dreams, myths, and mental illness—whatever may be the specific cause of fantasies, their content is remarkably alike. The difference between them seems to lie more in the time and mode of their appearance than in their nature.

We must therefore consider these new drugs from two points of view. We must ask, first, what they reveal about the complex chemistry of the brain. Do they provide support for the belief that all fantasies, from dreams to delusions, may have a common biochemical origin? It has long been suspected that schizophrenia and other mental disorders are caused by a toxic substance in the brain; the difficulty about this theory is that after many years of research no scientist has yet definitely identified such a toxin—though there have been some inspired guesses. Secondly, we must see what we can learn, from the experiences of those who have taken hallucinogenic drugs, about the psychic characteristics of fantasy. How far do these experiences confirm the insights of psychotherapy? Can we employ chemically induced hallucinations as active agents in the treatment of mental illness? Can we, indeed, use these drugs to discover much more about the unconscious processes of the mind and their effect on conscious behavior?

We speak of the hallucinogens as "new" psychiatric drugs, and it is true that they have been used clinically by Western medicine only since the end of the Second World War. But for thousands of years men have known that some drugs dramatically distort the workings of the brain. We can infer from the scant records of Assyrian, Egyptian, and Greek pharmacology that the ancient world had some working knowledge of such poisons, arrived at by trial and error—and we know that some tribal societies beyond the fringe of civilization long ago discovered means of using hallucinatory chemicals, extracted from roots, seeds, and fungi, that have only in comparatively recent years been discovered by Western science.

Two of the most famous of the fantasy-inducing drugs are not true hallucinogens—a term reserved for a distinct group of drugs, including mescalin, lysergic acid diethylamide (LSD 25), and psilocybin. These are opium, derived from the poppy, and hashish, otherwise known as marijuana, bhang, dagga, or "tea," which comes from the hemp plant. Both are known to have been used in China for at least four thousand years and both have been found in widely separated parts of the world. Belladonna and henbane have also been used for centuries both as poisons and as means of altering a man's mental condition; they were staple ingredients of medieval witchcraft. It is interesting to note that some other ingredients in the potions of witchcraft may have been hallucinogenic. Since the time of the ancient Egyptians, toad skins have been used in magic recipes—and bufotenin, which is hallucinogenic, can be extracted from the skin of a toad; the urine of animals and humans, which was another ingredient widely used in potions, may, under certain conditions, contain hallucinatory chemicals. No one knows what it was that the Greeks called "ambrosia," the food of the gods, but it was undoubtedly something more potent than honey.

It was in Central and South America, however, that Europeans first came across the "mind-loosening" drugs from which the modern hallucinogens are derived or to which they are chemically related. When the Spaniards conquered Mexico and Peru they found that the Aztecs had a "divine" drug named *peyotl*, and that the Incas made a sacred concoction called *coca*. More than 13 *phantastica* (the original botanical name given to plants that produce hallucinatory effects) were known to the Indians of Mexico alone, and others were found elsewhere in South America. The most common types are *peyote*, eaten in the form of the dried tops or "buttons" of a small cactus (this is the source of the drug we call mescalin), and the "sacred mushrooms" whose active component is psilocybin. The Indians in Mexico used also the seeds of a species of bindweed known to them as *oliliuqui* and to English and American gardeners as Morning Glory or convolvulus. In the Amazon basin the natives use the seeds of a plant called *cohoba*, and consume a drink called *caapi* which contains the hallucinogenic called harmine.

In the Congo many tribes chew the root *Tabernanthe iboga*, from which another hallucinogen called ibogaine has been extracted; and in northern Siberia the Tungus, Yakuts, and Koryaks use a fungus—fly agaric—as a means of inducing trances and visions. Now that chemists in European and American laboratories are investigating the extraordinary properties of these drugs and their refined derivatives, others may well be found in common plants (or even animals) used by tribes who long ago discovered their seemingly magical power to open what the poet Blake called "the doors of perception" into man's fantasy world. There is, for instance, a drug extracted from the Dream Fish—a species of mullet found in the Pacific—which can produce visions and cause other hallucinatory effects.

All these drugs—or the refined versions of them now used in psychiatry—have the capacity to stimulate fantasy. They are of great value in investigating the biochemistry of mental illness because they are "psychotomimetic"—that is, they can produce many of the characteristics of psychosis in normal persons. And they are a valuable asset in therapy because they are "psychodelic," or mind-revealing, inducing mental states in which an individual can recall long-repressed experiences and feelings. But there are other new drugs—generally grouped as "tranquilizers"—which have an opposite effect. They seem to block off hallucinations and bring the individual who is dominated by fantasies into closer touch with reality. Research into the chemistry of hallucination, therefore, concentrates on both aspects—on the drugs that cause fantasies and on those that diminish them.

The tranquilizers must not be confused with the standard medical sedatives, such as atropine, the barbiturates, morphine, chloral, and bromide—all of which are widely used to calm anxious people or enable them to sleep. The barbiturates, for instance, have been so far developed that over 2500 types have been synthesized; more than 50 types are in regular use, and they are prescribed so freely that at least 300 tons of them are consumed annually in the United States alone. Tranquilizers are a different type of drug, and some of them have already proved more effective in dealing with serious mental disorders than anything previously known.

Two Aztec codices, painted some time before the Spanish Conquest in the 16th century, that depict the temptation of the god Quetzalcoatl. Top right, the god is offered pulque—an intoxicating drink made from the heart of the cactus. Bottom right, the goddess of the sacred mushroom tempts him with the mushrooms. By taking them Quetzalcoatl loses his godly stature, upon which he destroys himself by sailing away into the rising sun. The Mexican Indians also chewed the seeds of a plant they called Ololiuqui but which we call morning glory or convolvulus. Left, codex (date unknown) shows the goddess Xochiquetzal with the plant in flower.

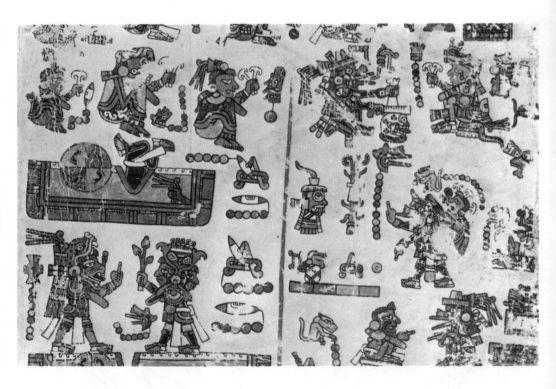

A few years ago, when they were just coming into general use, the eminent American pharmacologist, Dr. Harold E. Himwich, wrote that "they have introduced a new regime into the management of patients in mental hospitals. The drugs calm the patients without putting them to sleep ... they make even 'hopeless' patients accessible to psychotherapy by removing some of the barriers between the patient and the psychiatrist." It is now possible to discharge many patients who, without such drugs, would probably have been kept in hospital indefinitely, and to treat many more at home who in the past would certainly have been confined to mental institutions.

These drugs range from the minor tranquilizers, such as Equanil or Miltown (meprobamate) to the major ones, of which chlorpromazine (known commercially as Thorazine or Lagactil) is the best known. Two others are reserpine, derived from the snakeroot plant *Rauwolfia serpentina*, which has been used in a crude form for centuries as a specific for the treatment of mania and other mental illnesses, and azacyclonol (known as Frenquel).

The chemistry of the brain, which is so strikingly affected both by hallucinogens and tranquilizers, is highly complicated and difficult to study. Much has been discovered about the effects of these drugs, but many of the processes that produce these effects remain unknown. We say, for example, that LSD 25 produces hallucinations. But is it, in fact, this drug that causes the fantasies to arise? One theory suggests that there are chemical substances

Two 17th-century woodcuts of henbane (right) and belladonna or deadly nightshade (left), both of which can be poisonous but have medicinal qualities. They were used in medieval witchcraft potions, and can produce altered mental states.

in the body that can cause hallucinations, but that these substances are normally converted into other chemicals or eliminated from the body. When LSD 25 enters the system, however, it may interfere with the process of conversion or elimination by competing for stocks of some third chemical upon which the regular conversion process depends. The same problem arises in analyzing the effect of the tranquilizers. It seems probable that they work by assisting the conversion or elimination of chemicals that, if left in the body, would cause hallucinations and other types of mental disturbance.

The chemists and neurologists who study such matters have a difficult task. They are confronted by a brain that consists of approximately ten billion cells, controlling all man's thoughts and actions, his voluntary and involuntary responses to the problems of existence. Some parts of this brain direct the way a man breathes, the beating of his heart, and the circulation of his blood; some control the glands that influence his growth or sexuality, his responses to danger or pleasure, the functions of his digestion or excretion. Other areas of the brain are responsible for movement, speech, hearing, taste, smell, and sight. The eyes alone have over one million nerve centers, each carrying hundreds of impulses per second, and merely to register and store the flood of messages from without and within that reach the brain at a given moment would be a task beyond the capacity of any electronic computer yet devised. The human brain, moreover, evaluates as well as remembers; it thinks as

Hashish, which comes from the Indian hemp plant (right), was introduced into European medicine in 1838. The snakeroot plant *Rauwolfia serpentina* (left) is known in India as "the medicine of sad men." Both engravings date from the 19th century

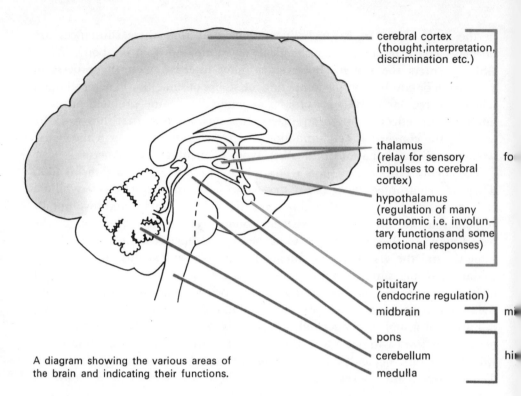

cerebral cortex
(thought, interpretation,
discrimination etc.)

thalamus
(relay for sensory
impulses to cerebral
cortex)

fo

hypothalamus
(regulation of many
autonomic i.e. involun-
tary functions and some
emotional responses)

pituitary
(endocrine regulation)

midbrain

m

pons

cerebellum

hi

medulla

A diagram showing the various areas of
the brain and indicating their functions.

well as giving automatic responses. It is, in fact, not one brain but several, intimately connected by circuits and chemical processes so delicate that most of them can only be guessed; they cannot be directly observed.

Man, in fact, has a hierarchy of brains, the latest of which (in evolutionary terms) is the cerebral cortex or upper brain, which alone has 15,000 cells in each square millimeter. This massive brain, which has far more potential than man seems able to use, has "silent areas" whose functions are less definite and precise. Injury to these areas, or their surgical severance from the rest of the brain, have an influence on a man's personality, though in many respects he can continue to lead a normal life. Other parts of the cortex govern the senses and the deliberate physical responses we make to their message. To put it simply, we may say that the cortex controls what we call rational thought and behavior.

In contrast, the parts of the brain that are biologically older are largely insulated against purposive activity. They control the instinctive and automatic activities of the organism—its growth, its sexuality, basic metabolism, reflex actions, and so forth. The lower brain, moreover, seems to be the source of profound emotional responses that are beyond our conscious control. We cannot deliberately decide to feel love or hate, anxiety or aggression any more than we can consciously influence our rate of growth.

There is, however, a continuous and subtle interplay between the upper and lower brains—a relationship that changes but persists when we sleep or when consciousness is otherwise diminished. Though we cannot examine this elaborate relationship in detail here, we must note that there is a crucial link between our sensory system and the parts of the lower brain—especially the hypothalamus—that control the activating processes of the human body. This brain structure contains the centers that link a man's emotional state with his breathing and pulse rate, with his blood pressure, with his ability to rouse himself in an emergency to fight or flee, and with his capacity to relax and go to sleep. Dr. Himwich has summarized this relationship:

"When the body is touched or stimulated in some way, nerve impulses go from the site of stimulation by pathways called the lemnisci to the thalamus in the center of the brain. From there the impulses are relayed to parts of the cerebral cortex which interpret the sensation—touch, pain, heat, cold, or the like. But there is also a parallel mental system, so to speak, which is affected by the stimulus. In the central core of the brain is a structure known as the activating system; it is located in the 'reticular formation.' When stimulated, the activating system produces an arousal reaction."

Such a reaction is translated into physical responses by the secretion of nerve hormones, such as adrenalin (called epinephrine in the U.S.A.), nor-adrenalin, and acetylcholine. Each of these helps to mobilize the system to cope with the demands and dangers of life. When we are afraid, or become angry or amorous, the glands release appropriate quantities of these and other nerve hormones which stimulate the beating of the heart, raise the blood pressure, and make possible the muscle movements that are needed to turn our feelings into actions. It has been suggested that if something has gone wrong with the chemical balance of the body—and the arousal mechanism is extremely complex and delicate, linking our physiological and psychological systems together—then the glands may secrete these nerve hormones (or closely related chemical substances) in the wrong quantities at the wrong times.

We do not know exactly why this should happen; nor can we yet show what complex chemical processes may lead to the breakdown of these nerve hormones into substances that produce hallucinations. But two outstanding Canadian researchers, Dr. Hoffer and Dr. Osmond, believe that the clue to all forms of hallucination lies in some defect in the chemistry of the system that converts impulses from the instinctual or "unconscious" areas of the brain into conscious thought and behavior. They have suggested that adrenalin, for instance, may break down into two other chemicals—adrenochrome and adrenolutin—both of which may be hallucinogenic. Against this theory is the fact that no one has yet demonstrated that either adrenochrome or adrenolutin exists naturally in the human body, although it is possible to produce a substance that seems very similar to adrenolutin from the blood serum of schizophrenic patients.

There are, however, other clinical and experimental reasons for thinking that Hoffer and Osmond are on the right track when they draw attention to the arousal system, and more specifically to the adrenal glands, as the probable source of hallucinogenic chemicals. There appears to be a close relationship between stimulation of the sympathetic nervous system and the onset of fantasies—a point that is underlined by the various physical characteristics of the REM period, from increased pulse and respiration rates to fluctuations in body temperature and blood pressure. In the search for an organic explanation of schizophrenia, it was discovered long ago that fear and stress (which affect the release of adrenalin and other nerve hormones) may produce hallucinations in normal persons, and yet produce at least a temporary improvement in schizophrenics. As early as 1840 mental patients were whirled in centrifuges and subjected to other frightening experiences. More recently, in the 1930s, Dr. Graves of England, in the belief that schizophrenia was due to a septic condition, removed the teeth, tonsils, and gall gladders of psychotic persons. He claimed that this improved their condition. But such improvements as there were are now thought to have been due to the strain of the anesthetic and the shock of the operation, just as the condition of some schizophrenics has been known to improve after they have had pneumonia or some form of high fever.

Though we have been stressing the possible importance of adrenalin, we must not overlook other possible biochemical causes of hallucinatory states. One suggestion is that there may be faulty metabolism of important protein substances in the body, notably in the functioning of the thyroid gland—the source of a vital hormone. Another theory stresses the significance of a hormone called serotonin, which occurs in many animals and in the human brain. This hormone plays a vital role in the function of the lower brain, especially those parts in it concerned with imagery and sensory elaboration. Some researchers have proposed that schizophrenia (and dreams) may be due to defective serotonin metabolism.

It is known that LSD 25 and mescalin have an effect on the secretion of serotonin; and it has been shown also that the supply of serotonin in the brain may be altered by the administration of chlorpromazine and reserpine. It is thus susceptible to both hallucinogenic and tranquilizing drugs. But it is far from certain what these drugs do—whether they raise or lower the amount of serotonin available to the critical regions of the brain. Some scientists believe that LSD 25 achieves its results by competing for the available supplies of this hormone; that when LSD 25 enters the system it uses up the stock of serotonin. Other scientists believe that the serotonin level rises when LSD 25 enters the system; in their view, LSD 25 competes with serotonin for some other substance that, in normal brain chemistry, would keep the supply of serotonin in balance. The same uncertainty exists about the relationship between certain of the tranquilizers and serotonin.

While the search for the mysterious "Toxin X" continues—and it seems increasingly probable that some schizogenic substance will eventually be identified in the lower areas of the brain—one important line of research is the study of drugs that diminish hallucinatory tendencies. Though most of this work concentrates on the clinical aspects of these drugs, because doctors are primarily concerned with both their therapeutic and their side effects on patients, some reports do notice their effect on dreaming habits. It has been found that some of the tranquilizers, as well as certain sedatives, appear to diminish the amount of dreaming at night, or at least change the intensity of emotional effect in dreams. Other drugs, which may reduce hallucinatory states in waking life, apparently lead to an increase in unpleasant dreams. The evidence of this kind is still fragmentary and inconclusive, and much more systematic work is needed before any substantial generalizations can be made about it. It does, however, seem to point toward the idea that some kind of equilibrium normally exists between dreaming and waking fantasies, and that any drug that influences one may have a result on the other.

It seems likely that, within the next few years, such research will reveal much more about the complex interactions of hallucinogens, tranquilizers, and other drugs with the chemicals in the brain. Already, a good deal of evidence exists for the belief that the arousal system may be the mainspring of all types of hallucinations, from dreams to the delusions of the insane. It

An engraving (1828) of a rotary motion machine that was used during the 19th century in the treatment of mental patients. It has been found that many psychotic patients temporarily improve under conditions of physical stress.

is particularly significant that both the hallucinogens and the tranquilizers seem to affect the arousal system—the hallucinogens apparently stimulating instinctual and emotional responses from the lower parts to the brain, while the tranquilizers block off or reduce the intensity of such impulses reaching the cerebral cortex. We also know that, in addition to their role in governing man's instinctive life, these lower centers of the brain control the basic autonomic rhythms of the body—including our ability to wake up and go to sleep. This leads to a crucial question. Is the dreaming process also a rhythmic function of these same centers in the brain?

We shall return to this question in the final chapter. We should, meanwhile, recall Dr. Dement's suggestion that the 90-minute sleep cycle may have its origin in a biochemical rhythm. The fact that this rhythm—originally lasting about 60 minutes—can be found even in newborn infants is highly significant. Babies seem to have the physical characteristics of the REM period from birth, and Kleitman has demonstrated that these REM periods are closely related to the infant's pattern of sleep and arousal. It is also significant that, as Dr. Dement's experiments in deprivation have shown, a person whose normal rhythm of dreaming is disrupted becomes increasingly confused and begins to develop psychotic symptoms. It is at least a working hypothesis that there are regular chemical transactions going on within the brain that are normally completed during the REM period, and that produce as a by-product the temporary hallucinations we call dreams. If these processes are disrupted by physiological or psychological stresses, then the hallucinatory material may well break through in waking hours.

This is why the hallucinogenic drugs are relevant. They enable men to experience waking hallucinations. Much valuable research on brain chemistry and neurology has been done with animal subjects, but ultimately drugs must be used on human beings if we are to know their psychological effects. This is what has been happening with the hallucinogens. The person who takes such drugs—and they must be administered only under the strictest medical supervision because they are a hazardous and often frightening disruption of normal life—can now experience himself and his environment in much the same way as someone afflicted by schizophrenic illness. There is, however, a significant difference. The experimenter knows that, although the drug will distort his awareness of reality, this strange state is merely temporary. He will be able to observe and comprehend what is happening to him, even though his conscious awareness is substantially diminished. The psychotic, on the contrary, does not know what is wrong; he is the prisoner of his fantasies and lacks the assurance of being able to regain contact with reality. In other words, the psychotic cannot make effective distinction between the fantasies coming from within and the sensory impressions from without.

It has been possible, however, to produce "model" or "experimental" psychoses only during the last 20 years, since chemists first began to isolate

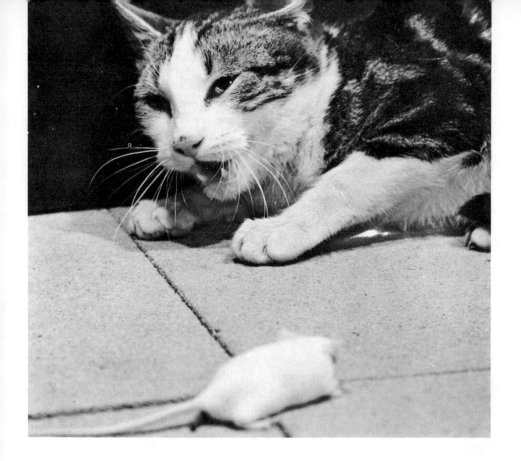

After being given a dose of LSD 25 this
cat showed confused reactions. Confronted
by a mouse it exhibited some normal
aggressive signs—dilated pupils, ears
flattened, etc. But instead of pouncing
on the mouse, the cat retreated.

the active hallucinogenic materials from the crude forms used by primitive tribes—and then were able to synthesize new derivatives. Before the Second World War, experiments involving chemically induced hallucinations were shots in the dark, haphazard and sometimes bizarre attempts using materials ranging from ether, nitrous oxide, and opium to mescalin; only the last of these belongs to the group of chemicals to which the general term "hallucinogenic" is now applied.

The effect of each of these drugs is different and it varies also from one individual to another. Yet some characteristic effects are common to them all, particularly an increase in visual imagery so striking that many reports of those who have taken them tend to concentrate on this theme. One of the earliest accounts of the effects of mescalin, for instance, came from an American doctor, Weir Mitchell, who gave this description:

"Stars, delicate films of color, then an abrupt rush of countless points of white light swept across the field of view, as if the unseen millions of the Milky Way were to flow in a sparkling river before my eyes ... zigzag lines of very bright colors ... After an endless display of less beautiful marvels I saw that which deeply impressed me. An edge of a huge cliff seemed to project over a gulf of unseen depth. My viewless enchanter set on the brink a huge bird claw of stone. Above, from the stem or leg, hung a fragment of the same stuff. This began to unroll and float out to a distance which seemed to me to represent Time as well as immensity of space."

A similar experience, from the same period, was reported by Havelock Ellis, who observed how the drug induced architectural and oriental visions reminiscent of De Quincey's opium dreams, and how it also changed the appearance of real objects:

"After watching the visions in the dark for some hours I became a little tired of them and turned on the gas. Then I found that I was able to study a new series of visual phenomena to which previous observers had made no reference. The gas jet ... seemed to burn with great brilliance, sending out waves of light, which expanded and contracted in an enormously exaggerated manner. I was even more impressed by the shadows, which were in all directions heightened by flushes of red, green, and especially violet. The whole room, with its whitewashed but not very white ceiling, thus became vivid and beautiful ... I was reminded of the paintings of Claude Monet, and as I gazed at the scene it occurred to me that mescal perhaps produces the same conditions ... as may be produced on the artist by the influence of prolonged visual attention."

Hundreds of subsequent reports, from those of volunteer subjects in clinical experiments to those of Aldous Huxley—whose book, *The Doors of Perception*, eulogizes the transcendental aspects of mescalin experience—are substantially the same. They all emphasize the vivid, colored imagery that mescalin induces, its enhancement of ordinary objects, such as pencils and biscuits, into things of iridescent beauty, the sense of detachment from ordinary cares and concerns, and above all the destruction of "normal" awareness of time and space.

Over and over again the takers of mescalin use such phrases as "the ordinary human sense of time seemed contemptible.... The sense of drifting in the infinite, of flowing into the ocean of eternity." The British politician Christopher Mayhew reported to a London medical conference in 1961 that he had taken mescalin during a television programme on hallucinogens and that it had totally disrupted his sense of time. Events that the screen showed in one order had been *experienced* by him out of sequence; he also felt that, at intervals, he had "gone away" for "countless years of complete bliss," although the camera record of his behavior and the transcript of his speech showed no apparent interruption. The experience left Mr. Mayhew feeling that: "... my dose of mescalin detached me so far from the current of events in the drawing room that 'I' actually stood outside the stream of time, and was aware of the events of two o'clock and three o'clock as things existing simultaneously, capable of being experienced by people in my position either before or after each other."

The feeling that the usual dimensions of time and space have been altered is characteristic of such hallucinogenic states, of dreams, and of the hallucinations of the psychotic. It is also found in the mental states of mystics after fasting, or prolonged meditation, or the exercises used in yoga. No satisfactory physiological explanation has yet been found for this type of derangement, which is so striking to those who experience it that they feel as if they have been translated into a new and ultimate dimension. Whether, in fact, the testimony of dreams and hallucinations is evidence of a new dimension of time is another question, which has recently been discussed at length by J. B. Priestley in his book *Man and Time*.

At the experimental level, however, there is no doubt that such "transcendental" distortions of our "normal" senses, which may be terrifying as well as elevating, are a common feature of hallucinatory states of all kinds. We have, for example, the testimony of Baudelaire who belonged to a group of Parisians who called themselves Le Club des Hachischins and met to take marijuana. Baudelaire spoke of the "peculiar state of joy and serenity" a man can achieve with this poison. He felt that everything magnificent in the world,

The British politician Christopher Mayhew
took mescalin in a televised experiment.
He experienced events out of sequence. In
brief moments of time, he said, "I enjoyed
an existence, fully conscious of myself,
for what seemed like several years."

Havelock Ellis remarked how under the influence of mescalin the structure and color of real objects were changed and enhanced. His impressions reminded him of the paintings of the French artist Claude Monet. Left, *Rouen Cathedral. The Façade at Sunset* (1894).

Top right, *Judith Returning to Bethulia* (about 1470) painted by Botticelli, and bottom right, *The Chair* (1888-9) by Van Gogh. Aldous Huxley refers to these pictures in *The Doors of Perception* (1954) as echoing the sensations that he experienced after taking mescalin. For instance, he became aware of normally unnoticed objects, just as Van Gogh did when he painted a chair or Botticelli did when he painted the folds of drapery in Judith's dress. "What the rest of us see only under the influence of mescalin," Huxley wrote, "the artist is congenitally equipped to see all the time."

"the labors of Science and the dreams of the Muses," had "been created *for me, for me, for me*! For me has humanity labored, been martyred, been immolated, to serve as pasture for my implacable thirst for emotion, for knowledge, for beauty!" And another early experimenter, Fitz-Hugh Ludlow, reported that when he had taken hashish:

"I looked abroad on fields and waters and sky, and read in them a most startling meaning. They were now grand symbols of the sublimest spiritual truths, truths never before even feebly grasped, and utterly unsuspected. Like a map, the arcana of the universe lay bare before me. I saw how every created thing not only typifies, but springs forth from some mighty physical law as its offspring."

Aldous Huxley and others have noted the similarity of such beatific experiences to those that underlie much oriental philosophy, especially Zen Buddhism. In the United States, a cult has now grown up that amalgamates chemical and introspective devices for inducing transcendental visions. For all its rewards, such a cult has serious dangers—both physical and mental—and it must be regarded as marginal to the controlled scientific experiments that chemists, physiologists, and psychotherapists are now conducting in many countries. Yet these experiments, too, are basically concerned with the problem of self-discovery, because one of the properties of the hallucinogenic drugs seems to be the enlargement of one's inner horizons—not merely while the drug is acting, but indefinitely. They permit much that has been forgotten or repressed, or that has never been truly apprehended during consciousness, to be recalled and even re-experienced, with enduring effects on the personality of those who take them.

There is now a large and growing literature describing the hallucinogenic experience, from the standpoint both of the therapist and the subject. Close to 500 papers on LSD 25 alone have been published in medical and scientific journals, apart from many popular accounts. Other experimental reports deal with mescalin, psilocybin, harmine, ibogaine, reserpine, and an unusual (but now abandoned) general anesthetic, phencylidine, which worked without inducing loss of consciousness but which induced something like sensory deprivation, followed by hallucinations. LSD 25, however, is the most widely used—sometimes in combination with a psychic energizer like ritalin or with some anxiety-reducing drug —and has been the most carefully studied.

The discovery that this drug had unusual properties was made in April 1943 by a Swiss chemist, Albert Hofmann. He was making an experiment with lysergic acid, which is a derivative of ergot, a black fungus that grows on rye. (This poisonous fungus was responsible, in the Middle Ages, for a widespread illness with many of the symptoms of madness.) Dr. Hofmann noticed that he had become dizzy and restless, and went home to bed. "When I closed my eyes", he reported later, "I experienced fantastic images of an extraordinary plasticity. They were associated with an intense kaleidoscopic play of colors." Hofmann concluded that he had somehow absorbed minute particles of the chemical substance on which he was working. He therefore went back to his laboratory and courageously took 250 micrograms of LSD— what proved later to be 10 times a potent dosage of this drug, which is so active that one kilogram of it would provide an effective injection for every inhabitant of London. Hofmann thus became the first person, experimentally, to experience the extraordinary powers of LSD. Since then, in laboratories

Left, an impression of an opium-taker's dream, taken from the *Mangwa*, a collection of 19th-century Japanese drawings. Right, the French poet Baudelaire drew this self-portrait after taking hashish.

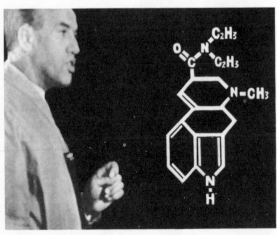

An engraving by Mathew Merian I (1593-1650) of the Christmas Eve Dance in Kölbigk churchyard—the beginning of the great dance epidemic of 1021 which is one of the earliest instances of St. Vitus' dance. When the people danced outside the church the priest's son tried to pull his sister out of the dancing ring, but her arm came off in his hand with no trace of blood. The priest excommunicated the dancers and ordered them to dance without ceasing for a year. St. Vitus' dance was almost certainly caused by ergot poisoning, and the incident of the woman's arm could be fact. Ergot is a poisonous fungus from which LSD 25 can be derived. Left, the Swiss chemist Albert Hofmann, who discovered LSD 25 in 1943, demonstrating the formula.

and clinics, thousands of volunteers and patients undergoing psychotherapy have shared this experience.

The drug can be administered orally or by injection, and it is usual to provide a calm and secure atmosphere for the session, with a doctor, therapist, or nurse within call. In most cases, the patient is alone for several hours, but some therapists remain with the patient. An American writer, Dorothy Newland, in *My Self and I*, has described a series of such sessions in which the therapist stayed with her and helped in the interpretation of her fantasies—to great therapeutic effect. Other doctors have made valuable trials of group experiences, in which several patients were enabled to work through the LSD period together. But though changes in the setting do undoubtedly influence the patient's reactions to the drug, they do not interfere with its fundamental action.

This begins a short time after the drug has been taken, and the patient passes through a series of states during the following six to twelve hours. The experience differs according to the individual and is itself different in the same person each time the drug is taken. Some persons are much more subject to anxiety; some resist the fantasies, some become deeply absorbed in them. A typical session begins with feelings of restlessness, and a number of somatic symptoms, from nausea and headache to localized pains and numbness. At the same time, the patient's sense of his own body alters, so that he feels larger or smaller, and becomes acutely aware of parts of his anatomy. He begins to lose touch with reality, to find his thoughts confused and wandering, to feel "out of time." At this stage he may experience vivid visual sensations, like those described by takers of mescalin or hashish, he may imagine that he hears sounds, music, or voices, become aware of smells and tastes for which there is no present real stimulus, and, above all, recall long-forgotten events and feelings—as if he were watching a film of scenes from his past.

Such recall comes in a curious manner that seems like a compromise between perception and experience. Some part of the patient's mind appears able to scrutinize and evaluate what is happening; another part becomes emotionally involved—tension, anxiety, fear, sexual pleasure, deep love, or profound sadness and transcendental joy can all emerge, sometimes as pure feelings and sometimes clearly associated with specific memories. It is as if the patient is *experiencing imagery*. He may feel himself to be an infant again, or an adolescent—many people have had experiences that seem like the reenactment of birth—or at the peak of the session he may undergo a sense of disintegration that feels like madness or death, or of identification with an object such as a toy, a flower, or an animal. As the hours pass, he moves into a reflective state in which he can review the memories and feelings that have been evoked from the hinterland of his mind.

So much material emerges into consciousness that the patient, especially if he is unaccustomed to the experience and reluctant to face the irrational

This painting, done after a dose of LSD 25, depicts the patient's sensation of the flesh falling off her bones and her body becoming a "kit of parts." The picture—of a type common in therapy—symbolically depicts the disintegration of the ego.

urges within himself, is often frightened and unable to assimilate all the feelings and memories that are aroused. Some of these may subsequently be identified in discussions with his therapist; some may be clarified in subsequent LSD sessions; some may reappear in later dreams; and some may not be fully recognized for several months.

One patient summed up her experiences in these words:

"I had other experiences later in the treatment. Twice I felt very babyish, I wanted milk. On the second occasion it was an exhilarating experience: I felt myself inside the womb, I felt myself being born; it was just as if I was starting life all over again, a turning point all over again. Eventually I started to begin to think in an adult fashion." In the Appendix to this book is an extended extract from a tape recording in which this woman attempted to interpret what she experienced. But interpretation seems to be the lesser part of the LSD experience. Whether or not the patient understands what has happened, a means has been found of releasing powerful emotions and forgotten events that he has hitherto failed to confront consciously. He may not, as a matter of fact, be able to describe very clearly what has happened, either while under the influence of the drug or afterward. Anyone who has taken a hallucinogen apparently finds it extremely difficult to communicate the experience (just as the psychotic encounters serious obstacles in his attempt to express his feelings or perceptions), for language fails when it is called upon to convey the inexpressible.

This is not simply a problem of communication—the lack of suitable words to describe what one is feeling. There appears to be a change in the actual thought-forms that underlie formal language, a regression to what Tauber and Green called "prelogical thinking," in which imagery and associations play the role that abstractions and reasoning play in rational thought. We have already seen how this conception has been applied to the dream. It is now clear—and it can be demonstrated experimentally by the use of hallucinogens—that whenever consciousness is disrupted, whether by sensory deprivation or by chemical means, these more primitive thought-forms come into prominence. They can appear at the beginning of sleep or on waking, as hypnagogic images; in sleep itself; in waking reveries; after fasting or strenuous exertion; as a result of shock, mental stress, or psychic illness; and from the administration of drugs. In every case, the nature of such fantasies appears to be the same, and the same type of problem arises when we endeavor to describe or comprehend them in the language of consciousness.

We may, perhaps, give them a generic name, such as "experiential images," because they carry an emotional charge, and because they affect all the sensory systems. It is true that they are predominantly visual, but they may also take the form of sounds and smells, hallucinate the senses of taste and touch, or give the impression of movement and even of changes in body functions. A characteristic of such imagery, moreover, is the phenomenon of *synesthesia*, in which one type of sensory impression is expressed in terms of another. This occurs to some extent in ordinary life. If we have to describe something unusual we sometimes displace adjectives, so that we may speak of *loud* colours, *stinking* ideas, or *blinding* pain, or invent new words, as a child does in its effort to convey its experiences.

What seems merely a passing oddity in healthy persons is a regular feature of all states of diminished consciousness. There is a reliance on the concrete. Or, to put it another way, symbolic language replaces formal language. One person under the influence of mescalin was asked to explain the proverb: "Too many cooks spoil the broth." But this proved impossible. The best he could manage was to report an immediate image of "little men in white overalls . . . there were two . . . two men." The proverb, that is, was reduced to a concrete image, accompanied by the association of "Too *many* . . . two *men*."

This type of pun, part verbal and part visual, was discussed at length by Freud, both in *The Interpretation of Dreams* and in *The Psychopathology of Everyday Life;* he regarded it as a common indicator that what he called "primary process" material was reaching consciousness. Modern experimental evidence seems to support Freud's opinion and to suggest that in the "free association" of psychoanalysis the sequence of ideas is much closer to prelogical than to logical thought processes. In "free association," as we have seen, it is the *similarity* of one image to its predecessor that provides the link, whereas in conscious thinking it is the *meaning* that makes the bridge. When we relax the control of consciousness, we become aware of a series of images based on former sensory and emotional experience, and linked by chance associations; when we think purposefully, we select, rearrange, and—most important of all—block off trains of thought that lead away from our purpose.

Thus, in fantasy states of all kinds, what has been called "knight's move" thinking is apparent. Like the knight in a game of chess, the prelogical thought process jumps about and progresses obliquely. When consciousness is no longer dominant, the mind is prone to follow divergent associations. In dreams or psychotic states, an individual may wander indefinitely in the maze of images, to emerge only on waking or on recovery. But one of the crucial differences between a psychosis and the condition induced by LSD is that the person who takes the drug is able to operate on two levels of thought, to be aware of simultaneous yet different types of mental activity. It is true that conscious thought patterns are disrupted and impaired, but for much of a session the person retains them to some degree and can, indeed, use them to evaluate what he is experiencing. The simplest way to understand this feeling is to imagine how one would feel if a daydream was as powerful as ordinary thought and consciousness was reduced to the strength of a daydream.

These two types of thought process have been usefully categorized by Dr. McKellar as R-thinking (reality-adjusted)—thought basically related to the outer world—and A-thinking (autistic)—thought turned inward. The first relies primarily on logic and abstract concepts, the second on association and imagery. R-thinking, so far as we can tell, is confined to waking thought, and is heavily dependent upon a sufficient and continuing sensory input, but A-thinking may occur at any time. Most people experience it only in sleep or in introspective moments, but the possibility of it is always there—and, of course, in the hallucinated person it has invaded and perhaps overwhelmed normal consciousness. The point was well put by Wilhelm Stekel, who suggested that "we never have single thoughts, but always many, an entire polyphony . . . I picture thinking as . . . orchestral music of which only the melody is audible." The melody is R-thinking; the complex harmonies are A-thinking. What appears to happen to the dreamer, or the person hallucinated by drugs or mental illness, is that the melody is lost and only the harmonies are heard.

In attempting to describe this concept, it has been necessary to use images drawn from one sense to convey impressions derived from another; the musical analogy employed here is an example of the way in which, even consciously, we employ such analogies. We know that A stands in a given relation to B; we therefore try to explain the relationship of C to D by saying it is like that of A to B. But we know that we are reasoning by an *as if* process. In dreams and hallucinated states, however, the awareness of *as if* is missing. The relationship between A and B on the one hand, and C and D on the other, may be demonstrated by placing them in juxtaposition, or even by fusing them. When we are hallucinated we cannot distinguish between analogy and literal fact; we may conclude from the *likeness* of AB to CD that they are the *same thing*. But they are not, they merely stand in the same relation. Thus, in a dream or a psychotic fantasy, a feeling that a policeman, say, is *like* one's father may appear as an image in which a policeman *is* one's father, or one's father *is* a policeman.

This view, which has been elaborately developed in psychoanalytic practice, may be subjectively experienced under hallucinogenic drugs. Complex transpositions and displacements occur, and many symbols emerge that carry an identifiable meaning or an emotional charge. Their resemblance to psychoanalytic theory on symbolism is so striking that Dr. Betty Grover Eisner, an American specialist in hallucinogenics, has remarked:

"In the course of five years' work with the psycholytic or mind-changing drugs—LSD, mescalin, psilocybin, ritalin, and the amphetamines—one can only be awestruck by the genius of Freud, Adler, and Jung, and be saddened by the forces which split apart this trinity. Their observations and theories should be integrated; for the split skewed so many fundamental conceptions and discoveries."

The essential concept in all forms of psychotherapy is that the patient should learn to bring repressed memories and feelings to the surface and

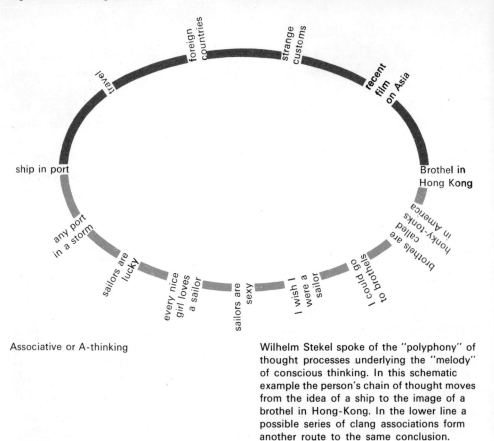

foreign countries
strange customs
recent film on Asia
travel
ship in port
Brothel in Hong Kong
any port in a storm
brothels are honky-tonks in America
sailors are lucky
I could go to brothels
every nice girl loves a sailor
I wish I were a sailor
sailors are sexy

Associative or A-thinking

Wilhelm Stekel spoke of the "polyphony" of thought processes underlying the "melody" of conscious thinking. In this schematic example the person's chain of thought moves from the idea of a ship to the image of a brothel in Hong-Kong. In the lower line a possible series of clang associations form another route to the same conclusion.

integrate them in consciousness. This is why much emphasis has hitherto been placed on dreams, because they embody the results of unconscious or autistic mental processes. But the products of A-thinking, as we saw in our examination of psychotherapy, are available in other forms. The therapist can ask the patient to tell him a story or to describe the pictures he sees on a Rorschach ink-blot card, he may then simply listen to the disturbed person talking about his relationships with other people or observe how he behaves in relationships with other people or observe how he behaves in relation to the therapist himself. In all these and other ways the experienced observer can see how A-thinking is erupting into consciousness and distorting the individual's perception of himself and of the environment in which he lives. The person who is psychotic, in fact, may be so much the prisoner of his A-thinking that he has lost his identity, does not know who he is, what he is doing, or what is happening to him. His psychic reality has swamped his natural reality.

But there are limitations on the value of dream material, as on that derived from other evidence offered from waking life. It is difficult for the therapist to help the patient understand the messages concealed in his dreams, and insight may be just as hard to achieve when the autistic symbolism is expressed in behavior to others rather than in visual imagery. There is little therapeutic value, as we have seen, in simply telling a person the meaning of a dream or of some aspect of his behavior. Psychotherapy, moreover, has been unable to make full use of the fantasies produced in sleep. As we saw in the previous chapter, there is usually no more than a fragmentary recall of a dream, and what is recalled may be distorted in recollection or report. The dream is rarely accompanied by intense emotional experience; that has to be evoked in the therapeutic session. Finally, the therapist has to find ways of detecting and overcoming the resistances of his patient—and this is, perhaps, the hardest of all his tasks. What is true of dreams applies to all the forms of A-thinking normally available in therapy or in psychological research.

But, when hallucinogenic drugs are used, many of these difficulties become less troublesome. Although the subject's consciousness is diminished, part of it is available, and much of an LSD session can be remembered as well as experienced. This means that the material that emerges is of enduring as well as of immediate effect. This is in marked contrast to the scrappy and distorted dream material, which is so evanescent that it requires great efforts to preserve it at all, let alone comprehensively and accurately. Under the influence of LSD a person can often interpret imagery that would seem meaningless in a state of normal consciousness. The fact that it is hard to communicate what has been experienced does not mean that it has not been comprehended—and possibly more fully comprehended than the flash of insight that rewards a long exploration of a dream. There is immediate, rather than retrospective evaluation. At the same time, the person under the influence of a hallucinogen is experiencing strong emotional reactions.

This difference is of crucial importance. For the therapeutic objective is to induce the patient to admit powerful feelings or uncomfortable repressed memories. But repression cannot be maintained under the influence of LSD: the subject's defenses against fear, anxiety, sexual feelings, or aggressive impulses—or even against love and tenderness—are broken down, the feelings are released, and their psychic terrors are exorcized.

The LSD experience seems, therefore, not merely an extension of dream interpretation but superior to it in intensity and in the wealth of material that it makes available. One of the outstanding British specialists in this work, Dr. R. A. Sandison, has said that it "is a kind of development of the dream life of the individual." Dr. Sandison thinks it possible, from observing hundreds of LSD sessions, that they offer a much more comprehensive view of unconscious mental life than the dream as it is consciously recollected. By the time we have woken up and tried to capture the fleeting images of a dream, we are left with no more than a fragment of it. Under LSD and other hallucinogens, several hours are available for the contemplation and experiencing of fantasy. It may be that the dream (if we could recall it in its entirety) would prove to be very similar, and that the distortion and loss that occur are subsequently imposed on the dream material by waking consciousness—that is, by the ego.

We can now see why LSD and similar drugs have begun to play such an important part in psychotherapy. Unlike sedatives and tranquilizers, which can temporarily allay severe anxiety or even bring severely hallucinated persons into closer touch with reality, the hallucinogenic drugs evoke a great deal of psychological stress and induce fantasies. But they do so under conditions that enable an individual to confront, rather than repress, what is disturbing him. As all schools of psychotherapy believe, the more an individual is able to achieve insight into the conflicts and feelings that trouble him, the better he is able to acknowledge them and to integrate them into normal conscious life. Psychoanalysis, which uses dream interpretation, is one way of doing this. But the hallucinogens may be a quicker and possibly more effective way of achieving the same result. In both cases, the objective is to break down the defenses an individual has created to protect consciousness from uncomfortable or disruptive feelings—and thus enable him to see himself and his relation to other people in a different perspective. We can put it simply by saying that the hallucinogens permit him to discover a fuller and richer sense of his own identity. They involve a change in his ego, in his consciousness of himself, as we can see in the cases presented as an Appendix to this book.

The development of the ego begins very early in life, and it is closely connected with the early emotional reactions of the infant to his surroundings.

The amount of love and care he receives, the way he is fed and handled, are decisive foundations for later life. From infancy onward, he learns to associate physical and emotional experiences—hunger with anxiety, food with pleasure—and the patterns laid down at this time will persist as he grows. He cannot separate his physical experiences from his feelings. By the age of seven, the child is self-aware; he has distinguished himself from the world he feels the sense of "I" as against "them," he knows his own body and his own emotions in contrast to those of his parents and his playmates. He has, to put it in psychological terms, identified his ego function with his own body and with the time and place in which he lives. He can say: "I am John. This is Tuesday. I am playing with my toys." At this age, for instance, it is quite common to find children writing in their schoolbooks a long identification of this kind:

John Smith
Form 5
New School
Maple Road
London
England
Europe
The World
The Universe

LSD 25 may be taken either orally or by injection. Far left, a nurse prepares a syringe for the doctor to use. Left, a patient takes his dose in liquid form.

Constant medical supervision is essential when LSD 25 is used in therapy, for patients need support and reassurance against the powerful fantasies evoked. Right, a nurse sits with a patient.

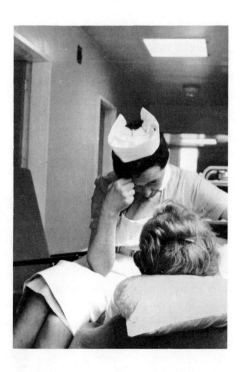

Above left, a patient under the influence of LSD 25 working out a visual fantasy by drawing on the wall in an English clinic. Above right, another patient's painting (referred to in the Appendix of this book) produced after an LSD 25 session.

Yet this growing awareness of reality does not exclude a sense of fantasy. The very small child runs round the room saying: "I am a lion." He does not clearly distinguish between the fact that he is a child and the feeling that he is a lion. The older child can make such a distinction, unless it is emotionally disturbed, but it will still play fantasy games—"let's pretend." The adult has not wholly lost this quality, but by the time adolescence is over his personality has struck a balance between reality and fantasy, between his outer and his inner environment.

A neurotic person, however, may develop a distorted ego, because he is using it to keep distressing unconscious material at bay. He will over-emphasize external situations and apparently rational relationships, and find security by identifying himself with, for instance, a political cause or the firm for which he works. He becomes an "alienated" person, who derives his sense of identity from sources outside himself. He has a strong defensive system—and very often he will say that he rarely or never dreams. Such a person is usually a rigid character, afraid of his feelings, who aggressively asserts his "rational control" of himself.

The psychotic, by contrast, has a weak or undeveloped ego and lacks defenses against unconscious material; he is unable to interpret his experience and he has a diminished sense of identity. Most people feel that such a weakness may be due to an unsatisfactory infancy, and especially to the loss or insufficiency of maternal love and care before the age of two.

The crucial effect of LSD and other hallucinogens seems to be an alteration in ego function. One of the commonest reactions to LSD is an onset of severe anxiety—and anxiety usually arises when there is a threat to the ego. But it is very important to note the way in which the person who has taken LSD responds to this threat. If he can marshal his defenses, he can cling on to "reality" and thus protect himself against the unconscious material that is welling up. Clinical reports show that he can do this in many ways. He may call for the therapist, walk around, dance, make notes, or draw pictures—he struggles to stay with familiar feelings and he tries to discharge the unfamiliar emotions by activity. He may, however, "go along" with the LSD; he surrenders to the new feelings and becomes fascinated by them, learning to explore sensations and insights he has never experienced before.

The doctors and therapists who supervise LSD sessions note the conflict between the two reactions—defense or surrender—and this conflict may be the source of the severe anxiety. It is sometimes resolved by a collapse of the ego defenses, and the subject then feels a terrible sense of disintegration. This is usually expressed as a distortion of the body image (the physical awareness of self), so that the patient feels that his flesh is falling away from his bones, that time and space have disintegrated, that he is nothing but a sound or a color or an emotion. This is called "depersonalization," and it may seem to the patient that he has gone completely mad or even died.

Somewhere within the total personality, however, there appears to be a continuing integrative force; though an individual may be overwhelmed by the LSD experience, some part of his mind still seems to observe, evaluate, comment, and even attempt to integrate this otherwise hidden material with the knowledge of conscious life. This may disappear for brief periods, when the fear of insanity or death supervenes, but for most of the time it is clearly at work. No one knows what type of "thinking" this may be. It appears to be different both from "reality thinking" and "autistic thinking," from the patterns of conscious thought and the imagery of fantasy—a kind of bridge between two types of mental process. Lawrence Lessing, in a *Fortune* article on recent sleep research, has written: "At the same time recent evidence shows that there may well be a second, lower level of dreaming extending down even into deep sleep, consisting largely of abstract thoughts or isolated symbols, much harder to recall than the generally vivid, active imagery of rapid-eye-movement dreaming."

The presence of this "third thinking" raises an interesting and important question that is relevant to dreaming. Suppose we say that conscious thought

When an individual who is faced by a difficult situation resorts to obsessional counting he is displaying a preoccupation with "magic" numbers as a defense mechanism against repressed feelings. The same device serves the Arab or Asiatic who is inseparable from his string of beads—nowadays these usually number 33.

is of one type, and fantasy thought (which appears during the REM period) is different, and that each type requires translation into the other. Could this "third thinking" be going on continuously, in waking and in sleep, so that it is at work even when we are not "dreaming" in the usual sense? There is a further question. Since this evaluative process does seem to scan problems, and to offer various types of solution for them—as we know from observing it at work in the LSD experience—can we suggest that it might be the source of the "problem-solving" capacity of the unconscious? Such an idea would certainly fit in with the idea that current difficulties are somehow unconsciously compared with similar situations earlier in life, and that new solutions emerge that are clearly related to previous successes and failures of the same kind. It would also provide a "model" explanation of the way in which dreams sometimes seem to be composed of successive attempts to find an answer to a difficult question posed by life—the "linked" dreams of one night, or the serial dreams of a period, or even the repetitive dream that indicates that the dreamer has reached an impasse and is unable to see a way out of a problem.

We know, moreover, that under the influence of LSD an individual tends to revert to earlier phases of life. He regresses to the ego-conceptions that belong to adolescence, childhood, and infancy. The analogy that is often used is one of peeling an onion; successive layers of the personality are stripped off and, as the adult ego-defenses give way, a flow of forgotten feelings and associations enters consciousness. It has also been noted that LSD sessions generally bring up repressed and emotionally charged material from definite and crucial phases of life—the points of transition from one phase of growth to another, when the individual has undergone particular stresses in his human relationships. The child who is turning into a teenager, for instance, has to pass through a period of physical and psychological adjustment in which his sense of himself and his attitude to other people has been radically revised in a relatively short period. Problems that were repressed, or inadequately resolved, at such a time tend to reappear in the LSD experience— just as they may, unconsciously, be "acted out" in everyday life.

In this respect, too, the LSD experience throws some light on the structure and significance of dreams. As we observed in previous chapters dealing with psychotherapy, the analysis of dreams usually reveals that they are a fusion of present and past experience. When an individual cannot cope with the strains and stresses of everyday life, he is frustrated. He then tends to regress to memories of previous situations where he was able to cope—perhaps with the aid of a parent, or by some "magical device" such as obsessional counting or lucky charms, or by being aggressive, or by humbling himself in some way. Such techniques had proved their value in the past, and he unconsciously hopes that they will again prove efficacious. But these earlier situations no longer exist, nor is the present reality truly comparable to childhood experiences. The discrepancy must therefore be overcome by retreating from reality into fantasy—by pretending, in some way, that present and past can be fused into a less frightening or frustrating set of circumstances.

Something like this seems to be happening in the dream. But under LSD the two elements in the process are more easily distinguished. It is possible for an individual to see the present reality and the earlier prototype situation, to recognize how they are related and how they differ, to understand how his adult behavior is being patterned on childhood experience. As a result, he develops a sharper sense of his own identity, an increased capacity to tolerate the pressures of everyday life, and the ability to accept the idiosyncracies of other people.

By the use of hallucinogens, therefore, scientific research has been given a new stimulus in the search for the physical causes of fantasy and in the study of the biochemical mechanism of what is usually called "dreaming." At the same time, psychiatry has found remarkable confirmation of many ideas about the content and significance of "dreams." These new drugs have not yet led to the discovery of what Julius Nelson called a "psycho-biological law" governing mental processes of all kinds, but the way they work and the kind of work they do raises the hope that we may at last be on the track of a general theory of dreaming and dreams.

11 Dreams and dreaming

There is an old fable about two knights who fought a duel because they disagreed over the color of a shield. One maintained that it was silver, the other insisted that it was gold. Each claimed that he alone was right; they quarreled and eventually fought. The combat was brought to an end by a bystander, who pointed out that they were both right: the shield was silver on one side, and gold on the other.

Much of the long debate about the nature and meaning of dreams has been a disagreement of the same kind. We have seen how one school of thought—whose views can be traced back as far as the dawn of scientific thinking in classical Greece—always sought a physical explanation of dreams, attributing them to causes as simple as bad digestion or as complex as subtle changes in the chemistry of the brain cells. But we have also observed another tradition, emerging from primitive magic and religion into philosophy and modern psychology, which regarded dreams as the result of hidden but vital mental processes, revealing much about the personality of the dreamer. The antagonism between those two basic types of dream theory has persisted for centuries, and has sometimes been acrimonious. Yet it is as foolish as the dispute between the two knights in the fable. The more we know about dreams, the more we must look for an explanation of them that takes account of both the physiological and the psychological evidence.

Toward the end of his life Freud complained that "the analysts behave as though they had nothing more to say about the dream, as though the whole subject of dream theory were finished and done with." His complaint had some justification, for much analytical work with dreams had been little more than the detailed elaboration of ideas originally formulated by Freud himself, Jung, Stekel, and other pioneers. One of the limiting factors was the analytical obsession with dream theory as an end in itself; because Freud had insisted on the crucial significance of dreams, there was a sectarian suspicion on the part of many psychoanalysts about other paths of inquiry into unconscious mental processes. Yet dream theory could not develop in isolation and mainly on the basis of accumulating case reports, selected to make clinical or doctrinal points, any more than psychoanalysts could "prove" that their methods were "scientific" by essentially subjective evaluations of their effectiveness.

New lines of advance had to be found. One of these was the extension of clinical and experimental psychology, using laboratory techniques to test a range of theories about perception, responses, learning, and memory, about fantasy, role playing, and social behavior. (We have drawn on these without examining them in detail, for they are seldom directly concerned with the problem of dreams.) Another was the breakthrough in sleep research that took place after 1953. Both of these changes, particularly the latter, provided new and verifiable evidence against which the propositions of Freud and others could be tested and from which new conceptions might be derived. "The development of the Kleitman-Dement technique," Dr. Harry Trosman of Chicago wrote in 1963, "thus serves as a challenge for the psychoanalyst to reexamine, develop, or modify basic dream theory and to discover where discrepancies lie between empirical findings and hypothetical constructs."

Dreaming may well be one important road to the unconscious (though there are other and increasingly useful paths to the hidden parts of the mind); but there is now little doubt that it is also the outcome of distinct physical processes in the human organism. It occurs at precisely the point where the functions of mind and body fuse into the mystery of personality—and where, therefore, all the disciplines that deal with the study of man have a valuable contribution to make. Merely to write this book, for instance, it has been necessary to use material drawn from anthropology, archaeology, history, mythology, religion, philosophy, sociology, and psychology, as well as from medicine, physiology, and biochemistry.

In the search for a unified theory of dreams, however, we should on no account disparage the role played by Freud and the other pioneers of psychoanalysis in directing serious attention to the content of dreams. It was their work, after all, that taught us to regard the dream as a meaningful expression of emotions and memories of which we are consciously unaware—and thus transformed the study of dreams from a kind of occult parlor game into a reputable and profoundly rewarding occupation. Freud himself foresaw that this would happen. In the first chapter of *The Interpretation of Dreams* he wrote: "A modification of our attitude to dreams will at the same time affect our views upon the internal mechanism of mental disorders ... we shall be working towards an explanation of the psychoses while we are endeavouring to throw some light on the mystery of dreams."

When Freud's book first appeared, it was greeted in some quarters with ridicule. Times have changed. Psychotherapy is now a recognized and valuable means of treating mental illness; and the search for the causes and cure of psychosis is being urgently pursued as a joint endeavor by psychiatrists, neurologists, and biochemists. There are institutes of dream research and well-equipped laboratories devoted to the study of sleep, and applied psychology has given us many new insights into the orders and disorders of the mind. The old dividing line between "mental" and "physical" theories—of dreams as well as of psychosis—is fast disappearing, if in fact it has not already been wholly erased. Whether or not one accepts Freud's specific ideas about the nature of dreams, it is impossible to deny the greatest of his achievements. By studying dreams he changed man's view of himself.

We began this book with a simple question: What are dreams? We cannot yet provide a comprehensive answer. But the answers we can give to matters men have speculated about for centuries have set the dream debate in an entirely different context.

We can now say that dreaming occurs as part of a distinct and biologically determined rhythm, which appears to be as natural and necessary as breathing. This rhythm, moreover, is related to a cycle of sleep and wakefulness that can be observed even in very small infants, and it probably goes on in some form in waking hours. The imagery of the dream, that is to say, is a psychological characteristic of a definite and identifiable physical state that differs from both wakefulness and non-dreaming sleep. This state, as we have seen, can be demonstrated in various ways; there are the tracings on the EEG machine, which registers the minute electrical impulses within the brain, the onset of rapid eye movements, changes in respiration, pulse rate, and the electrical conductivity of the skin, the disappearance of certain muscle tensions, and a diminution of body movements. Most recently, Dr. Charles Fisher has added a new feature—a cycle of penile erections in the male dreamer that coincides with the dream state—and it seems likely that further research will reveal other physical and chemical changes taking place within the body whenever dreaming occurs.

It follows from this evidence that dreams are a regular, not a random, phenomenon. The normal person, in good health and enjoying adequate sleep, dreams to a timetable scarcely affected by heat, or cold, or noise, or what he eats or drinks. He dreams when he is due to dream, and his first dream starts approximately 90 minutes after he has gone to sleep. Other dreams come at similar though shorter intervals throughout the night. As the intervals decrease, however, the length of the dream period increases. The first dream has an average duration of about 10 minutes, the second may last as long as 20 minutes, while the third and fourth may go on for half an hour or more.

This dream timetable, of course, is an average. Each of us has a slightly different dream pattern; in all of us—as Dr. Dement has shown experimentally—it can be drastically modified if we are unable to get our usual quota of dreaming. One important line of research is to look for significant differences between individuals. Do men dream differently from women? Are dreams more or less frequent in the aged, who tend to have rather different sleep habits? How far is the timetable changed by mental or physical illness, or by drugs, or fatigue, or climatic factors? Do dreams in color occur to everyone, or only to some individuals? We cannot yet answer such questions, but at least we now have a scientific technique that will enable us, in time, to find the answers.

But how can such evidence be reconciled with psychological theories of the dream? How can we sustain Freud's view that dreams are due to the upwelling of instinctive desires when Dr. Dement demonstrated that they occur at regular intervals? If dreams are psychic phenomena, why should they appear like the figures on an animated clock, which emerge to strike the hours and perform other complicated maneuvers?

We still seem to be faced by a choice between the psychic and physical theories of the dream. But must we make such a choice? Can we retain much of what Freud and others have taught us about the meaning of dreams, while accepting the new theories of their cause?

One valuable idea was advanced by the Czech psychiatrist Dr. Samuel Lowy in a book published in London in 1942. In his *Psychological and Biological Foundations of Dream Interpretation*, this pupil of Stekel's suggested that the dreaming process might be a rhythmic factor, "desirable and beneficial for life"—and it might be due to excessive secretion of hormones. Lowy argued that physical stimuli (such as poor digestion or the need to urinate), and psychic excitement (hate or anxiety, for instance), were both sources of dreams. There was, therefore, a "need for a unified conception of the total dreaming process, which would consider the two kinds of dream-stimuli as having a common denominator." He then went further, suggesting "that the dreaming process, which in the absence of waking consciousness results in the dream images proper, continues operating in the waking state." Thus he saw daydreams, psychotic states, and the delusions of the intoxicated as end results of the same organic mechanism. In all these ways, Lowy's difficult and somewhat neglected book anticipates the direction in which dream research has recently moved.

In 1958 Dr. A. Ullman, an American psychiatrist, made a further contribution. He noted that dreams appeared in so-called "light" sleep, and asked whether dreaming might be related to the biological mechanism that permits man to sleep yet maintains a state of vigilance so that he can quickly arouse himself if danger threatens. This readiness to fight or flee on awakening is instinctual in man—and in other animals. It depends on the supply of adrenaline and other nerve hormones, which translate the emergency signals from the brain into rapid physical responses. This is the reason why sudden waking sometimes makes one "feel queer"; the system is given a rapid stimulus by the adrenaline released and one may feel dizzy and even a little disorientated.

In the previous chapter it was suggested that adrenaline, and other chemicals of this type, may play a very important role in causing hallucinations and even mental illness of various kinds; if there is an excess of these chemicals, some researchers believe, the body cannot easily eliminate or convert them, and fantasies arise. If for any reason the body systematically produced such an excess in sleep and needed a period of time to accomplish the complex chemical processes required to dispose of these chemicals, we might find an explanation of the regular onset of dream states.

Why should this be the case? To answer this question we must move from what we know to what, at present, we can only guess. But the theory we now put forward does take account of a great deal of the recent evidence about sleep, dreams, and the chemistry of the brain.

It is conceivable that, in the long evolution of the human race, man's sleeping habits have changed. We know that, in small children, the basic rhythm of sleep is a 60-minute cycle; every hour or so the baby is on the point of waking, and it tends to take its sleep in multiples of one hour. As we grow older, as Professor Kleitman has shown, we develop the habit of the long sleep. Within this we find the 90-minute cycle, ranging from deep sleep to the "light" sleep that precedes arousal. It seems as if, biologically, man is a creature who is prepared to wake fairly often (as do dogs and cats, for instance), and that he has acquired the technique of long sleeps comparatively recently in the evolutionary process. Even though he now sleeps for several hours, the mechanism that kept him in a state of readiness for frequent arousals may persist as an underlying rhythm—the 90-minute cycle. We can go on to suggest that, in preparation for the contingency of sudden waking, he builds up stocks of adrenaline and other necessary chemicals. When these are not required, because sleep continues, they take some time to be eliminated—and during this period man enters what is called the dream state. When the conversion of the relevant chemicals is completed—and the assumption is that some of the by-products of this process are hallucinogenic—the dreamer returns to deep sleep. If some such process is going on in sleep, there would be a regular rhythm of dreaming. Such an explanation, moreover, would account for the fact that, as the night wears on, the interval between the dream states becomes shorter and the dream periods themselves become longer. After some hours, sleep is less necessary and waking is more likely. Thus, as a man moves toward the end of his "normal" night's sleep, his body might prepare larger stocks of the chemicals it needs for arousal. If waking did not actually occur, it would then take more time (a longer dream period) for these stocks to be eliminated.

The EEG tracings we examined in Chapter 9 give some support for this hypothesis. These showed that the sleeper reaches the dream state as he emerges from deep, non-dreaming sleep; he appears to be on the verge of waking, but instead of waking he dreams. When the dream ends, he returns to deep sleep. The dream, that is to say, becomes a substitute for waking.

Freud guessed that this was the case, even though he did not have the benefit of modern scientific equipment to reveal the electrical rhythms of the brain. He concluded from this fact that dreams were the "guardians of sleep." He assumed man had a need to sleep, that sleep was likely to be disturbed by instinctual wishes welling up in the sleeper's mind, and that the dream discharged these wishes in a fantasy form so that sleep could continue. It has been claimed that Freud's view is now untenable; after Kleitman and Dement established that there was a regular rhythm of dreams, it was asked why instinctual wishes should well up with such regularity.

It may indeed be necessary to modify Freud's theory, but need we reject its fundamental idea? If the chemicals released in the sleep cycle stimulate the "old" or instinctual areas of the brain—and, as we saw in the last chapter, there is reason to suspect that this is what happens—then the feelings and memories thus aroused will appear as dream images. (This process, or something closely analogous to it, seems to occur in psychosis or under the influence of hallucinogenic drugs.) But these dreams would not arise, as Freud put it, to prevent the dreamer being awakened by uncomfortable feelings. They might express certain instinctual and emotional tensions, but they would arise because the dreamer has no immediate need to wake—and the biochemical preparations he has made for arousal are therefore diverted into a fantasy substitute for waking life. We can extend this statement. If the dream mechanism is in some way a physical preparation for a return to conscious activity, then the dream content may also be regarded as a psychological preparation for the problems of everyday existence.

On this argument, the dream has a physical cause but psychological consequences—or, to put this another way, the rhythm of dreaming is the result of a primordial physical process, which occurs even in newborn infants, while the content of dreaming is a secondary and psychically significant process. There is a similar relationship between breathing, which is a basic function of the human organism, and speech; breathing makes speech possible, and man has gradually developed his ability to speak into refined systems of communication. Long ago, perhaps, man's ancestors developed the physical rhythm of dreaming; more recently, in evolutionary terms, man came to use the ensuing dreams to release his deepest and consciously unrecognized feeling, or even to anticipate his everyday problems and to seek possible solutions for them.

This would mean that, in certain conditions, a biochemical change in the body permits our unconscious conflicts, hopes, and fears to break through the barrier that normally separates them from consciousness. Such a change, moreover, occurs regularly in sleep but may take place at any time if the human organism is subjected to unusual physical or mental stress—fatigue, sensory deprivation, withdrawal into introspection and meditation, a worrying situation, unsatisfactory relationships with other people, or the use of drugs. When this happens, the consciousness of the real world is diminished and we regress into the world of fantasy. In extreme cases, such as psychosis, the power of the fantasy becomes overwhelming and the individual loses contact with reality.

The key idea in this theory was the suggestion Dr. Ullman made in 1958, that dreaming might be related to the arousal mechanism. As has happened so often in the tortuous evolution of our ideas about dreams, a new idea is little more than a new formulation of an older and neglected one. In this case, the original source was the valuable book *Conflict and Dream*, published in 1922 by Dr. W. H. Rivers, to whom we referred in an earlier chapter.

The book, which sharply criticized Freud's emphasis on infantile sexuality and argued that dreams are attempts to solve the conflicts of everyday life, has received too little attention. For this noted anthropologist had asked, in an appendix written shortly before he died, whether dreams had a biological role. Animals, Rivers had pointed out, need some agent to awaken them and prepare them to adapt to a new situation. This agency, in his view, had been much modified in man—above all by the development of an ability to discriminate between a sensory stimulus that made waking imperative and one that could safely be disregarded. Presumably, this ability was a function of the cerebral cortex, which receives sensory impressions, evaluates them, and transmits the appropriate response to the motor areas of the brain.

The suggestion of Dr. Rivers has found support recently in the work of Dr. Ian Oswald, who has demonstrated that one of the types of cortical activity that does continue in sleep is this ability to discriminate between the stimulus that can be ignored and that which demands arousal. A mother sleeps as trains pass her window, but wakes at the first cry from her baby; sleepers will ignore many names played on a tape-recorder but respond immediately to their own names.

We have been outlining a possible theory of dreaming that could overcome the old contradiction between the physical and psychological concepts of the dream. While it goes far beyond anything that can yet be proved, it does fit much of the evidence now available. Once we recognize that the physical state of dreaming opens the door through which the fantasies of the unconscious can emerge, it will be much easier to reconcile the new scientific discoveries with the older insights of the psychologists.

We have now reached the frontier of dream research, and while we may make guesses about what lies beyond, we cannot tell what routes we shall find through the dark territory of the mind. There are too many questions that we cannot yet answer. Why, for instance, should the cerebral cortex behave in a dream as if it is receiving real sensory impressions? What stops the brain from reacting to these sensory impressions as it would to the same situations in real life? What part of the mind *knows* that the images are merely fantasy? What has gone wrong when the capacity to tell fantasy from reality fails us, or when we become somnambulists? More important, perhaps, we must ask what is happening when we are not dreaming. Is there some kind of "third thinking" that is neither conscious nor fantastic, or is there a "true" sleep in which the brain does no more than sustain the autonomic processes necessary to keep us alive? We do not know. We do not even know how to set about answering some of these questions, or many others that we could ask —or whether, in fact, they are the right questions.

The same is true of other aspects of the dream to which we have paid very little attention, though they have intrigued men for centuries. Can dreams foretell the future, or reveal events at a distance? Are dreams evidence of a different dimension of Time, as J. W. Dunne and J. B. Priestley—among others—have suggested? Can we know things about other people in our dreams that we do not consciously know about them?

The difficulty about such questions is that we can only speculate about them, as the ancients did, for we are not in a very much better position to answer them than Aristotle or Artemidorus. But in view of modern experiments in extrasensory perception or telepathy, we should do well to keep an open mind. In view of scientific thinking about the nature of Time, we should be equally cautious about dogmatically insisting that there are no other dimensions to existence than those we know in waking consciousness. And, in the light of what we have learned about subliminal perception, we must concede that we "unconsciously" acquire a mass of information of which we are consciously unaware—including subtle assessments of the character and problems of other people—some of which later emerges in our dreams.

We need to explore all such problems, because we do not know when one of them will suddenly yield a vital piece of evidence. But the evidence at present available is so fragmentary and inconclusive, and so influenced by occult attitudes, that it would have been misleading to summarize it in this book. For the same reason, we have excluded some scientific research that is in such an early stage that its implications for dreaming are far from clear. There is, for instance, some evidence that the incidence of mental illness may increase during magnetic storms or other climatic changes, and that memory—and possibly genetic patterns—may be affected by intense magnetic fields. Before we can develop a real science of dreaming, we shall have to take account of many old guesses and new discoveries.

Nothing that has been discovered during the last few years, however, invalidates the hypothesis that dreams are meaningful and capable of interpretation—even if there is room for a good deal of controversy about what they mean and how they are best interpreted. This hypothesis, as we have seen, has persisted since antiquity, and survived every change in man's beliefs about the origins and nature of dreams.

In this century, thanks to Freud and other great psychologists, we have come to take dreams seriously, and learned to regard them as one of many fantasy states that provide clues to the hidden orders and disorders of the mind. That is a great gain. For man today needs every means to self-discovery and self-mastery, if he is to control the forces he has unleashed on the world. He needs to recognize the terrors and also the beauties that lie within him, and to confront them boldly. If he shrinks from self-examination, he cannot grow to maturity and full human responsibility; he remains a child in nature, emotionally crippled, and liable to vent on others the fears and fancies he cannot admit within himself. But, to the degree that he explores what lies within him, he learns to recognize his true feelings, to relate passionately to other people, and to face the problems of his life with dignity and courage. Because the study of the dream has opened the door on man's inner world it has been one of the golden keys to human freedom.

Appendix

Two clinical reports

How does LSD 25 help an individual become more aware of hidden feelings and forgotten experiences? In Chapter 10, this process was described in general terms. Here, in two transcripts taken from recordings of therapist-patient interviews in an English clinic, we can read how two women were gradually able to acknowledge powerful emotions that underlay their neurotic symptoms.

The first of them, Mrs. K., is a woman of 37 who had received LSD treatment at intervals over three years. The LSD experiences had enabled her to come to terms with repressed homosexual and incestuous feelings, with her confusion of aggressive and affectionate emotions, and with strong destructive impulses.

The second patient, Mrs. H., aged 39, had also had a series of LSD sessions in the past and had recently come back to the clinic for half a dozen "refresher" sessions. She had suffered from severe depressions, and (as her own words reveal) she also had strong feelings of hostility and jealousy—especially toward her brothers. Her previous inability to admit these feelings of anger, or a deep desire to punish men, may have been responsible for the depressions and the suicidal impulses she had experienced.

The accounts given by these two women are characteristic of those obtained from patients receiving LSD therapy, but they have been selected because both of them make interesting comparisons between the subjects' LSD experiences and their dreams. Mrs. K. had intense visual dream experiences but her LSD experiences were emotional rather than visual; Mrs. H. had a paucity of dream material but her LSD experiences had a more visual quality.

The notes are by the therapist concerned, and refer especially to the italicized passages.

The photographs in these appendices were taken in a British clinic especially designed for LSD 25 therapy. Above, one of the rooms. Facilities—like record players, toys, paints—are provided to help the patients to relax and express themselves.

Therapist	Mrs. K.
1 Could you start with yesterday, and go back to earlier treatments as your memory picks them up?	Yesterday I started off with this very intense feeling of affection for everyone. I suppose it was in a way a sexual feeling and it was quite a pleasurable feeling. I wallowed in it to some extent for a time. It was something I had never felt before. Then I got rather

Therapist	Mrs. K.

nervous about the feeling as I suddenly realised how intense it was and that it was enveloping me completely, and I got rather frightened and then that went into a feeling of frustration because I felt I had no outlet for this feeling. That added to my frustration because I felt I couldn't do it. I hadn't the means to do it, there was no positive outlet for it, I think that created a frustration and I became very tense after that. *Then I am rather hazy as to what exactly happened but I got into this rather distressed state over the fact that there may have been something toward my own sex in these feelings. That was the point at which I completely went to pieces and I felt that I couldn't live with the feeling and I just wanted to die and give up everything—I felt I couldn't go on after that.*

The patient is giving expression to the essential problem in her life; her desire for human relationships and her difficulty in accepting her sexual feelings both for her own and the opposite sex.

Even at the beginning of your LSD experiences have you ever had any kind of floating pictures?

"Hallucinations" do not always occur after giving hallucinogenic drugs. Emotional experience seems to be a substitute for visual imagery and suggests the close relationship that we know exists in the brain between centers responsible for "imagination" and emotional feeling.

No, never, that I can recall. It has been purely feelings.

What about the room itself, does that change?

No.

And you never get a kind of imaginative picture built up out of, say, a crack in the wall?

No, I have never had anything like that at all. The only time was when I had the feeling that I had become a monkey, I don't know whether you remember that . . . .

I remember.

Yes, I felt that if I touched my face it would be hairy just like the face of a monkey.

How did that feeling start?

Oh! I don't know. It's rather a long way back anyway, I can't remember what led up to it, it just happened.

I seem to remember that it was at a time when you were feeling that you were out of control and that you might do some harm to somebody and that you felt an animal-like thing coming in yourself.

Yes, that could have been. Yes, because I had a lot of those feelings, that I might lose control and hurt someone.

When you touched your face . . .

Well I didn't touch it, but I felt that if I did it would be hairy.

Therapist	Mrs. K.
Did this feeling frighten you?	
	No, it didn't frighten me; it only lasted for seconds, then it just disappeared.
Could you remember any other kind of experience under LSD? Something that was in some way different from the one you have told me about.	
	I have had a lot of experiences of insecurity recently under LSD. I think that what induced this recently is that you were going to leave the hospital. I felt that I had lost my prop. I seemed to feel that I was getting small. *I felt so tiny and the world and life itself seemed huge in comparison, and I felt a very pathetic individual really. I felt as though I was a mere nothing, I don't know how to put it into words. I felt like an empty shell I suppose, as though I had nothing in me, no resources of any kind.*
Yes, this feeling of being small, as though you had lost your feeling of being a person. Was it anything to do with being a child? *There is a distinction between feeling "small" (i) as part of a regression to childhood memories and feeling "small" (ii) as a result of ego defenses being threatened.*	
	It could have been, possibly, I don't know, I didn't think of it with that point of view, I just felt very tiny and small, in relation to life itself.
When you were here before for treatment you used to get very distressed. You would come up to me and pace up and down the ward saying you were falling to pieces.	
	I can't recall that at all, I don't know why. It must have gone from my mind, that particular occasion.
There were several, I think.	
	No, I don't recall it at all.
Can you remember what you did feel like?	
	Oh! I think I went through a period of hate toward my mother round about that time because I felt that she had had such a tremendous influence on my life and rather swamped my personality. In fact, that's what she has done; and I think I felt very bitter toward her. I got to such an extent that I felt I wanted to tell her exactly what effect she has had on me. I never got to the point of doing this, but I felt so strongly about it and I wanted to express to her what exactly she had done. In fact I think I almost got to the point where I wanted to kill her, my feelings toward her were so strong.
Was this during the LSD session?	
	Yes, yes.
I would like to come to that, because you did go through one or two sessions, round about the time we are talking about, when you had intense feelings of wanting to kill some-	

Therapist	Mrs. K.

Therapist

body. If I remember rightly you didn't know who it was at first, and then it became —

Could you remember how these feelings came to you under LSD?

This is the hallmark of awareness of unconscious material—"It comes out of the blue, it's something that hits you . . . ."

But it was a feeling of great intensity I take it, when it caused you a lot of distress.

How intense was it?

We gave you things to tear up didn't we, to try to relieve these feelings?

Note the remarkable sense of reality—which in itself became a defense mechanism.

You felt we were cheating you a bit?

Then we gave you some clay to knead.

Did that help?

A reference to the discovery that love and hate are closely related emotions. As love is more acceptable to this patient, "hate" becomes repressed and fixated at an early period of life, only to emerge as a violent emotion under treatment.

Did these feelings extend beyond the LSD sessions?

Mrs. K.

My husband!

There again, I don't know. *Some of these feelings just come for no reason, you don't seem to lead up to them—at least I found it seems to come from out of the blue, it is something that hits you or that's how it is with me. I don't know now what led up to that feeling.*

Well, yes.

Well it was so intense I thought, in fact I was afraid, I might well do it. Though I was aware I was under treatment I felt I might kill him at some point—outside of treatment, I mean . . .

Yes, I don't know that it did really, because I felt that it was only a substitute and not the actual object . . . .

Yes!

Yes.

There again I always had the feeling that perhaps we were working on the wrong lines. At that time I was just having the feelings of wanting to hurt someone, not necessarily to kill them but just to hurt them in some way. I had had these feeling for weeks and weeks and weeks, I just couldn't get beyond them. Shortly after, other feelings came up—feelings of affection toward Miss X, and then they fixed on one of the nurses, as you know. Although I still had the feelings of wanting to hurt, it wasn't that at all. It was just an extension of these feelings of wanting to love. Even now, when these feelings of wanting to love get intense, I feel I can only express the intensity of the feelings by hurting people.

To some extent. Not so much now, but I think there was a time when I used to have the feelings that I wanted to hurt apart from the treatment during the week. I used to get very frightened about it, because I wasn't

Therapist	Mrs. K.

aware of the reasons for these feelings and I wondered whether I might lose control and hurt someone.

Can you tell me something about the quality of your dreams—are they like the feelings that you describe under LSD or do they come as pictures?

They are definitely pictures, I mean I see people and faces quite clearly, I have even seen color on occasions. If you remember I mentioned that dream of butterflies—I don't know whether you remember—

Can you tell me this dream as well as you can remember it?

I was in a field and there were masses of these butterflies and other tiny insects and they were studded with what appeared to be brilliantly colored jewels. I was so fascinated and inspired by them. *I suppose in fact I had never seen anything quite so beautiful. I felt I wanted to call people to see them and I think I had a great desire to fetch my father to see them.* In fact, in the dream I did go and fetch him and took him by the hand and led him to see these things. That's all there was.

Analytically speaking, a highly significant dream—the treasure of the unconscious, the capacity to love, the desire to create, are all somehow to be shared and are invested in the patient's father.

This dream seems to have stayed with you.

Yes it was a very powerful dream in a way, emotionally—it raised some feeling of emotion in me. It must have done.

You have had a number of other dreams, which you have told me about, which have mostly been of a sexual nature. Could you say something about the general pattern of these?

Well, I have had various dreams where I have been having sort of—well not actual sexual relations, but at least making love to my own sex . . . not people I know, but figures . . . just female forms. And I think on one occasion there was a small child involved who eventually got smaller and smaller until it became a doll. Then I have had sexual dreams connected with various members of my family. I think it was my brother on one occasion. Then there was the one I told you of yesterday, when my father was making love to me. It was a very unpleasant one . . . and all these dreams have a very disturbing sort of feeling—atmosphere about them, in fact I usually wake. I think the unpleasantness wakes me as a rule. Distasteful.

Have these dreams of this kind only started since you have taken LSD or did you ever have them before?

Therapist	Mrs. K.

Therapist

It seems as if the unconscious is playing "hide-and-seek" between dreams and the LSD experiences—but if the therapist and the patient had ignored the dreams, knowledge of the incest problem would have been lost. We are clearly shown that these particular dreams only occurred after LSD therapy was commenced.

Where a man is making love to you?

What sort of quality do these dreams have?

Unpleasant?

So this is a feeling of pleasure and relief?

But the other dreams about your own sex and family you have had only since having LSD?

Yes, I am sure you are right. You only started to tell me about them after you had been on LSD for some weeks.

You have had these dreams more often since?

Do these particular dreams have the same kind of quality as the butterfly dream? Are they as vivid and is the dream seen as a picture?

Has this always been the case?

Do you remember if you had colored dreams before you had LSD?

Can you easily conjure up pictures in your mind—do you have day dreams?
The therapist was trying to assess the patient's capacity for waking visual imagery—she tends to dismiss this, suggesting that she has a defensive need to avoid clear imagery.

Well, we know that you easily create fantasy situations of unusual difficulty for yourself,

Mrs. K.

Before LSD I often had dreams where I was with men and I still get that now—I do have those sexual dreams . . . .

Yes, yes.

Oh quite a strong feeling, a physical feeling.

No.

Yes.

Yes.

Yes, I do actually remember a very long way back—in fact I think it's going back as far as my late teens or before I was married—when I did have a dream in which I was a man with a penis. I told my husband about it and we laughed, not realizing the significance of it at that time.

Yes, yes.

Yes. I think most of my dreams are very emotional dreams, my feelings are always very strong and they linger afterward. When I wake the feeling is still with me.

To some extent, but I think definitely more so since I have had LSD.

I can't recall anything. I don't normally dream in color, but in the butterfly dream I can recall it distinctly.

Not in that sense I think . . .

Therapist	Mrs. K.
but . . . when you are thinking about some past event does your mind conjure up a picture?	
	Yes, possibly. When I do think back, I do perhaps see events.
If I asked you to see your parents as they used to be, would you conjure up a picture of your mother as she used to look?	
	Yes. I have had some very horrific dreams since I started LSD, of a nightmare quality. I have a lot of those now. They are always extremely unpleasant and very frightening— it's a very weird sensation. I almost feel as though I am sinking, my mind is sinking and I have a feeling that my arms and legs are floating. There is always the feeling that I am being chased by some thing or someone, I can never quite work out quite what it is or who it is but there is a feeling that there is something horrible there. Sometimes they have even had a supernatural feeling about them.
Is there ever a kind of spiritual quality about your dreams?	
	Only in connection with and in an unpleasant way with these nightmare dreams—these usually occur just when I'm going off to sleep, just after I have got into bed.
They wake you, do they?	
	Yes. I shout as a rule . . . The only other significant thing that I can recall is that recurring dream I used to get a lot with water—connected with water—
Is this before you had LSD?	
	Yes, I have had this dream for years. I have always been swimming in the sea against overwhelming waves . . . I feel as though I am pushing as hard as I can with my arms and legs and that it is a tremendous effort to get anywhere. I don't think I ever did get anywhere. *As I have gone through LSD this dream has changed somewhat. I gradually found that I was swimming more easily. Eventually . . . one night it changed completely. I was in the water but I was going along quite merrily on my back—which I take to be quite a good sign. Then, the other night, I had a dream with water in it again, in fact two nights running. I can't recall the* first instance, but in the second one I was in a field and I was very distressed because a river was overflowing and it was gradually coming toward me. I felt I had to get away from it quickly and I sort of nipped smartly out of its way. I don't know whether that was related to these prior dreams of water, I imagine it could be.
We should accept this change in the pattern of the recurring dream as an index of improvement—of a better relationship to the unconscious. It is again of interest that we have to look to the dreams rather than to the LSD experience for information of this kind.	

Therapist	Mrs. K.

Therapist

Very possibly, I think. How old were you when you first started having the dreams of swimming against an overwhelming tide.

About how often would you have this dream?

Did it change at all after you were married?

Which do you think is the greater significance to you—the LSD experiences—or those you have in dreams?

Can you say why?

Mrs. K.

I have had it for years now, it may have started somewhere in my teens as far as I can remember—it is a considerable time, anyway.

Every few weeks I suppose.

No, I don't think so—except perhaps my efforts in the water became more difficult . . . more difficult after I was married.

I think, really, the experiences under LSD.

Because to start with, without having had LSD I couldn't see the significance of some of my dreams—they would have been pointless unless I had had LSD. I think the one works with the other. I mean, my dreams have got that much more intense since having had LSD; before, I just didn't feel such strong emotions in my dreams until I had had LSD. I think I am a more feeling person if you can understand what I mean. My feelings are more evident, I am aware of them more. I think before they were completely shut away.

Each patient is looked after by a nurse who stays with him throughout the course of the treatment. Left, one of the nurses and right, a patient drawing.

Therapist	Mrs. H.

Would you just like to talk about today's session?

You mentioned to me on Monday that perhaps my father played a more important role in my attitude at the moment. I thought I would try under LSD to think about him. Before, whenever I thought about him and certain incidents, I believed that they were finished with. Then I went back in my mind to being two years old when I felt that a terrible thing had happened to me, the realization that my mother had no love for me. I saw her holding a male baby and I felt in that instant that I hated males. I had just this fundamental feeling, a terrible feeling, and it grew and I became full of hate and I realized that it was directed toward the opposite sex. I felt that this had begun at an early age when I felt that my mother had given affection to the male members of the family and not myself. I was the only female. I realised that at that age she didn't love me and I must have felt jealous of the male. This grew up within me. Looking back on my life I realized that it was exactly what I had felt. I wasn't conscious of it but certainly over the last few weeks I have felt very strained with my husband. *I felt primitive, you know.*

What do you mean?

Well, primitive from the point of view of the fundamental issues, somehow. I occasionally see him naked when, in fact, he is dressed. I didn't consciously think he reminded me of my brothers, when I was little, but I suddenly felt a revulsion. I disliked the feeling. I tried to dismiss it and I couldn't understand why I should feel this. Then the other evening my son, who is 15, was sitting in the lounge. I had just made a drink and I must have been looking at him without really realizing it and he just said "Don't look at me like that." I said "Like what?" I didn't realise I had been looking at him in any particular way, and he didn't answer. Under treatment today I felt that there must have been a sort of hate in me, in my eyes.

Mrs. H. here identifies nakedness with the idea of exposure of "nature"—linked with primitive sexual impulses. She may well have misinterpreted her son's remark which follows here.

You know, in the past I always lavished a lot of affection on the family and particularly my children. I always felt they should never endure the unhappiness that I had felt as a child; the loneliness. Probably I overdid it. But before I had LSD I always thought that I was a very good mother, at least I tried to be in my way. During LSD I found out that I did withdraw at the age of two my feelings of loving (I think that was last week's treatment . . . or the treatment before). *I found*

Therapist

How common a story! Rejection by mother at a vital stage of emotional development followed by a "holding in" of love and inability to reach the opposite sex emotionally. In a naturally outgoing and affectionate child this leads to depression; in the more inhibited, it can lead to personality disorders or even schizophrenia.

Could we go back to the LSD experience of two weeks ago when you felt that you went back to mother, you were enveloped by mother and became part of mother?

The beginnings of freedom from mother which is experienced as the start of an ego-feeling, "I felt that nothing could destroy me now." Note that in this patient all this is worked out under LSD, whereas libidinal development in Mrs. K's case was worked out in dreams.

How did this particular experience come to you under LSD—did you see it as a vision or did it come as a feeling?

Mrs. H.

that I had stopped loving at the age of two and to me that seemed a terrible thing to do— to stop loving. I had this feeling of hatred toward the opposite sex, because they had taken what I felt I needed at that age. All through my years of adolescence I realised that quite often I would attract the opposite sex, that is early on in my years when I was about 18, I took a great satisfaction out of encouraging them and then rejecting them, which I suppose in the light of what I know today would tend to be a sort of manifestation of hate—to hurt. I think it's an awful feeling to admit, but I wasn't responsible in a way, you know I couldn't help being like that. The point is now whether I can salvage something from the wreck and begin to love and live a sort of normal emotional life.

Yes, I went back to this time when I was two and saw my mother there obviously loving another baby and I felt quite defiant and I said "You can't love me." Then I thought "Well, I'm a mother myself now," and I scooped up this child *that was me* and loved it as I do my own children now. Through the stages of life . . . certain incidents which I remember when I felt very forlorn . . . I picked myself up as it were and consoled myself—consoled this child that was me. I took her to the Grammar School, where I had always wanted to go, and suddenly the two together, mother and child, became one, wrapped around each other. *I realised that it was myself that I was loving and that fundamentally one must initially love oneself to be able to begin to love or to give out anything of value. Suddenly I saw myself in a church and I felt very strong—I felt strong and felt that I could stand alone and that I had at last, if you like, reached maturity and I felt very very strong indeed and I felt that nothing could destroy me now because at last I had found myself—and it was a very awe-inspiring feeling as though I had found the essential that was me and that I didn't despise myself or feel fear in any way.* I felt strong enough to go on living, I suppose, really.

Initially it was a feeling. I keep harping on this age two, but it seemed very strong in my

Therapist	Mrs. H.
	memory, the whole thing started at this age. It was a feeling, pure and simple; then I seemed to see the child there and then it became visual. I saw the place, the places in my childhood and that was visual in my mind but eventually the whole thing became a feeling, a strength and a completeness within. It is very difficult to define it.
Yes. I know it is. Looking back over the whole of your LSD treatment, have you ever seen anything you might describe as a visual experience—you know—outside yourself, in the room?	
	No, no, I haven't, I have seen flowers, but not visually—my eyes have been closed the whole time. My experiences were more dealing with reality as it were, rather than abstract thought.
How do you see this reality?	*I feel I see it as I did when I was small. You actually see the place, but you don't see the parent at all, that is a feeling. You don't see the physicalness of the parent. It is just the feeling that they are both within you at that time. When I say I felt that I was a mother and the mother and the child was me: consciously, I felt that I was me as I am now and this child wasn't me. I was looking at something portrayed before me and I wasn't the child. I was the mother looking at the child until eventually they became one. I remember rolling down a hill and I looked at a flower, and we were sort of curled together. I suppose the pictures are in the mind.*
The whole complex of reality, emotional experience, and fantasy is described here. As long as she is separated (psychologically speaking) from the fantasy experience, it remains visual and therefore "hallucinatory" in the sense that it is an image or picture in the mind. Once this separation is lost, the imagery changes—"I was the mother looking at the child." Perhaps this was what happened all the time to Mrs. K., although one suspects that in her case the defensive system prevented her from "seeing" the unconscious reality clearly under LSD.	
When you have painted some of your experiences, you do them in color.	*Under LSD, in the treatment, I don't. But when I go home after treatment . . . usually the next morning about 4 o'clock . . . there's the desire to bring color out into it and get away from the sort of the black and white of it. Then it becomes vivid. Under LSD red was very significant; I had to possess something red. I have never had anything red, but suddenly I had to buy something red and I bought a red scarf. It was an obsession to have something red. I don't really know why.*
The need to express emotional feeling! Again, this is a quality which Mrs. K. found so hard to bring out of herself.	
Would you like to tell me about these other two pictures that you painted; the ones that you sent me?	There was a rose.
This was a brilliant dark red. Was this about the same time that you had this feeling that you must possess something red?	
Never mind	I can't remember.

| Therapist | Mrs. H. |

Mrs. H.

But I can remember why I painted that picture. I felt that there hadn't been much beauty in my life, as a child, and *suddenly I wanted to try and reproduce some beauty and I think that the painting of the flower, which did to me seem beautiful—and suddenly I found myself without any thought behind it to paint a snake coming from the flower and I painted the snake and I thought, "That's what I see! ... there is beauty in the world but also there is cruelty and I must reconcile the two in my mind because that is a part of life, accept that they both exist."*

Now we see that Mrs. H's defensive system is perhaps not so different after all from Mrs. K's—only it is expressed differently. It is more creative, as she is naturally more extraverted.

So the snake means something evil and unpleasant and ugly?

To me, yes.

Would you go so far as to say the snake is a kind of threat to you?

It wasn't a conscious threat when I painted it.

Have you looked at a rose when you have been having LSD?

Yes, last week, actually.

How did it seem to you?

Well, I was thinking how beautiful it was. *A delicate pink, a lovely pink and then suddenly I noticed that it had thorns on the stem. I thought: "Well, that's it—the beauty is there but also you have got the viciousness of life as well."* Somehow I accepted it, I thought, "Yes, that's it. A rose is not just beautiful, it has its ability to hurt as well."

This is the capacity of LSD to heighten all emotional experience.

Yes, particularly with LSD.

Do you dream?

Do you mean that since you have been having LSD you dream more?

Yes, they seem to be more vivid. I have often felt very lonely in dreams.

How would you compare the dreams with the LSD experiences?

I would say that there was no comparison at all. I think LSD is bringing to the surface realities which you have experienced. But dreams I often find are a mixture of fears and desires, or even a mixture of conversation that you have had perhaps during the previous couple of days. LSD is quite a different thing altogether—for me anyway it's far more vivid and lasting.

You said that in dreams you sometimes dream about things which have happened during the past couple of days; does this ever happen under LSD, do you ever incorporate experiences in the past day or two into LSD?

Yes, I do initially. You start off as you are now and then you seem to go back in time. I know I have. I did quite a few violent things at the beginning which were very disturbing.

Therapist	Mrs. H.

Therapist

What were they?

Mrs. H.

Well, I murdered my father, initially, and destroyed the house where I used to live as a child and I did quite a lot of destruction. I feel now that was getting rid of something that had obviously been worrying me for some time.

While all that was happening in the LSD sessions, did you dream about these things as well?

I don't think so. It's the feeling more I have in dreams.

Could I ask you about your imagination? I am not talking about dreams now, or LSD. How do you see things, how do you remember people and past events?

Again, in contrast to Mrs. K., the defensive elements emerge more in dreams than under LSD. In neither case have we really seen how Mrs. H. uses her qualities for introversion as this only comes out when she is asked about waking imagination.

I wouldn't say I was very imaginative. I am affected by the sea, that has a profound effect. You know, I love the sea and that to me is very emotional and wonderful; and the sky is as well. I often stand looking at the sky for a long time. I often wish I could paint them. I have never really tried but, before the LSD I felt sort of withdrawn and unable to put things down on paper.

If I asked you now to recollect what the sea looks like, how would you recollect it—would you have a picture in your mind as to what is it like?

Firstly, it is the feel of the sea. I like to swim a little and I often like to swim out in the sea all alone and look inland and get a feeling of detachment.

Are these a sort of feelings rather than a kind of picture of the ocean?

Yes, I remember a long time ago seeing the sea in moonlight and that was very . . . . I was very touched by that. *I think I'm romantic, and I know my husband isn't. I think a lot of women are romantic and often they are frustrated in this direction.*

The lonliness of introverted feeling! This explains in part the depression. It also explains how LSD helped to free the depression and also how in some ways it accentuated it, leading to several suicidal attempts.

Why?

Why, well, I used to read quite a lot of poetry and I used to like talking about poetry and I like listening to music and I don't mean romantic from a silly point of view; but it's sort of deep within you: an attitude, a feeling within you of beauty, and sort of goodness which I think you get often in a child's eyes. If a child looks at me, there's a purity there and a beauty that's wonderful. I think that quite a number of women are frustrated from a romantic point of view especially if they

Therapist	Mrs. H.

<table>
<tr><td></td><td>have been married some time. A woman still wants romance then and I think the male doesn't . . . .</td></tr>
</table>

Therapist

You have had depressions for 20 years, haven't you?

Mrs. H.

have been married some time. A woman still wants romance then and I think the male doesn't . . . .

Yes, on and off for 20 years. People call them depressions . . . but I always felt that—well, to me anyway—that it was just waking up one morning and feeling that a switch had been switched off on the emotional side of my brain.

Yes?

And there was no feeling, neither fear nor of anything which is termed depression.

Well, yes, the term depression covers a multitude of sins. How was this depression treated?

In the first place I had electrical shock treatment which fortunately for me brought me out of it. After the first one I did begin to feel again. I had a succession of about six, then I went for another four years or possibly five—I can't remember—then this blankness would come down again without any particular warning.

Right from the beginning you had some notion that the depression might be something to do with your early life, didn't you?

Yes, I did actually mention it to the doctor at the time. I'm afraid all these years I have been trying to sort myself out—to find out why this happened . . . I mean it is abnormal and there must have been a reason for it and I wanted to find out the reason. Before I had LSD I could remember certain things which I thought had a bearing on my emotional life, but under LSD I found out a lot more which had a more profound bearing . . . there was this mother-child relationship which I think really is the most important factor.

Can you remember the first one or two occasions when you had LSD? What kind of experiences did you have then?
Dreams give the faint clues, LSD seems to give the real certainty in the sense that it makes the defense systems clear. This description also emphasizes the persistence of the neurotic drives leading to 20 years of self-seeking.

The first treatment nothing happened, but in the second treatment . . . as I told you, I destroyed the things that were tormenting me. Then later in the treatment I went back again and realised that I had to resolve them in a different way. Destroying them wasn't going to solve anything . . . .

You were saying that you went back into childhood early in treatment and then you came out of it and then went back again into childhood and thought again about the kind of feelings you had.

Under the treatment I became my mother and saw it from her point of view, that she

Therapist	Mrs. H.

Mrs. H.
had got children, she had got much to do and very little money and I thought it was essential to see her point of view and then I didn't blame her. I don't have any hatred really—I just felt rather sorry that the whole thing happened and I sorted out my problems then but I still haven't quite finished; but I thought on Thursday I had come to a logical conclusion and was very happy.

Twenty years ago you had this feeling that a clue to your depression lay in something in your early life. Do you still think this is true? Do you feel that going through all this has helped you in any way?

Yes, I feel I can see now the reason why I was withdrawn emotionally and I can understand it and if that in itself will help me then I am very grateful.

A group of patients, with a nurse and a doctor, at the end of the day's treatment.

Index

Acknowledgments

Key to picture positions: (T) top (C) center   (B) bottom; and combinations, e.g. (TL) top left. Brit. Mus.: British Museum, photographs reproduced by courtesy of the Trustees.

9   Musée Municipal d'Art Moderne, Paris: photo Giraudon

13   Dr. H. Leuner, Göttingen: courtesy of the Sandoz AG, Basel

14-5   Sigmund Freud *The interpretation of dreams* 3rd edition

16   photo Roger Mayne, London

18-9   *The Balcony*: dir. by Joseph Strick, distributed by British Lion Films Ltd., 1964

20   (L) photo Patrick Ward, London (R) photo Peter Keen, London © *Sunday Times*

22   (T) photo Charles Harbutt/Magnum (B) *Radio Times* Hulton Picture Library

27   by kind permission of the Archbishop of Canterbury and the Trustees of Lambeth Palace Library: photo John Freeman

28-9   Brit. Mus.

31   (T) Keystone, London (B) Brit. Mus.

32   Louvre: photo Archives Photographiques, Paris

33   Collection Clercq

34   Brit. Mus: photo John Freeman

35   Bibliothèque Nationale, Paris

37   Cathedral d'Autun

38   Bibliothèque Nationale, Paris

42   Brit. Mus: photo John Freeman

44   (TL) National Museum, Athens: photo Alinari (BL) Alinari (BR) Museo Nationale delle Terme, Rome: photo De Pretoris

45   (L) Alinari (R) Museum of Piraeus, Greece

46   (L) Greek National Tourist Office (R) Pictorial Press: photo Ambler

48   (T & CT) Brit. Mus. (CB) Brooklyn Museum (B) Brit. Mus.

51   Brit. Mus: photo David Swann

52   Brit. Mus.

54   Brit. Mus: photo John Freeman

57   Japan National Tourist Organization

59   Brit. Mus.

60   courtesy of Mr. & Mrs. D. I. R. Muir

63   Brit. Mus: photo John Freeman

64   Kunsthistorisches Museum, Vienna

65   Biblioteca Vaticana

66   Museum Unterlinden, Colmar: photo Hans Hinz, Basel

69   (L) National Library of Ireland, Lawrence Collection (R) National Library of Ireland

70   (T) Brit. Mus. (B) courtesy of the London Library

73   Brit. Mus: photo John Freeman

76   Mansell Collection, London

77   Brit. Mus.

78   (L) Brit. Mus: photo John Freeman (R) Warburg Institute, London: photo John Freeman

79   (TR TL) Brit. Mus: photo John Freeman (B) photo Mike Busselle, London

82   Brit. Mus.

85   Brit. Mus: photo John Freeman

86-7   by courtesy of the National Portrait Gallery, London

88   (L) Brit. Mus: photo John Freeman (R) Trustees of Sir John Soane's Museum, London: photo John Freeman

92   Brit. Mus: photo John Freeman

93   *Radio Times* Hulton Picture Library

94   Brit. Mus: photo John Freeman

95   The Raymond Mander and Joe Mitchenson Theatre Collection, London

96   Bibliothèque Nationale, Paris

100   The Danish National Museum: photo Lennart Larsen (TL, CR, BL) Brit. Mus. (BR) Museum of Navajo Ceremonial Art, Inc: photo K. E. Foster

103   National Museum of Canada

104   Museum of Navajo Ceremonial Art, Inc: photo K. E. Foster

106   courtesy of The American Museum of Natural History

109   Bibliothèque Nationale, Paris

111   photo J. E. Bulloz, Paris

112-3   photos Mike Busselle, London

114   (T) Culver Pictures Inc., New York (BL & BR) Paul Popper Ltd., London

116   Mrs. Marcel Duchamp, New York: photo Mike Busselle, London

118   Keystone, London

120-1   photos Mike Busselle, London

124   (T & B) Mansell Collection, London

125   (T) Brit. Mus: photo John Freeman (B) Keystone, London

127   Mansell Collection, London

128   Associated Press, London

130   (T) Brit. Mus: photo John Freeman (B) Jean Cocteau *Opium,* pub. Peter Owen Ltd. Librairie Stock, Paris

132   (T) Brit. Mus: photo John Freeman (B) Imperial Library, Teheran

Artists Credits

Text Credits

Acknowledgment is made for permission to
reprint excerpts from the following works:
The Clinical Use of Dreams by Walter Bonime,
published by Basic Books, Inc.
*A Cycle of Penile Erection Synchronous with
Dreaming Sleep* by Charles Fisher, Joseph
Gross, and Joseph Zuck, published in AMA
Archives of General Psychiatry
The Interpretation of Dreams by Sigmund
Freud, published by George Allen & Unwin
Ltd., and by Basic Books Inc.
Sleep and Wakefulness by Nathanial Kleitman,
© 1939, 1963 by The University of Chicago
Press
Imagination and Thinking by Peter McKellar,
published by Cohen & West Ltd.
Sleeping and Waking by Ian Oswald,
published by Elsevier Publishing Co.

House Credits

art assistants: Gilbert Doel, Jessica Greenbaun,
Marian Morris. research assistants: Sheila
Muir, Patricia Quick.